CORK BANDON &
SOUTH COAST RAILWAY

Ernie Shepherd

MIDLAND

An imprint of
Ian Allan Publishing

One of the Beyer Peacock 4-6-0Ts entering
Albert Quay station with an up passenger train
from Skibbereen. On the left is the raised
signal cabin and, in the background,
Hibernian Road bridge which replaced
Gas Works level crossing.
D Murray collection, IRRS

Cork Bandon & South Coast Railway
W Ernest Shepherd © 2005
ISBN 1 85780 198 9

Published by
Midland Publishing
4 Watling Drive, Hinckley
Leicester, LE10 3EY
England
Tel: 01455 254490 Fax: 01455 254495
E-mail: midlandbooks@compuserve.com

Midland Publishing is an imprint of
Ian Allan Publishing Ltd

Printed in England by
Ian Allan Printing Ltd
Riverdene Business Park, Molesey Road
Hersham, Surrey, KT12 4RG

Designed by
Midland Publishing
and Stephen Thompson Associates.

CONTENTS

Title page: **Headed by locomotive No 9, built by Neilson in 1894, a train crosses the most notable engineering feature on the CB&SCR, the Chetwynd viaduct.** Photographer unknown, Seán Kennedy collection

Front cover, top: **Ex-D&SER 2-4-2T No 432 of 1886 on a short train at Drimoleague while on the right is ex-WL&WR 4-4-2T No 274. The former engine was built in the Grand Canal Street Works of the DW&WR while No 274 came from Kitsons of Leeds in 1897.** Seán Kennedy

Above: **Skibbereen station looking south with its single broad-gauge platform on the up side. The goods store was located on the up side behind the photographer, while further out on the down side there was a small engine shed and turntable. The Schull & Skibbereen Tramway narrow-gauge terminus was located to the right, behind the wagons and the platform. Just visible to the left rear of the train at the platform in this undated view in GSR days are the arches of the Ilen River bridge, erected when the line was extended to Baltimore.** Photographer unknown, John Langford collection

ACKNOWLEDGEMENTS

It would not have been possible to have compiled this history without generous assistance from many people. First and foremost, the author must mention both the Secretary and the Archivist of Córas Iompair Éireann, the holding company for the present Irish railway system, and the keeper of the statutory records of all of the Irish railway companies which became part of the Great Southern Railways in 1925. The author was afforded free access to the Board Minute Books of the Cork Bandon & South Coast Railway and its predecessor and subsidiaries, with the exception of those of the Cork City Railways (not held by CIÉ).

Joseph Leckey, until recently the Archivist, Brendan Pender, the Assistant Archivist, and Tim Moriarty, the Librarian, respectively of the Irish Railway Record Society (IRRS) likewise allowed the author to research the vast collection of material in their possession. Other organisations which must receive mention include, the National Archives (previously known as the Public Records Office) in Kew, the National Library of Ireland and the National Archives in Dublin. Individual members of the IRRS have also rendered valuable assistance. The late Bob Clements' researches into the locomotive history of the 'Bandon' are held in the IRRS Archives. Herbert Richards has likewise undertaken in-depth research into the carriages and wagons and allowed the author to freely use this material. Eugene Field kindly provided the information on tickets for the relevant appendix.

Peter Rowledge had compiled a history of the line in manuscript form and generously allowed the present author free access to this material. Likewise, Walter McGrath of Cork provided copies of his articles on the line printed over a period of years in the *Cork Examiner*. Gerry Beesley spent many hours deciphering the vagaries of the rolling stock and enabled the author to produce the relevant chapter. He also very kindly read through the manuscript and made many constructive comments and suggestions, for which the author is extremely grateful. In addition, he gave moral support when the author's interest in the project wavered.

Others who have helped in various ways include the late Colm Creedon, Clifton Flewitt and Ken Manto. Seán Kennedy supplied the author with a number of the necessary photographic prints and these were up to Seán's usual high standards. Desmond Coakham also kindly provided the excellent photographs of the carriages and wagons, as well as the track diagram of Albert Quay. Photographs, as far as possible, are individually acknowledged. It has not been possible to identify the copyright in certain of the photographs used. The author would appreciate any information in this regard so that the matter can be rectified for the future.

In the event that any names have been omitted, this is entirely unintentional and the author asks anyone so omitted to accept his sincere apologies and regrets. Any errors or omissions of fact are entirely the responsibility of the author.

Ballinhassig station looking east with Goggin's Hill tunnel in the background. The train is the 11.00 down beet special for Clonakilty on 3rd November 1960.
John Langford

AUTHORS' NOTE

The spellings of place names used throughout the book are those used by the company. These spellings may differ from those used by the Ordnance Survey. In some instances, different spellings were used by the company, such as Innishannon and Innoshannon.

The twenty-four hour clock has been used throughout the book, except in direct quotations from other sources. Monetary amounts are shown in the currency of the period. Prior to 1970, the pound (£) consisted of 20 shillings, each shilling being made up of 12 pennies, there being thus 240 pennies to the pound. The abbreviations used were 's' for shillings and 'd' for pence, eg. £360 14s 6d. The post 1970 pound, known in Ireland as the 'Punt', was made up of 100 pennies, thus there were 2.4 old pence to the later penny. For metric equivalents of weights and measures, the reader is referred to a good encyclopaedia.

This volume breaks with the tradition of earlier works in the series in that it does not include any drawings of carriages or wagons. This is to be regretted, but none appear to have survived, apart from two or three very poor reproductions from the Metropolitan Carriage & Wagon Company collection in the Birmingham Public Libraries.

SOURCES

As already alluded to in the Acknowledgements, the author had access to the Board Minute Books of the various companies concerned. In addition there were a few Works Committee Minute Books extant, also a set of Letter Books dating from 1898 to 1924. The latter helped to add to the information already gleaned from the Minute Books. Other official records included station layout diagrams, signal cabin drawings, timetables and appendices. Regrettably, there appears to be a dearth of company timetables, and it was necessary to rely on Bradshaw and other similar publications.

Parliamentary papers, Acts of Parliament, BoT reports of inspections and accidents, Railway & Canal Traffic Cases, Ordnance Survey maps and reports of Parliamentary Committees also proved useful. The War Department reported on the line on several occasions; in particular a lengthy report dated January 1904 included station layout diagrams.

Railway periodicals included:
Herepath's Railway Journal.
Irish Railfans' News.
Irish Railway Gazette.
Journals of the Irish Railway Record Society.
Railway Gazette.
Railway Magazine.
Railway News.
Railway Times.

Other printed sources:
A History of Railways in Ireland: Conroy, J.C; Longmans, Green & Co, 1928.
Cork City Railway Stations 1849-1985: Creedon, Colm; Cork, 1985.
Dublin & South Eastern Railway: Shepherd, Ernie & Beesley, Gerry; Midland Publications, 1998.
Ireland since the Famine: Lyons, F.S.L; Fontana Press, 1973.
Irish Passenger Steamship Services, Vol.2: McNeill, D.B.; David & Charles, 1971.
Irish Steam Locomotive Register: Rowledge, J.W.P.R; Irish Traction Group, 1993

Official Hand Book of Railway Stations etc.; Railway Clearing House, 1912.
Railways in Ireland, 1834 to 1984: Doyle, O. & Hirsch, S; Signal Press, 1983.
Shipbuilding in Waterford, 1820-1882: Irish, Bill; Wordwell Ltd, Bray, 2001.
The Cork Bandon and South Coast Railway, Vols.1-3: Creedon, Colm; Cork, 1986-91.
The Cork, Blackrock and Passage Railway and River Steamers: Creedon, Colm, Cork, 1992.
The Cork Blackrock & Passage Railway: Jenkins, Stanley C; Oakwood Press, 1993.
The Cork & Macroom Direct Railway: Creedon, Colm; Cork, 1960.
The Schull & Skibbereen Railway: Boyd, James I.C; Oakwood Press, 1999.
The Schull and Skibbereen Tramway: Newham, A.T; Oakwood Press, 1964.
Topographical Dictionary of Ireland: Lewis, Samuel; London, 1837.
Tram Tracks through Cork: McGrath, Walter; Tower Books of Cork, 1981.

ABBREVIATIONS

ASRS	Associated Society of Railway Servants	CB&SCR	Cork Bandon & South Coast Railway	L&NWR	London & North Western Railway
B&FRP Co.	British & Foreign Railway Plant Company	CCR	Cork City Railways	LMSR	London Midland & Scottish Railway
B&TJLR	Ballinascarthy & Timoleague Junction Light Railway	CDB	Congested Districts Board	MGWR	Midland Great Western Railway
		CER	Clonakilty Extension Railway		
		CIÉ	Córas Iompair Éireann	NUR	National Union of Railwaymen
BBER	Bantry Bay Extension Railway	D&SER	Dublin & South Eastern Railway		
BBS Co.	Bantry Bay Steamship Company	DW&WR	Dublin Wicklow & Wexford Railway	PWLC	Public Works Loan Commissioners
BER	Baltimore Extension Railway	F&RR&H	Fishguard & Rosslare Railways & Harbours Company	S&ST	Schull & Skibbereen Tramway
BoT	Board of Trade			SofIW Co.	South of Ireland Wagon Company
BoW	Board of Works	GNR(I)	Great Northern Railway (Ireland)		
BCW	Birmingham Carriage & Wagon	GS&WR	Great Southern & Western Railway	T&CELR	Timoleague & Courtmacsherry Extension Light Railway
C&BR	Cork & Bandon Railway				
C&FR	Cork & Fermoy Railway	GSR	Great Southern Railways	TDA	Tourist Development Association
C&KJR	Cork & Kinsale Junction Railway	GWR	Great Western Railway		
		IRCH	Irish Railway Clearing House	W&LR	Waterford & Limerick Railway
C&MDR	Cork & Macroom Direct Railway	IREC	Irish Railways Executive Committee		
C&PR	Cork & Passage Railway			W&WR	Waterford & Wexford Railway
CB&PR	Cork Blackrock & Passage Railway	IRRS	Irish Railway Record Society		
		IVR	Ilen Valley Railway	WCR	West Cork Railway

Chapter One

TOWARDS BANDON

Bord Failte, the Irish Tourist Board, describes the West Cork region as being an area stretching from Ballinhassig in the east to Allihies on the western tip of the Beara Peninsula and from Macroom in the north to Mizen Head, the southernmost point of Ireland. It was broadly speaking within this area that the 'Bandon' was located. The area encompasses rivers, mountains, valleys, rugged coastlines and beautiful beaches, and includes many famous towns, amongst them Kinsale, Clonakilty, Bantry and Glengarriff. In the extreme west was the copper mining area of Allihies, which attracted miners from Cornwall. There are a number of Gaeltacht or Irish speaking areas within the West Cork area.

Prior to the coming of the railway era, much of west Cork was isolated from the remainder of the county and indeed the city of Cork due to the difficulties of travel on a very poor road system. Early in 1836, Charles Vignoles put forward a scheme for a main trunk line of railway from Dublin to Cork, including in this a branch diverging at or near Blarney and running through Macroom, Gougane Barra and Glengarriff to the coast at Dinish Island, Castletown Berehaven. This line would have run rather further north than the later Cork & Bandon

line, and would have involved the construction of a tunnel more than a mile in length and a viaduct 191ft in height; had they been constructed, these structures would have been respectively the longest tunnel and the highest viaduct in Ireland. The line referred to was part of the grand scheme of railway transport submitted to the Railway Commission, which had been set up in 1836 to consider the future development of transport within Ireland. When the final report of the Commission was issued in 1838, no mention was made of a line to serve West Cork, leaving it to local promoters to put forward their own plans. Incidentally, Vignoles was later to become the C&BR's first consulting engineer.

Another early scheme was the Direct Dublin Cork & Bantry Railway Co, provisionally registered in August 1845 for a railway from Dublin through Carlow, Kilkenny, Clonmell (sic), Cork and intermediate points to Bantry and Bantry Bay. Three London gentlemen were listed as having an interest in the scheme, which progressed no further.

Prior to the advent of the railway, the town of Bandon was the principal gateway to the western portion of the county and had in 1831 a population of 9,917. It was described in one contemporary guide as

being home to one hundred nobility, gentry and clergy, ten academies and schools, two breweries, two distilleries, two linen factors and four millers; there were no less than seventy-two licensed vintners! It was not until 1843-4 that proposals were again put forward for railway communication with Cork, this scheme being centred on Bandon rather than Cork, as might have been expected. Two Cork men were however principally involved, Edmund Leahy and J C Bernard. The former was the son of Patrick Leahy, a county engineer for Cork, the latter a well-known Cork solicitor.

The *Cork Constitution* reported that, 'a highly influential and numerous', meeting was held at the Devonshire Arms Hotel in Bandon on Thursday 28th September 1844 to consider the propriety of forming a company for the construction of a line of railway to connect Bandon with Cork. Leahy had already carried out the necessary surveys and reported favourably on both the proposed route and the anticipated traffic. The line was proposed to commence at Bandon Bridge, pass by the gasworks, and go via Doundaniel Castle, Innoshannon, Upton and Waterfall, crossing over the mail-coach road, for the third time, at Chetwynd. Finally, it was to pass Frankfield and Ballyphehane Bog to a terminus close to the Free

Opposite page top: **4-6-0T No 470 awaits 'right away' at Albert Quay on the 17.30 Baltimore train on 19th April 1952.**
J N Faulkner

Opposite page bottom: **'The Quarry' at Rocksavage with a typical line-up. In the back row (left to right) are 4-6-0T No 464, GS&WR 0-6-0ST No 299 & *Argadeen*; middle row the former MGWR 0-6-0T No 557, WL&WR 4-4-2T No 269; front 4-6-0T No 465 & GS&WR 2-4-2T No 41. This photograph was taken on 14th July 1957.**
C P Boocock

Right: **4-6-0T No 19 departing Albert Quay with the 16.15 passenger train for Baltimore on 25th July 1914. No 19 was barely a month old, having entered service on 7th June. She appears to have undergone no major repairs or alterations during her working life and was withdrawn in 1945 as GSR No 469.**
Ken Nunn collection, LCGB

Church at Langford Row, nearly opposite to the Cork Lunatic Asylum, later the South Infirmary.

Leahy did however state that the line could easily be continued to Anglesea Bridge near the Corn Exchange. The length of the proposed line was to be 20 miles and 275 yards. Leahy estimated the cost of land purchase, construction and the provision of stations, engines and carriages, 'at an excessive figure of £10,000 per mile'. No sooner had the details of the proposed route been published, than the Trustees of the Free Church voiced their apprehension at the likely inconvenience to the Congregation by the adoption of the intended terminus at Langford Row. Leahy however expressed his view that the terminus was sufficiently removed from the Church as not to cause any difficulties.

The title of the proposed company was the Bandon & Cork Railway and the *Cork Constitution* reported that no less than twenty-three worthy gentlemen had been requested to act as a provisional committee. These included Lord Viscount Bernard, MP, the Hon. Henry Boyle Bernard, Sir Edward Synge, High Sheriff of County Cork and the Reverend Somers Payne of Upton. Almost without exception all were residents of the immediate area. Robert Tresilian Belcher and William Conner Sullivan of Bandon were appointed local secretaries. Following on these appointments, the proceedings closed with a vote of thanks to Lord Bernard for the dignified manner in which he conducted the business of the meeting and for, 'his general attention to the interests of the Town of Bandon'. Two months later the provisional committee, with Belcher now appointed chairman, reported further. John M'Donnell had in the interim been appointed as secretary in Cork and Edward Billing as secretary and local agent in London. Meanwhile, offices were acquired at 59 South Mall, Cork, at a rent of £45 per annum. Another important change was the alteration of the company name to the Cork & Bandon Railway, the title by which it was known for almost 44 years.

In the intervening period, 'trustworthy persons were employed for the purpose of taking a daily traffic on the roads'. Between 23rd November and 16th December, an average of 687 passengers traversed the route daily – this figure did not include more than 500, 'on riding horses and on foot'. Some 208 tons of merchandise and 400 livestock passed daily; almost 75% of the latter figure being pigs. These figures, without any increase which would inevitably accrue when the railway was opened, were estimated to provide annual receipts in excess of £46,000. After deducting 40% for maintenance of way and working expenses, nett annual receipts were calculated at £27,688, sufficient to provide a dividend of 13½% on the capital of £200,000. Optimistic figures in the extreme!

A deputation from Kinsale waited on the provisional committee, but the consulting engineer, Charles Vignoles, who had approved of Leahy's plans, stated that it would be out of the question to deviate the railway to take in that town. They were to make further representations in March 1845 for a branch line to serve their town, at which time it was decided to assist in every way possible in the formation of a separate company for the construction of such a line. A Mr Anderson made a request in January 1845 for plans of the proposed railway to Bandon to enable him to prepare an estimate for, 'a wooden line of railway'; we shall return to this matter later in our narrative.

In April Mr Thomas Frewen wrote claiming damages for the town of Innoshannon as the result of the coming of the railway and it was agreed that he should receive the sum of £1,000, 'for the supposed injury to the town'. It was also agreed at this time that a station should be provided at or near Brinny. This latter later variously became known as Brinny & Upton, Upton & Innoshannon Road and finally Upton. Early in January 1846 the company concluded an agreement with Frewen for the construction, maintenance and keeping of a station near to the town of Innoshannon. The question of this latter station was to be raised on a number of occasions in subsequent years as we shall see later.

Tenders are sought

In April 1845 Leahy was instructed to place advertisements in various newspapers and railway journals seeking tenders for the works on the line, these being later postponed for a month. When they appeared in May it was clear that the line between Cork and Bandon had been split into six divisions. A special meeting of the board was held on 22nd May to consider the various tenders received, 38 in total. Some of the prospective contractors tendered for all six divisions, some for one only. After mature deliberation and consideration of each tender, it was resolved that the following be awarded the various contracts, the total of all six amounting to £52,300 5s 5d, viz. See table below.

These contracts were in fact awarded pending the obtaining of the Act of Incorporation, which received Royal Assent on 21st July 1845. Capital of the new company was £200,000. Also, in July it was agreed that the Secretary, John M'Donnell, should receive the sum of £200 for past services.

The first general meeting of shareholders was held at the company's offices in South Mall on 20th August. They were told of various projects afoot for lines in the general area of West Cork, including a line from Cork to Macroom and on to Killarney. There was also the prospect of a line to Bantry serving the intermediate towns of Inniskeane (sic), Dunmanway, Clonakilty and Skibbereen. In association with this project was a branch to Kinsale and a continuation by means of the Cork & Passage Railway through Douglas to deep water at the town of Passage. Such a line could not fail to render the Bandon undertaking still more productive. The Passage line would be of the utmost importance as the agricultural and commercial community of the county and city of Cork would thus be afforded the opportunity of transmitting their produce either to the markets of Cork or direct to Passage for shipment. Bearing this in mind, the directors strongly urged on the shareholders the adoption of measures for the amalgamation of the C&BR and the C&PR companies. Not only would this be the means of establishing the desired communication, but it would also bring about a considerable reduction of working expenses.

The engineer submitted his report on the appointment of contractors to the various divisions and stated that the line had been lockspitted throughout from Bandon to Evergreen in the suburbs of Cork. Revised plans had been drawn up for the viaduct to cross the Chetwynd valley as well as for the heaviest excavations between the viaduct and Evergreen which would reduce expenditure. It was hoped to have these major works completed before the following Christmas and the whole line by 1st August 1846. This was to be wishful thinking in the extreme on Leahy's part as we shall see.

Some doubts must have been on the minds of the directors as regards the curves and gradients on the proposed line as Leahy was summoned before the board early in

Division	Route	Length M F Y	Contractor	Amount £ s d
1	Cork to Old Kinsale Rd	2 4 132	Gerald Mahony & Co.	8,004 16 6
2	Old Kinsale Rd. to Inniskenny	3 5 11	Messrs. Henry & Henright	18,000 0 0
3	Inniskenny to Goggins Hill	3 5 33	W.E. Wright	8,085 11 0
4	Goggins Hill to Killeen	3 5 206	Theophilus Bolton	4,644 4 8
5	Killeen to Curranure	3 4 77	Matthew Parrett	10,131 0 0
6	Curranure to Bandon	2 4 66	Matthew Parrett	3,434 13 3

MFY = Miles, Furlongs & Yards.

Right: **CB&SCR head-office and terminal buildings at Albert Quay, Cork in 1938.** Photographer unknown, John Langford collection

Right lower: **Ex GS&WR 4-4-2T No 32 and an unidentified 'Bandon' 4-6-0T awaiting departure from Albert Quay c.1945. Trains were frequently double-headed as far as the first station, Waterfall.** W McGrath

September. He apparently convinced them that these were perfectly safe; he confirmed that he had referred to reports from the BoT and also to Whishaw, a work of great authority, and he had ascertained that the Newcastle & Carlisle Railway had lines, 'which are one continued succession of curves of every degree of curvature up to eight chains radius and with steep inclines having been worked for several years with economy and safety'.

Cutting the first sod
At the beginning of September a small committee was appointed to take the appropriate measures for a public demonstration on the occasion of the cutting of the first sod later in the month. The chairman was requested to solicit Lord Bandon's attendance, while invitations were to be sent to the shareholders and to the landed gentry along the line. Leahy was instructed to arrange for the erection of a temporary building for the occasion for the holding of the customary déjeuner. A Mr Lloyd of Cork agreed to supply the déjeuner at 15s per head for the first 100 and 10s per head above that figure; no charge was to be made for refreshments for the bands. The event in question took place on Thursday 16th September in a large field on the lands of Kilpatrick, just above the ruins of Doundaniel Castle, beside the Bandon River. The event was adequately described in the *Illustrated London News*. The sod turning ceremony was carried out by the Earl of Bandon in front of a crowd of several thousand local people, shareholders and gentry. A wheelbarrow of mahogany with a spade of bright steel, the handle of which was covered with red morocco leather and gilt lettered, were used for the occasion. His Lordship flung some spadefuls of soil into the barrow and rolled it off along a plank to the cheers of the crowd. The principal guests then retired to the handsome pavilion to partake of the déjeuner. It might be mentioned that the timber used in the pavilion was later sold off for £141 1s 5d.

A proposed scheme of 1845 envisaged a a rather circuitous route from Cork to Bandon and Kinsale via Passage, estimated to cost £250,000. In the same year, two other schemes were proposed, the Cork & Passage Railway, a revival of an earlier scheme of 1836 (with the Messrs Leahy as engi-

neers), and the Cork Blackrock Passage & Monkstown Railway. These three schemes in due course materialised as the Cork Blackrock & Passage Railway, which was incorporated by Act of Parliament dated 16th July 1846. A week after the C&BR sod turning ceremony a deputation from the C&PR attended the board and submitted propositions for the amalgamation of the two companies. Application was to be made to Parliament for an Act of Amalgamation to make the lines from Cork to Bandon and Passage the property of one company under one management. The C&PR were to lodge the sum of £8,000, being 10% of their capital to the credit of the C&BR. A special meeting of the C&BR shareholders was held on 9th October and the shareholders gave their approval for such a merger. On the same day tenders were approved for permanent way materials, including yellow pine and 21,000 beech sleepers at £237 10s 0d per thousand. Later in the month the tender of Sir John

Guest of London for rails at £12 10s 0d per ton, f.o.b. Cardiff was accepted, along with that of Messrs A Beale & Co of Cork for carriage from Cardiff to Collier's Quay at 13s.6d per ton.

An event of some note occurred at the board meeting on 27th November 1845 when Major North Ludlow Beamish was elected to the board of directors in the place of the Rev Dr Traill who had ceased to qualify as a director. Beamish was a noted military historian and soon became chairman of the board. In February 1846 a deputation went to London to wait on Sir Robert Peel and various local members of Parliament to solicit from the Government a loan to enable the company to afford as much employment as possible during the following six months. At the shareholders' meeting in February the chairman reported that there were four bills before Parliament which, if enacted, would afford benefits to the Bandon company. The C&PR Amalga-

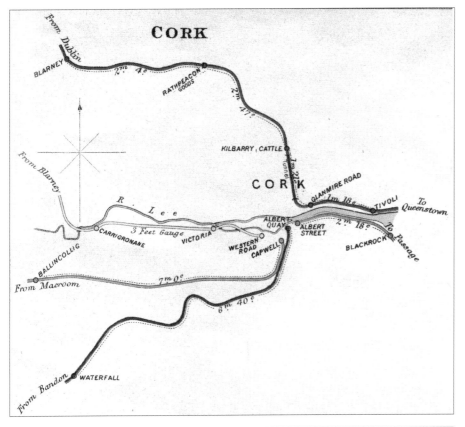

Left: **Railway Clearing House diagram of Railway lines in the Cork area.** Author's collection

Left lower: **Albert Quay station with the carriage shed on the right.** Ian Allan Library

due to, 'a combination of unforeseen circumstances'. He had been waiting five months for land and his tender had been based on, 'wages of last season, in full expectation of having the work nearly completed by this time, but which would be totally inadequate under present circumstances'. The board initially refused to accept Wright's resignation and threatened to enforce immediate execution of his contract. It was agreed that all measures possible should be taken to reduce expenditure and also to procure the report of an eminent engineer on the state of the line.

Work had stopped completely on the line by the end of March and Major Beamish was requested to make contact with Isambard Kingdom Brunel of the Great Western Railway to have an engineer appointed without further delay to inspect the line. In the interim it was reported that rails had arrived on site cut into various odd lengths from 12¼ft to 17½ft and without webholes punched in them. In addition many of the beech sleepers were not to specification. A deputation went to England to speak to experts and had personal interviews with Messrs Vignoles and Robert Stephenson, who both looked at the plans and sections of the line, but declined to come to Cork for a personal inspection. The deputation spent some time on the Birmingham & Gloucester Railway and met there J E McConnell, the line's locomotive superintendent. The deputation took a trip over the line, including the 1 in 37 gradient of the Lickey incline and expressed themselves satisfied with the gradients and curves, the latter little different from those proposed on the Bandon. They added a postscript to their report to the effect that it was imperative that the directors avail of the immediate services of a qualified person to manage the affairs of the company.

Vignoles reported on some of the deputation's queries. He stated that the crossing of the Chetwynd valley by a timber viaduct with two openings was perfectly safe; all the principal timbers should be of red pitch pine, with yellow pine for the flooring. Regarding sleepers, for which Leahy proposed to have a triangular section of yellow pine, Vignoles expressed the opinion that the latter was quite unsuitable for sleepers, as also was beech. In relation to the shape of the sleepers, he saw no positive objection. Regarding the bogie principle being applied to long carriages, he saw no objection, although Stephenson, commenting on this

mation scheme has already been referred to, the Kinsale Junction Railway Bill, the Bandon & Bantry Railway and its branches and finally the previously announced scheme for a line from Cork through Macroom to Killarney. The promoters had now decided to restrict this latter line to go only as far as Macroom, but it was hoped that a junction line would be made from Ballincollig to the C&BR. By means of this latter, troops might be carried to and from the military barracks at Ballincollig to Kinsale, Clonakilty, Crookhaven and Bantry. It was also proposed that the Macroom line should avail of the C&BR terminus at Cork.

At the February 1846 meeting, the engineer reported on the progress of the works to date, advising that a considerable portion of the land required had been obtained, particularly at the Bandon end and the works were actively going ahead on the fifth and

sixth divisions. Between Bandon and the Brinny River near Innoshannon the railway was for the most part formed, with the foundations and abutments of two river bridges in an advanced state. The viaduct at Castle White (Chetwynd) on the second division was also reported to be progressing satisfactorily with the centre pier sunk to the solid rock, with the railway on each side in process of formation. Leahy was able to report that the only division on which no work was in progress was the first one, closest to Cork. In all, about 400 men were employed and this was soon to be doubled.

However within days of this report being submitted, it was reported that one of the contractors, Mr W E Wright, had applied for compensation for loss of time awaiting possession of land on his contract. Worse was to come for Wright stated his intention at the beginning of March of resigning his contract

question, saw no decided advantage. Finally, neither gentleman perceived any objections to turntables large enough to accommodate such carriages. Stephenson commented that turntables of up to 35ft in diameter were now universal, but he was puzzled as to why the carriages should need to be turned at all. It is possible that Leahy had in mind the turning of the Adams engines and carriages, it being the initial intention to have these coupled together as were similar vehicles on the Eastern Counties Railway.

An engineer is dismissed

It should be mentioned at this point that Leahy had been courted by the Wooden Railway Company, an English concern, who were advocating the use of specially treated wooden rails. While Leahy did not actually purchase any of these rails, it seems likely that his ideas for light iron rails and beech sleepers may have been influenced by them. In the midst of all this uncertainty, M'Donnell, the company secretary, wrote tendering his resignation due to ill health, 'brought on by over exertion and anxiety in forwarding the interests of your Company'. Efforts were made to find a suitable person to act as managing director and in May the directors engaged the services of Charles Nixon of London to act both in that post and also that of secretary at a salary of £650 per annum with £50 travelling expenses.

Nixon was immediately requested to inspect and report on the progress of the works to date. His first report was presented to the board on 18th June, he having walked the length of the line. He had no adverse comments to make as to the actual laying out of the line which he found to have been arranged with a great deal of skill and caution. As regards the works actually carried out, Nixon disapproved of the masonry of the various viaducts and bridges, the interior of the works not being properly bonded, the mortar bad and many defective stones used. He suggested the addition of two additional piers to the Chetwynd viaduct, the substitution of level crossings for road bridges and, perhaps most interestingly, the substitution of a short tunnel for the open cutting between the Brinny and Bandon rivers.

A second report was put before the directors a week later in which Nixon reported in some detail as to the type of permanent way being laid by Leahy. The rails weighed 56lbs per yard on longitudinal timbers of triangular section, with the base 14in wide placed uppermost; the apex rested downwards on transverse sleepers of beech. The longitudinal timbers were not secured to the lower beech but were proposed to be maintained in the vertical position by blocks or short pieces of wood. Whilst the London & Greenwich and the London & Croydon lines both

used this type of permanent way, they both bolted the timbers together with the ballast solidly packed between them. Leahy had informed Nixon that part of the Dublin & Kingstown Railway had been laid in a similar manner to his scheme. Finally, Nixon did not approve of the use of beech sleepers.

It is perhaps hardly surprising that the board took the decision at the beginning of July 1846 to dispense with Leahy's services. Reluctant to go, Leahy suggested referring the various matters in dispute to an eminent English engineer. He stood over his proposed use of beech sleepers, which he commented had been used with some success on the London & Southampton Railway. Later, in 1848 a lengthy legal battle ensued as Leahy endeavoured to enforce a claim for £8,000 stated to be due to him in connection with his two years working for the company. The court case eventually ended with Leahy being awarded a sum of £325 plus a nominal 6d costs, the company however having to face a severe legal bill.

A further report on the state of the Chetwynd viaduct backed up the directors' suspicions regarding Leahy's lack of proper inspections of the work. The original rubble masonry had been put together in a loose and unworkmanlike manner, the mortar not adhering to the underbeds of the stones. Nixon again suggested the provision of two additional piers to the viaduct. Whilst he was of opinion that the Brinny and Bandon river bridges had been constructed of good quality materials, nevertheless in the case of the latter, he recommended a bridge of two arches instead of one as originally proposed. He was instructed to make the necessary application to the Drainage Commissioners, provisional sanction being granted at the end of July.

Nixon announced in July that he had appointed as his assistant, Joseph Philip Ronayne at a salary of £200 per annum. Ronayne had been born in Cork and in time became that city's leading railway engineer and contractor. Joseph had been apprenticed to the eminent engineer Sir John Macneill and had worked with him on the mainline of the GS&WR. After his departure from the C&BR, he went to the United States where he distinguished himself in the construction of aqueducts and reservoirs. His funeral in Cork in 1876 was reported to be one of the largest ever seen in the city.

In August, Nixon expanded on his ideas for substituting a tunnel for a deep open cutting at the hill between the Brinny and Bandon rivers, which he stated would make a saving of between £700 and £1,000. Based on Nixon's report, the board decided to proceed with a tunnel. Major General C W Pasley, the Inspector General of Railways and the gentleman who recommended the adoption of the 5ft 3in gauge in Ireland (which became law on 18th August 1846 by

an Act for Regulating the Gauge of Railways), advised that the substitution of a tunnel would in fact be an improvement on the open cutting. The BoT therefore issued a certificate in August approving of the substitution of the tunnel for a cutting at Kilpatrick. Arrangements were made to commence work immediately on the 170-yard long structure, but difficulties were encountered in finding navvies with the required expertise in tunnelling work. Nixon found it necessary to recruit a number of men from the West Carbery mines. Working on a 24 hour basis, the tunnel was completed within twelve months at a cost of £1,000 less than the proposed cutting. By the summer of 1846 almost 700 men were employed on the various contracts. One contemporary source referred to the navvies, many of whom were English, as being, 'sullen, ill-looking and as ignorant as 'Hotentots', not an expression which would find favour today!

Also in August 1846 the Land Committee were requested to inspect the land intended for the terminus at Bandon, following a claim by the Duke of Devonshire for the land in question. About this time, suggestions were made that application be made for a Government loan, the upshot of which was a decision to send a deputation to the Lord Lieutenant. It was feared that unless Government aid was forthcoming, it might be necessary to suspend works and put up to 800 men out of employment. In response, the Treasury replied in October stating that their Lordships, 'determined not to adopt Loans to Railway Companies as a means of relieving the suffering arising from the failure of the Potato Crop'.

Extension at Cork

Some important decisions were taken by the board in October 1846. As originally laid out, the line was to terminate at Langford Row. It was now resolved to extend the line across Monarea Marsh to a new terminus, 'at some convenient point to the rear of the Cork Blackrock & Passage Railway terminus', close to the river at Albert Quay and adjoining the Cornmarket. It was decided to leave the question of connecting the two lines for future consideration – it should be pointed out at this point that the CB&PR was initially planned and laid to a gauge of 5ft 3in, only being converted to narrow-gauge at the beginning of the 20th century. In addition, the terminus of the Passage line was until January 1873 situated to the east of the later Albert Street site, at the junction of Navigation Walk and Victoria Road (the original line as originally laid down ran close to the river to the north of City Park for the last mile). It was nevertheless hoped to obtain the co-operation of the Passage company in obtaining the Act for the extension to Monarea Marsh. Another important decision was that to complete the Bandon end of the line first, while arrangements were also made to obtain powers to divert the line at Goggan's Hill (sic) by means of a tunnel.

By January 1847 Nixon was complaining of the unsatisfactory progress by Matthew Parrett in the prosecution of the works on his contract No 5, he having made repeated promises to expedite bridge works, and as frequently broken these promises. Serious consideration was given to the forfeiture of his contract, he being duly notified to this effect. Soon afterwards it was reported that Parrett had suspended works on contract No 6. Henry Hill submitted a tender to complete the Bandon River bridge for a sum of £2,644, this being accepted. As regards the Brinny bridge, a decision was deferred as the board wished to consider whether to substitute stone arching instead of timber trussing. A similar decision was taken in respect of the Chetwynd viaduct. The Bandon road bridge was reported in April to be unsatisfactory inasmuch as the first course had been constructed without mortar and the foundation was so soft as to render it unsafe for erecting anything on it. April saw Nixon resign his position as secretary to the company, although he continued to hold the posts of engineer and managing director.

Reporting to the shareholders in February 1848 the directors stressed that non-payment of arrears on shares had pressed heavily on the company's finances. However, legal proceedings had been instituted to recover the amount due, £8,000 in arrears having already been paid. Agreement had now been concluded with the Duke of Devonshire for the necessary land for the station at Bandon, payment being made in shares at par. In April it became clear that Bolton was in difficulties with contract No 4 between Gogginshill and Killeen, when a large body of men employed by him turned up at the company's office in Cork claiming wages due to them. It was agreed to ascertain what wages were actually due and the company would pay them.

Nixon, in his report to the shareholders in August 1848, said there were some 600 men employed on the works and he hoped to have the section of line between Bandon and Ballinhassig completed within three months. The Bandon River bridge, previously declared to be a 'gewgaw' (a pretty thing of little worth, a toy), had been tested and found satisfactory. Over the next six months progress was retarded by Nixon being seriously ill for an extended period of time. The chairman told the shareholders in February 1849 that the directors had been told the line would never pay and that work had been commenced at the wrong end of the line. Hopefully the detractors would soon be proved wrong.

Inspection & opening

A trial trip was made on 30th June 1849. It was reported in the local press that the Cork and English directors along with a number of invited guests travelled from Cork to Ballinhassig in two horse-drawn carriages, while the western directors were brought from Bandon by train. The combined group left Ballinhassig shortly after midday, and, with Nixon driving the engine, 'they moved off swiftly amidst much cheering from the local populace'. The train reached Bandon in 18 minutes, following intermediate stops at Brinny station and just beyond the Bandon River bridge at Innoshannon platform. A déjeuner was held for the directors and invited guests at the Devonshire Arms Hotel, while the train made several return journeys. Nixon received a handsome tribute from the chairman, Major Beamish, for his attention to the construction, he having saved the company a good deal of money.

The line was inspected on 26th July by Captain George Wynne on behalf of the BoT. Although constructed as a single line, the railway at foundation level and the bridges were of sufficient width to admit of a second line of rails being laid when deemed necessary. Wynne reported that the stations and platforms were complete, with most of the signals up, the remainder being in course of erection. Whilst the masonry for the turntables at either end was in place, the ironwork for them had yet to arrive from England. However, as the company proposed using the small Adams engines, this was of less consequence than might otherwise have been the case. There were five level crossings, none of which had been authorised by the Act, although they had been approved by the Grand Jury. Despite these several unfinished matters, approval was given for this first section of line to be opened for the conveyance of passengers and parcels on Wednesday 1st August.

The company purchased five horse omnibus coaches, each capable of holding 25 people, to convey passengers between Ballinhassig and Cork. Messrs Magan & O'Connor of Cork provided the horses (four for each omnibus) and operated a service twice daily between Ballinhassig and the Imperial Hotel in Cork, through fares to and from Bandon being 3s, 2s and 1s 4d, respectively for first, second and third classes single; return fares were 5s, 3s and 2s. Journey time between Bandon and Ballinhassig was 20 minutes with the through journey to Cork being performed in 1½ hours. Trains were reported to consist of one composite, one third, one horse-box and a carriage truck, hauled by the 'light' engines.

Attention now turned to the completion of the line east of Ballinhassig. Under an Act of 1847 powers had been obtained to extend the line at the Cork end from Evergreen to a terminus at or near the east side of Cornmarket Street, and also for the deviation and tunnel at Gogginshill. A further Act of 1850 authorised a short 125 yards extension at Cork, which the chairman explained would give the company a complete communication with vessels on the river. A contract for the line was awarded to Messrs Fox Henderson & Co of London in an amount of £87,000, including the 900 yards long Gogginshill tunnel and the Chetwynd viaduct. It was a difficult enough contract with 19 embankments and 21 cuttings of varying lengths, and 15 road bridges, apart from numerous smaller bridges.

Government loan & a dispute with the contractors

A loan of £35,000 was received from the Public Works Loan Commissioners in February 1850 with interest due at 5% per annum. A stipulation was attached to the loan that the tunnel at Gogginshill should be wide enough for double track, adding in no small measure to the cost. Soon some 300 men were employed here working day and night. Six working shafts were sunk, enabling work to proceed at a total of 14 working faces. Later, three ventilation shafts were provided. The strata was such that masonry lining was required. Difficulties were soon encountered with the construction of the long embankment at Ballyphehane, about a mile outside Cork as much of it was constructed through bogland, making it difficult to obtain a firm base. A timber bridge over the Tramore River near Ballyphehane was later replaced by a culvert. The erection of the Chetwynd viaduct, which occupied several months, proved to be a great attraction with large crowds gathering to watch each of the 110ft spans being raised to a height of 90ft above the valley floor. Initially it was hoped to have the line into Cork completed by December 1850 but in February of the following year, Messrs Fox Henderson & Co reported that they would have the line open by 1st July.

In January 1851, Nixon had, however, reported to the board that the contractors were proceeding at a most unsatisfactory rate of progress and it became necessary to advise them of the possible forfeiture of their contract. It was clear however that the fault did not lie entirely with the contractors. By February, the contractors were demanding certificates of work which were not forthcoming. Payments to Messrs Fox Henderson & Co fell into arrears and they, rightly, suspected that the company's financial position was, despite the Government loan, unhealthy. In April it was reported that the third instalment of the Government loan had not been received to enable payment of £4,000 against certificates. Furthermore the company's bank account was overdrawn and the secretary was instructed to issue

Bills at two months date. Some of the directors declined to attach their names to these Bills, their signatures eventually being attached following a special board meeting on 14th April. One director, a Mr Swanston, still refused to sign and resigned his position, being later re-elected when he too was persuaded of the error of his ways!

The directors made a trial trip over the entire line on 31st July. Another excursion was arranged to take place on 7th August, for which invitations were issued to a large number of persons. Matters now, however, took a turn for the worse when the contractors' representative in Cork announced that they would prevent an opening taking place unless payments amounting to some £30,000 due to them were remitted forthwith. The directors refused to be intimidated by threats of this nature and proceeded

Albert Quay station layout photographed from Hibernian Road bridge with ex GS&WR 0-6-0T No 90 on yard shunting duties. The passenger station can be seen in the background to the left of the raised signal cabin. The latter's predecessor can be seen just to the right of No 90 with the goods yard in the background. An accident appears to have befallen one of the two goods brake vans on the left of the picture.
W McGrath

with their preparations. On the evening of the 6th August, Ronayne took an engine out from Albert Quay on a trial trip. The contractors now headed out behind with a rake of laden ballast wagons hauled by several horses. On reaching Black Ash bridge they stopped on the line and removed some sleepers. The driver of the returning engine spotted the obstruction in time and brought it to a halt.

It would appear that a physical confrontation now took place between the two parties in the dark. In due course, Ronayne and his men managed to propel the ballast wagons back into Cork. Having failed in their initial efforts, the contractors' men now proceeded along the line, dynamiting rocks in the Ballymah and Knockrea cuttings, completely blocking the line at both points with tons of stone and spoil. Rails were also removed from the Chetwynd viaduct. The BoT inspector, Captain Robert M Laffan in fact arrived in Cork on 8th August, intending to carry out an inspection of the extension. At Albert Quay, he found that no arrangements had been made to enable him to go over the line. At the first rock cutting, he found a number of men at work excavating and blasting, 'and the line altogether in such a state that it would have been impossible to have it ready for public traffic on the day fixed by the Directors for

the opening' (Monday, 11th August). Laffan was informed by the chairman and engineer that the unfinished state of the line had arisen from, 'an unseen misunderstanding with the contractors'.

The opening was postponed for a month, but it was to take considerably longer to clear the line of the blockages and it was not until Monday 8th December 1851 that it was opened for traffic, following a successful inspection by Captain Wynne. A service of four trains each way was provided on weekdays and two on Sundays. On the opening day the 250 guests had to endure torrential rain. Such was the weather that the first train had to be divided at Chetwynd viaduct, the first two coaches being uncoupled and taken on to Ballinhassig. The engine then returned for those left behind. The *Illustrated London News* commented that 'Few Railways have had such a hard struggle for existence as this Bandon line'.

In the interim, warrants were issued for the arrest of all the principal parties involved in the fracas on 6th August. The case was opened in Cork Courthouse six days later, Isaac Butt, later to be the founder of the Home Rule movement, acting as counsel for the contractors. The trial lasted for three days with the contractors being acquitted, although the obstruction to the line was clearly proved. In their defence, the

contractors contended that they had not handed over the line and were justified in their actions. The company for its part maintained that less than half the figure of £30,000 was actually due to the contractors. The company officials on the engine were charged with riotous conduct, the case against them soon being dropped. It was to be nearly five years before the contractors' claim against the company was finally settled. In the midst of all the legal wranglings, the company's solicitor, Mr Jameson, was requested to resign his office, his response being requested within half an hour. Jameson refused to give an answer until he was handed a copy of the board resolution, but the directors decided to bring matters to a head by dismissing him forthwith. Messrs Richard and William Coppinger were duly appointed in his stead, but they resigned within two months.

Left upper: **CB&SCR B4 4-6-0 No 470 on a Baltimore to Bantry train taking water at Bandon in the 1950s.** N Shelley collection

Left: **Waterfall station with an up laden beet special crossing a down goods, the latter in charge of a 'C' class Bo-Bo diesel electric locomotive.** W McGrath

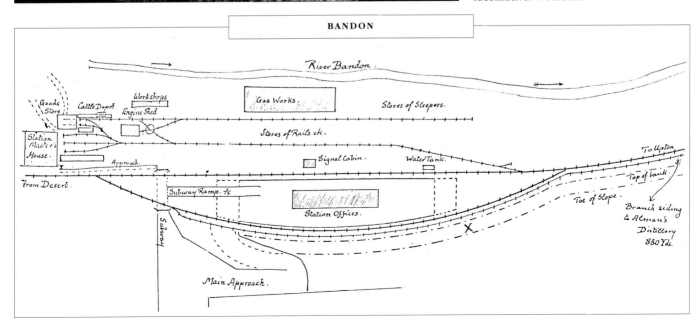

Chapter Two

A DECREPIT CONCERN

With the full extent of their line open it might be assumed that the directors and shareholders could now look forward to building up traffic and receiving the optimistic dividends which had been forecast. The reality was however somewhat different. The line had cost in the region of £20,000 per mile to construct and was grossly over-capitalised. This inhibited expenditure on much-needed improvements and it was not long before the directors were being severely censured for poor service, inadequate rolling stock and a lack of efficient management. The neighbouring CB&PR had cost more per mile to construct but it had the advantage of a greater traffic potential due in part to the suburban nature of its route. The C&BR directors, however, faced a more serious problem, namely the shortness of their line. It quickly became clear that western merchants were not prepared to tranship goods at Bandon and move them by rail for 20 miles to Cork, where they were again transhipped either for delivery in the city or for transfer to the GS&WR system. As late as 1859, a shareholder attributed the lack of a dividend to road competition, claiming that there were as many carriers as ever on the Bandon road. What was required was a further extension of the system to the west.

Removal to London
Initially the directors put on a brave face and attributed the low receipts to the loss of four months takings arising from the dispute with the contractors and the fact of having opened the line in the winter season. The approach of spring and the development of the western and Kinsale traffic could not fail, they believed, 'to create a favourable and material change in the prospects of the Company'. They could look forward to a good traffic in fish, flax and linen. The half-yearly meeting of shareholders in February 1852 turned out to be a lively affair with recriminations and disclosures regarding both the contractors and the company solicitor, who had as the *Railway Times* put it, 'been discarded'. References were made to the difficulties with the contractors who had sought to avoid the terms of their contract. Their agents had accepted that the line was to have been

opened to Cork on 8th August, so much so that a proposal was put forward by them to fit up the goods store at Cork for a grand banquet. Instead they had resorted to blowing up a rock cutting. The *Railway Times* seemed to take a different view of events and called for an instant refutation of the, 'slur upon the character of so reputable a firm, or even of their Agents'.

By February 1852 the directors were considering correspondence from some of their London colleagues. It was stated that a third party was prepared to advance a sum of £8,000 to the company provided six seats on the board were placed at his disposal and that the offices were removed to London and control vested in the London board. Considerable discussion ensued and it was finally agreed that the proposal be accepted, subject to certain conditions. A local committee was to be set up in Cork to manage the day-to-day operations and there were to be no redundancies amongst those currently employed. No appointments were to be made or any salary fixed or increased without the consent of the Cork committee. Agreement was reached in March whereby a traffic committee was set up in Cork consisting of three local directors to be selected by the London board. The latter agreed to use their utmost endeavours, 'to relieve the Company from its present embarrassments and they have no doubt of being able to do so'. Offices were taken at No 17 Gracechurch Street in the City of London at an annual rent of £45.

About this time, the engineer, Charles Nixon introduced the subject of his current position with the company, it being agreed that he be paid £250 per annum as remuneration for his services as engineer-in-chief; it was also agreed that he would accept sole responsibility for the locomotive and permanent way departments. Nixon was soon in difficulties with the board in relation to Messrs Fox Henderson & Co's claim, which was considered to be excessive. Apart from this, the local committee found it necessary to complain early in May of the slow progress in the construction of the works on the terminus at Cork. At the same meeting at which this item was discussed, the chairman, Beamish, tendered his resignation, in large part due

to the transfer of board meetings to London. Beamish however remained on as a local director and along with Messrs. Thomas Somerville Reeves and William James Shaw constituted the local committee. He was replaced as chairman by one of the London directors, Colonel J.C. Chatterton. In connection with notice that the Lord Lieutenant was due to travel over the line early in June, a Mr Honner applied for a free pass. He was politely informed that it was the intention of those English directors who planned to come over for the event to pay for their tickets as first class passengers, and he would be expected to do likewise.

Nixon approached the board again in June notifying his desire to resign as engineer-in-chief owing to the pressure of other professional engagements and duties, but offering his services on a consultancy basis. This request came as a shock to the board and less than a month later, following correspondence with the secretary, Nixon offered to withdraw his resignation. This was eventually agreed to and he was duly instructed to proceed with the measurement of the contractor's works on the line. About this time, Nixon reported on the state of the permanent way and recommended the purchase of some 500 larch sleepers as a number of the original sleepers were reported to be decayed.

At the half-yearly shareholders' meeting held in London in August 1852 it was announced that the directors had been successful in negotiating a reduction from 5% to 4% in the rate of interest on the PWLC loan of 1850; even at this reduced figure, the company found it difficult to meet the regular payments, such was the state of the finances. Once again it was announced that arrangements were now in place for securing the Kinsale and western traffic and the directors had no doubt whatsoever that the undertaking would soon become remunerative. As regards the Kinsale traffic, the board were reluctant to incur additional expenditure in the erection of a junction at or near Ballinhassig station and gave instructions for the repair of sufficient of the company's omnibuses. Tenders were then to be sought for the horsing of the Kinsale traffic, an agreement being concluded in September with a Mr Black.

Bandon low-level station, used for goods traffic following the opening of the new high-level through station in 1894.
W McGrath

Extensions are proposed

The Cork & Bandon Railway Amendment Act of 1852 enabled the company to raise additional capital up to £48,000 and to make arrangements with respect to the capital and mortgage debts. Thoughts now turned to an extension of the line westwards to Bantry, a special general meeting being held at the beginning of June to consider the matter further. Such an extension it was confidently stated would make the line one of the most remunerative in Ireland. It was claimed the extension could be constructed for as little as £5,000 per mile. A meeting of interested parties was held in Bandon on 28th October with Lord Bernard in the chair, Drimoleague now being put forward as a terminus with a branch to Clonakilty. A committee was formed to pursue the matter further and a resolution passed to the effect that certain baronies should guarantee a rate of interest not exceeding 4% per annum on the estimated cost of construction of £200,000 for a maximum term of 20 years.

Another meeting was held at Skibbereen early in December, the company solicitors informing those present that it had not been possible to have the plans for a branch to that town ready in time for lodgement by the deadline of 30th November. Yet another meeting in Bandon at the end of January was informed that the committee now proposed a maximum guarantee of 2% per annum. Clonakilty was not now to be connected to the network and the Barony would not therefore be asked for a guarantee. Some further discussion took place in relation to the guarantee, Mr Winkworth on behalf of the London deputation explaining that the promoters would not proceed unless 4% was guaranteed.

The Act as passed enabled the company to raise additional capital to the extent of £288,000. The authorised line, just over 32 miles in length, was to commence by a junction with the existing C&BR line close to the gas works at Bandon and pass through or close to Castle Bernard, Enniskeen, Ballyneen, Manch, Dunmanway and Dromdaleague (Drimoleague) to a terminus at Dromourneen Bridge in the parish of Caheragh about three miles to the south of Bantry. There was also to be a branch eight miles in length from a point near Gaggan Bridge and terminating close to the Poor Law Union Work House at Clonakilty. It was stipulated that certain baronies were to contribute at the rate of 3% per annum towards the Bantry extension in the event of receipts being insufficient. Section 100 of the Act was interesting in that the company were obliged to apply to Parliament in the next Session for an Act to construct a branch railway from or near Drimoleague to the town of Skibbereen. Powers were in fact obtained in 1854 for such a line terminating about 300 yards east of the bridge on the north side of the River Ilen in the parish of Abbeystrowry and town of Skibbereen. It should also be mentioned at this point that some consideration had been given to laying down a tramway from the terminus at Cork on to Albert Quay so as to provide direct access to shipping.

Lord Bernard suggested in October 1853 that consideration be given to an extension of the Bantry line from Dromourneen southwestwards to Dunmanus Bay, this suggestion being declined owing to the depressed state of the money market. His Lordship came up with other suggestions, all being turned down by the directors; on one occasion a memorial was submitted from the inhabitants of the Dunmanus Bay region, to no avail. In seeking powers for an extension of the line to Bantry, the directors also saw the possibility of a future branch to Crookhaven, yet another possible candidate as a transatlantic packet station. A communication was received from the Admiralty in London requesting to be supplied with plans showing how the railway might be extended towards Crookhaven on the Mizen peninsula. They also requested information on the capabilities of that port, considering it as yet another likely contender as a transatlantic packet station. The directors had already given their own attention to this prospect in 1853 and were of opinion that a saving of up to two days might be effected in the movement of mail between England and America. The necessary details were duly prepared and submitted to the Admiralty in February 1854. Whilst the latter considered the subject of a railway extension to Crookhaven to be, 'on the whole (of) a favourable nature', nothing further was done about it.

Back to Ireland

Despite the transfer of the undertaking to London, financial problems continued to beset the company. In January 1854 the PWLC solicitors wrote intimating the intention of the Commissioners to take possession of the line unless arrears of £2,400 were paid before the end of the month. Following negotiations the deadline was extended to April, but it was to lead to a meeting of shareholders in Dublin at the beginning of March seeking to transfer the direction of the line back to Ireland. At a further meeting in July, agreement in principle was achieved on removing to some convenient location in Dublin. Consideration was also directed to removing some or all of the current directors, or of adopting other measures to improve the financial affairs of the company. The local committee in Cork however expressed the opinion that this attack on the directors by a group of Dublin shareholders was at very least uncourteous in the extreme, suggesting that such a move should be resisted by all legitimate means. Other counsels prevailed and it was announced in April 1855 that the directors hoped that, 'an arrangement may be made for completing and carrying out that desirable movement for the salvation of the shareholders' property'.

At a special meeting held in Dublin on 28th March 1856, following the decision of the London directors to resign office in favour of an Irish board, a resolution was unanimously passed to appoint a committee to carry out the necessary arrangements for the formation of a new board. This committee included Sir James Dombrain, chairman of the Waterford & Tramore Railway, Valentine O'Brien O'Connor and David McBirnie (sic). An editorial in the *Railway Times* for 6th April stated that the company appeared to be struggling out of its difficulties, although the question of transferring the direction to Ireland was not going as smoothly as had been hoped. Later in the year the new board was set up with O'Connor as chairman, also including McBirney in its number. The company's offices were removed from London to No 3 Beresford Place in Dublin. This appears in GS&WR records as O'Connor's address.

Receipts for the first half of 1854 rose by 20% yet there was room for further improvement, a large volume of coal and corn traffic still going by road. At this time the directors were still awaiting Brunel's award in regard to the differences between the company and the late contractors. The latter were blamed for the delay, it being reported that they sought a postponement of discussions as Sir Charles Fox and others were reported to be absent from England. This matter dragged on for another 18 months, and it was not until March 1856 that the chairman was enabled to report that the award had been handed down in an amount of £19,874. It was finally agreed in June 1856 that Messrs Fox Henderson & Co would accept a sum of £17,380 made up of £10,000 in cash and the balance in No 2 preference shares.

A casualty of the settlement with the contractors was the engineer, Charles Nixon. He submitted a note of his expenses, which were considered to be excessive; having endeavoured to sue for their recovery, Nixon was promptly dismissed and was replaced as engineer by William R LeFanu. The latter remained with the company until he left in 1862 to continue a distinguished career and become a Commissioner of Public Works. There were some who felt that had LeFanu been in charge of engineering from an earlier date, the line might well have been constructed more cheaply. It was suggested that his predecessors were perhaps more interested in demonstrating their prowess in bridge and tunnel building than in constructing the line as cheaply as possible commensurate with the easiest and most practical route.

With the transfer of the company's management back to Ireland, the board in London acknowledged, 'their high sense of the ability, zeal and discretion with which, under circumstances of great difficulty', the secretary, Mr Williams Wood, had discharged his onerous duties. The directors went on to state that they regretted that the pecuniary position of the company during much of his period in that office had prevented them from adequately acknowledg-

ing his strict probity and general efficiency. Wood agreed to remain on as secretary for at least three months, subject to his being paid half a year's salary, viz £125. By September 1856, Wood decided that he had had enough and announced his resignation from the end of that month, agreeing however to act as London agent for the company. It was agreed to remunerate him at a rate of £50 per annum and, if his presence should be required in Ireland, he would additionally receive £10 as travelling expenses. Wood also very generously gave the company the use of his offices in London, free of charge. James Connell was appointed in his stead as from 1st October 1856.

Shortly before Wood's resignation, the new board in Dublin decided to appoint a traffic manager, the post being advertised in various newspapers in August. Various applicants were interviewed at the board meeting on 13th September and it was decided to appoint Richard Coghlan, the company's stationmaster at Albert Quay, on a three months trial basis. It was in fact to be almost nine months before Coghlan wrote

to the board requesting them to formally ratify his position. The local committee were instructed to fit up the terminus room at Cork as Coghlan's residence, a sum of £30 being allocated for the purpose.

Seizure of the line is threatened

Reference has already been made to the difficulties with the PWLC and the temporary extension of the deadline for payment of arrears. This matter was to rear its head again before long and the directors were under constant threat of having their line seized. In fact, a warrant for the sale of the line was presented early in 1855 and a technical 'arrest' was made in June of that year on the petition of a lesser creditor, the Beatty Minors, for an amount of £85 18s 11d, the company's engines being reportedly seized. It was also reported that two station clerks, Messrs Coghlan and Lyster, were placed in charge as bailiffs to prevent interruption of traffic. On each occasion the PWLC threatened seizure the directors themselves scraped together enough cash to avoid this indignity. As an example in June 1855 the Commissioners stated that they would not

Right upper: **Kilpatrick tunnel, the first railway tunnel in Ireland to be opened and used for public traffic.** W McGrath

Right: **The bridge over the Bandon river at Bandon providing access to the Beamish & Crawford bottling plant.** C L Fry, Seán Kennedy collection

extend the time for payment of interest and would take possession of the line within a week. An agreement was reached whereby the PWLC were paid £600 on account.

At the beginning of August, Mr Barnes, solicitor on behalf of the Commissioners, advised that he intended proceeding immediately to Cork by the evening train to take possession of the line. An advance of £640 was made by four of the directors with interest payable at 5% per annum, and an agreement made to pay the outstanding balance of £600 within a month. An agreement was made in October for the annual payments of the principal. However, in December, Messrs Barnes & Bernard advised that they had been instructed by their principals to take immediate possession of the line unless instalments due in 1855 amounting to £1,882 7s 0d were paid forthwith. A further extension of time was sought, but Barnes reported that he had been instructed to proceed by that evening's train to take possession. The new arrangement only recently arrived at was to be cancelled and the line seized for the amount now due under the original loan securities, viz. £14,000. The secretary requested the local directors to raise £1,000 provided the London directors raised the remaining £882, but the latter refused to intervene. Another party, unnamed, came forward and agreed to purchase the company's debentures for £1,740 at 6% interest for three years date, this generous offer being accepted. A new clause was now inserted in the arrangement with the PWLC authorising the cancellation of the arrangement in the event of future payments not being made on their due dates.

Matters improved for a time but in March 1861 the PWLC were again threatening proceedings over an amount of £744 odd some three months overdue, while in July 1865 it was reported that more than £1,400 remained unpaid. The PWLC wrote in September of the following year stating that it appeared from the company's accounts that they had ample funds in hand to pay arrears of principal and interest. The company responded by stating that these monies were required to pay interest on debenture debts and on the No 1 preference shares. More pleading in October 1866 cut little ice with the Commissioners and a cheque for £1,368 was reluctantly sent to them, with a further £971 odd in the following month. The loan was finally liquidated in 1870.

BoT intervention

February 1862 saw correspondence received from the BoT in London following receipt of memorials from, 'the Magistrates, Gentry and Inhabitants of Bandon', regarding the defective state of portions of the line and requesting an inspection by one of the BoT railway inspectors. These memorials were in direct opposition to the chairman's claim at the shareholders' half-yearly meeting that their line was, 'in good order in every respect', apart from the Innoshannon viaduct which was about to be replaced. Pending a BoT inspection, Thomas Conran, the locomotive superintendent, was instructed to take charge of the permanent way under LeFanu's directions. In addition, the local directors were requested to go over and examine the line once a month. Captain Tyler arrived from London in early March and carried out an inspection of the line, also taking the opportunity to investigate two minor accidents. Tyler found the track required lifting, draining and ballasting, as well as the renewal of sleepers, spikes and keys. He recommended that the rails be fish-plated to provide greater security and ultimately to reduce maintenance. Tyler also referred to the 'rickety' state of the wooden bridges, which should be replaced in iron or stone. Despite these various adverse comments, little changed during the next ten years or so and the BoT had to return in 1870 and yet again in 1873.

Reporting to the board in June 1870, Conran stated that he had walked the entire line and found it in better condition than it had been for some years. This statement was however made within the parameters that it was as good as the nature of the line's construction allowed, viz. short unjointed rails with poor ballast and the, 'usual percentage of bad sleepers and rails'. He recommended that attention be given in particular to the section of line between Macroom Junction and Albert Quay, which bore the heaviest traffic. Three months later, Colonel Rich wrote stating that he was about to visit the line to enquire into a recent accident at Crossbarry and also to proceed over the line itself following further complaints as to its condition. When he undertook the inspection on 19th September, he found the line in, 'very fair order'. Having returned to London however, he appears to have had second thoughts as a letter was received from the BoT in October expressing the hope that the directors would take immediate steps to improve the condition of their line. The upshot of this correspondence was the appointment of Mr A Dargan as inspector of permanent way at a salary of £2 per week.

Dargan submitted a lengthy report on the state of the permanent way in December 1870. The principal defect in his view was the manner in which the rails were jointed, which would not now be allowed on a new railway by the BoT. Chair joints were extremely difficult to maintain in proper order and were dependent on constant attention by the milesmen. As a matter of urgency, Dargan strongly advised that the line as far as Kinsale Junction should be fish-plated. He also strongly urged the replacement of 15ft rail lengths by a minimum of 24ft lengths. Dargan pointed out that there were in the region of 10,000 defective sleepers on the line, about one-fifth of which were in need of urgent replacement. The line also required lifting and ballasting in most of the cuttings, which would help to improve drainage and thereby extend the life of sleepers. Two other matters were referred to in his report, viz. the defective condition of fencing and the fact that many of the milesmen lived long distances from the line. In the latter context, Dargan suggested the building of small houses as was done on other lines.

Once again, we can see the parsimonious approach adopted during O'Connor's term as chairman. Three more years went by and little appears to have been done to remedy defects, as the Earl of Bandon took upon himself the responsibility for again communicating with the BoT in November 1873, calling for a further investigation of the company's line and engines. It also seemed clear that the company were reluctant to advise the BoT of accidents, probably feeling that distance from London would enable them to avoid interference from the regulatory authorities.

Colonel Rich returned again in December, having been in Cork only two months previously to enquire into the derailment of a goods train in Innoshannon tunnel. Rich reported that 13 of the 20 miles of track had deteriorated, apart from which there was a lack of distant signals and catch points. In their defence, the company stated that they had sustained no accidents resulting in death or injury. Rich retorted that this could only have been due to the dedicated care and effort of the enginemen and permanent way staff. O'Connor died in September 1873, and was replaced as chairman by David McBirney of Dublin. Under new leadership, the directors soon realised that the method of operation of the railway in previous years was false economy. Gradually the permanent way and rolling stock was improved. Steel rails began to appear in 1877 with the first six miles from Cork being so fitted. These rails, in 30ft and 42ft lengths, weighed 68lbs per yard. Many new sleepers spaced 3ft apart were laid down and broken stone ballast put down.

The year 1873 began badly for the Bandon. On 16th January, serious flooding breached an embankment about 1½ miles from Bandon, displacing about 60 yards of permanent way. An approaching train was derailed as the driver, although able to see the rails, did not realise that the ground underneath had been washed away. Fortunately the passenger carriage remained upright, although four passengers suffered minor injuries. As was the practice at the time, the carriage doors were locked, and none of the train crew appears to have made any attempts to release the passengers. The

Ballinhassig station showing the terminal of the Ballinphellic Ropeway.
Photographer unknown, National Archives, London

driver and the company's traffic manager, who happened to be travelling on the train, set out on foot for Bandon to summon assistance. Arriving there, they discovered that the telegraph had been damaged, and Coghlan decided to proceed to Cork to enlist help. In the interim, the clerk at Bandon arranged to dispatch a cart to the scene to rescue the stranded passengers and bring in those who had been injured. Later, Colonel Rich, reporting on behalf of the BoT, censured Coghlan's action in going back to Cork. Coghlan retired in December 1877 on the grounds of serious illness, in part brought on by his experiences in January 1873, by which time he had served more than 25 years with the company.

Distillery siding
Messrs Allman & Co of Bandon are described in the 1886 edition of the *Postal Directory of Munster* as being distillers of the finest Irish whiskey from pot stills only. Established in 1825, the premises was situated approximately half a mile to the east of Bandon railway station. Fifty years later the firm was employing about 300 men. In October 1868 Richard Allman approached the board seeking the provision of a siding connecting the line with the coach road running parallel to their distillery to facilitate the loading of grain for Cork. Subject to the company's approval, Allman stated his intention of applying to the Grand Jury to make a tramway from the railway company's boundary into the distillery itself, a distance of about 200 yards. They would also give the company the carriage of their coal from Cork, rather than via Collier's Quay. The board agreed to provide the siding if guaranteed the carriage of coal, this proviso being accepted. In September 1872 Messrs. Allman requested that the siding be lengthened, but this was declined on the grounds of expense.

In February 1874 the distillery offered a sum of £100 towards the expense of a tramway from the railway to their premises. It was, however, June 1876 before the cost of the tramway was estimated at £220. It was reported to be in a very forward state by September of that year. It left the company's siding close to the distillery and crossed the main road diagonally to enter the distillery premises, where it crossed an open square and then divided in two, one section serving an engine shed, the other a coal bank. Messrs. Allman agreed to keep that portion of the public road occupied by the tramway in proper order. It was not until July 1878 that the engineer reported that his men were just completing the tramway into the

distillery yard. In the following November, Messrs Allman offered to pay £100 per annum if the company would provide an engine to do their shunting at Bandon. The locomotive superintendent saw no difficulty in this but suggested that ordinary permanent way be installed instead of tramway rails. A special engine would be required, the cost of working which would amount to at least £225 per annum.

It is assumed that the company did in fact work the tramway for several years although there is no reference to this in the company's minute books. What we do know is that it was in 1885 or 1886 that Messrs Allman & Co purchased a second-hand Manning Wardle 0-4-0ST, maker's No 773, which they retained until 1920. In the latter year it was replaced by a new 0-4-0ST built by Messrs Peckett. Details of both engines can be found in Chapter Thirteen. The last distillation took place during the winter of 1925 but the siding remained in use for a further five years to clear the stock of spirits. In 1930 the second locomotive was taken over by the GSR as their No 495.

The Macroom connection
It will be recalled that Charles Vignoles brought forward plans in 1836 for a line from Blarney through Macroom and Glengarriff to the coast at Castletown Berehaven, a scheme which was stillborn. Three separate schemes for connecting Cork with Macroom were put forward in 1860. The 'southern route' proposed a line forming a junction with the C&BR at or near Ballyphehane and running along the south side of the valley of the River Lee to Macroom, a somewhat similar scheme having been proposed by Sir John Benson four years earlier. The 'northern route', under the title of the Cork Blarney & Macroom Railway, was to run from a terminus at York Street in Cork (now Thomas Davis Street) through Blarney, Dripsey and Coachford to Macroom, with a 3½ mile line connecting with the

GS&WR near Monard. Extensions were also envisaged to Kenmare, Bantry, Glengarriff and Castletown Berehaven. The scheme, which subsequently formed part of the separate Cork & Muskerry Light Railway, was proposed by Sir John Macneill and had the backing of the War Office. The 'middle route' was to run more or less all the way along the banks of the River Lee. This and the northern route foundered for a number of reasons and it was the southern route which was finally chosen.

An approach was made to the Bandon board in October 1860 on the part of the promoters of the Cork & Macroom Railway making certain propositions. These included the formation of a junction with the C&BR at Ballyphehane, about ¼ mile from Albert Quay, and joint use of the latter station and offices. Enquiry was also made as to whether the C&BR would work the proposed new line or provide the necessary facilities to enable the new company to operate their own line. The use of one station would, the Macroom deputation believed, 'materially assist the traffic of both companies and economise on expenditure', and they expected the Bandon to meet them in a fair and liberal spirit. These various suggestions were agreed in principle, subject to the remuneration to be paid to the C&BR being left to the arbitration of the chairman of one of the principal Irish companies.

Plans for the proposed new line were examined and reported on by LeFanu in March 1861 and on 1st August of that year the Cork & Macroom Direct Railway Company was incorporated by Act of Parliament. Capital was to be £120,000 with the usual borrowing powers. The chairman of the new company was Sir John Arnott, a former Mayor of Cork. The contract was awarded to Joseph Ronayne, a person already familiar to us. The first sod was turned by the chairman close to the point of the proposed junction with the C&BR and the line was in due course opened throughout on 12th May

1866. Prior to this however, a number of matters required clarification and agreement with the Bandon.

Some consideration was given in May 1861 to the laying down of a second line of rails from Ballyphehane, which would have allowed the new company independent access to Albert Quay. Discussions took place in November 1864 regarding the remuneration expected by the C&BR for the use of the various facilities, a sum of £2,000 per annum being suggested. In support of this figure, it was pointed out that additional buildings and other works would be required. The C&MDR deputation however refused to countenance such a high figure and reverted to their board. Writing in March 1865, the Macroom secretary stated that his board were of opinion that there seemed to be little likelihood of an amicable agreement being reached and suggested referring the matter to the arbitration of the BoT.

In due course the BoT appointed Captain Mark Huish of the Isle of Wight, and one-time general manager of the L&NWR. However the C&BR announced in April that they could not agree to such an arbitration, which they believed to be contrary to the provisions of the C&MDR Act, the BoT being similarly informed. Despite this Huish was appointed and the Bandon directors reluctantly agreed to go along with it. Whilst awaiting the outcome of the arbitration, Charles Cotton was appointed by the C&BR to act as engineer to direct and superintend the execution of the junction works at Ballyphehane. The award was made in November 1865, arrangements being made for the provision of the various facilities suggested, which included a signal cabin at the junction, engine shed and a goods shed.

A plan of the proposed engine shed was prepared by Cotton and submitted to the C&MDR for approval. Following some alterations, the tender of Barry McMullen of Cork was accepted for £620, whilst in June 1866 arrangements were made for the introduction of staff working between Albert Quay and Ballyphehane. Also in June, the C&MDR wrote regarding the use by their clerk of office accommodation at Cork, referring thus to it – 'the stench being so unbearable that no clerk would consent to remain in it, as in all probability it would cost him his life'. Instructions were issued to provide a more suitable office.

Further complaints were made in February 1869, this time with reference to the arrival platform at Cork being used for the storage of coal and timber. In asking for this practice to be stopped, they went on to state that the facilities for working the station were very imperfect. The C&BR local committee declined to take any notice of the complaint, this lack of action being taken to a similar complaint in December

1871, when, 'they did not consider themselves called upon to enter into any explanation'.

In April 1874 it was reported that the C&BR considered they were losing heavily on the provision of facilities for the C&MDR due to increased labour charges, an approach being made to the latter company seeking a review. The Macroom directors however saw no reason to increase what they already considered to be an excessive payment of £2,000 per annum. This matter added to the friction already existing and it is hardly surprising that proposals were put forward in December 1876 to enable the C&MDR to extend their own line into Cork and to provide their own terminus, an Act giving effect to this being obtained in the following year. Consideration was also given about this time to the construction of a branch from Crookstown to join up with the WCR at Enniskeane. A site was procured to the west of Albert Quay at Capwell in 1877 and construction of the new line was commenced in February of the following year. The new station and extension line, completed at a cost of about £20,000, were brought into use on 27th September 1879, the connection with the C&BR at Ballyphehane being severed. We shall return to the C&MDR in regard to its future relations with the Bandon in a later chapter.

Station improvements

A number of alterations and additions were made to stations during the period reviewed in this chapter, and for convenience these are now grouped together. Albert Quay station was in the news in October 1857 when the board accepted the tender of the United General Gas Co of Cork to supply gas to the terminus for three years at a rate of 4s 6d per 1,000cu ft. In February of the following year, Conran reported that the turntable on the arrival side of the station, over which trains had to pass, was unsafe and unnecessary for traffic purposes. Instructions were given for its immediate removal; however a station layout in volume 1 of the late Colm Creedon's book purporting to date from 1869 clearly shows this or a replacement turntable giving access to a carriage dock and to the Hay Market siding. In November 1858 Conran was directed to lay down a crossing, 'to meet the Corporation Footway', the stones being taken from Goggin's Hill tunnel. Eleven years later, on 1st October 1869, Conran felt obliged to report on the dangers of this level crossing, the matter being referred to the local committee for their attention. One of the problems was that the gatemen were unable to adequately mind the crossing itself and the various points under their control. It was agreed that an additional hand be employed, leaving the gatemen free to attend only to the gates.

By the mid-1860s it was becoming clear that additional facilities were required at Cork, as a result, Conran submitted plans for additional goods accommodation, while in March 1870 authorisation was given for the provision of an additional siding into the C&MDR ground so as to provide covered accommodation for their rolling stock.

Following a dispute with the Corporation in February 1871 over land which might be required for road-widening purposes, it was suggested that if the Corporation would sanction the closing of the crossing, which was considered dangerous due to the number of daily movements to and fro over it, the local committee would recommend to the board that they should provide another strip of land rather than the one sought by the Corporation. Following further discussions, it was decided to retain the level crossing. The crossing was in the news again in August 1875. So much opposition was being raised to the company's suggestions for closing it that the local committee were of the opinion that no concession would be made short of erecting a footbridge over the line at this point.

The old turntable at Cork was reported in March 1871 to be out of repair, a new wrought-iron one of 18ft diameter being recommended at a cost of about £120. After inspecting an old GS&WR turntable at Cork in May, and finding it to be totally unsuited to the company's requirements, nothing appears to have been done for almost three years. Finally at the end of January 1874 the tender of Messrs. Courtney & Stephens of Dublin was accepted at £105.

A further expansion of facilities being deemed necessary, the engineer submitted plans in May 1876 for an additional goods store, estimated to cost £1,350. Consideration was given to the purchase of the old roof and walls of the platform of the CB&PR, which had been advertised for sale. In June it was decided to proceed with the erection of the new goods store about 210ft long and 55ft wide, along with a new carriage shed, making use in their construction of the material from the old Passage terminus at City Park. In addition, it was hoped there would be sufficient lattice girders to erect a footbridge at the Gas Works level crossing. In the following October, the tender of a Mr B McMullen, 'a most respectable and reliable man', was accepted at £679. By February 1877, Conran was able to report that the eastern side of the new store was almost finished, the arches over the doorways having all been closed in.

The station at Waterfall does not appear to have been opened with the line as a complaint was made in April 1852 in relation to the very slow progress being made by the contractors in constructing the station. Conran advised the board in November 1870 of the necessity to lengthen the up platform at

Waterfall as tickets were normally collected here. In addition, ground was being prepared for a goods siding. In April of the following year, instructions were given for the erection of a down distant signal here. Plans for a new station at Waterfall were considered in March 1879 and it was decided to proceed accordingly. It is not clear whether this referred to accommodation for the stationmaster or station offices, the former being commenced in September 1881. It was noted in January 1896 that the wooden structures at both Desert and Waterfall were falling to pieces, approval being given for their replacement by corrugated-iron station houses at a cost of about £150 each. We certainly know that there was a corrugated-iron building at Waterfall by 1904.

In March 1852, Nixon reported on the probable cost of erecting a goods store and platform at Upton. In April, Mr Payne proposed to build the intended goods store for whatever sum Nixon might estimate for it, but he was informed that his position as a director precluded him from entering into a contract with the company. The tender of Mr Parrett to construct the shed here for £240 was in due course accepted, as was a tender from Edward Preston for extending the goods shed at Bandon. Consideration had been given to erecting a permanent stone structure to replace the existing timber one, Nixon advising against this on the grounds of cost. In July, Payne requested to be allowed to take away the materials of one of the stables at Ballinhassig and to erect a shelter at Upton for the accommodation of passengers, 'travelling in their own vehicles or on horseback'. Payne corresponded with the board again in September 1853 offering to construct a permanent station at Upton and rent it to the company, with an option to purchase. This was agreed to and the engineer was instructed to prepare a plan and specification for the proposed building, estimated to cost £200. Payne agreed to accept debenture shares in payment. However in May 1854 he reneged on his agreement and the directors decided to take no further action in the matter.

Instructions were given in January 1859 for the removal of the goods shed at Ballinhassig, this having been recommended by LeFanu. The platform was lengthened by about 100ft in May 1875 so as to allow Sunday excursion trains to be checked there instead of at Waterfall. It was stated that there was a public house close to the latter, this leading to considerable delays in consequence of passengers indulging in alcoholic beverages!

Bridge repairs & renewals

By the end of 1860 it was becoming clear that a number of the timber bridges were reaching the point where they would soon require renewal. Particular reference was made to bridges at Ballyphehane and Innoshannon. On being requested in December 1860 to inspect the former, LeFanu advised that he was confined to his house with an attack of rheumatism, but he instructed C P Cotton to carry out the necessary inspection. It is not clear whether this inspection was in fact undertaken as reference was made again in June of the following year to the urgent necessity for an inspection of the bridges at both locations. In regard to that at Innoshannon, it was stated that the upper beams were rotten and broken, while the lower beam at the centre pier was cracked. It was suggested that the track should be moved to the opposite side of the bridge. Luckily, the piers of Innoshannon bridge had been built for double track and this would enable traffic to continue while the new bridge was being erected. Clear instructions were given that a prompt inspection of the bridges was to be undertaken, to 'prevent reports being circulated calculated to alarm the public mind and injurious to the Company's interests'.

Following a personal inspection by LeFanu in July 1861, he informed the board that he could not advise them to spend money on timber renewals. He also stated that if additional piers were built they might obstruct the course of the river and cause flooding, which might involve the company in litigation. His recommendation was for an iron bridge which would cost about £2,000. By the time of the half-yearly shareholders' meeting held in September – postponed from the previous month due to the non-attendance of a quorum – LeFanu was able to confirm that the rails had been shifted across the bridge and that he was in course of preparing the necessary plans for an iron topped bridge. Various parties were contacted seeking plans and estimates, the

only ones to reply being Messrs Richard Perrott & Sons, Iron Founders of Cork. They advised that they were not in a position to offer plans but if supplied with same they would estimate for the work. Urgent instructions were now given for the preparation of plans as the directors believed that the recent falling-off in passenger traffic might be attributable to, 'the reports still abroad, and continuing to gain ground, as to the instability of the structure'.

Messrs Fairbairn & Co of Manchester quoted a figure of £3,976 in December, including delivery and erection, or £3,218 in sections f.o.b. in Liverpool. These figures were considered excessive and further tenders were sought, that of the Cork Steamship Co at £1,882 being accepted in January 1862, half to be paid in three months and half in six months. The old bridge was of the American lattice type and consisted of two 105ft spans and was, at rail level, 41ft 6in above ordinary summer level of the river. A fuller description of this bridge can be found in the *Transactions of the Institution of Civil Engineers of Ireland* for 1866. The new bridge, still of two spans, consisted of four iron girders, which were initially put together in Cork and then taken apart for transport to Innoshannon.

Reverting to the Ballyphehane bridges, Cotton reported in November 1862 that in his view the best course was to replace them by iron bridges on stone abutments at a cost of about £400 each. Three months later, LeFanu advised that he could no longer be answerable for them, such was the extent of decay to the timber. He confirmed that he would prepare drawings and specifications for iron bridges as soon as possible. Further problems were however reported in April 1864 when 13 tons of Memel timber was ordered for emergency repairs. The nearby Tramore River bridge was condemned following Colonel Rich's inspection of the line in December 1873, a stone culvert being decided upon, Dorman being requested to proceed accordingly.

B4 4-6-0T No 470 on an up train near Cork in July 1953. David Murray, IRRS

Chapter Three

EXTENSIONS TO SOUTH AND WEST

We have seen in Chapter Two how the C&BR directors wished to extend their line westwards from Bandon, but although Acts were obtained to go to Bantry and Skibbereen, the powers were not taken up and it was left to the independent West Cork Railway to carry the line onwards to the west. Similarly, a branch line to Kinsale was constructed by an independent company. This chapter deals with these two extensions.

Cork & Kinsale Junction Railway

A public meeting was held in the town of Kinsale on Friday 19th February 1858 in connection with the provision of railway accommodation to that town. Following a survey of existing traffic between Cork and Kinsale, the large fish traffic of the port and the low cost of construction, the promoters were of opinion that such an undertaking

would prove remunerative. The C&BR directors having considered the matter, were of the view that it would also be beneficial to that company. The board even went as far as offering to work the proposed line for 30% of the gross receipts and to convey traffic between Kinsale and Cork free over two miles of their own line. The agreement offered was to be for a period of three years from the date of opening of the new line, the latter to be subject to the approval of the C&BR engineer as regards permanent way and other matters. The proposed point of junction was to be at or near Crossbarry rather than Ballinhassig as had been initially considered. The promoters of the Cork & Kinsale Junction Railway sought an increase in the term for working to 15 or 20 years, but this the C&BR directors were not prepared to concede; they did later agree to alter this to five years.

The opening of the Cork & Kinsale Junction Railway depicting the arrival of the train at Kinsale.

At the half-yearly meeting of shareholders in February 1859, the chairman stated that the Cork & Kinsale Junction Railway Bill had successfully passed Standing Orders of both Houses of Parliament. The Act of Incorporation for the C&KJR received Royal Assent on 19th April 1859, with Lord Kingsale (sic) as chairman and Lt Col North Ludlow Beamish as deputy-chairman. Other directors included Thomas Winkworth, William James Shaw, Sir John Benson, Frederick William Sedgwick and Sir Patrick Cusack Roney, who had been secretary to the Great Eastern Railway in England and was also a director of the London Chatham & Dover Railway. Several of these gentlemen were also directors of the C&BR. Lord Kinsale appears to have had little influence over the affairs of the new company and he was soon succeeded by Sir Patrick Roney.

As passed, Section 18 of the Act of Incorporation also provided for, 'a Branch Railway or Tramway diverging from the Railway at or near the barracks in the town of Kinsale, and terminating at or near the Long Quay', a distance of about 1,100 yards. Speaking at the half-yearly meeting of shareholders in August 1860, Lord Kinsale reported that four miles of line from the junction had been completed and only awaited the laying down of permanent way. Difficulties with landowners had however delayed the obtaining of land nearer Kinsale. Consideration had been given to partially opening the line for the summer traffic, but, having consulted with the C&BR directors, it was deemed advisable to defer this until the whole line was completed. The chairman then made reference to the proposals for the tramway to the Long Quay. The directors decided that such an extension was essential for the development of both the railway and the town, to facilitate the transfer of goods, and particularly, fish traffic on to the railway.

The contract for construction of the line was awarded to Messrs Trowsdale & Co and it was announced in August 1860 that it was hoped to open the new line to Kinsale in the early part of summer 1861. It was also reported that a large body of workmen were engaged in preliminary works for the construction of a hotel and floating baths in the town, which would hopefully be completed at the same time. Delays were encountered when two cargoes of rails were lost at sea. The continuing inability to purchase land at Kinsale itself also led to delays and the original plans were altered to terminate the line near to the military barracks overlooking the town. This in turn proved to be the cause of further delays as the ground was found to consist largely of rock, requiring a deep cutting.

A separate company, the Kinsale Hotel & Baths Co was incorporated in March 1863 to further the hotel project. It shared the company's offices at No 17 Gracechurch Street in London, with none other than Humphrey Williams Wood as its secretary. Capital of the new company was £10,000 and early subscribers included a number of C&BR and C&KJR directors, as well as Wood. The objects of the company were quoted as being, 'the purchase of land and tenements at Kinsale, the erection, furnishing and maintenance of an Hotel, and of laying down floating baths in connexion with the Hotel'.

In October 1860 the C&BR engineer reported on the various plans and sections for the new line and expressed his reservations as to the severity of the curves and gradients. The C&KJR engineer, Henry Coneybeare, attended the board meeting and informed the directors that they were necessary due to the nature of the country through which the proposed line was being built, and that they were no worse than similar branch lines in England. Part of the new line having been completed, the C&KJR secretary, H Williams Wood, approached the board of the C&BR in June 1862 suggesting that the line should be opened as far as Jagoe's Mills in the following August and the remaining three miles to Kinsale some six weeks or so later. The C&KJR would arrange for the provision of conveyances between the two points. When it was pointed out that a turntable, signals and engine house along with a house for the signalman would be required at the former point, the Kinsale directors sensibly decided to postpone the opening until the entire line was completed.

Opening to Kinsale

The directors made inspections of their new line in February. Following a request from the company, Captain Rich visited Cork on 11th May 1863 to carry out an inspection of the new line. It was described as being about eleven miles long, single throughout, with sidings at the Junction, Kinsale and at the only intermediate station, Farrangalway. A second intermediate station was opened at Ballymartle in April of the following year. Iron flat-bottomed rails weighing 65lbs per

Right upper: **Crossbarry station on 19th June 1959. Known simply as Junction until 1888 and later Kinsale Junction, it was the junction point for the branch to Kinsale until the closure of the latter in 1931. The down platform on the right was an island, Kinsale branch trains using the reverse side. This platform included the corrugated-iron station building and 26 lever signal cabin. 'Stations UK'**

Right: **Crossbarry station (previously Kinsale Junction) with a three-piece diesel railcar set on a down train. The leading railcar is No 2660, one of six built at CIÉ's Inchicore Works on AEC underframes and with Bulleid designed bodies.**

yard were used, the joints being fished and fastened with four dog-headed bolts to the sleepers, the latter mainly of memel and laid transversely at an average of 3ft apart. Ballast consisted of broken stone and was laid about 12in deep beneath the sleepers. The gradients were severe, over half the line being at 1 in 80. Rich commented that though reasonably adequate, in some locations triangular posts and rails were provided as fencing; this type of fencing was liable to be stolen or knocked down by cattle making rubbing posts of them.

The only work of note was the viaduct at Farrangalway, which consisted of nine spans of 27ft each, the viaduct being about 35ft in height on a curve. The piers were of masonry, the superstructure and girders being timber. Whilst apparently strong enough, Rich was of opinion that the carpenters' work appeared to be indifferent, with joints being packed and badly fitted; the bridge creaked and strained in places, and he called for this to be rectified, as well as the fitting of guard rails. Several other bridges on the line also required strengthening. The station at Kinsale was reported to be incomplete. It was reported that a small and very tasteful station had been provided at the Junction with a timber top from the Innoshannon bridge. Captain Rich stated that there were two junctions with the mainline, about 300 yards apart. One of these should be removed, the signals and points at the other to be properly connected. Rich returned on 12th June, on which date the line was passed for opening.

LeFanu was requested to inspect the works on behalf of the Bandon and he laid down some further requirements which delayed the official opening until 27th July, although a special excursion had been run from Cork on 16th May for about 350 guests. The special train departed from Albert Quay at 10.30 carrying a large number of important personages, 'who scrutinised the line very carefully', and were, 'delighted with the substantial nature of the works'. One report stated that they were overawed at the grandeur of the town and harbour at Kinsale, 'which presented the aspect of a beautiful picture seen through the lens of a camera' (a comparatively new phenomenon at the time). Following the arrival of the train, which was greeted by the firing of small arms by the West Cork Militia, a military band headed the procession to the nearby barracks for an inspection, after which the dignitaries partook of a tasteful dejeuner in a hotel in town. They then witnessed the laying of the foundation stone of the Marine Hotel and Baths, a project intended to stimulate tourist traffic to the town. The guests later travelled on to Bandon to take part in the turning of the first sod of the West Cork Railway, where they were again treated to a repast.

The first year's receipts were disappointing, amounting to only £1,958, hardly surprising as the company charged the lowest third class fares in Ireland. On 8th June 1864 the Courts granted a writ of sequestration appointing the contractors sequestrators over the company's funds for moneys due to them. In due course they applied to the C&BR but could only obtain £5, such were the poor receipts. The C&KJR directors were however still optimistic that the line would pay once the hotel was opened and a connection made with deep-water at the harbour. Receipts continued to be poor in 1865, Sir Cusack Roney, who was by now chairman of the company, accusing the C&BR of mismanagement due to a want of energy and interest in the line. In March the Kinsale board requested the C&BR to provide building tickets to those who built properties close to the line, in addition to lower excursion fares, more advertising and more trains. In the latter context the Bandon companies felt the service was adequate but agreed to provide more trains if paid 2s per train mile. Free building tickets valid for five years were eventually issued in 1869.

The year 1866 also proved to be a bad one for the company, which was still in the hands of S M Hussey as Receiver acting for the Chancery Court. An amount of equipment, including platform seats, was seized by the sheriff in June and it was necessary for the C&BR to buy back this equipment to enable services to be maintained. Further bad news was that the fifty bed-roomed hotel on which so much store was placed to increase receipts was abandoned and left to decay. The Hotel company was finally dissolved in March 1882.

There was little doubt that the C&BR had struck a bad bargain when the original agreement for working was drawn up, but this was in part due to their being anxious that the English parties involved in both the C&KJR and the WCR should proceed with construction of the latter. Good notice was given that when the agreement came up for renewal in 1868 improved terms would be sought. When the agreement did expire in June 1868, a temporary arrangement was arrived at charging 2s.3d per mile for a two train a day service, this being confirmed as permanent in August. In February 1868 the directors submitted a scheme of re-organisation to the shareholders providing for the withdrawal of law actions for £60,000 of debts and settlement of these by the issue of £24,000 of 5% debenture stock. An Act was obtained for more effectual provision for working and borrowing of £15,000 was approved for the provision of rolling stock and an approach road at Kinsale. This scheme in due course received approval from the Court and the receiver was discharged in August, the directors regaining control of the company.

Farrangalway viaduct

As early as July 1863, a Mr Heard of Pallastown called the attention of the board to the fact that the arch of Farrangalway Viaduct was, 'disturbed at both sides, (and was) showing several openings'. It was duly inspected by Cotton who advised that it was unsafe and required immediate steps to prevent the possibility of an accident; he suggested that two baulks of timber be laid across beneath the rails instead of the cross sleepers. Remedial works were carried out but in January 1874 Dorman reported at some length on the bridge's condition. By this time, the longitudinal timbers had decayed, two spans at the Cork end being described as getting very shaky. It was estimated that 108cu ft of timber was immediately required. The report, which dealt with a number of other defective matters in relation to the Kinsale branch, was sent to the C&KJR secretary for the immediate attention of his board. However eight months later nothing had been done and the bridge was, 'as bad as it can be'. The view was that it should be renewed and the C&KJR charged with the expense. The latter company were given a week to do something or else trains would cease to run to and from Kinsale. The C&BR chairman went so far as to say that it should never have been built as there was no necessity for a viaduct there.

Some urgent remedial works were in fact undertaken but it was agreed that further work was required in the longer term. In April 1875 the engineer advised that six or eight new beams must at once be put in, while the whole of the decking also required renewal. A 5mph speed limit was imposed pending the completion of repairs. Dorman however strongly urged the renewal of the entire bridge in iron at a cost of about £1,200. Before these repairs were carried out, Dorman informed the board that he had had to replace the truss at the southwestern corner. Once again he stressed that repairs must be put in hands immediately, failing which he would be compelled to stop traffic.

Despite these repairs being put in hand, a report in September 1881 stated that one of the bottom span beams put in in 1875 was cracked. Further minor repairs were carried out. Dorman suggested that a large portion should be filled in and the remaining three spans renewed in iron. This work would cost in the region of £1,100 or £55 per annum capitalised, whereas repairs to the bridge were currently costing about £100 a year. He was instructed to seek tenders for the necessary works, he in turn suggesting that the work of filling-in be done by his own people. To carry this into effect, he would need four ten-ton hopper trucks. These were in due course ordered from the Swansea Wagon Co at a cost of £75 each. In all, about 15,000cu ft of filling was carried out, the work being finally completed early in 1885.

In receivership again

Constant complaints were made by the C&BR engineer as to the poor state of the track and also of Farrangalway Viaduct. Fencing also came in for criticism, particularly that at Kinsale station which had been blown down in a storm in 1870. It became necessary in March 1872 to again appoint a receiver; this time it was Richard Coghlan, the traffic manager of the C&BR. It was hoped that the Government might provide loans to larger companies to buy out smaller ones, a course of action which would assist in solving the company's problems. Henry Coneybeare, who had by now become the chairman, had an interest in the horse tramway system in Cork and he hoped that a connection might be made with the GS&WR so as to better transport fish. A request for a reduction of the working charge was rejected and in fact it was increased in January 1875 to 3s per train mile.

Ballymartle station was in bad condition to the point where the building could be shaken by hand. Ballymartle was also mentioned in the context of signalling, when it was stated that the signal lamp was never lit because the signalman was afraid of heights! It was in the news again in December 1877 when it was stated that it was in a very bad condition, the engineer suggesting a stone built replacement as he had the necessary materials on the ground. The Kinsale board went along with this but it was February of 1879 before plans and estimates were submitted. A new house for the stationmaster was estimated to cost £230 and offices £187. Four months later, the platform was declared to be unsafe and in danger of giving way at any time. By now the C&KJR board declined to incur any expenditure pending amalgamation of the two lines and it was decided to leave the matter in abeyance.

To protect himself, the engineer reported in July that the platform had been so often patched and repaired he thought it impossible to do any more. He also pointed out the heavy cost of stopping and starting trains on the 1 in 80 gradient at this location, implying perhaps that the station should be closed. Another year went by and it was 30th July 1880 by the time the new platform and buildings were reported to have been completed.

An Act was obtained on 8th August 1878 endeavouring to sort out the company's financial problems. Interest arrears now amounted to £8,147 and the receiver had to pay out all money received by him. The Act authorised the issue of new debenture stock and the receiver was discharged. Provision was also made for rolling stock, if purchased, to be protected against seizure or legal action for five years. Another Act of July 1879 made provision for the purchase by the C&BR of both the C&KJR and the WCR. The sale price was to be decided by arbitration, this latter to be completed by 1st January 1880. The future working of the Ilen Valley Railway was also dealt with in the Act. So came to an end the independent existence of the C&KJR.

West Cork Railway

An extension to the west of Bandon was always considered to be essential to stimulate growth in revenue of the fledgling company. In this context, we have seen how Acts were obtained in 1853 and 1854 for extensions to Bantry and Skibbereen with a branch to Clonakilty, and also how these extensions were to be dependent on baronial guarantees. Nothing was, however, done towards progressing these lines and the question was revisited by the board in 1857, by which time serious consideration was being given to restricting the new line to Dunmanway. This raised the question of baronial guarantees being sought from the landholders of the Bantry and Clonakilty districts and it was decided to allow the powers under these Acts to lapse.

Mr. H. Williams Wood, who had been appointed secretary to both the Cork & Kinsale Junction Railway Company and a new company being promoted to again consider an extension to Dunmanway or Drimoleague, approached the C&BR board in May 1859 enquiring upon what terms they would work the new line if constructed. The initial response was that the matter required mature consideration. Wood persisted in his enquiry and suggested to the Cork committee that it be worked for 30% of gross revenue, the committee in turn suggesting to the board in Dublin that they seek a rate of 35% for a period of five years. The board in their wisdom decided to postpone any consideration of the matter. By the following July it became clear that proposals for an extension to the west of Bandon were being initiated by influential inhabitants of Skibbereen and district. It was announced that the services of an engineer, Henry Coneybeare, had been secured. Coneybeare, who was also engineer to the C&KJR, based his survey on that carried out some years earlier by Edmund Leahy, and he advised the promoters that he would be prepared to make a 25 mile line to Drimoleague for a sum of £125,000; he was to obtain a subscription of £45,000 with the balance coming from the contractor.

In February 1860 further correspondence was entered into regarding a figure for working the new line, an increased offer of 45% of gross receipts coming from the West Cork people, a figure which they considered a fair sum. The Bandon directors decided that they would prefer to work the line on a mileage basis and sought a figure of 2s 3d per train mile for the line, making an annual charge in the region of £5,500 for a service of two trains per day between Cork and Skibbereen. The West Cork were not in favour of a mileage rate and suggested 40%, but the company stuck to their offer and stated that, 'they (WCR) will find that no other railway is charging less'.

Enthusiastic meetings were held in Cork, Bandon, Dunmanway, Drimoleague and Skibbereen to further the new project, although opposition was reported from an unexpected quarter, namely William O'Neill Daunt. Daunt was highly regarded in the Carbery district and was a member of an old and highly-esteemed family which had in fact given its name to Daunt Rock, just outside Cork Harbour. He had been received into the Catholic Church by the renowned Father Matthew, of Temperance fame, and it was believed that his strenuous opposition to the railway may have had its origins in some religious differences. That said, Daunt was noted for his benevolence to the poor people of the Ballineen district during the Famine years. Gradually however the combined influence of other dignitaries such as the Lords Bandon and Carbery, T McCarthy Downing and The O'Donovan (The O'Donovan or Chief of the O'Donovan clan of West Cork) overcame the opposition.

The Act of Incorporation of the West Cork Railway Company received Royal Assent on 28th August 1860. It is of interest that whilst the company title was in the singular, the legislation itself was entitled the West Cork Railways Act, 1860. Capital was £200,000 with additional borrowing powers up to £66,600. The first directors included Sir John Arnott, Thomas Somerville, David Connor, Henry Winthrop O'Donovan (The O'Donovan), Henry John Townsend and William Henry Hall. The railway as authorised was to commence in the townland of Cloghmacsimon at Bandon by a junction with the C&BR and to terminate near the town of Skibbereen in the townland of Marsh and parish of Abbeystrowry. The line, the length of which was not quoted in the Act, was to be completed within a period of five years from the passing of the legislation.

Section 41 empowered the company to enter into traffic arrangements with the Bandon company, including the supply of rolling stock and locomotives. Section 49 allowed for the C&BR to subscribe a figure not exceeding £20,000 to the new undertaking, while Section 55 laid down that certain Baronies might subscribe at a rate of 4½% on a figure not exceeding £66,600, payable half-yearly. On this occasion all of the townlands in the Poor Law Union of Clonakilty were excluded from the contribution. The Baronial Guarantee was to last for a period of 20 years from the opening of the railway for public traffic. They were also only permitted on borrowings, an application to Parliament to allow half the capital to be in the form of borrowings being declined.

Three months prior to the obtaining of the Act, it had been announced that Alexander Gordon had agreed to construct the line for a sum of £230,000, this figure to include the purchase of land, construction of the line, building stations and erecting the electric telegraph. Of this figure, he agreed to take £150,000 in shares, this being later increased to £223,000. Gordon also requested that he be given first refusal for the provision of rolling stock and working of the line. McCarthy Downing stated that if the C&BR were not prepared to subscribe £7,400 capital up front, the shareholders releasing a similar amount, then consideration would be given to completing the section of line from Skibbereen to Dunmanway with a view to making a connection with the contemplated line from Cork to Macroom. This suggestion was to lead to some isolated construction taking place on the western section of the authorised line.

The O'Donovan was elected chairman of the new company in September, and Mr H R Marmion, who had offered his services, was appointed secretary at a salary of £120 per annum. It was stipulated that if at any time, 'all communications and accounts and other business be not promptly attended to', the board would be at liberty to dismiss him at a week's notice. In October the board found it necessary to pass a resolution to the effect that no discussion taking place at board meetings was to be made public and for the future, that in case of any requirement for the printing of letters or notices from the board, except for advertising, Mr Potter be requested, if so employed, to abstain from giving the same publicity in the *Skibbereen Eagle*!

The contractor goes bankrupt
The board expressed its dissatisfaction with Coneybeare in December as he had not taken steps, as he had intimated he would, to arrange for the purchase of land and enable the contractor to have plant and machinery on the ground by 10th January. Reference was made at the first half-yearly meeting of shareholders in February 1861 to the high character and experience of Mr Gordon, who was bound by his contract to have the line completed throughout by 1st September 1862. No work was commenced, one reason being Gordon's attempts to use an inferior type of rails and it soon became clear that the anticipated completion date could not be met, when it was reported that Gordon had been declared bankrupt.

Arising from the bankruptcy of the contractor, a committee was appointed in October 1861 to proceed as a deputation to meet Sir Robert Peel in Dublin in the hope of obtaining a loan to enable work to commence. Later, in January 1862, the chairman and one of the directors went to London to press for a Government loan and also to endeavour to find a suitable contractor, either with or without such a loan. In April it was suggested that William McCormick would undertake construction work under the superintendence of Sir John Macneill. Later in the month however a draft contract was approved with Messrs Moore Bros and they announced that they were most anxious to make a start on the Bandon to Ballineen section, but this was all to be wishful thinking.

In April 1863 the company transferred its offices to No 17 Gracechurch Street in the City of London, the new chairman being Sir Patrick Roney. Irish born, Roney was a prominent railway promoter and administrator. Marmion resigned his position as secretary and was replaced by H Williams Wood at a salary of £500 per annum. At a meeting held at the new offices on 21st April it was confirmed that a contract had been concluded with Messrs Wheatley Kirk & Co of Manchester. Mr Edward Corry, manager of the British & Foreign Railway Plant Company, attended the meeting and confirmed that his company would supply all necessary rails and sleepers, allowing two years for payment.

The ceremony of turning the first sod of the WCR was performed by Lord Carbery close to the gates of Lord Bandon's demesne on 16th May 1863. A procession, headed by the combined bands of the West Cork Artillery and the 11th Regiment, led the procession from Bandon station. It was reported that Lord Carbery used, 'a handsome silver spade and a wheel-barrow of polished oak made by Messrs Howell & James of London'. The barrow included an allegorical design in silver illustrating the construction of a railway; this showed a locomotive front forming a shield which bore an inscription, and leaning against it a group of spades and pickaxes, with a wreath of wheat and olives, representing peace and plenty. The spade also had a blade with engraved sprays of wheat and olives. Many of those who attended had earlier been at the opening ceremony of the C&KJR at Kinsale and they partook of a second déjeuner in Bandon Town Hall, which was reported to have been gaily decorated for the occasion. Following the meal, Sir Patrick Roney said it was hoped to complete and open the first ten miles of line within a year. He also commented that local investment had been stifled by the inability of the poorer Irish to speculate or wait for financial return.

Construction begins
Construction work started in June at a number of locations, even as far away as Skibbereen, and initially good progress was made. Reporting to the shareholders in September, Roney said the works were in a state of great forwardness and the contractors were, 'indefatigable in their exertions'. The district through which the line was being constructed was described as being one teeming with agricultural produce, while the station at Dunmanway was of great importance as from here roads led to all parts of the western coast. Roney was hopeful that Crookhaven, 16 miles distant from Dunmanway, would obtain a fair share of the North American traffic. The telegraph had recently been completed to this point, thus reducing by some six hours the receipt in London of intelligence from America. It was also hoped that tourist traffic to and

Innoshannon viaduct. Note the piers were constructed to accommodate double track which proved useful when the bridge was rebuilt in 1862. W McGrath

Ballineen station looking east on 28th April 1938. The small engine shed and water tank on the down side were for the use of the ballast engine. The ballast sidings were behind the platform. W A Camwell, IRRS

from Killarney would be attracted to the new route rather than going via Mallow.

By February 1864 it was reported that the Government arbitrator, Mr Fishbourne, had made his final award in respect of the entire of the lands required for the 33 mile long extension. By this time the company were in possession of about 18 miles, and 13 miles of railway had been made. The greater portion of this latter was ballasted and ready to receive permanent way. However, having gone over the works for some four miles west of Bandon in April, Mr Corry expressed his disappointment and dissatisfaction that no land had been taken up at that end of the line, and, as a consequence, no works had been carried out there. In fact, minor deviations were carried out to avoid difficulties with land. Also in April, attention was directed to the provision of locomotives and rolling stock; orders were placed in August for delivery in October, details of which can be found in the relevant chapters.

Presenting the half-yearly report in August, Roney advised that all but one and a half of the seventeen and a half miles westwards to Dunmanway might now be consid-

ered complete, with permanent way in course of being laid. It was confidently expected that the line would be ready for opening within a few months. Four miles of the section eastwards from Skibbereen were also completed with rails on the ground ready for laying. The completion of this isolated stretch was most likely linked to the plan for a connection with the proposed westward extension of the C&MDR, thereby obtaining an alternative route to Cork. The directors were more than ever convinced of the bona fides character and merits of the undertaking, which would quickly become the means of realising the hitherto undeveloped and profitable potential of the agricultural and commercial interests of the district.

Problems at Bandon

Although the railway was as yet incomplete at Bandon, the directors decided to make a trial trip over their new line on 14th March 1865, borrowing one of the C&BR Tayleur engines for the purpose. We must assume that this and the company's own rolling stock were moved across by road. The short unfinished section at Bandon required an Act in 1865 to make a deviation so as to avoid Lord Bandon's demesne. The Act, which received the Royal Assent on 5th July, also enabled the company to raise further capital to the extent of £120,000 and to extend the time for completion to Skib-

bereen by a further two years. William Parsons, previously manager of the Cork & Youghal Railway, was appointed to the post of traffic manager in March at a salary of £300 per annum, to be increased to £400 as soon as the Skibbereen extension was opened for traffic. Despite the incomplete state of the works, notification was given to the BoT early in April 1865 of the company's intention to open the line, similar notice being given, and quickly withdrawn, only four months later.

In June, Messrs Cotton & Flemyng, who had replaced LeFanu as consulting engineers to the C&BR, wrote regarding the junction arrangements at Bandon, the WCR being requested to supply full plans of the intended junction. Also about this time, the WCR agreed, in pursuance of an agreement with the Earl of Bandon, to provide a flag station at Roundhill, near Castle Bernard. In August it was reported that the WCR had begun laying permanent way on C&BR land and had erected a signal box without prior permission. They were later given permission to remove the latter to the other side of the Bandon line at their own expense. The WCR provided a station of their own in line with the Bandon company's station, but at a higher level. Goods traffic was apparently dealt with about half a mile west, adjoining the later Bandon West passenger station. Through goods wagons were placed on a siding on the down side of the WCR line at the junction for collection and delivery. Goods traffic continued to be dealt with in this manner until all goods facilities were concentrated at the C&BR's low-level station in 1894. Regarding communication between the two companies' stations at Bandon, the WCR had intended that all passengers for their line should pass through the C&BR station. The latter however considered this to be most objectionable and agreed to allow temporary access through a side door and through their yard. In return for this they were to receive a nominal rent to safeguard their rights.

Giving evidence to the Devonshire Commission on railways in Ireland in June, a Mr W B Jones strongly criticised the WCR, saying that everyone except the labourers had been paid in shares, and that the company had, 'wooden viaducts, little slight wire fences, and everything as trumpery as it could be'. He attributed the delay in completing the line to Bandon to lack of funds and added the comment that, 'they have stuck at that last half mile, with a manager, staff and engines actually standing in the middle of the fields from inability to raise money'. A harsh and slightly exaggerated comment, but the financial state of the company was certainly far from healthy at this time.

It was reported in August that some WCR shareholders who also held a large interest in the C&BR had urged an amalgamation of the four companies in west Cork into one uniform system of management. As a result an approach was made to the C&BR suggesting that their line along with the C&KJR and the C&MDR should be leased and worked by the West Cork. Apart from the obvious financial benefits accruing, this would also stimulate further extensions to Clonakilty, Bantry and Crookhaven. Needless to remark this suggestion was not seriously considered by the Bandon directors. Somewhat later, however, in September 1866, the C&BR were asked to take over the working of the new line and they agreed to do so at a mileage rate of 2s per mile per day. This offer was not pursued.

In September 1865, Edward Corry wrote in scathing terms stating that he was so dissatisfied and disappointed with the contractor, 'and not being able to restrain my temper, it will be prudent for me to abstain from attending the Board Meetings in the future'. He went on to state that in his view the contractors had been paid far more than they were entitled to for work done. He concluded by stating that he was, 'anything but satisfied with my connection with the West Cork Railway'. About this time, Mr Wood was given extended leave of absence due to ill health, his position as secretary being taken by Frederick Corke; it was resolved that Wood's salary be discontinued during his absence. When Parsons enquired in

November as to through booking arrangements with the C&BR, it was decided that such could not be justified until the WCR were in a position to work traffic with sufficient engine power.

BoT inspection & opening
It had been hoped to open the line as far as Dunmanway in November 1865, but it was to be 1st May of the following year before a trial trip was made, following which the BoT were notified of the company's intention to open the line. The line was duly inspected on 1st June by Captain Rich. The new railway was quoted as being 17m 49c in length, with stations at Bandon (close to and joined by a covered way to the C&BR station), Ballineen and Dunmanway. The line was single throughout, permanent way consisting of 65lbs per yard iron flat-bottomed rail in 21ft lengths, fished and fixed with fang bolts to sleepers laid about 3ft apart. Rich commented that the rail joint was on the sleeper, and the fish only about 15in long, making for, 'a very inferior mode of jointing to the suspended fish'. The line was well ballasted, with excellent gravel. Turntables were provided at the terminal stations.

Some criticism was made of the bridges, some of them being described as being not strong enough as permanent work, while others required pointing. The buffer stops at Dunmanway were within inches of the public road, and in their present state, 'could easily be pushed down by a runaway engine'. In response, the company claimed that this was only a temporary measure, pending the extension of the line westwards. Nevertheless, they were requested to fill up the stop blocks with about ten tons of masonry rubble. Level crossing gates required alteration so that they could not be opened outwards. Some doubts existed as to the status of two of the line's level crossings, one leading to the Chapel at Bandon, 'which appears to be a private crossing belonging to the Roman Catholic parishioners', the other at Enniskeen (sic).

On receipt of written clarification later in the month regarding the various matters from Roddy, the company's engineer, BoT approval for opening was finally given on 20th June, although the official opening appears to have taken place eight days earlier. At about this time, William Kirk went bankrupt and the C&BR had to look to his principals, the British & Foreign Railway Plant Co for rent for sleepers lying at Albert Quay. This company had forced the seizure of plant, machinery and rolling stock against debts owing to them. In fact in April 1866 it had been necessary to obtain a loan of £500 from the B&FRP Co to enable stations to be completed for the BoT inspection. Further financial difficulties hit the company when Messrs. Brown Marshall & Co sued them for £12,392 in respect of rolling stock supplied,

this being one of a number of such legal cases. A judgement for £12,643 was handed down in 1867.

With the line open, the WCR directors now sought payment of the £20,000 due from the C&BR under the terms of the Act of 1860, which would enable them to clear debts and proceed with the Skibbereen extension. The resident engineer, Mr Roddy, submitted estimates in July 1866 for the erection of temporary stations and sidings at Castle Bernard, Gaggin and Desert, in a total figure of £271, they being considered vital for the development of traffic. It was decided to apply once again to the B&FRP Co for a loan of this figure, repayment to be made by instalments as promptly as practicable. The Plant Co were also requested to place an order for rails in respect of sidings. Later, Messrs Swanton and Todd, mill owners, agreed to advance a sum of £250 for the erection of a station and siding to accommodate twelve wagons at Desert. On completion, all ordinary passenger and goods trains were to stop there.

Before the WCR opened their line, consideration was given to the provision of a station at Castle Bernard, in connection with anticipated traffic to and from Timoleague and Courtmacsherry. The Earl of Bandon himself made strong representations through his solicitor in October 1867 for the opening of such a station, the WCR pleading inability due to being unable to raise the necessary finances and suggesting His Lordship might himself carry out the works against company debentures. This he declined to do, insisting on an agreement of March 1867 between himself and the company being carried out. A month later however, the Earl enquired whether the company would repay him any advances he might make in erecting temporary stations here and at Gaggin. The company agreed as regards the former to repay the cost, 'out of the first assets of the Company available for the purpose'. They expressed their opinion that no agreement existed as regards a station at Gaggin.

In August 1870, a further communication from the Earl's solicitor enquired when a road, made necessary by the railway destroying His Lordship's entrance to Castle Bernard, would be completed. Again the company declined to carry out the necessary works due to lack of funds. Ten years later, Messrs T Crowley & Son of Bandon approached the C&BR board requesting a siding. It was agreed to put one in on trial provided they paid 2d per ton extra and undertook to load and unload their own goods. No siding was installed at this time, General Hutchinson agreeing to the provision of one in August 1885. This work was finally completed in January 1887, the necessary signal fittings being provided by the Railway Signal Co Ltd of Liverpool at a cost of £26 11s 10d, the siding itself costing £116. Later, with the closure of the station itself in 1891, the company agreed to retain the siding. This latter remained in situ right up to the line's final closure in March 1961.

It was also reported in August 1870 that the Earl of Bandon had complained of lack of station accommodation at the above locations, he being informed that the directors were seeking Counsel's Opinion as to their ability to construct them by means of a loan from revenue. In this context, it might be mentioned that Parsons had withheld some traffic receipts towards the cost of these temporary works. This was to lead to his dismissal towards the end of August and his replacement pro tem by Joseph H. Beattie. Beattie however refused in November to continue in this role and his place was taken by John Moore, again on a temporary basis, at a salary of £2 per week. Moore was clearly instructed to pay into the bank at Bandon traffic receipts and all other monies received on a daily basis.

At about the same time as Parsons was dismissed, Wood wrote complaining that he had been working for the previous six months without pay, or even having his salary defined. It will be recalled that Wood had been on leave of absence due to ill health, without pay. Corke, who had been appointed to stand in for him, resigned in February 1866 and Wood was then duly reappointed. At the time, it was made clear that Messrs Wheatley Kirk & Co were not to interfere in any manner with the secretarial or accountant's offices, or the duties appertaining to them. In his letter, Wood went on to state that he had only reluctantly returned to the position at the specific request of the chairman and some of the directors, and on a promise that his position would be regularised once the line was opened. This had not been done and Wood was now in dire straits financially, so much so that he had found it necessary to borrow £10 from a tradesman in connection with preparations for the opening of the line. Whilst he deplored the unfortunate financial position of the company, he now requested payment of £162 4s 6d due to him.

In response to a reply from Mr Sedgwick, the chairman, Wood again wrote stating that as the company either could not or would not pay his just claim, he now tendered his resignation. However, to cause as little inconvenience as possible, he was prepared to resume his position should the company agree to pay him the back money and agree a salary of £250 per annum with an additional £50 a year for rent of offices, both to be payable weekly. The directors now accepted Wood's resignation, 'subject to his having the opportunity of reconsidering the same'. Mr G Jordan was in the meantime appointed to act as secretary, without salary for the present. It was agreed that £13 1s 0d in respect of petty cash be forwarded immediately to Wood, but the balance of his claim was to be considered. Wood reverted to the board in October advising them that his decision was final, and he called for some arrangement to be made regarding the monies due to him, when he would happily hand over all the books and documents belonging to the company. Following some further correspondence, Wood agreed to hand these over, he being paid £50 for out-of-pocket expenses. He was also given written confirmation of the outstanding debt due to him, which the directors were unable to meet at that time.

A Committee of Investigation is appointed

The traffic manager reported in September 1866 that office furniture and stores at Bandon and Ballineen had been seized by the sheriff at the suit of Mr Hamilton Breen for £294 and a Mr Ryan for £90. The half-yearly meeting of shareholders held in August had been adjourned due to the serious financial state of the company. When it resumed, a lengthy discussion ensued regarding the accounts rendered by the directors, which were found to be incomplete. Arising out of this meeting a committee of investigation was set up to inspect and examine all the books and documents of the company, Mr Wood, who still was in possession of the various books, being requested to make them available to the committee.

Arising from the committee's investigations, various suggestions were put forward in March 1867. The company's registered office was transferred to Cork, where a resident committee was made responsible for regulating the ordinary traffic of the line. A group of London directors remained as a committee for managing the company's finances. A further connection with the C&MDR was the appointment to the post of secretary of George Purcell, who held a similar position on the Macroom line. The committee also commented that payments made to the contractors appeared to have been made with much irregularity, and were greatly in excess of what they were entitled to receive. Despite this re-organisation of the company's affairs, the fact was that the C&BR continued to be obstructive in relation to connections at Bandon, thus making it difficult to increase traffic. A further Act of Parliament which received Royal Assent on 12th August 1867 granted the company power to attach shares authorised under their Act of 1865, and which remained unissued, towards completion of the Skibbereen extension. Additional borrowing powers were also granted, along with a two year extension of time for completion of the Skibbereen line.

Financial matters still occupied the attention of the directors in 1867/8. It was reported in October 1867 that a sum of £10 8s 10d remained in the company's bank account, and it was agreed that this be withdrawn for petty cash. In response to correspondence from the B&FRP Co, the board advised that they had no objections to the removal of unused plant, but were hopeful of receiving Government assistance to enable them to purchase rails intended for the Skibbereen extension. Any withdrawal of rolling stock would place the company in even greater difficulties and might even occasion the

A down train ready to depart from Dunmanway. The coach nearest the photographer is No 1, an eight-compartment bogie third supplied new by Metropolitan in 1905. Note the typical CB&SCR porter's barrow on the up platform. Lawrence collection, National Library

Dunmanway station looking east on 27th June 1951. The down evening train is in charge of 4-6-0T No 463. Behind the down platform were the goods facilities, consisting of cattle pens, loading bank and a 98ft long stone-built goods store.
W A Camwell, IRRS

closing of the line. There is a reference in the C&BR Board minutes in September 1868 to WCR locomotives and rolling stock about to be disposed of to the Dublin Wicklow & Wexford Railway. We do know that the latter company's locomotive superintendent, Mr. Wakefield, inspected this stock lying at Bandon and subsequently the secretary had an interview with the B&FRP Co relative to prices. The Bandon chairman also mentioned at a board meeting that this stock was for sale, but nothing further was done in this regard.

Little of note occurred during the next couple of years, with the company continuing to struggle financially for its very existence. In September 1869 it was suggested that the board might finally consider abandoning the Skibbereen extension but no decision was taken. By July 1870 the C&BR were continuing to renege on their subscription of £20,000 as authorised under the Act of 1860 and consideration was given to taking an action against that company to compel them to subscribe. Messrs Radcliffe Davis & Cator, solicitors, were appointed to take all such proceedings as they deemed necessary to compel payment. It was suggested that the WCR should go to Parliament seeking an Act for free running powers over the Bandon line to Cork until such time as the payment was made. Parliament in due course considered the Bill and decided that it was most unusual in its terms and it failed on Standing Orders following strenuous opposition from the C&BR. The latter company's argument for not paying the subscription was that it was based on an

estimated construction cost of £6,000 or £7,000 per mile, whereas it had actually cost £20,000 per mile to construct. In addition, the WCR shares which were to have been given to the C&BR had been distributed amongst the contractors and others.

In the meantime, proposals were submitted for a scheme of arrangement with the company's creditors, which it was agreed should be filed with the Court of Chancery. This matter was finally concluded in April 1872 when a scheme of arrangement was approved by the Chancery Court in Dublin. Under this arrangement, the company were empowered to create and issue various categories of debenture stock totalling £246,600 and bearing a perpetual and preferential interest of 4% per annum.

Problems at Bandon

The junction at Bandon continued to be a source of problems. It had been reported in December 1866 that the signal house at West Cork Junction was in a very bad state of repair. The WCR were informed that unless they immediately carried out remedial works, the C&BR would do it for them and charge accordingly. In the following November, the C&BR were requested to undertake the working of WCR traffic at Bandon, agreeing to do so for a sum of £4 per week, excluding rent or tolls; this figure was to include a sum of 12s per week for the signalman's wages, currently paid by the C&BR, but the responsibility of the WCR. It was also clear that the West Cork had encroached on the Bandon company's premises and had come within 6ft of their

running line. This latter precluded a doubling of the Bandon line should it ever become desirable, without having to purchase additional land. The question of rent for the use of Bandon and tolls for the use of half a mile of the C&BR line had also yet to be finalised. Reporting in April 1868, Messrs. Cotton & Flemyng advised that a siding 400 yards in length had been installed by the WCR entirely on C&BR land.

In July 1871 the C&BR suggested a figure of £1,000 per annum as a fair rent for the use of their facilities at Bandon, this being declined by the WCR. This was to lead to arbitration between the two companies. In January 1873 George Ilberry, the GS&WR traffic manager, agreed to act on behalf of the C&BR. The West Cork board persuaded Edward John Cotton, manager of the Belfast & Northern Counties Railway, to act on their behalf. The award was handed down in the following August and was in favour of the Bandon, an amount of £1,643 6s 8d being awarded against the West Cork. The latter company refused to pay this figure, having been totally opposed to the idea of arbitration in the first instance. Application was made in February 1874 and again in April, the WCR again refusing to pay over either the award or their proportion of the arbitrators' fees. The Bandon now instructed their solicitors to issue proceedings for recovery of the sum due. The directors were informed in May however that George Purcell had returned the writ after holding it for ten days, and stating that he was no longer the company secretary. This was clearly an attempt to prevent the case coming before the next sittings. Having said this, the C&BR and their solicitors had slipped up badly as Purcell had in fact been appointed WCR general manager in December 1873 at a salary of £250 per annum. Purcell's place was taken by Mr. Mitson at a salary of £80 per annum.

The solicitors recommended making an application to the Court for liberty to enter judgement; if unsuccessful, they would have a writ served for the Assizes. To enable them to proceed, they requested an affidavit from the secretary stating that he had written to Purcell as late as March 1874, addressing him as secretary of the WCR, and that Purcell had not repudiated the position and must have opened the letter so addressed. Messrs Barrington were able to advise in June that they had obtained an order from the Court of Queen's Bench to substitute service of a writ by serving Purcell as manager in Cork and by sending a registered copy to Mitson in London. In response, the WCR pleaded several defences, amongst them that the arbitrators had not signed or executed the award at the same time and place, nor even in the presence of one another. Messrs Barrington advised that the defendants must succeed on this plea, Counsel advising that a consent to judgement for the defendants and for their costs be given.

The WCR wrote in March 1874 regarding the proposed opening of their new station at Bandon West. This station, which was situated just to the west of St Patrick's Roman Catholic Church and the adjoining level crossing, in the townland of Cloughmacsimon, was used between 1874 and 1880 by WCR trains. The platforms and buildings were situated on the down side. The C&BR directors agreed to through running of traffic between Cork and Dunmanway on completion of certain repairs and on the examination of the extension by their engineer. They also confirmed that they were prepared to accede to the transfer of through passengers' luggage from their terminus to the current West Cork station, but not to the new station, situated as it was nearly half a mile away. They suggested that passenger traffic should continue to be worked as normal pending a new agreement for through running. As regards goods traffic, all wagons going to the west would be placed on the WCR siding.

To avoid the inconvenience of through passengers to and from the WCR line having to walk the half mile between the two stations, a temporary, uncovered, wooden platform was opened on the down side of the WCR line at West Cork Junction in November 1876. This platform remained in use until all traffic began to use the low-level station in January 1880. To cater for the extra traffic at the latter station, a new platform and water tank were installed there early in 1880. Following the closure of Ballyphehane Junction, the company purchased the locking frame from the C&MDR in December 1879 and added extra levers to enable it to be used at Bandon. At the same time, the WCR interchange siding was extended to connect it with Messrs Allman's siding.

Later in the year, it would appear that the Bandon company's staff were suffering harassment from WCR officials. In October it was resolved that the C&BR officials should be protected in the discharge of their arduous and responsible duties from any dictation or interference outside that company as to how traffic was conducted. It was agreed that WCR trains should always be subservient to trains of the 'Parent Line', latterly made more difficult to work by the removal of the WCR station about half a mile away, thus obliging passengers to and from the west to walk, 'a most intolerable nuisance in wet weather, and there was, very properly, a general and indignant outcry'. The removal of the original station also caused problems with the maintenance of punctuality.

Twelve months later, in October 1875, complaints were received from the WCR of undue delays to wagons belonging to that company, charges which were unfounded and were fully refuted by the C&BR. Similar complaints were made a month later, when it was pointed out that the Bandon were utilising the WCR wagons for their own private uses. The board minute entry commented that, 'there appears to be a decided resolve on the part of the West Cork Railway, represented by Mr Purcell, to obstruct the working of this Company'.

The WCR wrote to the Bandon in June 1876 regarding accommodation at Bandon station, reference also being made to the latter company's claim for the settlement of the outstanding rent. It was suggested that the C&BR should accede to the erection of a platform between the two companies' lines near the junction points. About this time the question was again raised of constructing a connecting line between the WCR and the C&MDR, the proposed junction to be at Crookstown, 16½ miles from Cork and 7¾ miles from Macroom on the latter company's line. This suggestion, which came from Sir John Arnott in his capacity as chairman of the Macroom company, was declined by the WCR due to their having no monies at their disposal. If however the Macroom board

wished to promote a Bill, the West Cork would throw no obstacles in the way. Regarding the proposed platform at Bandon, the C&BR decided that matters should be left stand pending the determination of various matters in dispute between the two companies. When the Bandon's engineer looked into the matter he came up with an estimate of about £80 for a 60ft long covered-in platform, the WCR requesting that one 100ft long be erected as soon as possible. This temporary wooden platform was opened for traffic by 28th November 1876.

Ilen Valley Railway

An inspection of the Skibbereen extension was carried out on behalf of the C&BR in June 1871, when it was confirmed that the partially finished line extended from the latter town for some four miles. A 6ft wire fence had been erected nearly all this length, but most of the posts were by now decayed at ground level. Whilst cuttings had not been taken out to full width, the extra material was suitable for ballast when the road was laid. A number of small bridges had been completed, topped with timber. It was reported that the remaining 12 miles were through more difficult terrain. Exactly why this survey was carried out was not made clear, but it was announced in November 1871 that a scheme for an extension of the line to Skibbereen was being put forward by an independent company. Having considered the matter, the WCR directors came to the inevitable conclusion that such an extension would be of considerable advantage to them and, as they were not in a position to carry out the scheme themselves, they agreed to make over to the new company all claims which they had for earthworks previously carried out near Skibbereen. In addition they agreed to offer every reasonable facility and assistance in obtaining an Act.

Although nominally independent of the WCR, the first subscribers are shown in the Act of Incorporation of the Dunmanway & Skibbereen Railway Company as The O'Donovan, McCarthy Downing and Thomas Somerville, all currently directors of the WCR. The Act, which received Royal Assent on 25th July 1872, authorised a railway 15m 6f 7c in length commencing by a junction with the West Cork Railway and terminating in the parish of Abbeystrowry to the northeast of the bridge known as Colonel Townsend's or the Steam Mill Bridge just to the east of the Skibbereen to Bantry road. Capital was £80,000 in £10 shares with additional borrowing up to £20,000. Certain baronies were authorised to contribute for 35 years at a rate of 5% on £53,000 of that capital. In addition to the three above mentioned gentlemen, the first directors were to include Sir Henry Wrixon Belcher and John Warren Payne.

Advertisements were placed in February 1873 seeking tenders for construction, a number being received and considered at a board meeting on 24th March. The D&SR had a new Bill drafted for submission to Parliament in 1874. Clauses were to be inserted allowing for the new line to be worked by the C&MDR, but following strenuous opposition from the C&BR these were removed. The Act in modified form received Royal Assent on 30th July 1874, the most obvious point being the company's change of name to the Ilen Valley Railway Co. Provision was made for the C&BR to subscribe £10,000 towards the new undertaking and for working agreements to be entered into with the C&BR and/or the WCR. In the following month the Bandon directors decided that they would give £5,000 when the line was completed as far as Drimoleague and the remaining £5,000 when the line was finished to Skibbereen and ready for traffic.

A contract for construction of the line was awarded in March 1875 to Messrs G B Crawley & Co. of Bishopsgate Street in London in an amount of £119,200, of which £40,000 was to be paid in cash and the balance in shares. The line was to be completed within eighteen months from 1st March 1875 and the schedule attached to the agreement included eight public road level crossings, 50 field crossings, the four bridges, one 36ft turntable and stations. In respect of the latter, the contractor was not bound to expend more than £5,000. Rails were to be a minimum of 65lb per yard and sleepers were to be either Baltic redwood or larch.

In April the board appointed Albert Sillifant as secretary to the company at a salary of £50 per annum, and Henry O'Neil as corresponding secretary at Skibbereen at a salary of £35 a year. The company's offices were at 4 Bishopsgate, London, coincidentally the offices of the contractor. Under the contract, the line should have been completed and ready for opening by September 1876, but at that time and despite 650 men at work, only some 1½ miles at the Dunmanway end had been brought to formation level. In fairness to the contractor notice had been given to the PWLC in the previous

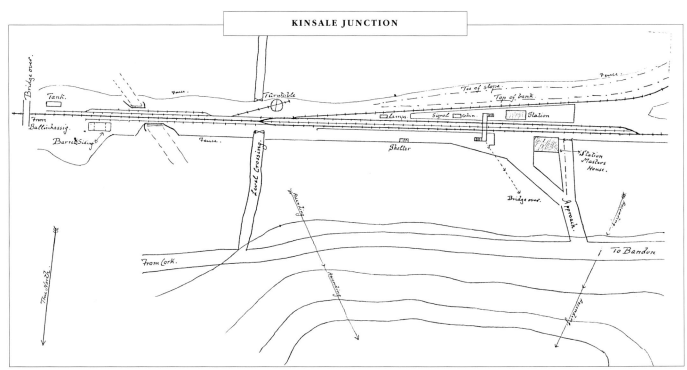

KINSALE JUNCTION

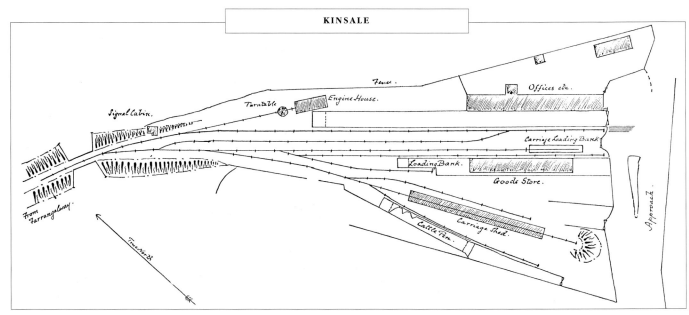

KINSALE

September that work would be suspended owing to lack of funds. The contractors were later in fact congratulated that they had worked, 'with wonderful speed', and had carried out the work, 'uncommonly well'.

The matter of the C&BR working the Dunmanway line was raised again in 1876 when it was proposed that they work it at 52% of gross receipts, also taking over the working agreement for the Ilen Valley line. The traffic on the three railways should be worked by a joint committee and the C&BR would take over the WCR rolling stock at an agreed valuation. The Bandon directors agreed to all these proposals except for that relating to a joint committee. They now proposed that a station, to be agreed upon, should be constructed at Bandon. We shall now leave the affairs of the WCR line for a short while and take a look at the further extension of the line to the west.

Consideration was now being given to which company should work the new line. The C&BR would be the preferred option as they had more experience of working and they had, or could more easily provide, sufficient rolling stock, whereas the WCR were lacking in both fields. The advantage of the latter company was of course that they enjoyed a physical connection at Dunmanway. The C&BR expected to be given the working and could avail of the IVR running powers over the WCR system. Negotiations took place with the Bandon but in due course the latter declined to agree to terms and an agreement was made with the WCR. This drew objections from the C&BR directors and the matter was referred to the decision of the Railway Commissioners. In April 1876 they came down in favour of the agreement with the WCR. It was about this time that the company made contact with the Treasury seeking a loan of £40,000, this being approved provided the BoW were satisfied that the working agreement with the WCR was binding.

Plans for the proposed new stations were submitted to the WCR board in December 1876. As far as Dunmanway was concerned, little required to be done to adapt it for the requirements of the increased traffic. Purcell had endeavoured to persuade the contractors to build a shed for the third engine but without success. The IVR would have to provide signals, points and crossings for their requirements. It was agreed that on the opening of the new line, it would be necessary to provide for the crossing of trains at Castle Bernard and Ballineen at a cost of about £150. Later, in May 1877, William Barrington wrote regarding the two small intermediate stations at Madore and Knockbue, which the contractors proposed not to erect until after the opening of the line. It was agreed that they be erected immediately after the opening. The contractors

announced early in May that they expected to have the line completed and ready for opening by 2nd July. In connection with ballasting work, they had borrowed from the C&BR an engine and eight wagons. A derailment occurred at the end of May involving this borrowed stock. The C&BR locomotive superintendent was sent to examine and report on the incident. By the time of his arrival, one wagon had been recovered from the bog, two were in course of being removed and he could only see a small portion of the wheels of a fourth. The driver, who was most likely a C&BR employee, was praised for his conduct on the occasion of the derailment.

The line was inspected by General Hutchinson on behalf of the BoT and a ceremonial opening took place on 21st July. It was reported that a special train, which left Cork in the forenoon, was greeted by a volley of shots as it passed Drimoleague. On arrival at Skibbereen a déjeuner was held in the goods store which had been specially decorated for the occasion. The Rev Fr Davis, PP of Skibbereen, said the town had waited 17 years for this blessed day. The public opening took place two days later although Hutchinson had drawn attention to some matters requiring attention. He returned at the end of August and found the ballast still inadequate. Hardly had the line been opened but the board turned their attentions to a proposed branch from Drimoleague to Bantry, details of which are related in the next chapter.

McCarthy Downing, who had been the chairman of the IVR, was succeeded in 1878 by Sir William Tyrone Power of Kensington in London. Shortly after taking office he had the unpleasant task of announcing the sudden death of the secretary, Albert Sillifant. The secretaryship was offered to Hector F Munro at a salary of £100 per annum as from 29th September. Munro accepted the post pro tem. It was reported that Sillifant had passed away shortly after receiving an increase in salary. About this time a letter was read from the Skibbereen Board of Guardians as to the desirability of a siding at Madore. In reply the secretary stated that the company had no funds at its disposal for such a purpose.

Amalgamation in West Cork

By now it was clear that moves were afoot to bring about an amalgamation of the companies operating in West Cork. It was no surprise therefore when talks took place between the boards of the C&BR, WCR and the C&KJR regarding the purchase of the latter two companies by the C&BR. The C&KJR obtained an Act in 1879 allowing for the takeover as from 1st January 1880, the purchase price of each of the two lines to be decided by George Leeman, chairman of the Railway Companies' Association, assisted by

Henry Oakley of the English Great Northern Railway. The IVR remained independent and was for the future worked by the C&BR. It eventually lost its independence in 1909. The powers for the Bantry extension obtained under the Act of 1878 were passed to the Bandon company.

Leeman sat in London for a total of eleven days in November and December 1879, the evidence put forward running to almost 900 pages, dealing with a wide range of topics. Much emphasis was placed on the poor train service to and from Kinsale, which had stifled the growth of various categories of traffic, fish being particularly singled out. It was stated that the port of Kinsale was home to almost 10% of the country's total fleet of fishing vessels. Due to a lack of proper facilities, not least the location of the town's railway station, much of the fish traffic went by boat; a smaller proportion was carted by road to Cork, involving a journey of nearly six hours.

As regards passenger traffic, connections at the junction involved considerable delays of up to an hour and fifty minutes. A journey from Cork to Kinsale consequently took 2¾ hours for a distance of 24 miles, with but two stops. Furthermore, the service consisted of only two trains each way daily, described by Counsel for the C&KJR as, 'hardly reasonable accommodation for passengers'. Another complaint centred around excessively high fares. Wood, the C&KJR secretary, complained that there were as many public cars and conveyances and private vehicles on the coach road as before the line opened.

A similar pattern emerged in the case of the WCR. Complaints in this instance included the fact that the sum of £20,000 promised as a subscription by the C&BR had not been paid, this leading to the necessity to hire, rather than purchase, rolling stock. Frequent complaints were made that the C&BR held on to wagons at Cork, these frequently being used for the Bandon company's own traffic requirements. In their defence, the C&BR maintained that wagons were often received at Bandon with only small items contained in them, rather than being utilised to their full capacity. The other complaint related to lack of through booking at Bandon, both passenger and goods. Many traders were called to give evidence of a lack of facilities, leading to the use of road transport. It was reported that cattle and pigs were sometimes driven by road to Macroom for onward transport to Cork.

At the half-yearly shareholders' meeting of the C&BR in February 1880, the chairman reported that Leeman had handed down his awards in respect of the purchase monies for the two companies, £48,009 in respect of the C&KJR and £141,934 for the WCR. This latter sum included a figure of £13,300 for rolling stock. Although the IVR was not finally absorbed until 1909, the four companies came under the control of one management as from 1st January 1880. It was confidently expected that the traffic along the whole line would be largely developed and increased, with a corresponding reduction in expenditure.

Under the arrangement with the WCR, the company agreed to undertake monthly payments to the B&FRP Co, amounting to £176.5s.0d per month. By March 1880, the WCR were claiming £926.10s.2d interest on the purchase money and advised that the rate of interest would rise from 4% to 5% as from 1st March. The Kinsale company went

further, issuing a writ for recovery of interest due to them. This dragged on for another two years, payment finally being made on 19th October 1882, and then only after the WCR had obtained the appointment of a Receiver. It was on that latter date that the WCR was formally transferred to the C&BR.

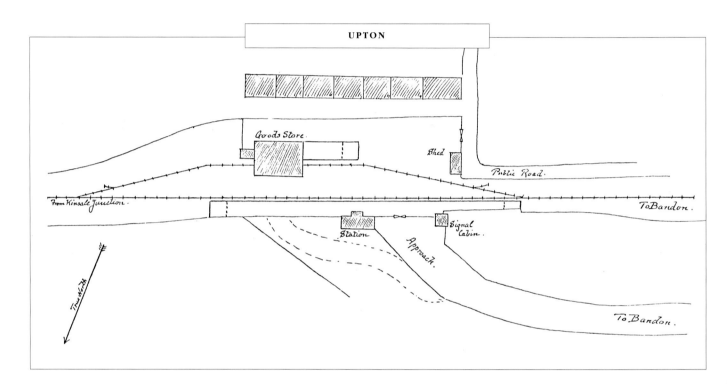

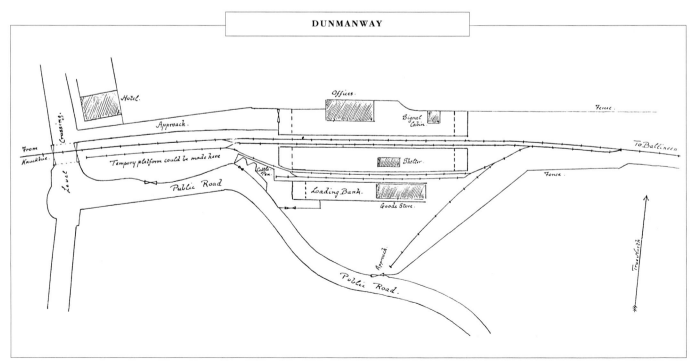

Chapter Four

LINES TO BANTRY & CLONAKILTY

We now briefly leave the parent system to take a look at the extensions which were to bring the railway to the west coast at Bantry and also to the south coast at Clonakilty. These two lines were authorised by independent companies, although the Ilen Valley Railway's powers for the former were, as we have already seen, assumed by the C&BR with the take over of the WCR in 1880. Further extensions to Timoleague and Courtmacsherry, made by companies independent of the C&BR, are dealt with in Chapter Five.

Extension to Bantry
As stated in Chapter Three, during 1877 the IVR had decided to extend their line a further eleven miles to the coast at Bantry, the draft Bill for which was submitted to their board in December. Whilst approving the wording of the Bill, the directors decided to reserve the right to withdraw from its promotion should it appear that capital was insufficient. In May of the following year the IVR board decided to offer the contract for construction in the first instance to Mr Crawley, who had constructed their own line; however, in February 1879 Crawley declined to become involved. The Ilen Valley Railway (Bantry Extension) Act received Royal Assent on 8th August 1878 for a line 11m 1f 9c in length commencing in the townland of Dromdaleague by a junction with the IVR near Drimoleague station, and terminating in the townland of Carrignagat and parish of Kilmacomogue in a field occupied by Patrick Cotter, at or near the town of Bantry. The plans for the new line were based on the original scheme of 1852/3. Capital was set at £70,000 and of this figure a sum of £40,000 was to be baronially guaranteed at a rate of 5% for a period of 35 years from the opening of the line. Two addition-

al shareholders were to be appointed as directors to represent the extension railway, these being named as J Warren Payne of Bantry and John Edward Barrett.

With the Act passed, attention turned to the working of the new line when constructed. In December 1878 a letter was read from the WCR enclosing a copy letter addressed by them to Mr Thomas Downes, a solicitor of Skibbereen, suggesting terms on which they might work the new line

when completed. They were informed however that Downes was not acting as an agent for the IVR and there the matter appears to have rested. Under Section 35 of the Cork & Kinsale Junction Railway Act of 1879, the Act which gave powers for the taking over by the C&BR of the Kinsale and West Cork companies, arrangements were made for the transfer of the IVR's powers to construct the Bantry extension to the C&BR in return for a financial consideration.

Right upper: **Railcars 2636 and 2637 working the 17.40 Cork to Baltimore train await the 'right away' at Clonakilty Junction on 15th June 1954. On the right is ex D&SER 2-4-2T No 432 on the 19.00 to Clonakilty.** B K B Green

Right: **4-6-0T No 467 (originally CB&SCR No 14) on an up train at Clonakilty Junction.** Ian Allan Library

The C&BR engineer, J W Dorman, became involved in the extension railway, causing the local committee to comment in March 1879 that he could not possibly be spared as he had sufficient work on the Bandon line to keep him fully occupied. The contract for construction of the line was in due course awarded to Thomas Dowling of London, a director of the IVR, in an amount of £105,000. The chairman urged early acceptance of the tender, but a Mr Morgan requested that consideration of the offer be postponed so that the local committee might have an opportunity to consider it. The chairman refused the request and the tender was duly approved, Morgan handing in a protest which went unheeded. In September it was decided to seek powers to authorise a deviation between the 6 and 9 mileposts, J J Johnstone, the WCR engineer, reporting that he had walked and laid out the revised route; his view was that he would be able to improve even further the proposed gradients. He also confirmed having walked down from the proposed terminus to deep water and he reported that there would be no engineering difficulties and only one viaduct of importance; he estimated the cost of an extension to deep water at about £12,000.

The extension from Drimoleague included sixteen bridges and culverts, most of which were to be constructed to accommodate a double line of rails. The terminus at Bantry was to be situated some 75ft above water level, adjoining the Workhouse and with a magnificent view of the harbour and town of Bantry below. Under his contract, Dowling was required to construct the terminal station similar to that at Skibbereen, but in the event that at Bantry was superior in design and construction.

Work commences

Work was commenced in November 1879, initially at Drimoleague but later this was transferred to the Bantry end, where difficulties were encountered with a clay cutting. Considerable interest was noted in the use of 'tonite' as a new explosive for blasting. A stretch of bogland near Drimoleague was also to cause problems in finding a firm base. With work underway, the engineer reported in July 1880 that alterations necessary at Drimoleague should now be carried out as he anticipated that the line would be ready for opening within six months. Having spoken to Dowling and requested him to assist in undertaking work on the new platforms and the moving of the station, the contractor declined to do any portion of this work which, he claimed, was not in his contract. In addition, he was providing a better station at Bantry than he was bound to do.

Clonakilty Junction looking east. On the left No 463 (ex CB&SCR No 4) awaits 'right away' on a train for the west, while on the right, ex WL&WR 4-4-2T No 269, stands at the platform used for the Clonakilty branch trains.
Sean Kennedy

Initially the two platforms at Drimoleague lay in the vee of the junction of the Skibbereen and Bantry lines, being removed slightly to lie just to the west of the level crossing at the Cork end. The permanent junction was reported to be in place by February 1881, the new platforms being almost complete in May, at which date the signals and points had been connected to new locking apparatus supplied by Messrs. Saxby & Farmer. The station buildings were removed to the new up platform in June 1881, while the engineer reported that the turntable at Bandon had been loaded on to three wagons for transfer to Drimoleague. The original turntable here had been located on the down side adjoining the level crossing, the new one of 30ft diameter being placed in a corresponding situation on the up side. It was decided in November 1881 that an engine shed should be erected for the branch engine at Drimoleague, portion of the carriage shed at Dunmanway being utilised for this purpose.

Plans for proposed sidings at Bantry were submitted in October 1880 but they were reported to be insufficient for both cattle and goods traffic. With the imminent arrival of General C S Hutchinson to carry out an inspection on behalf of the BoT, consideration was given to various matters, including the appointment of a stationmaster at Bantry (although this was postponed for future consideration at a later date), the fixing of rates and fares and a train service, the furnishing of the station at Bantry and whether or not a refreshment room should be provided there. Two further items were listed, viz. the question of having a déjeuner at Bantry on the day of opening and the provision of a steamer service to Castletown Berehaven.

BoT inspection.
The BoT inspection was carried out by General Hutchinson in mid-June 1881. The new

An unidentified 'Bandon' 4-6-0T on a Dunmanway to Cork beet special at Clonakilty Junction in December 1955. Sugar beet was an important traffic on the line in its latter years. The Clonakilty branch diverged from the mainline just beyond the road overbridge in the background.
Photographer unknown, J W P Rowledge collection

line, 11m 15c in length was single throughout, although sufficient land had been obtained for doubling it at a later date if desired. Steel rails, 30ft long and weighing 65lbs per yard, were used, secured to half-round, creosoted, Baltic timber sleepers, while ballast was a mixture of broken stone and gravel. There were no intermediate stations at this time. Alterations had, as we have seen, been effected at Drimoleague to make it suitable for branch trains. Hutchinson laid down a number of requirements. These included additional ballast, improved rail fastenings at two small viaducts, alterations so that all occupation gates were prevented from opening inwards, and the provision of adequate clearance between the sides of carriages and several rock cuttings, the side of one over-bridge and the post of a level crossing gate.

A second inspection was undertaken on 29th June. Most of the earlier requirements having been attended to, permission for opening was given, subject to the observance of a speed restriction of 15mph pending yet a further inspection. The third, and final, inspection was carried out early in August, when there was still a deficiency of ballast, especially on embankments, which had settled in the interim. Hutchinson also stated that rock cuttings would require careful watching for some time to come. The new line was in fact opened for goods traffic on 1st July, the opening for passengers

taking place three days later. The *Cork Constitution* reported at some length in its issue of 5th July on the opening and on the running of a special train from Cork on Sunday 3rd July with directors and officials. Interestingly there is no mention of a déjeuner or any other celebration being held at Bantry. It did however go on to advise that horse-buses would operate to Glengarriff and Killarney in connection with Vickery's Hotel. Initially a service of two trains each way was provided on weekdays with one on Sundays. It might here be mentioned that when the telegraph was extended from Drimoleague to Bantry, the wires were erected along the main road and not along the railway, as was normal practice.

The BoT report clearly states that the only new station was at Bantry. The board minutes for 20th July 1881 make reference to a memorial requesting that the station for Durrus, 'be placed at Scart instead of at present'. A further minute of 17th August refers to verbal notification from the contractors that the station at Durrus Road was ready, with a request to have it opened for traffic. The local committee declined to open the station and ordered Dowling, 'to go on with the platform at Scart and to remove the station to it'. The board however decided, inasmuch as the station at Durrus was already made, to have it opened at once and, if found later not to be suitably placed, to remove it to Scart. It would appear therefore

Above: **Clonakilty Junction station.**
W McGrath

Left: **A diesel-railcar set taking the mainline for Bantry at Clonakilty Junction in 1957. The line to the left is the Clonakilty branch.** J L St. Leger

making a foot passage 110 yards in length from the station to the steps through the adjoining Workhouse grounds. Also at Bantry, the locomotive superintendent had reported in September 1881 that the turntable was unsafe. It was reported to be in the same condition in the following May when the line was almost ready to be handed over by the contractor. The local committee were unhappy with the state of the Bantry line, which they believed was incomplete in a number of respects. Nevertheless, the line was handed over, although it was necessary to refer to the solicitor the matter of collection for an account in a total of £1,014 due for engine and wagon hire and maintenance by the contractor.

A branch to Clonakilty.
Clonakilty (Clanna Chaoilte, or O'Keelty's sept) is one of the more important towns in West Cork with a population in 1831 of 3,307. The town was founded by Sir Richard Boyle, who afterwards became the First Earl of Cork. During the 1830s the town's staple trade was that of linen manufacture, up to 1,000 people being employed on 400

that Durrus Road was opened towards the end of August 1881. Probably in an attempt to retain Durrus Road where it was, a Dr. Levis and his tenant offered in September to give ground at the station free for the provision of a goods shed and siding, and these had been erected by February 1882. The platform at Durrus Road was lengthened in 1889.

Another intermediate station was opened in February 1882 at Aughaville, four miles west of Drimoleague. This station was, however, closed between March 1891 and May 1904, ostensibly to avoid the costs associated with signalling necessitated by the Regulation of Railways Act of 1889. A new siding connection, facing to up trains, was inspected and passed by Colonel P G von Donop in April 1905. Aughaville station was again closed for a brief period in February and March 1921. The engineer reported in April 1882 that he had men engaged at Bantry

looms. Cotton and corn were also important and there was a harbour fit for small vessels. Brief reference was made in Chapter One to the C&BR schemes of 1853/4 for extensions to Clonakilty, Skibbereen and Bantry. Another scheme of 1864 envisaged a route from Gaggin, near Bandon, via Clonakilty and along the south coast to Rosscarbery, while several years later another scheme involving Clonakilty was put forward by the Irish Tramways Co Ltd. None of these ideas progressed beyond the initial planning stage and it was not until 1880 that another proposal was put forward, the Clonakilty Extension Railway Act receiving Royal Assent on 22nd August of the following year. Included among the promoters were Thomas W Wright, who became chairman, and T J Canty of Clonakilty, a well-known brewer. The C&BR, having been approached, had agreed to subscribe £4,000 in guaranteed shares. They had also agreed to work the new line, when completed, at 60% of gross receipts up to £65 per week, reducing to 55% thereafter.

Long before the Act was obtained, the C&BR local committee reported that the company's engineer, John W Dorman, appeared to be working for the new company. He was duly informed that the board considered that his whole time and attention should be devoted to looking after C&BR engineering matters. The board found it necessary to raise the issue once again in December 1881, when they commented that he would have no spare time after attending to the company's business, considering that he already had 76 miles of line to superintend. In addition, the directors could not forget the inconvenience attendant on his acting as engineer to the Bantry Extension Railway.

The subject of providing a station at Gaggin, the point of junction between the mainline and the proposed branch, was discussed in December 1881, the board being of opinion that a station was not necessary and would, in any event, be very expensive. Brief consideration had previously been given to the provision of a station here as early as 1866, long before there was any idea of a branch to Clonakilty, but this came to nothing. Only a month later, in January 1882, the board were of the opinion that the making of the extension railway was, 'a very doubtful matter'. Once again, comments were made as to the amount of time Dorman was expending on the CER company's affairs. Dorman approached the board in August 1884 advising that he had made arrangements with the CER to construct that line. He resigned his position in

September to become contractor for the Clonakilty extension, his place as C&BR engineer being taken by John Kerr, while in December it was reported that Singleton Goodwin was appointed engineer to the CER during the construction period. A request was made to James Tighe, engineer to the W&LR, to inspect the plans and contract and to report thereon. Shortly after his appointment, Goodwin was also requested to go over the CER works and report his findings. This led to certain changes and additions, Dorman agreeing to be bound by these.

During the three year period following the passing of the 1881 Act no moves had been made towards construction of the line. Under the provisions of the Cork & Bandon Railway and Clonakilty Extension Railway Companies Act of 1884 a further period of two years was allowed for the compulsory purchase of land. Perhaps more importantly for the CER, the C&BR subscription was increased to £7,500. In January 1885 the CER secretary was instructed to apply for payment of one-quarter of this figure. Plans for the proposed station at Clonakilty were submitted to the Bandon board in March and were in due course approved, subject to some minor alterations, including the extension of the roof covering a portion of the platform to provide shelter for carriages. Reference was also again made to the provision of a station at Gaggin, and as to whether it should be a station or simply a run-through junction. The latter would involve alterations at Bandon to cater for traffic. Dorman had previously written to the C&BR in regard to the provision of a bridge or level crossing at Ahalisky public road crossing at 4m 48c. The C&BR considered that a level crossing should be constructed as laid down in the Act. Dorman however advised that if the C&BR would open Gaggin station as soon as completed and work it as a station until the remainder of the line was finished,

then he would agree to build a bridge at Ahalisky crossing. The board decided that the expenses of the proposed station would be too heavy, but agreed to try and meet the contractor's views if some arrangement could be agreed. Dorman also requested permission to run his engine, *Bantry*, to Gaggin on Sunday mornings; this was agreed to, subject to its being sent by goods train and not in steam.

Good news was received in August 1885 when it was announced that the Treasury had approved a loan of £20,000, the first instalment of £10,000 of which was paid in November. By this time the C&BR had also paid over their subscription of £7,500. In September 1885, Messrs Bennett & Co, who owned and operated a mill at Shannonvale, sought the installation of a siding to their premises, the subsequent construction of which is described in Chapter Five.

BoT inspection

Further good news in May 1886 came in a letter from Dorman stating that the BoT inspector was expected to make a first inspection of the line mid-month. He requested the loan of whatever engines the inspector might require and a carriage. This was agreed to at a minimum charge of £5 and subject to Dorman giving a guarantee to make good any damage to the stock. With the line virtually completed, the C&BR appointed three stationmasters and a clerk early in June. William Coe was appointed stationmaster at Clonakilty at 21s per week plus a house, George Tuck becoming a clerk there at 15s per week. James Wagner was appointed to Ballinascarthy at 14s per week and Michael Ring to Gaggin at 18s per week.

General Hutchinson carried out a first inspection of the new 8m 67c line on 29th June. He reported that there was a small junction station at Gaggin (later renamed Clonakilty Junction), a small station at Ballinascarty (sic), the junction for the recently

The terminus of the Shannonvale Mill siding with Paddy *preparing to take a laden wagon up to the junction.* W McGrath

authorised light railway to Timoleague, and a large terminal station at Clonakilty. The line was single, with no provision made for future doubling. Permanent way was the usual 30ft steel flat-bottomed rail weighing 65lbs per yard. Sleepers were half-round Baltic redwood with the usual ballast of broken stone and gravel. Works consisted of 15 over-bridges and eleven under-bridges. The River Argadeen was crossed by a three span viaduct, each span of 60ft, constructed of wrought-iron lattice girders on masonry piers and abutments. All of these structures appeared to have been substantially constructed and were standing well. Hutchinson commented that sufficient accommodation had been provided at stations. At each of the stations, signalling was controlled from raised signal cabins, that at Gaggin Junction containing nine working levers, Ballinascarthy four working and five spare levers, and Clonakilty, five working levers. Turntables were located at Gaggin and Clonakilty, large enough to turn the tank engines expected to be used on the line.

General Hutchinson laid down a number of requirements, including the necessity for additional ballast, both on the permanent way itself and on some of the under-bridges. Public road level crossings should be prevented from opening outwards, and home signals provided, while the occupation gates were to be prevented from opening inwards. There was inadequate clearance at some over-bridges, requiring some re-alignment of track, while a good deal of lifting and regulating was needed on parts of the line. Notwithstanding these various requirements, Hutchinson approved the line for opening, subject to certain speed restrictions, viz. 20mph between Gaggin and Ballinascarthy, and 15mph from the latter station to Clonakilty. No time was to be lost in completing these requirements, and the line was to be worked on the 'single engine in steam' principle.

The inspection was unusual from Hutchinson's point of view as Thomas Sheehan, the tunnel man at Ballinhassig tunnel, was killed by the engine of the special train. Despite BoT approval, the C&BR declined

to open the line on 1st July as had been requested, as they insisted on further works being completed, not all of which Dorman considered necessary. It was also reported that the contractor had retained an engine and kept the crew on duty for more than 28 hours, endangering not only their lives, but also those of others, and one wonders if this the same crew that was involved in the Ballinhassig fatality!

Kerr reported, following a visit to Gaggin on 19th July, that a siding capable of holding 50 wagons could be put in between the mainline and the turntable. Instructions were given that the CER should make the siding at once, they refusing to provide further accommodation. Kerr was requested to lay down a shorter siding to hold ten or 12 wagons, the question of siding accommodation generally to be referred to arbitration between the two companies. Kerr was instructed on 11th August to inspect the branch once more and he again submitted a list of outstanding requirements, which he considered necessary before the line was taken over for working. Following the issuing of a report and certificate by Goodwin on 19th August, it was reluctantly agreed to open the line for traffic on Saturday 28th August. It was, however, made clear that such opening was in no way to delay the carrying out of the outstanding works or to prejudice any matters arising therefrom later referred to arbitration.

At the time of the opening, the station at Ballinascarthy was still incomplete, it being finally opened on Saturday 9th October. At about the same time it was reported that the stationmaster's house at Gaggin, by then named Clonakilty Junction, was damp. General Hutchinson carried out his final inspection of the branch towards the end of March 1887 and found everything more or less in

Left upper: **Clonakilty terminal station looking towards the buffer stops on 5th June 1958. Constructed on a hill overlooking the town it served, it was so built to facilitate a possible extension of the line westwards towards Glandore and Rosscarbery. Clonakilty had its single platform on the down side, which included the usual passenger facilities. Opposite, on the up side, were extensive goods facilities. The signal cabin of eleven levers was at the Cork end on the up side, almost opposite which were a 30ft diameter turntable and a small, single-road, shed capable of stabling one engine.** John Langford

Left: **Clonakilty station with the single 400ft long platform and station buildings on the right. On the left is the goods store, beyond which were extensive cattle pens. The crane was rated at four tons.**
Photographer unknown, John Langford collection

Above: **Ex D&SER 2-4-2T No 432 of 1886 on a short train at Drimoleague while on the right is ex WL&WR 4-4-2T No 274. The former engine was built in the Grand Canal Street Works of the DW&WR while No 274 came from Kitsons of Leeds in 1897. The goods shed can be seen on the right of the picture.** Sean Kennedy

Right: **Aughaville halt taken from a down Bantry-bound diesel-railcar on 19th June 1959. There was a single platform on the down side.** Late Douglas Thompson, 'Stations UK'

order. As a result the temporary speed restrictions were removed. He did however ask for the provision of caps on the turntable locks at Gaggin and Clonakilty, so as to prevent the locks being interfered with. Notice was served on Dorman by the CER that they had taken possession of all plant, engine, wagons and rails left by him on the line against monies owed by him. His brother, E H Dorman, resigned his position as secretary about this time, most likely because he was only offered a salary of £50 per annum. He was replaced by Denham Franklin at the same salary. Franklin in turn remained until he resigned in April 1903, being replaced by R H Leslie. Following on Dorman's resignation, the offices were removed from No 74 South Mall to Albert Quay, Messrs John Wallis & Sons being paid a sum of 15s for the removal of the safe.

In July 1887 it was announced that the company had received an amount of

£31 10s 0d, representing 3s 4d in the £ on £189, this latter being the total amount owed by Dorman to the company. Three months later the BoW advised that Dorman had requested them not to pay the balance of the Government loan as the company allegedly owed him money, whereas the accounts appeared to show the opposite. The company wrote to the BoT in October 1888, stating their intention to alter the system of working the line from 'one engine in steam' to the absolute block and train staff and ticket system, and enquiring whether they might be allowed to lay the block wires on the post office poles. The BoT replied that they saw no objection to this course of action.

A requisition was received from 21 share-holders in March 1889 asking the directors

to hold an extraordinary general meeting for the purpose of appointing a committee of management. This committee would have wide-ranging powers, including entering contracts on behalf of the company, the appointment and dismissal of officers and including the fixing of their salaries, taking custody of the company's books and documents, and the receipt of all monies due to the company. A second resolution barred the existing directors from exercising any of the powers of the company. The committee in question comprised Captain A Warren Perry, J W Payne, G Vickery and J W Dorman. In July, consequent on the opening of the Timoleague line, the CER agreed to pay one-quarter of the cost of blocking their line and providing the necessary signalling at Ballinascarthy Junction.

Alterations at Clonakilty

The CB&SCR wrote in November 1890 enquiring whether the CER would contribute towards the cost of substituting a bridge for a level crossing at the Clonakilty Workhouse, this receiving a negative response. Reference was also made in November to the great inconvenience being experienced due to Dorman's absence abroad. He responded by informing the board that his leaving the country again should be regarded as, 'equivalent to (his) resignation as a Director'. Francis Johnson-Travers was appointed to the post of engineer in March 1891, the CB&SCR refusing to grant either him or the secretary a free pass over their line. They were politely informed that the directors and officials had up to now been travelling first class as a right rather than as a favour; their acceptance of tickets was no more than a courtesy. Travers (and presumably Franklin) could now travel whenever he liked without a ticket.

The question of accommodation at Clonakilty station was raised in September 1891 when it was intimated that the CER were prepared to expend between £800 and £1,000 on re-modelling the layout. Plans submitted to Kerr were however turned down as being inadequate for the working company's requirements. It was decided in January 1892 to renew the cattle pens here, but only if the CER agreed in advance to pay for the work. Further correspondence led to

an offer from the latter company in June to subscribe £900 - £250 immediately, £250 within six months and the balance in the following half-year. Considerable delay ensued, and as late as January 1899 the CER advised that they now had £1,200 available towards the necessary enlargement of the station.

Five months later the CB&SCR stated that the alterations would cost a minimum contribution of £1,500 from the smaller company. They would be prepared to accept £1,200 so long as the balance was paid within three years. This was accepted subject to the CER having the necessary funds available at that time. By December 1899 the cattle bank was complete, the foundations for the goods shed were laid, progress was being made with the engine shed, and additional sidings were in place. When the Bandon sought payment of the £300 balance in February 1902 they were informed that there were no funds available. The question of further alterations was raised in November 1905, including the provision of offices and waiting rooms on the new platform and a carriage shed, but it was April 1909 before it was reported that a new station had been opened here at a cost of £540.

The question of making Clonakilty Junction a crossing station was considered by the Bandon board in August 1893, a decision being postponed. The matter was raised again in May 1895 when it was agreed that a

sum of £500 saved on proposed signalling at Desert station be utilised in providing suitable accommodation at the junction. In April of the following year a footbridge was ordered from Messrs Arrol Bros at a cost of £447 6s 8d, a weather-proof shelter being provided on the up platform in November 1907.

Amalgamation between the CER and the CB&SCR was raised in July 1908, this being referred to a small committee from each company. It was suggested that should the baronies forego an amount of £5,031. 4s.10d then due to them, then the Bandon would agree to relieve them from any future guarantees. Similar proposals were put forward in March 1911 but they were turned down on both occasions. The troubled years from 1914 onwards precluded any further moves to bring about an amalgamation, and the Clonakilty Extension Railway remained an independent concern until eventually absorbed by the Great Southern Railways under the terms of the Railways Act of 1924.

Bantry Town station in the early 1930s. In the lower right of the picture is the engine shed, with water tank overhead. Standing on the turntable is one of the Bandon's 4-6-0Ts. It will shortly cross over to head the short train back towards Drimoleague. The roof of the station building appears to be undergoing some repairs. 'Stations UK'

Change of title

The draft of a Bill for various alterations was submitted to the board for consideration on 21st September 1887. Included in the powers to be sought were the diversion of the railway at Ballinhassig so as to avoid the tunnel, the closing of the level crossing at Cork and its substitution with a bridge, purchase of lands at various locations and powers to run along the quays at Cork. At a subsequent meeting one of the directors suggested that powers also be obtained to make a connection with the CB&PR, Kerr being instructed to prepare the necessary plans.

As regards the Ballinhassig deviation, the proposed line was to be 1m 41c long round the shoulder of the hill through which the tunnel passed. This would have involved the resiting of Ballinhassig station. The estimated cost of the deviation was £10,702. Although powers were obtained in the 1888 Act, the works were never undertaken. Opposition came from Cork Corporation to the closure of the Gas Works level crossing and to the quay extension, both of these being later completed in connection with the cross-city connection. The Passage railway connection, however, never came to fruition.

The Act also included powers to change the name of the company to the more embracing Cork Bandon & South Coast Railway. The local committee had as far back as June 1879 suggested that the continuing use of the individual company names would lead to confusion and came up with the idea of the Cork Bandon & West Coast Railway. So it was that the company title was altered by the Act of 1888, which received Royal Assent on 5th July of that year. In the next chapter, we will look at the further expansion of the system with the construction of the Balfour lines.

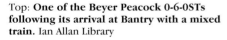

Top: **One of the Beyer Peacock 0-6-0STs following its arrival at Bantry with a mixed train.** Ian Allan Library

Centre: **On 5th June 1958, Bantry town station looking west with the 15.00 up Cork train standing at the single platform. Note the small engine shed on the right-hand side and the bilingual nameboard on the signal cabin. The connection to Bantry Pier ran to the left of the engine shed. The goods store can also be seen immediately to the left of the train.**
John Langford

Below: **Bantry Pier, the most westerly point on the CB&SCR system, and terminal for the steamers of the Bantry Bay Steamship Co, which operated steamers to Glengarriff and Castletown Berehaven.** Ian Allan Library

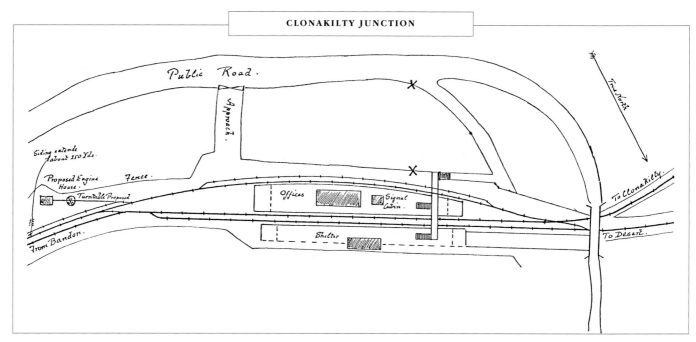

CLONAKILTY JUNCTION

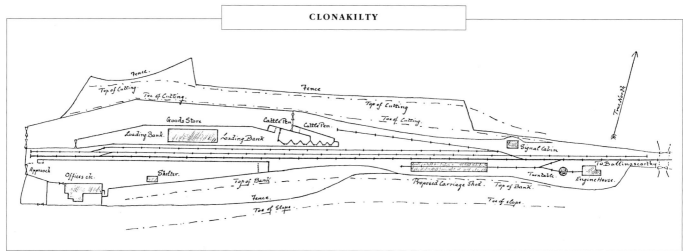

CLONAKILTY

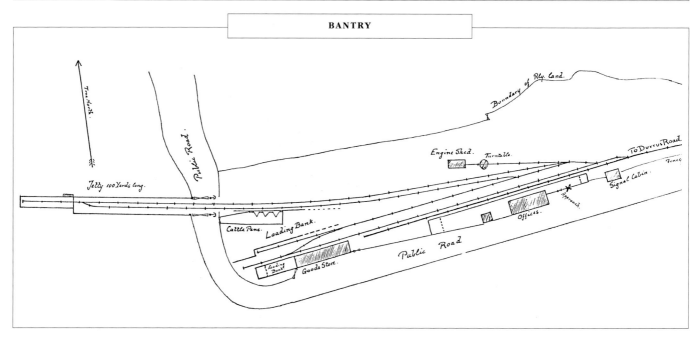

BANTRY

Chapter Five

INDEPENDENT DEVELOPMENTS

Chapter Four saw the extension of the system to Bantry and Clonakilty. Even before the latter extension had opened, plans had been drawn up to construct a light railway from the intermediate station at Ballinascarthy to Timoleague, and, by means of a tramway, on to the coast at Courtmacsherry. This extension was to remain independent right up to 1925, although to all intents and purposes it was a part of the 'Bandon' system. Without the latter, the extension would probably never have been constructed as it would have been isolated from the remainder of the railway system. In this chapter, we also take a brief look at the narrow-gauge Schull & Skibbereen Railway in so far as it affected the C&BR system.

Shannonvale siding
For some years prior to the coming of the railway to Clonakilty, the Bennett family operated a thriving flour-milling business beside the River Argadeen in the village of Shannonvale, about two miles north of Clonakilty. Realising the potential of the railway, Messrs Bennett & Co wrote to the C&BR in September 1885 requesting a siding. Correspondence was entered into with J W Dorman, contractor for the Clonakilty extension and he agreed to complete the necessary work, estimated to cost £100, although construction did not start for another year or so. Later, in September 1886, Kerr reported having examined the site of the proposed siding and now estimated that it would cost £300 to install. Messrs Bennett & Co agreed to give the necessary ground free of charge, to pay half the cost of construction and the cost of keeping it in repair. The tender of the Railway Signal Co was accepted in October at £31 10s 6d for signal fittings required.

The half-mile long siding was duly completed in January 1887 and was inspected

and approved by General Hutchinson on behalf of the BoT and opened in March 1887. An extension was requested in October 1889, Messrs Bennett & Co offering to do the earthworks to the satisfaction of the company's engineer. The siding diverged from the Clonakilty branch by a facing connection on the up side just before the branch crossed the Argadeen River Viaduct. The junction points were controlled by a key on the branch staff. The siding, which closed in March 1961, was unusual as regards its motive power as it was always worked by horse.

An independent extension
The area to the east of the Clonakilty branch includes the villages of Timoleague and Courtmacsherry. Timoleague, or Tigh Molaga (the house of St Molaga) includes the Abbey founded by the Franciscans about 1240 on the site of St. Molaga's ancient cell. Courtmacsherry is an attractive village and favourite seaside resort on the bay of the same name. The village of Kilbritain, to the south of Bandon, lies to the east roughly midway between Clonakilty and Kinsale. The passing of the Tramways & Public Companies (Ireland) Act of 1883 brought forth a number of schemes for the provision of railway accommodation to the area in question. A public meeting was held on 5th November 1883 with a local JP, Robert A Travers in the

chair. A scheme was put forward for a line from Bandon to Timoleague, passing over Scardone Hill, and which would have involved a gradient as steep as 1 in 18; a connection was also suggested to a proposed tramway at Kilmacsimon on the Bandon River. The chairman referred to two other possible routes, one a variation of the first one passing through Kilbritain and thus avoiding the severe gradients associated with Scardone Hill. The other was to be a branch diverging from the newly planned Clonakilty branch.

Whilst the latter line would be cheaper to construct, Travers favoured the Kilbritain line. There may have been two reasons for this, firstly that it would be six miles longer to Bandon by the Clonakilty route and, more importantly, it would involve a break of gauge as the new line was at that time intended to be constructed as a narrow-gauge line. Whilst the 1883 Act did not specify a gauge, other projects put forward under that legislation were to the 3ft gauge. It should also be mentioned that the line deviating from the Clonakilty branch would have been constructed along the Argadeen valley, a route described by J W Dorman thus: 'nature almost having made it for the railway'. It would in addition have generated extra traffic for the Clonakilty branch and thus have been of benefit to the guaranteeing baronies.

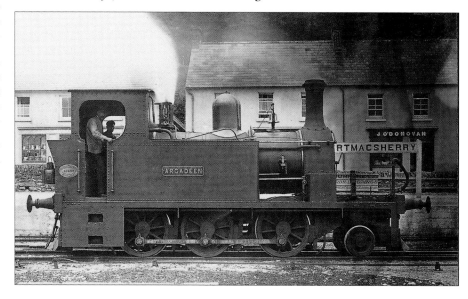

Ex T&CELR 2-6-0T *Argadeen* awaits her next turn of duty at the terminus at Courtmacsherry. O'Donovan's was possibly the most photographed retail establishment in the village!
Ian Allan Library

Ex T&CELR 0-6-0ST *Slaney* 'on shed' at
Timoleague. *Slaney* was delivered new
from Messrs Hunslet of Leeds in September
1885 to the contractor, Robert Worthington
and was used in the construction of the
Palace East to New Ross contract in County
Wexford, hence the name. She was sold in
December 1890 to the T&CELR and was
withdrawn in August 1920. As built, she
had only a slightly turned weatherboard, a
backless cab being fitted about 1892. She
also sported skirts for a period of about ten
years. The bell and the cow catchers were
required for running along the roadside
tramway. Timoleague Abbey is visible in
the background. Ian Allan Library

Notice appeared in the *Dublin Gazette* for 1st December 1883 to the effect that the promoters of the Bandon & Timoleague Steam Tramway intended seeking a presentment for a 5% baronial guarantee on various baronies. Just over five months later a similar notice appeared for the Ballinascarthy & Timoleague Junction Light Railway involving the same baronies. This was the line intended to diverge from the Clonakilty branch at Ballinascarthy and it was quickly announced that the gauge was to be 5ft 3in and that steam or other mechanical power would be employed in its working. It is worth noting that this was the only line to be constructed to the Irish standard gauge under the 1883 legislation.

Robert A Travers, Francis Beamish and George Lamb were appointed directors of the new concern in October 1884 and, in the following January, J W Dorman was awarded the contract for construction at a figure of £25,000. S A Kirkby was requested to act as engineer during the construction works. Nothing happened for the next three years and it was 10th December 1887 before a fresh contract was entered into with Robert Worthington for the construction of the line. It was stipulated that Worthington was to construct the line to the same standard as the Cork & Muskerry Light Railway and he was to be liable for the line's maintenance for six months after it was opened for traffic. Mr S G Fraser was now appointed engineer to the company. Denham Franklin was appointed as company secretary, a position he already held with the Clonakilty Extension Railway. It was agreed that he would not receive any salary until the line was opened for traffic. Despite these various appointments and contracts, it was not until August 1888 that the company was formally incorporated. In fact as late as April 1888, permission was granted to Worthington to issue a prospectus at his own expense.

An approach had been made to the CB&SCR in January 1887 enquiring if that company would enter into a working agreement, but they declined, even after T W Wright, the Timoleague company's solicitor, offered to increase the weight of the rails to be used and have the sleepers closer together. Further approaches were made suggesting either mileage or percentage rates, these all being declined. Some irregularities appear to have arisen with the registration of the new company, as the Master of the Rolls directed early in August 1888 that several persons' names be removed from the Register of Shareholders. These included Robert Worthington. It was requested that the original agreement between Worthington and the company be filed with the Registrar of Joint Stock Companies and notice of the Master's Order be given to the Registrar, following which the shareholders so removed be issued fresh certificates of the same value and bearing the same serial numbers.

Further extension to the sea

About the time of this minor problem with the company's registration, plans were announced for a possible extension of the line to the seaside village of Courtmacsherry. In connection with this, the Bandon company's engineer, Kerr, reported to his board in August 1888 following an inspection of the plans and route. He stated that there were several curves of seven chains radius, although the line was virtually level apart from gradients on the approach to Courtmacsherry. This visit to the Courtmacsherry section followed a similar inspection two months previously of the first section of line. Once again, gradients were not a major problem, but there were eight or nine curves of ten chains radius. Kerr advised that it would not be possible to use long (bogie) carriages and that engines would tear up the

road. He suggested that the Timoleague company should themselves provide at least two engines and three carriages. He estimated the cost of maintenance at £9 10s 0d per week for materials and labour, but the board decided, however, against entering into a working agreement.

Worthington submitted a plan of the proposed junction at Ballinascarthy in October but it was decided to wait until arrangements had been made for the working of the station itself before any junction arrangements could be approved. A draft working agreement for the station was submitted to Worthington later in the month, payment for the use of the station to be at the rate of £100 per annum. It was also stipulated that the B&TJLR should pay for the blocking and signalling of the Clonakilty section, a requirement which they found impossible to accept.

In October 1888, notice appeared in the *Dublin Gazette* regarding the proposed extension to Courtmacsherry. It was announced that the County Cork Grand Jury had sanctioned the Timoleague & Courtmacsherry Extension Light Railway Company but had altered the baronial guarantees by reducing the capital of the B&TJLR down by £2,000 to £23,000 and increased the extension capital by a similar amount to £12,000. This in part was because the original project had been shortened by 33 chains in connection with the re-siting of the station at Timoleague.

The chairman reported at the February 1889 meeting of the B&TJLR that the construction works were well in hand and he confidently expected the line to be open for traffic within a short time. A good deal of work had also been done in relation to the causeway on the seaward side of the road between Timoleague and Courtmacsherry. Following this meeting of shareholders, instructions were given for the solicitor to press an amalgamation of the two lines as speedily as possible. This made good sense as the companies shared common directors, they were guaranteed by the same baronies and in due course they would share one set of rolling stock. Despite this instruction, and a recognition of the anomaly by the Lord Chancellor at a Privy Council meeting, the lines were to remain legally separate until arrangements were made for their absorption into the Great Southern Railways under the provisions of the Railways Act of 1924.

The question of blocking and signalling the Clonakilty branch was raised with Worthington in April 1889, he agreeing to pay a sum of £150. However, in the following August the CB&SCR were informed that the B&TJLR would contribute half of the cost provided the term of the lease was extended; the latter was in fact extended to 90 years. Whilst these matters were being discussed, General Hutchinson came over from London and inspected the intended layout at Ballinascarthy, proposing three alternatives, viz. [1] a simple crossover road for wagons only and locked by the Clonakilty staff, with no signals and the B&TJLR to make their own station, [2] the latter company to carry out the station plan and agreement as approved by the CB&SCR, the connection to remain as in the last, and [3] the station plan as approved by the CB&SCR to be carried out and the station to be fully signalled and interlocked and the block system to be introduced between Gaggin, Ballinascarthy and Clonakilty. This plan the general strongly recommended as either of the others must, he said, be only temporary. He was of the opinion that the cost of blocking the Clonakilty branch and the junction signalling, which that would entail, should be divided between the two companies as it was not, in his opinion, an absolute necessity and would in any case have to be done by the parent company at some time. To this latter scheme the Bandon company agreed, provided the CER paid one-quarter and the B&TJLR one-half of the cost. This was agreed to by both companies.

Difficulties with the CB&SCR

The *Cork Constitution* for 9th September reported at some length on a recent shareholders' half-yearly meeting of the B&TJLR. The chairman said that the line should originally have been opened in June, but this had been delayed due to being unable to come to terms with the CB&SCR for the use of Ballinascarthy station and the provision of wagons. An approach was made to the

Bandon in the following December seeking the hire of some wagons, the latter company stating they had none to spare. It was suggested that the Timoleague company should provide not less than twenty wagons themselves and give an undertaking to provide more if found necessary in the future. Subject to this, the Bandon company were prepared to agree to an interchange of wagons on the usual IRCH terms. Later, in March 1890, the B&TJLR arranged to hire ten wagons on a five year lease from the Birmingham Carriage & Wagon Co.

As matters now moved towards the day of opening the line, consideration was given in May to the appointment of a traffic manager; Alex Gordon being appointed to the post at a salary of £60 per annum for both lines, provided the board of the CB&SCR had no objections. Also, in May instructions were issued for Worthington's locomotive *Slaney* to be put in perfect working order. It was later inspected on behalf of the Timoleague company by the Bandon locomotive superintendent and purchased from Worthington in the following December. Worthington approached the CB&SCR in June 1890 seek-

ing the loan of a carriage and two or three wagons for use on the new line until their own rolling stock was delivered. He was advised that the Bandon had no rolling stock to spare, but they did agree to the alteration of two carriages provided the cost was paid in advance.

The engineer, S G Fraser, was instructed in July to communicate with Worthington expressing the extreme dissatisfaction of the board at the delay in opening the line, which they considered was entirely down to Worthington. Nathaniel Jackson, the Cork West Riding surveyor, contacted the BoT in August 1890 expressing his concern in regard to the tramway line where it crossed public roads; in one place, a bridge had been built and the road altered. Jackson was unclear of his responsibilities, and enquired whether it was his duty to report on the entire tramway or only where the roads had been interfered with. He was also concerned that legal fees had not been paid. The BoT advised that his responsibility was limited to level crossings and road bridges, and their approaches, which required to be completed to his satisfaction.

Right upper: ***Aghadeen* at Courtmacsherry Pier. Bringing up the rear of the train is the T&CELR brake van No 5J.** Locomotive Publishing Company, courtesy Sean Kennedy

Right: **Either No 90 or 100 hauling a short goods train, consisting of three wagons and brake van, the former including a GNR open, on the T&CELR.** W McGrath

BoT inspection

The two lines were inspected by General-Hutchinson on 18th September 1890. He made particular reference to the lengths of the two lines, the T&C one being 5m 41.8c long. This was 33.2c shorter than authorised by the Order in Council, this being for the purpose of avoiding the construction of an expensive river bridge near Timoleague. The B&T line was quoted as being 3m 9.84c in length. All of the latter and about half of the former were on private land, about 2½ miles of the T&C line being constructed along the side of the road. Gradients on the two lines as actually constructed differed from those authorised, lateral limits of deviation also having been exceeded in three places. These changes had been made in the interests of economy in construction and, as there had been no objections from landowners, Hutchinson suggested obtaining authority for the deviations.

Rails on the two lines weighed 50lbs per yard, laid on half-round sleepers, the latter being a mixture of Baltic redwood, Scotch Pine and Larch. The only work of note was a river bridge of 59ft span, of wrought-iron girders on masonry abutments; this and other bridges appeared to have been substantially built. Hutchinson commented on the sea wall adjoining the tramway section, which had not been constructed to the satisfaction of the county surveyor. The latter suggested lodging a sum of money to cover the expense of repairs which might become necessary after the wall had been exposed to the ravages of the winter weather.

Signalling arrangements had been properly attended to, the only raised signal cabin being at Ballinascarthy Junction, containing 15 working and two spare levers. At both Timoleague and Courtmacsherry, points were worked from ground frames, unlocked by the train section staff. Rolling stock as supplied was not only insufficient, but also required alteration for tramway working and the fitting of automatic brakes. Further details of the locomotives and rolling stock can be found in the relevant chapters.

Hutchinson laid down a total of 14 requirements, a number of which referred to the permanent way. Wickets on some of the level crossing gates and some trees were foul of the line, along with the railing of the river bridge, which required lowering. Clocks at all three stations were either inadequate or lacking. Hutchinson also advised that it was most desirable that the entrances to the national school and the smithy at Courtmacsherry should be made at the sides, rather than, as at present, opening directly to the tramway.

Hutchinson returned on 29th November to re-inspect the lines, and whilst most of the requirements had been attended to, some trees had still to be removed; rails on

some curves also required additional bending. He confirmed that the first section, from Ballinascarthy to Timoleague, might now be opened for traffic. When in November Worthington declined to hand over an amount of £70 2s 9d for the crossover at Ballinascarthy, the CB&SCR threatened to, 'pull up the line'. This matter was in due course resolved and the first section of line was opened for public traffic as from Saturday 20th December 1890. As regards the tramway section, damage had in fact occurred to the sea wall in recent gales, and this required careful attention. He stipulated that a sum of £200 should be lodged to cover repairs. His main difficulty, however, was in relation to the provision of additional rolling stock, properly equipped for tramway working, and he therefore refused permission for the opening.

Work was now concentrated on the Courtmacsherry extension. The BoT requirements led to further delay in opening the final section of line, a third inspection taking place on 23rd February 1891. Hutchinson now referred to a dispute between Worthington and the company in relation to the additional rolling stock. If Worthington was found not to be liable to provide this, the company guaranteed to acquire it. Hutchinson called for a careful daily watch to be carried out on the sea wall, especially after storms. He imposed a speed limit of 6mph between Timoleague and the point where the line left the road, as well as through the village of Courtmacsherry, and 12mph elsewhere on the line. The tramway was finally opened for traffic towards the end of April 1891; the exact date is not recorded, but the BoT certificate was received on 22nd April and it is generally felt that the line opened the next day. A note inside the front cover of the B&TJLR board minute book however refers to the opening having taken place on the 22nd. Whatever the date, considerable local resentment had been expressed at the delay in opening the line. It was also stated that the line had been used during the previous winter to convey train loads of potatoes for the poor of Clonakilty.

An intermediate halt was opened on 9th May at Skeaf, between Ballinascarthy and Timoleague, to serve the nearby village of Clogogh. A shelter was requested here in June 1892, the board being sympathetic to the provision of this. Mr Armstrong reported in September however that the provision of a shelter would necessitate the removal of portion of a bank. Nevertheless it was agreed to proceed, and in the following November a Mr Foley was instructed to erect a shelter about 12ft in length, 'provided the old station at Innoshannon could not be got'. It was agreed that a lockable door be provided and that any person of respectability applying, should be allowed to keep a

key for it. It was agreed in June 1893 to lengthen the single platform here, while the board asked that cattle pens be provided as soon as possible. Complaints came before the Committee of Management in November 1898 about this halt being removed; it was requested that it be put into perfect order at once. In August 1912 it was agreed that the train guards should use a book for the issue of tickets from this halt, except for excursion tickets which were to be issued as usual. In May 1892 a request was made to the Bandon for a reduction in the rent of £100 per annum for the use of Ballinascarthy station, a figure of £30 being considered more appropriate; this request was refused.

It was quickly found that the CB&SCR bogie rolling stock was too long for the restricted loading gauge of the new lines and instructions were issued that no carriages be loaned to them. Later, new short bogie carriages were constructed for use on the extension lines, of which details are given in Chapter Fourteen. Reporting to the shareholders in August 1893 the chairman referred to increased passenger receipts arising from excursion traffic to Courtmacsherry. He stated that the provision of a hotel at the latter point would be a wonderful improvement to the line. There was one serious drawback however, Courtmacsherry being apparently the only village in the south of Ireland without a water supply. He also suggested that the inhabitants of the village might consider tidying it up and remove heaps of manure and filth of every description. There was a small pier at Courtmacsherry, powers being obtained for its extension in 1892; later, instructions were given for the laying of rails on this pier. The chairman also informed the shareholders that a carriage shed had been erected at Timoleague, but as this was only sufficiently large to accommodate new carriages, it might be extended to provide covered accommodation for all the company's carriages.

Finding that ballast was urgently required on the line, orders were given in October 1894 for the laying forthwith of a siding into the company's ballast pit at Ummera, situated close to mp5, between Skeaf and Timoleague. The expenses of working the lines, in particular the hire of rolling stock, meant that the receipts were lower than expenditure. Thus the baronies had to make regular payments under the guarantee. Continuing losses led the Cork County Council, as the successor to the Grand Juries, to exercise their power under the 1883 Act to take over the management and working of the line. The first meeting of the new Committee of Management was held on 25th July 1896, and comprised of five gentlemen so authorised to act by the County Council, viz. R Travers, T J Canty, R Bence Jones,

Right: **Ex GS&WR 0-6-0T No 90 shunting at Timoleague. In the left background are the ruins of the Abbey.** Robin Linsley collection

Right lower: **0-6-0Ts Nos 90 and 100 after arrival at Courtmacsherry with a summer Sunday excursion from Cork. These trains were very popular and frequently filled to capacity.** W McGrath

D O'Leary and Captain Townsend; Travers being duly elected chairman. The County Council refused to make any additional payment for administrative costs and it became necessary to levy a fee of ½d per share for that purpose. The working of the line was formally taken over on 12th August 1899. In August 1903 the secretary, W H Spiller since the previous April following the resignation of Franklin, drew the attention of the directors to the fact that the Committee of Management were using the company's headed notepaper and also that the Committee's bank account was in the company's name. The secretary was instructed to communicate with the Committee requesting them to desist from such practices.

The County Council suggested in 1903 that there was no necessity for the directors to remain in office. Consequently they all resigned, only to be re-elected at a shareholders' meeting on 1st June 1904. An interesting aside was referred to in February 1910 when it was stated that owing to the fact that J J O'Connor, the auditor appointed at the previous meeting, was currently undergoing a term of imprisonment (not in any way related to the affairs of the company), the accounts had not been audited. Spiller resigned his position as secretary in January 1920 and was replaced by Robert Morley.

The little company was in the vanguard as regards wage demands when the staff wrote in November 1897 seeking an increase in wages as laid down under the National Programme. As this would increase the wages bill by £186 per annum, the staff were informed that as the line was no longer being worked by a board of directors but by a Committee of Management appointed by Cork County Council, it would not be possible to accede to their demands. The reply went on to state that if the men were dissatisfied with the response, they were quite at liberty to retire, either individually or collectively. Having once quit their employment however, they would not under any circumstances be reinstated.

Plans for Rosscarbery & Glandore
To the southwest of Clonakilty are the coastal villages of Rosscarbery and Glandore. The famous Irish patriot, O'Donovan Rossa, was strongly connected with the Rosscarbery area and St Facthna founded a monastery there in the sixth century. The

village is attractively situated at the upper end of a narrow sea inlet. Glandore, about five miles west of Rosscarbery, is an extremely pretty village overlooking a harbour. At the mouth of the latter are the twin islands of Adam and Eve. The coastline in the area is strikingly picturesque.

The Irish Tramways Co. Ltd proposed a number of horse tramway schemes in 1872, one such being for a line from Clonakilty to Rosscarbery. Nothing further came of this and it was to be more than ten years before further proposals were put forward, resulting from the passing of the Tramways Act of 1883. During that year, J W Dorman, the C&BR engineer, carried out a feasibility study on various tramway schemes to serve the areas east and west of Skibbereen. James Swanton, JP, an important merchant in Glandore and Skibbereen, had at his own expense, promoted the idea of a tramway to serve Glandore and Rosscarbery, the latter generally referred to simply as Ross. Dorman advised against going to Ross due to the narrow roads and severe gradients.

Whilst attention turned to a tramway westwards to Schull, which in due course led to the construction of the narrow gauge

Schull & Skibbereen Tramway & Light Railway, consideration was still given to the eastern line. In December 1883 the West Carbery Tramways & Light Railways Co. was registered, its proposed line was called the Skibbereen Glandore & Union Hall Tramway & Light Railway. The directors included J W Johnstone and E.H. Dorman, respectively engineer and secretary to the WCR. Further meetings were held and a fresh survey was carried out in May 1887. Following the passing of the Light Railways (Ireland) Act in 1889, the supporters of the eastern extension held another meeting in August of that year but nothing further came of it.

In December 1890 the Very Rev Reeves, Dean of Ross, wrote to the CB&SCR board with reference to the working by them of an extension from Clonakilty to Rosscarbery. A deputation attended the board meeting on 10th December and informed the directors that they had been promised a Government grant of £25,000 in aid of the extension, provided the company would agree to work it. The deputation suggested that the Clonakilty Extension Railway working agreement should be extended to work the Ross line. Having considered the matter the board decided that it would not be in the best interests of their shareholders.

Not satisfied with this response, a larger deputation attended the board a week later and outlined the advantages such a line would bring both to the district and to the company. Despite a further rejection it was announced in January 1891 that the plans of the Clonakilty & Rosscarbery Light Railway Co. for the Ross extension had been lodged with the Grand Jury. It was decided that if the IVR decided to oppose the scheme, then the Bandon would offer them every assistance and contribute half of the cost of such opposition. No mention is made of the extension in the IVR board minutes and it is difficult to see how they would be materially affected as their eastern terminus at Drimoleague lay some distance away to the northwest of Glandore. Irrespective of any extension, it would seem that traffic from the Glandore/Ross area would naturally flow towards Clonakilty. Nevertheless, in July 1893 the IVR sought an amount of £52 2s 8d, being 50% of the opposition costs.

The next move came in September 1895 when a deputation from Skibbereen waited on the board to advise that an application had been made to the Treasury for a grant for the construction of a railway from Clonakilty via Rosscarbery to Glandore. In October, a Mr Waldron, on behalf of the promoters, enquired how much the company would charge for preparing plans, laying out the line and for legal and other expenses. The board agreed to charge £150 for preliminary plans, surveying and preparing the books of reference, but informed Waldron that all other expenses were the responsibility of the promoters.

Initially the Bandon company expressed an interest in working the new line if built to their satisfaction but they withdrew this offer in January 1896. Two months later, the Dean of Ross, Robert Travers, T H Wright, J W Canty and Sir George Colthurst comprised a deputation which asked the board to again consider working a line from Clonakilty to Rosscarbery if made to the company's satisfaction. They stressed that prospects appeared good for the line, which could expect considerable revenue from the carriage of Indian Corn and other goods now landed at Glandore and transported to Clonakilty by road.

It was decided that the general manager should inspect the proposed line and report back to the board. This report was considered in May, the cost of construction and the provision of two additional engines for working the line being estimated at £68,200. Receipts were likely to fall short of expenditure and it would be preferable if the promoters worked the line themselves, as the CB&SCR could then run their stock

through for cattle fairs and excursions. Taking all matters into account it was decided that the company should not undertake the working of the line. This was to be effectively the end of any further expansion into the area west of Clonakilty although as late as August 1899 a brief attempt was made to revive the tramway project from Skibbereen to Glandore, while a further abortive request for a line from Clonakilty through Rosscarbery to Skibbereen was made as late as July 1909.

Narrow-gauge connection at Skibbereen

Before taking a look at the Baltimore extension, we will first briefly narrate the story of the narrow-gauge Schull & Skibbereen Tramway, a comprehensive history of which, by J I C Boyd, was published by the Oakwood Press in 1999. Some brief details are necessary here however to explain how it impinged on that of the Bandon system. As early as October 1883 a letter was read from James Swanton, a merchant of Glandore, asking the company's assistance towards the undertaking of a tramway scheme to connect Skibbereen eastwards with Leap, Glandore and Union Hall. Whilst the C&BR directors were happy to subscribe £50 towards the preliminary expenses, this was to be contingent on the balance being subscribed locally; this figure was later increased to £100. By the following January it was reported that Parliamentary Notice had been submitted under the title of the West Carbery Tramway & Light Railway Co, the title of West Cork Tramways also being mentioned. Further correspondence took place in February 1884, when a rent of £50 per annum for three years was agreed for the use of the company's station at Skibbereen. About this time the suggestion was made that the new line could be worked by the C&BR so as to relieve the Grand Jury of the responsibility. Having considered the matter, the Bandon board suggested that the line be worked for ten years, they to receive the gross receipts in full until they amount ed to £4 per mile per week, after which the tramway company would receive any excess up to 40%; above this figure the Bandon would take 60%.

By the following October agreement had been reached that the permanent way, station buildings and rolling stock should be constructed and supplied to the satisfaction of the C&BR engineer. A letter was read from Messrs McKeone, Robinson & d'Avigdor to the effect that they had now concluded a contract for the completion of the Schull & Skibbereen Tramway and requesting that a portion of the company's ground at Skibbereen should be rented to them. They also sought the carriage of materials from Cork to Skibbereen at the lowest possible rate, along with free passes to their

managing partner and engineers. A rate of 20s per truck not exceeding six tons in weight was quoted, all materials to be carried over the Bandon, in default of which a penalty of 10s per six tons was to be paid. All loading and unloading was to be performed by the contractors' men. Free passes were to be granted to the managing partner and two passes at half fares for their engineers. A reduction was sought in the rate for the carriage of materials, but this was declined.

As late as June 1885 it was still expected that the C&BR would work the new line when it was completed, while in November it was agreed that a platform might be erected at Skibbereen for the narrow-gauge line, this to be removed on a month's notice. Kerr inspected the S&ST line in April 1886, and reported the permanent way to be good with rails well laid and fastened, the bottom ballast was reported to be plentiful and of good quality, whilst the bridges were very substantial. Portions of the fencing of the line were however not good whilst station buildings were not sufficiently far advanced for Kerr to report on them. The line was officially inspected by General Hutchinson on behalf of the BoT in August, his report being dated 2nd September. Hutchinson requested attention to a number of outstanding points. Notwithstanding these outstanding matters, a special train ran from Schull to Skibbereen in connection with the pig market on 7th September, the official opening apparently occurring two days later. It might be mentioned at this point that J W Johnstone was appointed traffic manager and locomotive superintendent in the following December at a salary of £11 per month.

Traffic, however, ceased as from 6th April 1887, there being no locomotive fit to operate the service. In addition there were still defects in curves and gradients. In the following year a new locomotive, *Erin*, was obtained from Messrs Nasmyth Wilson & Co enabling services to resume. The company never prospered financially and a Committee of Management was appointed by the Grand Jury in 1892. In the interim, problems arose in 1889 with the lease and agreement for the use of Skibbereen station, the S&ST people threatening to refer the matter to the Railway Commissioners. This dispute led to the tramway company's receipts being withheld for a time. Complaints were also made against the tramway manager by the stationmaster at Skibbereen. At one point, the tramway company made arrangements for their wagons to be loaded on the public road so as to avoid payment to the Bandon, leading to the C&BR declining all liability for such goods. Eventually, common sense prevailed and the S&ST agreed to pay a rent of £25 per annum for the use of Skibbereen station and yard, along with £25 quarterly for the working of the station.

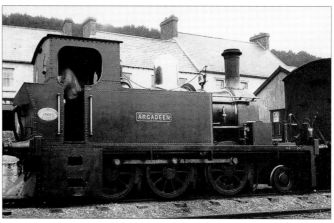

Top left: **0-4-2T** *St. Molaga* **on a goods working at Courtmacsherry. O'Donovan's shop must have been the most photographed such establishment in the village!** Ian Allan Library

Top right: *Argadeen* **at Courtmacsherry.** Ken Nunn collection, LCGB

Above left: **Ex GS&WR 0-6-0T No 90 or 100 on the tramway section of the T&CELR.** W McGrath

Above right: **C232 on an excursion train at Timoleague. On the right is the goods loading area, used in the latter years of the line's existence for the loading of sugar beet for onward transmission to Mallow sugar factory via the CCR. In the background can be seen Timoleague Church of Ireland.**

Right: **In the last years of the tramway, modern motive power in the form of CIÉ's 'C' class diesels were often used. No C217 is seen on an excursion at Courtmacsherry in 1958.**

Bottom right: **Ballinascarthy station, point of junction with the independent T&CELR to Courtmacsherry. Like many stations on the Bandon system, it had only the one platform, on the down side. In this view, taken on 4th November 1960, we are looking south towards the junction of the two companies' lines. The line to Clonakilty swung off to the right to cross over the Owenkeagh River, while the Timoleague line diverged to the left through a level crossing. In the distance is a 17ft diameter turntable, the smallest on the system, adjacent to the 15-lever signal cabin.** John Langford

Left: **Ex MGWR 0-6-0T No 552 and train after arrival at Courtmacsherry.** J L St. Leger

Below left: **A good view of a down excursion train on the tramway section of the T&CELR line between Timoleague and Courtmacsherry on 26th August 1951. The train is double-headed by 2-6-0T** *Argadeen* **and 0-6-0T No 90.** O H Prosser

Below right: **Ex GS&WR 0-6-0T No 100, one of two diminutive tanks used on the T&CELR extension in CIÉ days.** Ian Allan Library

Left: **Timoleague station on 4th November 1960 with ex MGWR 0-6-0T No 552 taking water as she prepares to leave for Ballinascarthy with the 12.00 up beet special No BM25 from Courtmacsherry.** John Langford

Left: **Ballinascarthy station with a Timoleague branch passenger train.** John Langford

Above: **An old CIÉ wooden wagon being loaded by hand with sugar beet at the terminus of the T&CELR line at Courtmacsherry on 4th November 1960. The engine is 0-6-0T No 552 which will take this and other wagons as Special BM25.** John Langford

Above: **2-6-0T *Argadeen* with a mixed train on the roadside section of the T&CELR.** W A Camwell, IRRS

Below: **Timoleague on a fair day. This photograph gives some indication of the volume of livestock handled.** W A Camwell, IRRS

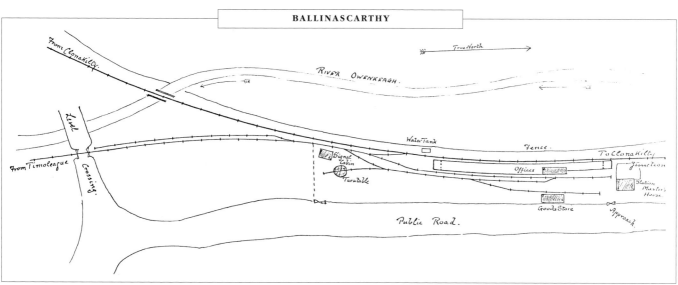

BALLINASCARTHY

Chapter Six

FURTHER EXPANSION, 1889 – 1899

With the change of title, the company now set about completing the final extensions to the CB&SCR system to Bantry Bay and Baltimore, which effectively brought it to its full extent of 93¾ miles. Baltimore had always been an important centre of the fishing industry in the county, rivalling Kinsale, while Bantry was a jumping-off point for travellers to Kerry and the tourist resorts of Kenmare, Glengarriff and Killarney. The completion of the railway to Bantry led to the introduction of a steamer service in Bantry Bay. These extensions were in fact completed by nominally independent companies under the auspices of the Light Railways Act of 1889, to which we shall now turn our attention.

Light Railways Act, 1889 & the Congested Districts Board
In the 1880s, the government recognised that direct assistance was needed to improve economic and social conditions in poverty stricken districts, mostly along the west coast of Ireland. These were the so-called 'congested districts'. The construction of roads, harbours and railways were seen as important elements in the developing these areas. A royal commission, the Allport Commission was set up to investigate Irish public works. out of the recommendations of the commission came the Light Railways (Ireland) Act of 1889, also known as the Balfour Act, after the Chief Secretary for Ireland at the time, Arthur Balfour. This allowed, for the first time, direct state aid in the form of grants and loans from the Treasury, to be given towards the construction of railways in the poorer districts. The Act was to apply only where either the promoters of the light railway were an existing Irish railway company open for traffic or where they had made an agreement, approved by the Treasury, for the working, management and maintenance of such a line, or finally a baronial guarantee was given to the promoters for payment of dividends on a portion of the paid-up capital. State aid might consist of either a free grant or a loan, or a combination of both.

Before proceeding to look at three particular lines proposed under the Act, this might be a good opportunity to refer to another institution formed about this time, namely the Congested Districts Board. Arthur Balfour set up the CDB, which consisted of two land commissioners, five experts appointed by the Government and the Chief Secretary himself as an ex-officio member. The Board's objects, broadly speaking, were four-fold; to promote local industries by subsidies and technical instruction, to amalgamate uneconomic holdings by land purchase, to assist migration from impoverished areas to the newly amalgamated holdings and finally, to improve the quality of agriculture in the congested areas.

At the outset the CDB was rigidly limited in its geographical operation by the decision to define a congested district as one in which the total rateable value divided by the number of inhabitants amounted to less than 30s. per person. In 1891 this definition produced an area of just over 3½ million acres and a population of about half a million spread over parts of the counties of Donegal, Leitrim, Roscommon, Sligo, Mayo, Galway, Kerry and Cork. Gradually the Board extended its area of operations to almost double the acreage involved by 1910. Starting life with a modest income of just over £41,000 (drawn from the Irish Church surplus), the Board attracted to itself all sorts of supplementary revenue until by 1912 its income was over £530,000, though even this was probably too small for it to discharge its manifold responsibilities to its own satisfaction.

The CDB also made for intelligent appli-

Skibbereen station on 7th July 1950 with ex GS&WR 2-4-2T No 33 ready to depart for Cork. R S Carpenter Photographs

cation of existing resources. These were expended in a multitude of different, but generally constructive projects – the encouragement of cottage industries, the building of roads, bridges and harbours, the stimulation of the fishing industry, the provision of expert advice on the raising of crops and livestock, above all, perhaps, land purchase and re-settlement. By 1923, when it handed over its responsibilities to the Irish Free State, it had bought more than two million acres at a cost of over £9 million.

What was most needed was employment and this was found partly through an increase in the road and bridge building programme, but even more through a radical extension of a scheme for light railways first set on foot in 1889. Despite the considerable expense of building these railways in difficult and sparsely populated country, Balfour pressed on with his plans, which resulted in the creation of a dozen different lines and the employment of 16,000 people.

Deep water extension at Kinsale
Petitions were received by the CB&SCR in the autumn of 1889 from the Town Commissioners and inhabitants of Kinsale urging the company to extend their line to the harbour, the Harbour Commissioners also becoming involved in the negotiations. Some difficulties were encountered in relation to the acquisition of land, objections being voiced by those owning or occupying properties with a sea view. The company decided at the end of 1889 to abandon the proposed extension due to there being little chance of obtaining the entire amount of the estimated cost of £33,000 as a free grant. In response to correspondence from the Kinsale Harbour Commissioners in November 1890 the secretary was instructed to inform them that the company would consider the matter further if at least three-quarters of the capital required was provided by the Treasury.

The general manager suggested in February 1896 that consideration be again given to an extension to deep water. In fact, three years later the company announced that powers would be sought for, inter alia, the construction of a ropeway to the pier at Kinsale. The engineer, however, expressed caution as there were at least two major objections to such a line. Firstly it would have to pass right over the Barracks, which would undoubtedly lead to objections from the military authorities, and secondly it would have to cross the harbour and berths at a height of at least 70 feet. It was decided to drop the matter and this was to be the last reference to a connection being made into the town of Kinsale.

Bantry Bay extension
The Bantry extension was promoted by a Bantry born man, William Martin Murphy of

Top: **Baltimore Pier, Ireland's most southerly railhead.** W McGrath

Above: **Creagh looking west towards Baltimore on 21st June 1959. The single platform, 249ft long on the down side included a small station building and accommodation for the stationmaster. There were no goods facilities, signals being controlled by a four-lever ground frame.** Douglas Thompson, 'Stations UK'

Dublin, who was at the time coming to prominence as a railway builder. Murphy wrote to the board in October 1889 strongly urging them to notify the Privy Council of their willingness to pay a proportion of the cost of the extension; a failure to do so might well result in a failure to have the line constructed. The board decided that the time was not right to volunteer this information, although they hinted that Murphy might let it be known, off the record, that they would subscribe one-quarter of the estimated cost.

Two months later an estimate was prepared showing the cost of the 1½ mile extension at £23,000, the company agreeing to contribute one-quarter if the balance was provided by means of a free Treasury grant. It was suggested that a jetty should be included in the estimate and this was accepted. The BoW wrote in March 1890, their estimate for the entire works, including the jetty, being £30,000; they suggested a free grant of £20,000 provided the company subscribed the remaining £10,000. It was decided to appear before the Grand Jury first to see if they would sanction the line; the question of financing the extension was to occupy the parties for the next six months. Eventually, in September 1890, the Treasury refused to budge above £15,000 (the actual amount granted was £14,940) and the directors accepted this with reluctance, the remaining £15,000 to be raised if possible by Debenture Stock.

Tenders were sought in November 1890 for the construction as the BoW were by that time pressing to have the works started. At the beginning of December Murphy offered to carry out the construction of the Bantry

Bay Extension, including the purchase of land, for £30,000. This figure was deemed to be too high and was declined. Three formal written tenders were submitted to the board at their meeting on 17th December, varying from £18,000 from Messrs Collen Bros to £26,000 from Murphy. The two lower estimates did not include land and permanent way and, as these were estimated to cost about £8,500, Murphy's tender was accepted, subject to BoW approval. None of the estimates allowed for the construction of the terminal station. It is clear that the Order in Council had not been signed at this point as Murphy wrote early in January 1891 stating that occupiers were refusing to hand over land, and he was therefore unable to proceed. In this regard, nothing could be done until the Order in Council was signed, thus giving the company compulsory powers of purchase.

Plans and specifications were prepared in August 1891 by the engineer, an amended design for the Bantry station being submitted the following January, to which the general manager objected on the grounds that the roof only came half way across the platform. Nevertheless, this plan was approved and a copy sent to Murphy so that he might tender for the station. His tender, at £3,800, to include the station master's house, was accepted in February 1892. In March Murphy reported that he hoped to have the extension completed by the end of April. This proved to be optimistic and in July he was having difficulties with the excavation work. The same month a connection was installed to enable the contractor to bring in an engine to the extension works. Early September was mentioned as the new completion date. The line was in fact inspected on 29th September by General Hutchinson who authorised its opening. The actual opening to passenger and goods traffic took place on 22nd October 1892, from which date the old (hilltop) station ceased to be used.

The old station and grounds were sold to a Mr R Leslie (the board minutes do not state whether this was the R H Leslie who was shortly to become the company secretary) for £650, an additional small piece of ground being sold at the same time to a Mr William O'Sullivan for £81. In both cases the company reserved their right to take water – this condition was stipulated as the Bantry Union refused to provide a water supply to the new station. In October 1892 Leslie sought and obtained an additional piece of land to the west of the bridge beyond the Workhouse. He also requested about thirty wagon loads of surface clay, 'before the permanent way into the old station was removed'. This was provided at a charge of 12s per laden wagon.

In November 1894 a committee of the board met William Murphy to arrive, if possible, at a settlement with his firm of various matters in dispute in relation to both the Bantry Bay and Baltimore extensions. In the case of the former, the company claimed penalties for delays in completion of the contract totalling £306 18s 10d. Murphy countered that although the company had opened the line on 22nd October 1892, they had retained a figure of £6,564 of the contract money for a further year. On this they had accrued interest and he felt that this more than compensated for any penalties due. The board, in due course, agreed to waive the penalty claim.

Baltimore extension

The third of the Balfour lines was the eight mile extension from Skibbereen to the fishing port of Baltimore. It is interesting to note that a suggestion for such an extension was made by the GS&WR as early as October 1887 in the course of a discussion between the two companies' boards in connection with plans for connecting the two lines across the city of Cork. Once again, William Murphy became involved, writing to the chairman in June 1888 stating that he was paying the preliminary expenses in connec-

tion with the promotion of the scheme and, that if such a line was made it would obviously be of advantage to the CB&SCR to work it, and therefore soliciting their assistance. As regards the Baltimore line a free grant of £56,700 came from the Treasury, the total cost of the line being estimated at about £60,000.

A new company, the Baltimore Extension Railway Company, was incorporated with a nominal capital of £70 made up of seven shareholders each with a £10 share. In June 1889 the engineer was instructed to go over the ground and report on the route he would recommend. Having made a rough survey, Kerr reported that he disapproved of the plans laid out by the Baltimore company's engineer, Mr Barrington, on the grounds of steep gradients and the necessity to reverse all branch trains out of Skibbereen station. Kerr suggested following the River Ilen, thus avoiding the steep gradients. He later went over the proposed route with Barrington and the plans were considerably altered so as to avoid a back shunt at Skibbereen.

A working agreement was signed with the CB&SCR in December 1889 for the operation of the branch by that company, and Barrington agreed to substitute 65lb per yard rails for the 50lb rails initially intended to be laid. A petition was received in February 1890 requesting a flag station at Oldcourt; no decision being taken at that time. In September 1890 it was agreed, however, that the intermediate station on the branch should be, 'about 3¾ miles from Skibbereen on the top of the incline near the road to Lough Hyne and that it be called Lough Hyne station'. In the following January the Rev C Davis again approached the board requesting the provision of a flag station near Oldcourt Bridge instead of at Creagh, as well as a station at Reengrogue Bridge. Both stations were declined in consequence of the steep gradients pertaining. It was realised in February that the plans for the station at Baltimore made no provision for the construction of a pier or jetty there, which according to the general manager, 'would be a serious loss and which he understood up to the present was to have been provided'. It was in fact to be more than 20 years before an extension to the pier was provided.

Murphy approached the board in November 1891 offering £1,000 for alterations to be carried out at Skibbereen, including signalling and a level crossing. It was decided not to accept this offer unless Murphy omitted the two latter items. Mr Barton of the

Drimoleague station with the church in the background. Late Douglas Thompson, 'Stations UK'

Right: **Ex WL&WR 4-4-2T No 274 on a Baltimore branch train near Skibbereen on 1st July 1938.** H C Casserley

Right lower: **Drimoleague Junction, simply referred to on the station nameboards as Drimoleague, on 19th June 1959. The diesel-railcar set on the down platform is most likely headed for Bantry. The up platform was an island and included the main, corrugated-iron, station buildings and a thirty-one lever signal cabin. There was a small engine shed at the Cork end of the station and a 30ft diameter turntable; the former was demolished in the autumn of 1958.** Douglas Thompson, 'Stations UK'

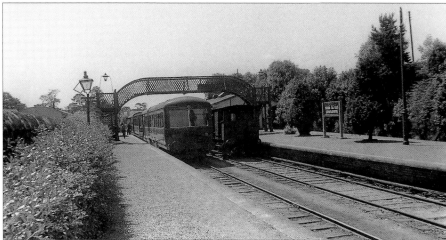

BoW estimated the works here at £900, a figure which was accepted by the company. Rapid progress with the new line was reported in March 1892 and Murphy confidently hoped to have the line finished by 1st June, 'and as soon as this Company have the station yard at Skibbereen ready'. Murphy informed the board on 20th April that trucks could run through to Baltimore and suggested that fish might now be brought up over the line. This was agreed to, subject to the company not incurring any liability until delivered at Skibbereen station.

Estimates were submitted in May for new station buildings at Skibbereen, that of William Jones of Dunmanway at £667 being accepted. When Murphy wrote early in July 1892 to the effect that the new line would be ready to open before the end of the month, his attention was drawn to the large amount of works still uncompleted, some of which had not even been commenced. Difficulties were becoming evident in relation to Street Crossing at Skibbereen and the provision of a footbridge there. Despite this, one month's notice was given to the BoT on 1st July. A Mr George Robinson of Coronea, near Skibbereen, wrote to the BoT complaining, 'very seriously of the manner in which my Demesne and other lands have been injured'. He went on to state that the works generally, at least as far as he was concerned, had been done in an imperfect and unsatisfactory manner. The BoT politely informed him that he should relay his concerns to the arbitrator appointed by the BoW.

Nevertheless, General Hutchinson inspected the extension on 10th August. He confirmed that the line was 7m 44.21c in length, single, and ran from an end-on junction with the IVR at Skibbereen to a terminus near the pier at Baltimore. There was one intermediate station at Creagh, where there were no sidings. The ruling gradient was 1 in 60 and the sharpest curve was of eleven chains radius. The permanent way consisted of flat-bottomed 60lb steel rail in 30ft lengths, fished at the joints, with creosoted

sleepers at 3ft 1in centres; ballast was of broken stone and gravel. There were 14 under-bridges on the extension, the most important being the Ilen River bridge at Skibbereen. This bridge had a single span of 120ft, the main girders being of lattice form.

Specific mention was made of the street crossing at Skibbereen, which Hutchinson referred to as being especially dangerous, and which had been objected to by the BoT when plans were submitted in November 1890. He now required a signal cabin with signals, the gates, without wickets, to be worked from the cabin. The gates themselves were to be covered with strong wire netting and a row of spikes on top to deter trespassers. Finally, he asked for the provision of a footbridge. A number of other requirements were listed. These included the provision of mileposts and gradient boards, additional clearance in some of the cuttings, signals for the protection of level crossings, the fitting of targets and lamp irons to all level crossing gates and the moving of the up distant signal at Creagh so as to be visible from the signal cabin (actually a ground frame of four levers). Pending attention to these matters, approval for the opening of the line was postponed.

Matters dragged on and even the intervention of the BoW did not speed up the

outstanding works, mainly the provision of the footbridge which Murphy declined to construct under his contract. Others walked the line and found dangerous points. Mr J E Barrett wrote to the company in March 1893 drawing attention to nine under-sized culverts, which he believed would be unable to carry off excess water. On John Weir's farm, 'where the line touches the sea', the retaining wall was bulging and threatened to tumble down, while on John Brown's farm a quarter of a mile away, the embankment was being eaten into by the sea.

Meanwhile, the BER wrote to the BoT in January 1893 to the effect that the Order in Council did not require the BER to erect a footbridge over the level crossing at Skibbereen, nor to comply with the BoT requirements, save as related directly to the plans. The BER were therefore of the opinion, having taken legal advice, that it was the working company who were obliged to comply with the requirements. Hutchinson has appended a note to this correspondence stating, 'It is a novel position for a Railway Company to take up that the carrying out of a requirement on their own line is not one devolving upon them, but upon the Company which is to work the railway when completed'.

Questions were raised in the House of

Commons in February, and again in April, asking when the line was to be opened. The BER wrote again in March advising that most of the requirements had been completed, although nothing had been done regarding the footbridge. This work had never been contemplated or provided for; furthermore the company had neither the powers nor the means to erect it. Hutchinson was adamant; the crossing in question should never have been authorised, but having been, it was his duty to safeguard it by every available means, and he was not prepared to incur the responsibility of recommending the BoT to allow the opening of the line without the footbridge, or at very least a satisfactory guarantee that it would be erected without delay.

General Hutchinson returned again on 7th April 1893 and agreed to give the necessary certificate for the opening of the line, the BER having agreed to give the necessary undertaking to erect the footbridge within six months. Despite this the CB&SCR refused to work the line and it was not until 2nd May 1893 that it was finally opened. There appears to have been little interest in

Skibbereen station with an ex GS&WR 2-4-2T on a Baltimore branch train. Behind the train is the single-road engine shed, opposite which is the goods store.
W A Camwell, IRRS

the opening as far as the public were concerned. The *Cork Constitution* commented, 'There was absolutely no interest. When the train crossed Bridge Street, there was nobody to see it, only a few idlers. On arrival at Baltimore it was no better. There were no cheering crowds, no display of bunting, and no signs of rejoicing that the fishing port was now in direct communication with the city'.

Even now there were difficulties with Murphy, who refused to pay for the cost of fitting the electric train staff on the branch. He offered £200 in lieu of certain works for which the company had asked £500 and in July notice was served on Murphy by the County Surveyor to compel him to carry out certain works. When Murphy announced his intention of withdrawing his men from maintaining the line at the end of his six months maintenance contract, Kerr reported that he was not happy with the state of the permanent way and it was decided to call on the BoW to carry out their undertaking and to compel the contractor to put the line in proper order. Attempts were made to have the BoT insist on an iron footbridge at Skibbereen rather than the wooden one proposed by Murphy, but they refused to interfere. This footbridge was to lead to further difficulties later as will be related in due course. Although chronologically out of order at this point it is, however, now appropriate for us to take a look at the extension

to the pier at Baltimore.

Extension to the pier at Baltimore
There is no doubt that the opening of the Baltimore extension proved to be advantageous to the fishing industry based there. It was soon realised, however, that a further extension of the line and the provision of a proper pier would enable Baltimore to achieve its full potential. By January 1894 the railway company had submitted plans for a hulk landing stage estimated to cost between £300 and £500, the actual figure being dependent on the actual size of the hulk provided. The CDB engineer inspected the site proposed in company with the Bandon's own engineer and expressed the view that a larger pier would be required, stating that if the company would undertake the future care and maintenance of the work, they would probably meet the company in a liberal way towards the erection of a pier. Baltimore Harbour Board now entered the arena and suggested that the company should contribute two-thirds of the cost of the pier, the CDB providing the remainder. The company, however, declined to make such a large contribution.

In February, the engineer reported that the boatmen at Baltimore had expressed the view that nothing but a large and long pier would suffice and that they would not bring their vessels alongside a hulk in the bay; a hulk would in fact stand a great chance of being broken up there. Such a pier as envis-

DRIMOLEAGUE

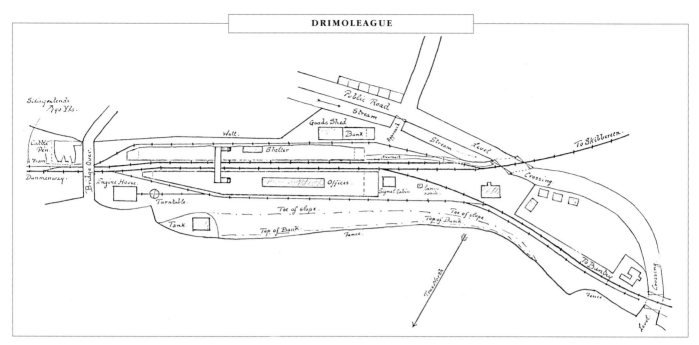

SKIBBEREEN

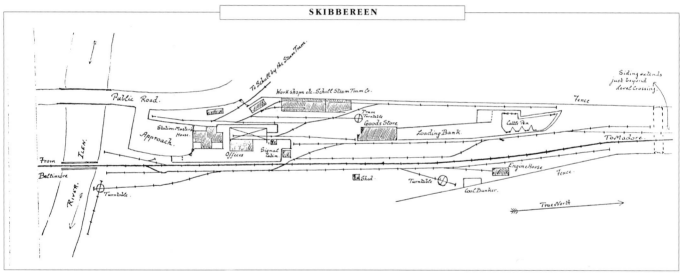

aged would cost in the region of £10,000. As the CDB were unlikely to construct such a pier, plans were submitted for connecting the line with the old existing pier; excluding the purchase of land, this was estimated to cost £1,500 and the company decided to postpone any decision to see what, if any, proposals the CDB might have. The Baltimore Harbour Board meanwhile endeavoured, unsuccessfully, to persuade the company to join with the CDB in constructing a new pier.

The next move was made by the CDB who offered £500 towards a wooden pier, a suggestion immediately turned down by the company. They then offered to contribute one-third towards the cost of a permanent pier if the company and the BoW would contribute the balance. This idea was quickly knocked on the head when the BoW announced that they had no funds available. Nothing further transpired until January

1898 when the CB&SCR announced that the directors did not feel justified, in the current state of the railway labour market, in adding to capital expenditure. With the labour situation improved, the company found another reason not to contribute in March 1900, namely the lack of a rail connection across the city of Cork.

Matters dragged on and it was not until March 1911 that the general manager reported on correspondence with the CDB, which latter body intimated that an application might be made to the Development Commissioners for a grant towards a pier at Baltimore. Various meetings were held over the ensuing months and optimism was expressed that the project might finally achieve success. This led to the company offering to contribute £1,000, also agreeing to lay sidings on the proposed pier and to connect these with their mainline at the station, the latter works at their own expense.

Success finally came in November 1912 when a grant of £7,500 was made by the Development Commissioners, Cork County Council agreeing to contribute a further £1,000.

The general manager reported in July 1918 that the pier had been fully completed in accordance with the drawings. He did comment, however, that it had been shortened somewhat, leaving a rock showing outside the pier head, and thus making the latter unavailable for berthing. The siding and extension works were carried out by the company's own workmen at a cost of £734 9s 1d, two sidings being provided on the pier. There was some correspondence with the CDB in February 1918 regarding the provision of an ice plant on the pier, the company expressing their willingness to construct an ice house at cost plus 10%. The company had previously provided this facility in the mid-1890s by means of the hulks

Chapter Seven

OTHER DEVELOPMENTS TO THE SYSTEM, 1880 – 1899

Prior to considering the final 25 years of the company's independent existence in the first quarter of the 20th century, consideration must be given to some important events which affected the company in the twenty year period ending in 1899. These included the growth of the trade union movement in the railway industry, which led to a potentially damaging strike of staff in 1898. Also, the notion of introducing electric traction to proposed extensions of the system was contemplated.

The engineer reported in April 1880 that the viaduct just outside Bandon station required extensive repairs, and he recommended that the portion of it opposite the station should be filled in, and retaining walls built, at an estimated cost of £200. He also recommended that two engines coupled together should not be allowed to run over it. It was not, however, until July of the following year that Dorman confirmed that he had men engaged in removing the timber sheds in French's yard beneath the viaduct. By this time, the viaduct was reported to be in a very bad state, Dorman advising that he could no longer be responsible for its safety, unless he got immediate instructions to repair it. In the meantime, he recommended a speed restriction of 15mph over it. Instructions were now finally given for repairs to be carried out, and by the beginning of August masonry work had been commenced. This had progressed sufficiently by the end of September to allow of the removal of about 40ft of timber. Work was however held up for a time by a demand for a wage increase.

An errant engineer
Some difficulties surfaced towards the end of 1881 in relation to directors. Captain Perry wrote in November stating that James H Payne, one of the C&BR directors, had accepted money from Thomas Dowling, thus making himself ineligible to remain as a director. In response, the chairman stated that he was fully aware of the situation and saw no objection to it. Perry was not inclined to accept the situation and took Counsel's opinion, the upshot of which was that Payne duly resigned in February 1882, being immediately re-elected.

At a meeting held on 28th April 1882, Messrs William Stewart and John McMahon entered the boardroom and were at once requested to leave, they having apparently been illegally elected directors at a board meeting the previous week. It appeared that Messrs. McBirney and Aitken and Captain-Perry had moved, and had passed, two illegal resolutions at the meeting of 21st April, not having given the requisite 14 days notice, one proposing to rescind a resolution of the board, the other appointing four additional directors, including the two above named. At the meeting of 5th May, the chairman proposed, seconded by Payne, that an extraordinary meeting of shareholders be called to appraise them of what had happened, and also to receive the resignation of Messrs. Aitken, McBirney and Perry. Failing this being forthcoming, they should be removed by resolution of the shareholders in pursuance of sections 82 and 83 of the Companies Clauses Act of 1845.

A meeting not having been convened in the interim, a requisition from 41 shareholders was received in June 1882, calling for the convening of an Extra-ordinary General Meeting to consider the position of the company. Only a week later, a receiver was appointed to the company, at the request of the WCR for non-payment of the purchase money, although a stay had been put on the order for one month; the receiver was none other than James H Payne. The shareholders' meeting was held on 15th July to determine the position of the company, the constitution of the board, a reduction in the number of directors, and the resignation or removal of one or more directors. It was resolved that the meeting be dissolved and a further meeting called for three weeks. McBirney refused to accept the resolution and put forward an amendment simply adjourning the meeting for a fortnight. The amendment was declared lost, being defeated on a vote being taken.

At an EGM held on 11th August, a new board was appointed. Thomas Austen tendered his resignation as chairman, being replaced by William Shaw, MP. It was resolved and approved that the business of the company be removed to Cork, and Albert Quay was to become the location for all future board meetings of the company.

Reporting to the board on 11th November 1881, Conran referred to engine No 3 which had been lying up in the shops since September 1873 awaiting repairs. Conran confirmed that she was no use as a train engine, even on the branch lines. Work had however been proceeding as time permitted

Timoleague station looking towards Ballinascarthy on 4th November 1960. Wagons are being loaded by hand with sugar beet. On the right is the station building with the local Church of Ireland in the background. John Langford

and it would, in course of time, be used for shunting duties. It transpired however that Dorman, the engineer, had independently, and without informing the local committee, informed the board in Dublin of the engine's lengthy sojourn in the shops. Dorman was severely censured for not having advised the committee as they were responsible for day-to-day working of the line.

Dorman was in further difficulties in December when it was announced that he intended to become the engineer for the Clonakilty extension works. More disturbing news regarding the engineer surfaced in May 1882, when it became clear that he had solicited signatures to a requisition of shareholders (referred to above) seeking to remove certain directors. The local committee now called for his resignation, but, strange to relate, they were not backed up in this by the board in Dublin. Subsequently, he wrote promising not to interfere in future in the election of directors. Dorman resigned his position as engineer in August 1884, on his appointment as contractor to the CER, being replaced by John Kerr. He did however remain in a consultative capacity until the end of 1886. Shortly after completing the CER contract, Dorman left for British Guiana to take up a position as engineer, and later general manager, to the Demerara Railways. He returned to Ireland in 1903 and resided at Kinsale until his death in 1911.

A change of officers
Obviously with the pending retirement as secretary of James Connell, George F Townley was appointed assistant secretary in November 1882. Only three months later, Connell did in fact retire and he was replaced by Townley. The latter gentleman was however in trouble with the board in November 1883, when it was reported that he had been advanced a sum of £90 by Mr

Pericho, the audit clerk. The latter gentleman was suspended pending an investigation of the matter by the board. Within twenty-four hours however, it was decided to also suspend Townley, Alexander Gordon being requested to take possession of the company's books and keys, and to act as secretary, pro tem. A special board was summoned for 23rd November, Townley being ordered to attend. Having admitted applying the company's money for his own purposes, he was duly dismissed. J J Mahony was appointed in January 1884 to succeed him, while Pericho was left in charge of the audit office. Mahony's salary was increased to £200 per annum as from 1st January 1886, but he only remained in office until April 1887, when he announced his resignation. Gordon once again stepped into the position until E H Dorman, the brother of the engineer, J W Dorman, was appointed as secretary and accountant a month later.

Thomas Conran, who had held the position of locomotive superintendent since April 1857, died of heart disease on Saturday, 29th January 1887. It was decided to appoint John J Johnstone, the district superintendent at Bantry, to the vacant position at a salary of £250 per annum. It was agreed to continue to pay Conran's salary to his widow until 30th June 1887. In the interim however, an appeal was received from Archdeacon Coghlan asking, 'kind and favourable consideration'; there is no further reference to the matter and we must therefore assume that the payments ceased at the end of June.

Exactly a year after Conran's death, Johnstone also passed away, his son, James, applying for the vacant post. Initially, Maurice Reen, the locomotive foreman at Cork, was placed in charge pending a further consideration of the matter. James Johnstone was appointed on trial in mid-February at a salary of £200 per annum. It was reported

Bandon high-level station on 3rd November 1960. Diesel-electric No C202 on a down beet special has been shunted to allow it to be overtaken by the 12.15 down railcar set. John Langford

that he was so youthful looking when he was appointed, that he was requested to grow a beard to give him more of an air of authority. Johnstone was to remain in charge at Rocksavage until the amalgamation of November 1924. He eventually retired from the service of the GSR on 11th February 1927 when he was 64 years old.

Shareholders' revolt
The chairman, William Shaw, announced his resignation at the board meeting on 9th December 1885. Only a week later, a requisition was handed in to the board, signed by 66 shareholders representing stock to the value of £110,044 calling for an extraordinary general meeting for a number of purposes. These included ascertaining the current position of the company with a view to isolating the cause of the great depreciation in the value of shares, also to ascertain the position of the company in relation to the Clonakilty Extension Railway. There was felt to be a necessity to appoint a competent, independent, engineer to oversee the construction of the Clonakilty line and its stations. before that line was taken over. It seemed advisable to appoint an independent auditor to inspect the company's books. The requisition also called for the appointment of a committee of shareholders to investigate the company's affairs, to accept the resignation of, or to bring about the removal of any or all of the directors, and to appoint new ones in their stead. Having considered the matter, the board agreed to summon such a meeting in Dublin on Tuesday 5th January 1886. It was pointed

out however that the directors considered the holding of such a meeting would be injurious to the interests of the proprietors and the company.

In the interim, the January meeting was postponed, the secretary meeting with Sir Croker Barrington as to the legality of the notice of the meeting. Following this consultation with the solicitor, it was decided to hold the meeting on 17th February. On that day, a deputation of shareholders met with the board and put forward the following points, viz.

(a) the Dublin shareholders considered that they should have a larger representation on the board, and suggested adding John Findlater as a director.
(b) the February half-yearly shareholders meeting should be held in Dublin each year.
(c) the expenses incurred by the Dublin directors when attending board meetings in Cork should be paid by the company, and that the board should only meet once each month.
(d) that an independent engineer be appointed to inspect and pass the Clonakilty line.

The meeting having discussed the various points raised, it was decided that it would not be necessary to appoint another engineer, the deputation expressing their confidence in Mr Goodwin. As regards the other points, the board said they would, as far as they possibly could, meet the views of the shareholders, including the appointment of Mr. Findlater to the board. It was agreed that the August meeting each year would be held in Dublin. Having been later put to the half-yearly meeting, the various proposals were unanimously adopted.

On the mainline, the viaduct at Bandon was in need of extensive repairs in April 1880, and once again it was recommended that portion of it be filled in and retaining walls built. Pending remedial works a prohibition was placed on double heading of engines across the bridge. Some difficulties were encountered in obtaining some additional land from the local landowner, a Mr French. Repairs however commenced in July 1881 and were completed by the end of the year.

Underground repairs

A report was received from the engineer in January 1879 that a slip had occurred in the cutting close to Innoshannon tunnel. It appeared that during the construction of the tunnel, a shaft had been sunk in and later blocked off with timbers which had now rotted. This led to the roof of the tunnel at this point being unsound and it was recommended that about 20ft be arched with Youghal brick. Some 10,000 bricks were used in this repair at a cost of about £150. About the same time, it was reported that a blind shaft had also been discovered about 7ft from the No 3 shaft in Ballinhassig tunnel. It appeared that pieces of timber had been used to close off the bottom of this shaft and that approximately 39ft of rubbish had been dropped in on top. Having examined the tunnel from the top of a horsebox, it was decided that there was no danger of a collapse. Nevertheless, a section of loose rock about 18ft in length was cut away, making the tunnel six yards shorter.

The winter of 1880/1 was a severe one in west Cork. On 21st January 1881 the engineer reported that the frost had been so severe for the past week that most of the water pipes along the line had frozen. In addition, large lumps of ice had formed on the roof of Ballinhassig tunnel. Attempts had been made to knock this ice down with picks and crowbars but these had been unsuccessful. He recommended that the speed of trains through the tunnel be limited to 20mph so as to reduce vibration; in addition loads should be restricted so as to reduce engines slipping. This latter also caused excess vibration which would be liable to bring down ice on carriage roofs after partly thawing due to exhaust steam. The ballast through the tunnel was reported to be covered in a thick layer of ice and a second man was put on as a temporary measure to walk the tunnel. Some of the large icicles taken down were reported to weigh at least 180lb.

It was reported in June 1887 that the tunnels at Ballinhassig and Innoshannon were in need of urgent repairs. This led to a joint inspection by the company's own engineer, J R Kerr accompanied by Albert Gordon, the

GS&WR engineer. Gordon reported that the rock in both tunnels was in a very unsound and precarious condition, with a serious risk of pieces fracturing off without prior notice. He recommended the lining of 956ft of Ballinhassig tunnel and 170ft of that at Innoshannon. Consideration was now given to a deviation of the line at Ballinhassig so as to avoid the large expense of lining the tunnel, estimated at £11,851. In the event, a deviation would in fact have cost as much. Pending a decision on this matter, Kerr was instructed to protect both tunnels with timber sheeting. Powers were in fact taken in the company's Act of 1888 for a deviation 1m 4f 1c in length, which would have passed to the south of the hill through which the tunnel was bored. The deviation, which would have included a new station at Ballinhassig, would have involved curves of 15c radius.

An order was placed at the end of June 1887 with Messrs Drury & Sons of Youghal for 250,000 Youghal bricks for Innoshannon tunnel at a cost of 30s 6d per thousand. As reported later in our narrative, Creedon stated that a brickworks existed at Ballinphellic, about 3¼ miles southeast of Ballinhassig since 1880. If this was the case, it is surprising that the company went as far as Youghal to obtain bricks. On the other hand, the Cork Brick Manufacturing Co Ltd was only formed in 1897 and it may be that only limited production was undertaken at Ballinphellic prior to this.

It was to be November 1888 before the board minutes refer to a report being received from a Mr Mills, quite possibly the GNR(I) engineer, recommending that the entire unlined portion of 601 yards of the Ballinhassig tunnel be lined. Having considered this report, Kerr now recommended that the worst affected 350 yards be done at a cost of £7,500, this suggestion being accepted by the board. To enable the work to be carried out, sidings and stores were provided at both ends of the tunnel and Ballinhassig was made a staff station for the duration of the works. Two sets of narrow-gauge rails were laid in the tunnel for the carriage of materials, some small trollies also being obtained. At the northern end of the tunnel it was found necessary to obtain about an acre of ground.

Work commenced in February 1889, timber required for framework being recovered from Milleenarrig bridge, then in

Although of very poor quality, this is the only known photograph of Bandon West station. It was used by the WCR between 1874 and 1880. The level crossing referred to in the text can be seen to the right of the locomotive; it was later replaced by a 'tunnel bridge'. W McGrath collection

0-4-0ST No 495 at Hibernian Road bridge, Cork. This locomotive was purchased new in 1920 from Messrs Peckett for use on Allman's Distillery Tramway at Bandon. Following closure of the distillery, the engine came into the possession of the GSR who numbered her 495. The Peckett remained in service until 1949.
Photographer unknown, Seán Kennedy collection

course of being re-timbered. About this time, Peter O'Neill, a farmer at the southern end of the tunnel, threatened legal proceedings for pollution of water on his land and for trespass through his fields. This matter was in due course resolved, but only after O'Neill had caused serious interference and obstruction. Work on the tunnel was finally completed in September 1889 with the sidings and stores being removed in the following month. This was not however to be the end of the matter, as an approach was made in July 1890 by the local Parish Priest requesting a crossing over the line at the northern end of the tunnel. This request was declined but the Rev. Eugene McSwiney took the matter up with the BoT. They in due course wrote to the company suggesting that a footbridge be provided, the company declining on the grounds that they did not recognise any right of way. Following protracted correspondence, the company sought a contribution from the Presentment Sessions, and a footbridge was finally erected in February 1899 at a total cost of about £100.

In recounting the repairs to Ballinhassig tunnel reference has already been made to the use of timber removed from Milleenarrig bridge near Dunmanway, which had some repairs carried out in 1889. A new bridge was completed here in 1896, which brought problems of a different nature. It was reported in December 1895 that the first cylinder being driven had hit solid rock at only 19ft below rail level.

Bandon level crossing

The watchman at the Chapel crossing at Bandon, adjacent to the old Bandon West station, requested the board in February 1890 to carry out repairs to his house. Kerr however suggested that as a new house would cost £125, consideration should be given to closing the crossing. The parish priest saw no objections, provided an ornamental wall was erected. However, Messrs Allman, who owned the adjoining land, refused to grant it to the company. About this time, Messrs Allman were anxious to make some alterations near the distillery on the far side of town, and it was suggested to them that they should negotiate an agreement with the company. Whilst the two were obviously not linked, they subsequently agreed to hand over to the company a millpond and chimney shaft at Cloughmacsimon (Bandon West).

The BoT were duly approached for permission to close the level crossing and to substitute a bridge, General Hutchinson carrying out an enquiry in November 1893. He agreed that the existing level crossing was, 'no doubt of a dangerous character, being approached on one side through a tunnel bridge, which prevents a train being seen till being close at hand'. Approval was given, subject to a number of minor requirements. One was that the crossing be retained as a private crossing for Bellevue House, apparently occupied as a convent. Work on the new road was commenced in January 1895 and was completed in the following July.

Yet another station at Bandon

The practice of reversing through WCR trains over the half mile of line between West Cork Junction and the C&BR's low-level station was inconvenient, not to say dangerous, and plans were therefore drawn up in 1893 for the provision of a new station at Bandon, to be located close to the original WCR station of 1866. The new works were completed in February 1894 and were inspected by General Hutchinson towards the end of that month. He described the new layout as consisting of a long loop with an island platform, which included commodious offices and waiting rooms. Access to the platform was by means of a ramp and subway at its western end from the entrance of the low-level station, and from a road to the south. A new raised signal cabin of twenty-one levers, three of which were spare, was brought into use to control both stations.

The old West Cork Junction was now removed. Subject to some minor matters involving the interlocking of point and signal levers, and the provision of fencing for the pathway between the two stations, the works were passed by Hutchinson. For the future, the original C&BR station was used for all goods traffic, access to it being by means of a trailing connection off the up (loop) line just beyond the Cork end of the island platform. The new station was brought into use on 1st March 1894.

Crossbarry siding

A deputation from the Cork Corporation waited on the board in March 1883 on the subject of putting in a siding near Kinsale Junction for stone traffic in connection with the supply of stone for the city streets. The company declined to undertake the work as the Corporation declined to contribute to the cost of such a siding. A further deputation waited on the board on 25th April, advising that the stone contractor, a Mr O'Brien, had offered to construct a siding at the south side of the station. The company again declined on the grounds of the cost of signalling, but agreed to inspect the place and see whether arrangements could be made to allow O'Brien to load materials on the loop siding. Following an inspection, it was agreed to provide this latter facility.

The traffic manager suggested in December 1889 that the stone loading siding at Kinsale Junction should be extended to accommodate eight wagons, thus doubling its capacity. Kerr subsequently advised that this would cost £110 if carried out on the company's ground, but if extended at the other end, it would cost in the region of £50. Kerr was duly instructed to try and purchase thirty perches of land for the purpose. This he failed to do and it was decided to check whether the stone contractor, Barrett, would in fact obtain the Corporation contract for stone, before proceeding any further. Reporting in July 1890, Kerr estimated the cost of the siding for O'Brien (presumably the same gentleman referred to in 1883) at the junction at £130, work again being postponed. A minute of 10th September again refers to O'Brien, the stone contractor, apparently being obstructed by the company's servants while discharging stone into the Corporation yard at Cork.

It was agreed, provided that O'Brien gave security that if he lost the Corporation contract within 12 months, he would pay the company £30, or £15 if lost within two years, the siding would be laid in at Crossbarry. Orders were given in October for the siding to be laid. However, William Dunlea, a solicitor of Cork, wrote to the BoT in December, advising that the proposed siding would be a source of danger to the travelling public. He also referred to the fact that the BoT had previously declined to sanction a similar siding unless protected by a distant signal.

The company advised the BoT that the proposed siding would be outside Kinsale Junction station limits and would be secured by an Annett's key – it was in fact situated 2¼ miles from the junction close to Upton station. The siding was in due course laid in and was inspected by General Hutchinson in February 1891, and was passed, subject to the facing points being provided with a bolt to ensure their being locked close to the stock rail. A similar condition was applied to a new facing connection to a ballast pit at Desert.

Two into one
Dating from the opening of the WCR two separate stations had existed at Ballineen (referred to in some timetables as Ballyneen) and Enniskeane, serving their respective villages, although only about ¾ mile apart. In January 1880 the manager recommended that a siding be put in at Enniskeane to enable goods traffic to be handled there as he regarded it as a competitive point for Crookstown on the neighbouring Macroom line. Johnstone advised the board on 20th February that the siding was complete and ready for traffic. In November 1888 a Mr R A Orpen of Enniskeane complained that portions of trains did not come up to the platform there and the board agreed to lengthen it by 100ft at a cost of £32.

Only 12 months later however, in December 1889, the agent for the Duke of Devonshire wrote enclosing an extract from an agreement in relation to Enniskeane, which stated, inter alia, that, 'the Company bind themselves… to build, make and provide a station house… at the village of Enniskeane for the purpose of enabling the trains on the said Railway to stop there on all occasions'. The secretary was instructed to write to Hodson and inform him that the board proposed to abandon the two stations and to build a new one between them, he being requested to put the matter before the Duke for his sanction. In reply, Hodson enquired why a site had not been chosen midway between the two stations, the com-

pany informing him that the site chosen was the most suitable from the point of view of gradients and the nature of the ground.

Petitions were presented from the inhabitants of Enniskeane in January 1890 against the proposed removal of the station, and again asking if the new one could be placed at the midway point. Hodson suggested that if the road leading to the new station could be sited closer to Enniskeane, then some accommodation might be reached. By April, all opposition had been withdrawn and moves were made to obtain the necessary land. This in turn led to difficulties and delays. Meanwhile in August 1890 it was decided to name the new joint station 'Ballineen & Enniskeane'. It was also decided to incorporate accommodation for the stationmaster into the office at a total cost of £550. The tender of the Railway Signal Co was accepted at £380 for the necessary signalling.

The new station was ready for use by 15th May 1891 and it was duly opened to the public on 23rd June, having been inspected and passed by General Hutchinson for the BoT. In the interim it had been found necessary to erect a gatehouse at the level crossing at the old Enniskeane station, while the old Ballineen station building was rented in August 1893 to a Mr R Lombard. In March 1894 the manager recommended the provision of a second platform at the new station so that it could be used as a crossing station, instructions being given for this to be done forthwith. It might be mentioned here that it was not until the passing of the CB&SCR Act of 1900 that legal approval was obtained for the closure of the two original stations.

It was reported in August 1894 that an agreement had been concluded with a Mr Patrick Fitzgerald for the letting to the company of a small parcel of land at Ballineen at a rent of £8 10s 0d per annum for an entrance to a ballast pit. In March 1896 Johnstone reported that the timber-built engine shed at Ballineen (the station was by now being simply called Ballineen) had been burnt down, as far as he could see, through the carelessness of a cleaner, the ballast engine being slightly damaged. It was to be almost five years before the shed was replaced. Attempts were made in 1897 to purchase additional land so as to extend the ballast pit as the existing pit was expected to be exhausted within twelve months. It took a considerable time for the legal matters associated with this purchase to be settled, and as the little ballast that remained had to be retained for emergencies, the engineer found it necessary to lay off the ballast gang in March 1899. The last item of note regarding Ballineen was in July 1901 when the engineer reported that the whole of the signalling there had been overhauled, this having been the first major signalling work

undertaken on the line under the provisions of the 1889 Act.

Desert bridge received attention in 1888. In June 1895 the engineer reported that a settling of the land spans had been noticeable for some time, although the reasons for this were unclear. The most likely explanation was that the old short piles were gradually sinking through gravel to the peat below. Reporting to the board in February 1896, Kerr said that a new bridge, by now a matter of some urgency, would need to be placed to one or other side of the existing bridge. If placed to the south, it would be necessary to provide a new intake and sluice for the nearby Desert Mill, although land required would be cheaper than on the north side. In the event, it was decided in July to put the new structure on the site of the old one. Tenders were submitted in April 1897, that of Messrs Arroll Bros of Glasgow being accepted. Work was seriously affected by flooding in the river and it was not until August 1899 that Kerr was able to report that trains had begun using the new bridge.

A serious trade dispute
During the second half of the 1890s workers began to express anger and frustration at what they saw as low pay and poor working conditions. This led to the formation of the Associated Society of Railway Servants which put forward proposals for reduced working hours and a minimum wage scale. This was not to the liking of autocratic boards of directors who were more concerned at looking after the interests of shareholders than those of their employees. The board of the CB&SCR was certainly no different in this regard. In May 1897 they reluctantly gave three days leave of absence for two of the men to attend a meeting of the Society in Dublin, but only after consultation with the GS&WR who had allowed some of their workers to attend. The chairmen and managers of the principal Irish railway companies held a meeting in Dublin at the beginning of November 1897 to consider the demands of the ASRS. At this meeting it was agreed that none of the companies represented would recognise the Union, they would not negotiate, even with the men themselves, in relation to hours of work, which they contended was a matter for the BoT. Nor would they submit any claim to arbitration.

On the same day as this meeting took place, 3rd November, an application was read from one Michael Buckley, a signalman in Cork Cabin, requesting the directors to receive a deputation of the company's men so that they might explain the National Programme as laid down by the ASRS. The directors agreed to meet Buckley on his own but he insisted on a deputation consisting of all grades; this latter was declined.

Timetable of the service on the Cork & Bandon Railway, April 1887; although Killarney is mentioned in it, the Tourist Car service did not operate outside the summer period.

An extract from the Company's timetable of April 1887.

In due course a total of eleven groups attended the board on 29th November, each group or grade being seen individually. Attempts to have the secretary of the ASRS attend or to have observers present were strenuously opposed.

Matters came to a head on the morning of 7th January 1898 when the Cork station-master reported that on examining the Train Record Book in Cork Cabin he noted that no record had been entered of a special engine departure for Clonakilty Junction at 07.00. The signalman in charge at the time was none other than Michael Buckley. When the stationmaster checked the register again at 11.25 he discovered that an entry had been made in the interim. Buckley was duly summoned before the board and freely admitted his omission and he pointed out that he had returned immediately he realised his mistake and put the register right. The general manager was duly instructed to remove Buckley to another station, Ballinascarthy Junction. This had an immediate and dramatic result. Notice was

given that unless Michael Buckley was rein-stated to his position in Cork by mid-day on 24th January, the men would walk out with-out giving the usual week's notice.

It would appear that Buckley was regard-ed by the company as an agitator and in their defence the directors claimed that he had been reprimanded and cautioned on a num-ber of occasions as far back as 1894. The only concession they would make was that if he took up duty at Ballinascarthy Junction, and then made an application for re-consid-eration of his case, they would accede to his request. The men however struck work and the board took steps to institute legal pro-ceedings against them and to employ men to replace them. These replacements were to be provided with food and lodgings on the company's premises. Instructions were also issued for the removal of gatekeepers and their families, by legal means if found necessary, where they had walked out. In fact, one gatekeeper who had refused to work, resulting in a train striking the gates, had legal proceedings taken against him.

An approach by the secretary of the ASRS brought a refusal to meet him, a subsequent letter demanding Buckley's reinstatement receiving a similar response. Towards the

end of January however the directors did advise that if the men returned to work unconditionally and Buckley took up duty at Ballinascarthy, all pending prosecutions would be abandoned. A request from the Cork United Trades Association, asking the directors to meet with the secretary of the ASRS, was declined but they did agree to meet a deputation of the men. The Presi-dent of the Cork Chamber of Commerce also intervened with a suggestion that Buck-ley be suspended rather than moved; this request was also declined as was one from the Lord Mayor, Alderman Roche, for arbi-tration of the dispute.

The directors determined not to alter their position and in fact offered those hands who had remained loyal double pay for the duration of the dispute, while clerks who acted as guards or stationmasters were allowed a bonus of 10s per week. Mean-while the Paint Shop in Cork was fitted up as living quarters for men hired from the Free Labour Association in London. Both the GWR and the City of Cork Steamship Co afforded the company facilities by way of free passes to men travelling from London to take up employment, while letters of sup-port were received from other English railways. Attempts were made in February to derail trains when it was reported that stones had been placed on the line at the 6¼MP, while in March a rail was loosened about 3¾ miles from Cork, derailment of the 06.00 down train being narrowly avoided. A reward of £300 was offered for any evidence leading to conviction of those responsible. Another serious incident occurred when three soldiers who had arrived in civilian clothes aboard the SS *Innisfallen* were savagely beaten up, being mistaken for 'blacklegs'. These and other incidents led to terms of imprisonment and hard labour up to 15 months being handed down to some of the railway staff.

Kerr reported in March that men obtained from England for the Permanent Way Department had proved, 'nearly useless', and he proposed to let up to 15 of them go. It was decided however to retain them for the present and Kerr was instructed only to dismiss those who either misbehaved or were insubordinate. Yet another approach was made to the board in April 1898, this time by the Roman Catholic Bishop of Cork, who suggested that the new men taken on during the dispute might be bought out, thus allowing the strikers to return to work. The directors expressed their unwillingness to even consider such an idea, but did advise that there were vacancies in both the traffic and permanent way departments. Finally, following a meeting between management and a deputation of the men held early in May, the matter was resolved, a good number of the old hands returning to work, but only to fill vacancies. The directors were asked if they would re-employ those men who had been committed to prison, their response being that the time of their release was so far distant that no promise or guarantee could be given.

It is hardly surprising that there was initially a good deal of ill feeling against the new men who had been taken on and the late strikers. There is no mention in the minutes of the fate of Michael Buckley, but it seems likely that he did not resume employment with the company. In due course the company received a payment of £2,000 towards the cost of the dispute from the Railway Companies' Association. Patrolling of the line by the Royal Irish Constabulary was stopped in May, normal train services resuming on 1st July. So came to an end a bitter and acrimonious dispute which caused great disruption and loss to the company.

Electric railways to Kenmare & Kilmacsimon

The closing years of the nineteenth century saw various schemes being put forward for the electrification of railways. West Cork was not left out of this, proposals being introduced for an electric tramway from Bandon to Kilmacsimon Quay and for an extension of the Bandon system from Bantry to Glengarriff by a tramway or light railway to be worked by steam or electricity. Croker and Kerr visited Kilmacsimon Quay early in December 1899 and found there four vessels discharging cargo for Messrs Allman, one of grain and three of coal, representing a loss to the company of about 700 tons. This was in direct violation of Messrs Allman's commitment to give all their business to the railway in return for considerably reduced rates. Croker stated that it was the intention of the tramway company to carry passengers between Innoshannon and Bandon at 1d per head. He feared that the railway company were likely to lose a large share of the coal, oil and liquor trade if the tramway was constructed. Subsequently it was reported that the supporters planned to extend the electric tramway from Bandon northwards to Crookstown on the C&MDR system. Luckily for the Bandon, nothing further was heard of the scheme. A much earlier tramway scheme of November 1860 had planned a route from Bandon to Collier's Quay. Both lines were planned to connect the town of Bandon with deep water on the Bandon River.

In the case of the second scheme, the Glengarriff route was put forward to counter plans to connect that town with Kenmare on the GS&WR system. The general manager and engineer having surveyed for light railways to Kenmare and Castletown Berehaven, Croker was of opinion that the line would never pay if the company had to provide the necessary capital. He suggested instead that Government assistance should be sought. The BoW in due course declined to advance money on the grounds that the line would not pass through a congested district within the meaning laid down for such assistance.

In May 1900 Croker reported that a London American syndicate intended to make Long Island a port of call and introduce a transatlantic service to Ireland. In addition, the syndicate planned to extend the railway from Bantry to Castletown Berehaven as an alternative to the GS&WR scheme. The company offered their moral support but no financial assistance. In the following December, notice was published by the promoters of the above scheme under the title of the Irish Electric Railways Co. Their proposal now was to construct and equip an electric railway from Bantry to Kenmare via Castletown. The line was to commence out of the Headford branch of the GS&WR some 350 yards from the northeast corner of the station building at that point and to terminate by a junction with the CB&SCR opposite the northwest corner of the station building at Bantry.

In giving their moral support to the scheme, the CB&SCR made it clear that they expected the entire scheme to be carried out and not just the section between Castletown and Kenmare. Sanction was given by Cork County Council at a meeting held on 8th January 1901, subject to the entire scheme being carried out. However, as we know, none of the works were even commenced.

Amalgamation proposals

Various amalgamation schemes were considered around the close of the 19th century. In December 1893 a John McCarthy enclosed a requisition from a body of shareholders for an amalgamation of the Bandon system with the neighbouring C&MDR and CB&PR companies. The latter at this time still operating on the 5ft 3in gauge. However when the board of that company suggested the formation of a committee to consider the matter further, the CB&SCR replied that they considered amalgamation impracticable. In March 1895 the C&MDR again raised the issue of amalgamation of the two companies. The response was positive in so far as enquiries were made as to the compensation which that company would pay to their entire staff in Cork. Having said this, the Bandon directors made it clear that they were not implying that all of the Macroom staff would be let go.

Reports were submitted to the board in June on the condition of the Macroom permanent way and rolling stock. These reports suggested that an expenditure of about £28,000 would be necessary to put the system into thorough order and to form a new junction between the two lines. This figure did not take into account a major upgrade in facilities at Albert Quay, which would soon be necessary for the handling of the company's own traffic. A special board meeting was held at Albert Quay on 15th July, attended by representatives of the C&MDR board, some discussion taking place regarding the likely price to be paid for their concern. Correspondence passed back and forth, but the Macroom board advised in February of the following year that the Bandon company's offer was, 'totally inadequate and there was, therefore, no point in carrying on the negotiations'.

Despite this, a fresh approach was made in April 1899, an improved offer being declined although a counter-proposal came from the Capwell boardroom. This in turn was declined, an amended offer by the CB&SCR being again considered to be insufficient. Another four years passed by until the subject was raised yet again in May 1904. This time the matter rumbled on until July 1906 when the Bandon called a halt to the negotiations. In a submission made to the Vice Regal Commission on Railways in February 1908, the company expressed their willingness to consider the amalgamation with or purchase of the lines south of the River Lee.

Chapter Eight

CORK CONNECTIONS

The city of Cork is low lying with hills to the north and west. The former had to be penetrated by Glanmire tunnel to allow the GS&WR system access to the city while the Bandon approached the city on a long falling gradient terminating in a deep rock cutting on the approach to the terminus. The city is also unusual in that the River Lee divides in two just to the west, becoming one again to the east, thus forming an island in the city centre. These two geographical features, particularly the river, in a large measure inhibited the linking-up of the various railway lines serving Cork.

On the north side the GS&WR originally had their station beside the river at Penrose Quay, before re-locating to a new station in 1893 at Glanmire Road immediately to the south of the tunnel. Adjoining Glanmire Road, on the north side and at a higher level, was the Summerhill station of the Cork & Youghal Railway, in use from 1861 until 1893. In the latter year trains to and from Youghal and Queenstown (now Cobh – pronounced Cove) began using the GS&WR terminus. To the west, the narrow gauge Cork & Muskerry Light Railway had their terminus on Western Road, while on the south side there were three railways.

The C&BR was by far the largest of the three southside concerns with a terminus at Albert Quay, close to the South Channel of the river. A little to the east, adjoining Victoria Quay, was the Victoria Road station of the Cork Blackrock & Passage Railway. On 6th February 1873 the company opened a deviation to a new terminus at Albert Street almost next door to the Bandon station. In August 1896 an Act was obtained empowering the CB&PR to extend their line to Crosshaven. The decision was taken to construct the new line to the 3ft gauge and to convert the existing line. The extension does not concern us here but the line from Albert Street to Passage was converted over the weekend of 28th and 29th October 1900.

Reference has already been made to the C&MDR. Between 1866 and 1879 this company made a connection with the Bandon system at Ballyphehane and used the latter company's terminus at Albert Quay. For reasons already discussed, the connection was removed in 1879, in which year the C&MDR opened their own terminus to the southwest at Capwell. Apart from a short period between 1918 and 1921 there was no physical connection between the two lines until after the 1925 amalgamation.

Cork tramway systems.
The tramways of Cork can be divided into two distinct periods, a shortlived horse-operated system between 1872 and 1875, and the electric tramway system, which ran from 1898 right up to 1931. As originally envisaged in 1860 by its promoters, George Francis Train and Henry Hugh Roche, the horse tramway was to connect the various railway termini, both to facilitate transfer of passengers from one railway to another, and to foster travel within the city itself. It was however to be Thursday 12th September 1872 before the line was eventually opened, running from Victoria Road, along Albert Quay and over Anglesea Bridge, then along South Mall, Grand Parade, Patrick Street and via St. Patrick's Bridge, Bridge Street, King Street (now MacCurtain Street) to a terminus at Alfred Street, beside the

original GS&WR terminus. Various extensions were proposed, which might have had the effect of prolonging the operation of the tramway.

The line was laid to the standard 5ft 3in gauge and was just under two miles in length. Included in the original plans was a siding into the C&BR terminus and it was anticipated that wagons would be hauled across the streets to the GS&WR station. As far as is known, the siding was never laid in to the Bandon yard and in any event, the tramway's working life was short and it was reported to be in a derelict condition by early 1875. This was probably due in part to the circuitous nature of the line's route, necessitated by the layout of the city, as well as the fact that it did not extend into the suburbs. The final nail in the coffin came on 22nd October 1875 when the decision was taken at a Cork Corporation meeting to pull up and dispose of the rails. Trams ran every twenty minutes from the Passage and Bandon stations between 08.40 and 19.40 daily to the GS&WR and Summerhill stations. On Sundays, the service did not commence until 13.00, but it continued until 22.25. It is worthy of mention that our old friend, H Williams Wood of the C&KJR, played a large part in promoting the notion of a tramway system for Cork. It was Wood who stressed the advantages of running wagons along city streets between the various termini.

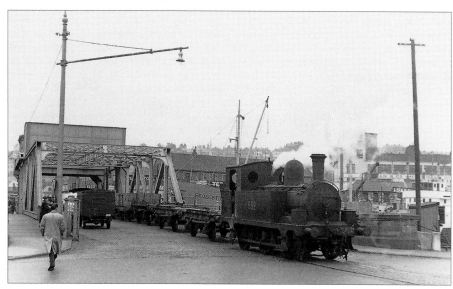

0-6-0T No 552 with a cross-city goods train approaching Albert Quay on 25th March 1961. J N Faulkner

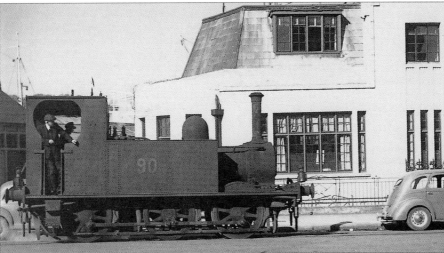

Left: **Ex CB&SCR 4-6-0T No 466 on a light-engine movement between Glanmire Road and Albert Quay on 4th June 1958.**

Left lower: **No 90 working the Cork Milling Company traffic on Victoria Quay c1950.**
Both photographs W McGrath

seeking approval to a proposed bridge across the river. The Bandon were however already experiencing difficulties with the latter body in relation to the proposed closure of the Gas Works level crossing and its replacement by a footbridge. This dispute had got to the point where the company had threatened to remove their works from Cork altogether and had gone as far as instructing the locomotive superintendent not to proceed with the erection of additional machinery until a final decision was reached. Pending a resolution of this matter, the board felt it would be inexpedient to become involved in the proposed cross-city link-up, and it was not until February 1889 that the Bandon agreed to join in an application, declining however to contribute financially.

The Royal Commission on Irish Public Works (Allport) reporting in 1888, made reference to the shortcomings of not having a cross-city connection, particularly in relation to fish and other perishable traffic. Owing to this break, the cost of carriage from the west of the county and the delays in transhipment were detrimental to the advancement in traffic. Reference was made to the above-mentioned discussions between the Bandon and the GS&WR. In 1888 another line was planned, connecting with the Bandon at Waterfall and running northwards to Carrigrohane, from which point a third rail was to be added to the Cork & Muskerry Light Railway as far as Blarney. From here the new line would climb parallel to the GS&WR mainline, joining it at Waterloo. There was also another scheme which would deviate from the CB&SCR at Chetwynd Viaduct, cross the city at high level and then tunnel under Patrick's Hill to connect with the GS&WR at Blackpool. Yet another idea was for an extension of the Bandon and Passage lines eastwards by means of a tunnel beneath the River Lee to join up with the GS&WR Cobh branch.

A rather more ambitious scheme was announced with the passing of the Cork & Fermoy and Waterford & Wexford Railway Act in August 1890. This scheme was to form part of a new route to London, taking over the powers of the Waterford & Wexford Railway, details of which are mentioned below. A central terminus was proposed at Marina Walk on the site of the pre-1873 CB&PR station, from which point a line would run initially south-westwards as far as Evergreen Road, then westwards to the Bandon Road from whence it would curve around the city

It was 23 years after the closure of the horse-operated tramway that the Cork electric tramways began operating under the title of the Cork Electric Tramways & Lighting Co. Ltd. This company had close connections with the electrical contractors, Messrs British Thomson-Houston. William Martin Murphy, who had constructed, inter alia, the Bantry extension of the CB&SCR, was appointed contractor for the permanent way, the entire introduction of the system being supervised by Charles H Merz. Merz, as one of the partners of the firm of Messrs Merz & McClellan Ltd, was later to become involved in the Drumm battery train experiments on the GSR and CIÉ. Merz in fact met McClellan whilst supervising the construction of the Cork tramways

This rather more extensive system opened for business on 22nd December 1898 and had routes extending out of the city to Blackrock, Douglas, Sunday's Well, Blackpool and Tivoli. The total length of the system was just under ten miles. The city 'terminus' was at Father Mathew Square at the northern end of Patrick Street, otherwise known as 'The Statue'. Father Mathew, a Capuchin Priest, was a tireless worker for temperance in the 19th century, the statue in his honour being erected in 1864. The tramway depot and power house were situated at Albert Road, separated only by a wall from the CB&PR Albert Street terminus, and but 200 yards from the CB&SCR terminus. The system finally closed on 30th September 1931. Whilst it ran past the various railway termini, there was no possibility of wagon transfers as the tramway was laid to a gauge of 2ft 11½in.

Early connecting schemes
The situation therefore around 1900 was that, apart from the GS&WR, there were two narrow-gauge and two standard gauge lines, the latter two not on speaking terms. The only meaningful connection would therefore be to bridge the gap between the CB&SCR and the GS&WR. The first recorded proposal for the linking of the railways north and south of the river was in 1861. A line was proposed to run from Penrose Quay to Victoria Road with an opening river bridge, but nothing came of the proposals.

Discussions took place between representatives from the C&BR and the GS&WR in October 1887 to consider several schemes for connecting the two lines, the possibility of a connection with the CB&PR also being discussed about this time. The GS&WR enquired in January of the following year whether the Bandon would join them in an application to Cork Corporation and turn eastwards just to the north of the northern entrance to the GS&WR Glanmire tunnel. From here it would pass via Gouldings Glen to Fermoy. The direct connection with Fermoy would obviate the necessity for through traffic to and from Rosslare having to go by the circuitous route via Mallow. A short spur at Farrancleary would run northwards to connect with the GS&WR, connections also being envisaged with the CB&PR, CB&SCR and the C&MDR. This ambitious scheme like all its predecessors failed to go any further.

In January 1902, Mr Price, the Cork Harbour Board engineer, called on the general manager in connection with the proposed bridging of the River Lee, and also requested details of the amount of interchange traffic between the company and the GS&WR. This latter information was refused. Kerr, who also attended the meeting, mentioned that there was a difference in the loading gauges of the two companies' lines, pointing out that a number of the Bandon company's bridges were too low for GS&WR wagons; these restrictions did not apply to passenger stock.

Messrs Barrington & Son wrote to the company in November 1904 drawing their attention to a Parliamentary notice for a Bill seeking powers for a connecting railway. This was the Cork Junction Railways, which proposed two connections with the Bandon, one of which was to form a new link with the C&MDR. It was decided to lodge a waiting petition and to await developments. It was agreed in January 1905 to approve of the CJR Bill in principle, but not to contribute in any way towards the cost of it. The CJR Bill was in fact thrown out in July 1905. One of the reasons cited by the promoters was, 'the refusal of the CB&SCR to put 6d into the venture'. In the interim, the CB&SCR were in communication with the Cork Harbour Commissioners seeking to have a connection from Albert Quay to the deep-water quays.

Our good friend, J W Dorman, made contact with the board towards the end of February 1905 enclosing a plan for an alternative connecting railway and for a line along the south quays. He suggested that the various companies concerned should each contribute £1,000 per annum as interest on part of the necessary capital. Dorman listed what he saw as the advantages to the Bandon, including the closing of the Gas Works level crossing and its substitution by a bridge. He pointed out that the cross-river

bridges would be both symmetrical and pleasing to the eye. Whilst they were intended as swing bridges, the design could be altered to replace them by the bascule type, if required by the harbour commissioners. The directors however decided not to give their support to this scheme, in view of their attitude to the CJR scheme.

Dorman wrote again in July 1905 with an amended plan and seeking a subscription of £30,000 from the company. He pointed out that the company would at some future stage have to expend more than this sum on necessary alterations and improvements at Albert Quay. Double-deck bridges were now proposed, with the railway crossing the river about 20ft above quay level, while Albert Quay itself would be widened by 50ft to accommodate several sidings. This line was to commence at Albert Quay goods yard, and would have passed over Anderson Street, Ship Street and Alfred Street on piers, before descending into the GS&WR yard at Glanmire Road. It was estimated to cost £270,000. Dorman was informed that the board were prepared to consider approving the plan on the understanding that they would be at liberty to approve any future scheme, but were not prepared to make any financial contribution. Yet another proposal was for a line from Albert Quay to descend under the Passage line and, by means of a tunnel under the River Lee, would form a connection with the Queenstown branch at the city side of Dunkettle.

Cork City Railways
Then in October 1905, the Harbour Commissioners submitted plans for a low-level scheme with rolling bascule bridges for the two crossings of the River Lee. This scheme also envisaged new streets and was estimated to cost between £100,000 and £130,000. It was favoured both by the Harbour Commissioners and Cork Corporation, and had been prepared jointly by the harbour engi-

neer and Mr Walter Meik, MICE, of London. The company now agreed to contribute up to £1,000 towards the cost of promoting the new railway, on the understanding that the Bill would provide for a connection from their line to the south jetties and for the closure of the Gas Works level crossing. With all parties now in agreement, arrangements were made to issue notice for a Bill to be presented to Parliament in the 1906 Session under the title of the Cork City Railways & Works Company. Messrs Joseph Pike and Savage French were put forward as representatives of the CB&SCR, others including the Lord Mayor, the High Sheriff of the city and Mr Long, chairman of the Harbour Commissioners.

Following much discussion, a compromise route was agreed. This involved a line commencing at the west side of Albert Quay station and crossing the north and south channels on combined road and rail lifting bridges and along Alfred Street to the west side of the GS&WR goods yard, making an east-facing connection with the latter's goods loop at the rear of Glanmire Road passenger station. The construction of this line would also necessitate the provision of a new road (Brian Boru Street). The line would be sufficiently far up-river so as to cause minimum disruption to the port's shipping berths.

The Cork City Railways Act received Royal Assent on 4th August 1906. Capital was £150,000, subscriptions being authorised as follows, viz. Great Western Railway £75,000, GS&WR £25,000, CB&SCR £15,000 and Cork Harbour Commissioners £10,000. The remaining £25,000 was to be a Treasury loan. Apart from the construction costs, substantial compensation was to be paid to the Clyde Shipping Co, through whose premises the new line was to run. Joseph Pike, the CB&SCR chairman, informed his fellow directors that they would in fact be getting excellent value for their subscription since

Ex-GS&WR 4-4-2T No 37, an Ivatt 2-4-2T design of 1894, working a transfer freight over the CCR in August 1950. Note the street side railway signal, with telegraph on top of the post, immediately to the right of the engine. C Hunter

they would at some stage in the near future have to consider the removal and replacement of the level crossing in the middle of Albert Quay yard. In addition they were obtaining access to the quays and a cross-city link. At the end of the day the directors were quite happy to contribute when it was reported that the GS&WR were contemplating an extension of their Kenmare branch to Castletown Berehaven; such a line would seriously impinge on the Bandon company's Bantry traffic.

Cross-channel connection

The reader might reasonably enquire why the GWR were the major contributors to the CCR project. To answer this query we must go back many years to look at cross-channel developments. Back in the 1840s plans had been drawn up to connect Fishguard with Chepstow and thus with the GWR. The story of the Fishguard connection warrants a history all to itself but we will here confine ourselves to a summary of the main events. The South Wales Railway, in effect a subsidiary of the GWR, was incorporated in 1844 to provide the final piece in what would have been a through route between London and Dublin. Construction got under way in 1846 but was soon suspended, in a large measure due to the Famine in Ireland. The proposed line from Dublin to Wexford and Waterford was restricted in 1851 to going only as far as Wicklow, and in fact the connection with Waterford by this route did not finally materialise until more than 50 years later. The SWR directors had also proposed a branch line from Clarbeston Road to Haverford West, and instead of going north to Fishguard, they decided to go south to Haverford and then on a short distance to the

coast at Neyland. This latter port, which later became known as New Milford, was reached in April 1856 and a steamer service was opened with Waterford.

In 1872 a short line, 8¼ miles in length, was constructed from slate quarries at Rosebush to a junction with the SWR at Clynderwen. Seven years later the Rosebush & Fishguard Railway Co was incorporated to connect Clynderwen with Fishguard; whilst work got under way, this was shortlived as the company soon went bankrupt. It was resurrected in 1884 as the North Pembrokeshire Railway, having been bought by two Birmingham gentlemen, Messrs Rowlands and Carter. The company was initially offered to the GWR who declined to purchase it. In 1895 they obtained an Act for a line from Clynderwen to connect with the London & North Western Railway at Abergwili. Not wanting their arch-rival to have further access to the coast, the GWR now bought out the North Pembroke. Meanwhile, in 1893 a further Act was obtained by the Fishguard Bay Railway & Pier Co for the construction of a pier at Fishguard and a mile of line to connect the new port with Goodwick, the GWR in due course completing the line from Clarbeston Road to form a through route to Fishguard. The FBR&P Co. acquired the W&WR and the pier at Rosslare under an Act of 1894, the name of the company being altered to the more familiar Fishguard & Rosslare Railways & Harbours Co.

In 1864 the Waterford & Wexford Railway had been incorporated to form part of a connecting railway between these points, a branch also being authorised to Greenore Bay (Rosslare) where a new harbour was to be constructed. Work did not get under way

until March 1873 and the line was finally opened for traffic between Wexford and Rosslare on 24th June 1882, being worked by the DW&WR, which had finally reached Wexford from the north ten years earlier. The line towards Waterford was abandoned, while the line to Rosslare had a somewhat unfortunate career and was closed between May 1889 and August 1894, when it began to be operated by its new owners, the F&RR&H company.

The last piece of the jigsaw fell into place when the GWR completed negotiations with the GS&WR regarding the purchase of the Waterford Dungarvan & Lismore Railway and the Fermoy & Lismore Railway. Under a further Act of 1898 the F&RR&H Co obtained powers to construct a line from Rosslare Strand, where it joined up with the W&WR, to Waterford. The GWR, through the Fishguard company, now in effect had access to the south of Ireland. The line was in reality based on the C&FR and W&WR Act of 1890. It was the construction of these various lines on both sides of the Irish Sea which finally led to the connection of the railways in Cork and the GWR involvement in it.

There were one or two other interesting clauses in the 1898 Act. Under Section

An overall view of Albert Quay from Hibernian Road bridge. In the foreground is ex-GS&WR 0-6-0T No 208 on yard shunting duties. The line curving off sharply to the left behind the signal cabin is the connection to the CCR. The low building directly behind the wagon in the left foreground is the old signal cabin in use until the provision of the new raised cabin. Photographer unknown, Author's collection

Right: **4-6-0T No 464 operating an Irish Railway Record Society special between Glanmire Road and Albert Quay on St Patrick's Day 1961, just two weeks prior to the closure of the 'Bandon' system.**
W McGrath

Right lower: **Ex MGWR 0-6-0T No 552 on a cross-city freight approaching Albert Quay on the 15th August 1961.**
C L Fry, Sean Kennedy collection

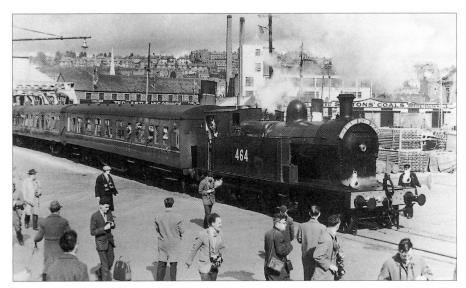

68[11] the company was obliged to return to Parliament in 1899 to obtain powers to construct a line from Fermoy to Dunkettle on the Youghal branch of the GS&WR. This would provide a more direct connection to Cork. Powers were obtained in 1899 for the Dunkettle connection but this was never constructed and led to the company forfeiting part of a Government grant. In addition, under Section 68[12] the company was to use its best endeavours to obtain the co-operation of other companies and apply to Parliament for powers to construct a direct communication across the River Lee so as to connect the system of the GS&WR with those of the Bandon and Macroom companies. When completed, this link was to become part of the undertaking of the F&RR&H Co.

Construction begins
It will be recalled that the C&MDR had removed their connection with the Bandon line in 1879. Talks took place early in 1906 when the CB&SCR directors expressed their willingness to join with the Macroom company in making a new connection between the two lines. This followed a resolution from the Macroom Rural District Council, who obviously saw the benefits of being able to bring goods traffic across the city. The C&MDR board however declined to become involved. Discussions took place in the summer of 1906 regarding draft terms for the working of the CCR. Interestingly in May 1910 correspondence was read regarding the working of the extension to Victoria Quay, it being agreed that if the line was to be completed for electrical working, the CB&SCR would provide the necessary electric locomotives and obtain power from the Cork Tramways Co. In fact there was even a suggestion that the entire CCR might be worked by electricity.

The contract for the two river bridges was awarded to Sir William Arrol of Glasgow, the bridges themselves being supplied by the Cleveland Bridge & Engineering Co The bridges were on the Scherzer rolling-lift principle, the first example of which had been constructed across the Chicago River. Both bridges, each of which incorporated a 62ft lifting span, were, unusually, constructed in the upright position so as to minimise disruption to river traffic. At the inner end of each opening span, a curved iron hollow

rolling structure was erected and then filled with cement and iron bars, thus creating a counterweight so that the full weight of the link span would not rest on the machinery during the lifting operation. The opening spans were electrically operated, power being initially supplied by the Cork Electric Tramways & Lighting Co, and later by the Electricity Supply Board. Messrs Crompton & Co Ltd supplied the necessary electrical gear for the bridges. The Clontarf, or south, bridge was 197ft in length, that over the north channel, Brian Boru bridge, being 232ft long. Rail tracks of tramway type, flush with the road surface, were provided. In later years the two bridges, rebuilt and fixed in 1980, became an important part of the city's transport infrastructure.

The road and rail works were awarded to Messrs W Muirhead & Co of London. It was found necessary to construct two new streets in connection with the CCR works. Brian Boru Street, on the site of a former coal and timber yard, ran from the bridge of the same name to the junction of Lower

Glanmire Road and King Street. The railway in fact only used part of this new street, curving away sharply through the premises of the Clyde Shipping Co to reach Alfred Street. Clontarf Street was constructed on the site of demolished warehouses and extended from Clontarf Bridge to a junction with Dean Street. Apart from the 'mainline', spurs were constructed to serve Penrose Quay and Anderson's Quay on either side of the north channel and Lapp's Quay on the north bank of the south channel. In addition to these three connections, a line ran from the northeast corner of the Albert Quay complex out on to Victoria Quay for a total length of forty-five chains. This line served both the Ford Motor Co and the Cork Milling Co.

The Cork City Railway brought the ideal opportunity for the Bandon to re-model the layout at Albert Quay. Finally, after many years of debate on the subject, the level crossing at Gas Works Road was removed in June 1911, and was replaced by the newly constructed Hibernian Road bridge. The company also now improved and extended the works at Rocksavage, while the two old engine sheds were removed to provide more room. Construction works on the city railway were completed towards the end of 1911, and following a number of trials, the line was inspected on Friday 30th December by Colonel Von Donop on behalf of the BoT. He arranged for the bridges to be tested by running two GS&WR locomotives coupled together over them along with a Corpora-tion steam roller and a petrol lorry belong-ing to the Tramways Co. He was accompa-nied by various railway officials, including E J O'Brien Croker, by now Irish traffic man-ager of the GWR, J R Kerr and W C R Coe, respectively general manager and traffic manager of the CB&SCR. Von Donop found everything to his satisfaction and the line was opened for goods traffic on the follow-ing Monday, 1st January 1912, being worked by the GS&WR. The Victoria Quay

siding, isolated as it was from the remainder of the CCR, was worked by the CB&SCR.

So at long last the city had acquired its rail connection across the river. One of the early dividends was that the new bridges relieved traffic congestion on the existing road cross-ing at St. Patrick's Bridge. There had been talk of through passenger tourist traffic from Rosslare to West Cork but this never materi-alised, and in fact a limited passenger ser-vice operated over the city railway only for the summer season of 1914. The world war and the post-war explosion in road traffic did away with any prospect of passenger traffic.

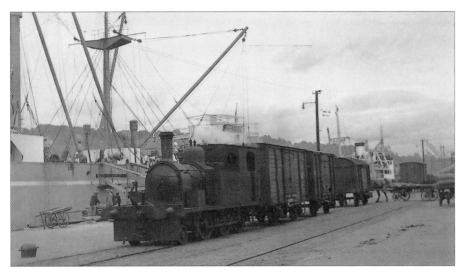

Left: **Ex T&CELR 2-6-0T *Argadeen* on Victoria Quay, Cork on 19th August 1949. The vessel alongside is the MV *Irish Cedar*, from which sacks of corn are being unloaded into the wagons. Between the chimney and the dome, it is just possible to see the bell fitted for working on the tramway section of line between Timoleague and Courtmacsherry.**
O H Prosser

Below: **Ex GS&WR 0-6-0T No 217 in charge of a stock transfer train crossing the CCR from Glanmire Road to Albert Quay on 15th July 1957.** C P Boocock

Chapter Nine

THE LAST TWENTY-FIVE YEARS

In March 1899, Kerr submitted a detailed list of works, which he suggested might be included in future legislation. These included the purchase of Cork Corporation's stone yard adjacent to the station, the erection of a reservoir at Cork, the acquisition of land and the construction of an aerial ropeway from Ballinhassig to Ballinphellic brickworks, the extension of the railway from Clonakilty to Rosscarbery and Ring Pier, the taking of shares in and improvement of the steamer service operating in Bantry Bay, to build or contribute towards the building of a pier at Baltimore, and to acquire and work existing road coach services. He also suggested that the company should legalise the position in relation to stations which had previously been closed, viz. Innoshannon, Castle Bernard (for passengers), Ballineen and Enniskeane. It was agreed by the board that the majority of these matters should be included in the company's Bill for the 1900 Session of Parliament. It was also decided to seek the views of the City Engineer on the closure of the level crossing and the laying of rails on to the Quay. The question of constructing a reservoir was rejected, the extension to Rosscarbery being deferred for further consideration. The various works in Cork were later carried out as part of the Cork City Railways project, described in Chapter Eight.

The board meeting of 15th January 1902 was adjourned as a mark of respect to John Warren Payne-Sheares, the chairman, who had passed away on the previous day. A week later, Joseph Pike was elected in his stead. Eighteen months later, E J O'Brien Croker, the general manager, informed the board that he had been appointed Irish traffic manager of the Great Western Railway at a salary of £1,000 per annum. He requested leave to take up his new appointment on either 1st July or 1st August, the latter date being agreed. The board, in recognition of his services to the company, voted to allow him his salary for July at the same rate as he had been offered by the GWR. Three weeks later, on 24th June 1903, John R Kerr was appointed to succeed Croker at a salary of £500 per annum; in addition to his new responsibilities, he was to remain in charge of permanent way. William Coe, the traffic superintendent, was promoted to the position of traffic manager, at a salary of £175 per annum. Both of these appointments were to date from 1st August 1903.

An unusual branch
Ballinphellic lies some 3¼ miles south-east of Ballinhassig station. The area around Ballinphellic was rich in clay deposits of two varieties, one a rich, strong, plastic blue clay suitable for the manufacture of flooring and roofing tiles, the other a brown marl for red-brick making. Creedon states that a brickworks had existed here since 1880, but it was early in 1897 that the Cork Brick Manufacturing Company Limited was formed with four Cork business men as directors – Benjamin Haughton, Alfred Beale, John Sisk and William H. Hill, the latter an architect and civil engineer. Charles Olden was appointed as the company secretary.

The brick company first approached the company in February 1898 suggesting the provision of sidings at Ballinhassig station and seeking special rates for the transport of brick to Cork and coal in the reverse direction. A fortnight later they wrote again, suggesting the construction of a branch to the brickworks, Kerr being instructed to obtain particulars of a 'Chair Railway'. Subject to the brick company guaranteeing the whole of their traffic to the railway, the company agreed to contribute £1,000 towards the cost of such a line. The brick company then decided to approach the Grand Jury for powers to construct a 5ft 3in gauge railway under the provisions of the Railways (Ireland) Act of 1896. This scheme failed to pass the Grand Jury and towards the end of 1898 thoughts again turned to the construction of an aerial ropeway. In the meantime there had been rumours of a line from the brickworks to Carrigaline on the CB&PR being approved by that company.

Negotiations with the brick company had by February 1899 progressed to the point where Croker suggested to the board that he and the engineer should inspect a ropeway in operation at Reading. This was agreed to and in due course arrangements were made for Mr J Pearce Roe of the Ropeways Syndicate Co of London to come over to West Cork to inspect and report on the likely route of such a line. Roe visited Ballinphellic at the end of March 1899 and

submitted a report stating that the proposed route would not cause any undue problems. The line was capable of being worked in one section and would provide an operating capacity of 12 tons of bricks and tiles per working hour, with a normal velocity of rope travel of 100 yards per minute. The only feature of note on the route was the crossing of a valley 1¼ miles from Ballinhassig, necessitating a clear span between trestles of 250 yards, well within the normal parameters for aerial ropeways. Roe went on to state that 43 trestles would suffice, giving an average spacing of about 140 yards. The system would be powered by an engine to be situated at Ballinhassig station. He saw no reason, from a safety point of view, of special requirements where the line was to cross roads, unless it was desired to hide the buckets from horses. Later, the County Surveyor sought a clear headway of 16ft wherever the ropeway crossed a public road, and the erection of a screen to protect anything from falling on to the roads.

The brick company agreed to give the company a lien on their works, subject to a first charge of £3,000 for debentures if a connection was made with them by an aerial railway. They also agreed to pay a rate of 2d per ton per mile or 4s per truck of six tons for the rope line. Whilst the plant and machinery was capable of producing 100,000 bricks weekly, they could not guarantee to dispose of that quantity (the average delivery during 1898 had in fact been closer to 40,000 per week). O'Brien informed the board about the potential traffic this would generate; 2,000 bricks equated to six tons, which at 6s per truck between Ballinhassig and Cork, would yield £780 annually, plus an additional £120 for coal brought in by rail for the brick works. Powers were sought and obtained when the company's Bill went to Parliament in 1900 for the taking of additional land at Ballinhassig and the construction of a wire ropeway thence to the brickworks.

Tenders for the construction of the line were not sought until June 1900, two tenders being considered at the end of October, that of the Ropeway Syndicate being accepted at £6,625. In the interim, this firm had constructed on behalf of the brick company a shorter line from the brickworks to

Dübs built 4-6-0T No 10 near Cork while working the 12.00 midday to Baltimore on 25th July 1914. She differed from her three sisters in that they all started life as 4-4-0T engines, Nos 3, 9 & 18 being rebuilt as 4-4-2Ts. Although four sets of materials were ordered from Dübs for conversion of all four, evidence suggests that she remained as a 4-4-0T until rebuilt as a 4-6-0T in June 1906. She was certainly still in original condition when photographed by the late Harold Fayle in 1902. On the other hand, a new crank axle and connecting rod were ordered for No 10 in 1903. It is unlikely that she would be heavily rebuilt again in 1906, by which year the first of the Beyer Peacock 4-6-0Ts had been ordered and delivered.
Ken Nunn collection, LCGB

the Kinsale Road. From this latter point, a seventeen ton road traction engine, the *St Patrick*, was put to work hauling three trailers for the conveyance of bricks to Cork. The company had been approached enquiring if they would convey these bricks from the Kinsale Road to Ballinhassig station, but this they had declined to do. Reference was made to the operation of this shorter ropeway in the brick company's annual report in March 1900 and their Mr Hill stated at the end of April that it was carrying 30,000 bricks per ten-hour working day.

The tender of Messrs Robey & Co Ltd was accepted in January 1901 for the provision of a 12hp Compound Robey Undertype engine and boiler for £423 4s 0d delivered free on Quay at Cork. Its cylinders were 6½in and 11¼in by 14in. Some difficulties were encountered in obtaining the necessary land. Peter O'Neill, who owned land adjoining Ballinhassig station, had agreed compensation with the company's engineer, but later sought unsuccessfully to increase the compensation when he saw how the Arbitrator was dealing with other claims. Later, O'Neill argued that a previous agreement respecting the provision of water at Ballinhassig station applied only to locomotive engines and not therefore to the ropeway engine.

With work only just commenced the previous day, the general manager reported to the board on 26th June 1901 on the probable starting up of a brickworks at Rathpeacon and the connection of this by means of an aerial ropeway with the GS&WR. He therefore urged the necessity of completing their own ropeway at the earliest opportunity. The line was in fact completed and commenced operations on 9th September 1901. Within three weeks the large driving wheel cracked and had to be temporarily repaired pending its replacement by the manufacturers. In December it was reported that the military authorities at Ballincol-

lig had decided in favour of the Ballinphellic bricks, with an initial requirement for 250,000 bricks, equivalent to 130 wagon loads, and five times that quantity within a year. Plans were therefore drawn up for the connection to be reinstated with the C&MDR, but no agreement could be reached with the latter company. About this time, the brick company sought to recover from the CB&SCR the cost of the temporary ropeway to the Kinsale Road; a figure of £800 was reluctantly accepted.

In December 1902 an agreement was concluded with a Mr John Willis of Ballinphellic for the conveyance of sand and lime to his farm for a period of five years at a rate of 4s per six-ton load from Ballinhassig, the company agreeing to put up an unloading platform on his land. Willis was to tip the buckets at his own risk and labour. Also at this time a dispute arose with the brick company regarding the weight of bricks. Initially it had been agreed that 2,000 bricks constituted a six-ton wagon load. Following some damage to wagons, it was discovered that they were 'dangerously over six tons'. Two wagons were loaded with 1,800 bricks each and these were in fact weighed at just over six tons. The brick company contended that their bricks were the same weight as they always had been and sought a credit for overcharging when loads dropped to 1,800, the company in return retorting that they had obviously previously undercharged.

In May 1905 the brick company applied for the provision of a siding in Cork yard, this being agreed to at an estimated cost of £200. The brick company can hardly be said to have been a financial success and in October 1912 the general manager informed the CB&SCR Board that negotiations had been entered into with the Youghal Brick Co for an amalgamation or purchase. The company refused to agree to any arrangement which would not provide for the carrying on

of the Ballinphellic operations in accordance with their existing agreement with the railway company. In due course the Cork Brick Manufacturing Company was taken over by the Youghal Brick Co and a new agreement concluded. In the event of the latter company failing to transport one million bricks annually by rail, they were to pay the company £100 per annum for a period of twelve years from the date of the agreement – August 1913.

A severe storm on the night of 21 February 1914 caused considerable damage to two of the ropeway trestles, one being blown down and smashed, the second having its top blown off. Moves were made in 1917 to sell off the ropeway, there having been no traffic over it for upwards of four years. The solicitor confirmed that, subject to obtaining the Youghal Brick Company's permission, there was nothing to prevent the company disposing of it. It was duly announced in November 1917 that the British Ropeway Engineering Company had offered £1,000, this being accepted subject to this amount being paid before the ropeway was dismantled. Only three months later, the Youghal Brick Co went into voluntary liquidation and the company later received one last payment of £100. The ropeway engine at Ballinhassig was offered for sale for £500 in February 1919, but there was no mention of this sale being finalised.

So ended an this episode in the company's history. It is of interest to note that the route of the ropeway remained on the ½in OS Sheet 25 maps up to at least the 1961 edition. A description of the line is to be found in Chapter Fifteen.

A dispute over water
Reference has been made above to Peter O'Neill, the landowner adjoining Ballinhassig station. In December 1902, O'Neill served a civil bill on the company for alleged wrongful use of water for the ropeway

engine, seeking £20 damages and an injunction restraining the company from taking the water for this purpose in future. When the case came up for hearing in January 1903, the Recorder gave judgement for 5s damages to O'Neill, but refusing the injunction. Both parties appealed the decision. The company's solicitor, Mr Julian, recommended that the board should endeavour to compromise by offering a sum of up to £15. Otherwise, if the case went in O'Neill's favour, they would have difficulties in future with water supplies. This the board agreed to and it was reported in the following April that O'Neill had accepted the sum of £15, and agreed to assign to the company the right to take a sufficient supply of water for the ropeway engine.

Chetwynd viaduct is rebuilt

The major engineering feature on the entire Bandon system was the viaduct at Chetwynd, just five miles from Cork. By July 1888 it was found necessary to prohibit double-heading, which led in turn to additional shunting. Nevertheless, it was to be another eleven years before Kerr advised that the board should obtain, 'a first class opinion on the present state of the bridge and how it might if possible be strengthened'. A Mr G A Hobson of London carried out such an inspection in December 1899. Pending the issue of his full report, a speed limit of 8mph was imposed over the bridge.

The lengthy report began by describing the bridge in some detail before proceeding to describe the tests carried out and work considered necessary. Hobson had used four of the company's heaviest locomotives coupled together and even with this load the maximum deflection on the centre of each of the spans was miniscule. The only noticeable deflection was on No 3 span. He recommended that the four arch ribs in each span be reinforced with additional cross-bracing of steel, which would add some 40 tons to the structure's weight. In addition, he recommended the removal of the cast-iron floor plates and their replacement with a new steel floor system designed to distribute the live load more evenly. It was agreed that the old parapet could be used again. To carry out the necessary repairs it was necessary to put in a short siding at one end of the bridge.

Messrs Andrew Handyside & Co of Derby, who had supplied many bridge girders to the DW&WR in the 1890s, tendered for the work at £4,345 in April 1900, this figure to include the services of a Head Erector and two skilled assistants. It was also based on the use of timber floor decking, Hobson having agreed to this to save expenditure. It

was estimated that the work would take about seven months to complete. If not completed within this time scale, they would charge an additional £148 11s 6d per month. Additional men and plant to be provided by the company increased the basic cost to £5,025 and £188 11s 6d per month after seven months. By August 1900 it had been decided to incorporate steel decking as originally suggested and this caused an increase of £1,322 in Messrs Handyside's figure.

In addition to the provision of a siding, a number of huts were erected for the use of the men working on the project and for storage of materials. An air compressor was also found necessary to power the pneumatic drills. In addition, a portable three-ton crane, lighting apparatus for night work, and a hanging scaffold and associated safety netting for one span, were all provided. Work proceeded slowly but by the beginning of October 1901 it was reported that only the riveting remained to be completed, which was finished towards the end of the month and full services resumed on 20th October.

During the First World War, the Argadeen and Ilen River bridges were both replaced, but only after objections from the Ministry of Munitions were overcome. In the case of the Argadeen or Shannonvale bridge, it had been hoped to obtain a bridge from Messrs Mann & Co in Scotland. This bridge had been built for China but could not be delivered owing to the war, but purchase by the CB&SCR was not, however, proceeded with. Both bridges were supplied by Messrs R A Skelton & Co, work being completed by the close of 1916.

The final bridge to be considered was that over the Bridewell River at Castle Bernard. A letter was received from Lord Bandon's agent in December 1902 stating that this bridge required the company's attention. The board however replied declining all liability. The agent responded to the effect that

Lord Bandon would hold the company responsible for any injury or damage resulting from their inaction in the matter. Reference was made to the company having carried out repairs previously. Despite this the company maintained their denial of liability and there the matter appears to have rested as there is no further reference to it in the board minutes.

Messrs Allman's siding

Messrs Allman & Co, whiskey distillers at Bandon, made contact with the company in April 1902 pointing out that the siding from their premises to the mainline at Bandon was in a poor state of repair. They enquired whether the company were prepared, as had been done on similar occasions in the past, to contribute half the cost and substitute good second-hand rails for the tramway ones in use, as well as second-hand sleepers. Repairs were estimated by Mr Kerr at £92. Whilst agreeing to bear half of the expense, the directors could not agree to substitute steel rails for the old tramway ones, as the former were now being used in the company's own sidings; they could however be sold for £5 per ton.

A year went by when Kerr reported having had several meetings with Messrs Allman. They were insistent on arrangements remaining as they had been in the past, namely that the company provide second-hand rails and sleepers and pay half the cost of labour. On 20th March, they wrote advising that as the siding was becoming, 'practically useless and dangerous to work, they would accept four or five days notice to discontinue the passage over it of the Company's rolling stock'. The company now relented and agreed to relay the siding on Messrs Allman's terms, provided any rails put in now or in the future were to remain the property of the company, the distillers being allowed to retain the tramway rails if they so desired.

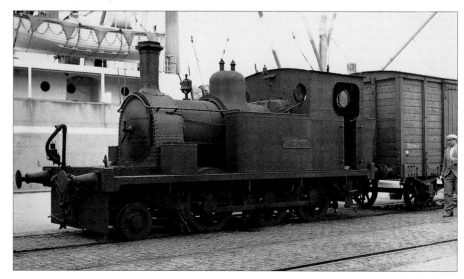

Argadeen **shunting on the quays at Cork on 17th August 1949.** I L Wright

A greyhound & a gun

Two interesting cases came before the board in January 1903. A greyhound booked from Skibbereen to Bandon in the previous October had, on arrival at the latter station, been put into the tank room, fastened to a stake and locked in. When the consignee's man arrived to collect the dog, the station porter accompanied him. On opening the door, the greyhound jumped out over the men's heads and made off, having broken a link in his chain. Whilst every effort was made to find the animal, including calling in the police, it was later reported that the dog was discovered some distance away at Newcestown, apparently starved and mad, and was shot. A writ was served by the owner, a Mr Walsh, for £20, the alleged value of the greyhound. The case came before Mr Justice Bird in February, he holding that the company's notices at stations were insufficient to relieve them of liability of common carriers. The solicitor informed the board in July 1903 that the case had been dismissed, no costs being awarded in respect of the hearing.

The second case involved a Mr Kerry, JP, of Springvale, who inadvertently left his gun in a sheath on the platform at Dunmanway station on 9th January. On being advised of his loss, Kerry requested that the gun be forwarded to Cork, where he would collect it. However, when the head porter at Dunmanway was lifting it from the luggage barrow into the van of the next up train, the gun went off, luckily without causing any injuries. Mr Kerry was later severely censured for transporting a loaded gun by rail.

Whilst on the subject of general matters, it might here be mentioned that an aviation meeting was held at Clonakilty in August 1910, resulting in a considerable loss to the organisers. The company were approached for assistance, a sum of £5 being contributed towards expenses.

Further amalgamation proposals

Financial statistics were submitted to the board in December 1907 for the Bantry and Clonakilty extension railways and the Ilen Valley Railway, as well as for the T&CELR and the S&ST. These figures were produced in the context of evidence to the Royal Commission on Irish Railways. Arising out of these, proposals were put forward for an amalgamation with the IVR. It was proposed that £40,000 of CB&SCR 4% Debenture Stock be given in exchange for the existing £40,000 IVR 4% debentures. In addition, £53,000 Bandon non-cumulative 4% preference stock of 1900 was to be given for an equivalent amount of IVR baronially guaranteed stock, with a further £27,000 of the same Bandon stock being handed over for IVR ordinary stock. The CB&SCR agreed to take over the Ilen Valley company's liabilities and assets as regards the guaranteeing baronies.

In evidence before the Commission in February 1908, the company advised their willingness to consider the amalgamation or purchase of the lines south of the River Lee. Three of them, the BER, CER and IVR were already worked by the company and were, to all practical purposes, owned by them. They foresaw little difficulty in taking over the C&MDR, so long as an agreement could be concluded on the value of that company's ordinary shares. The Bandon company however saw no public advantage in taking over the narrow-gauge Passage and Muskerry lines, unless both were extended into a central location at Albert Quay and a connection made to the Cork City Railway. The CB&SCR would themselves be financially unable to carry out these extensions, but would be quite willing to carry them out if the public authority provided the necessary money.

Some consideration was given in July 1908 to a possible amalgamation with the CER, the matter being referred to a sub-committee to consider fair terms for amalgamation. In September, the CB&SCR board agreed to relieve the guaranteeing baronies from any further liabilities if they agreed to forego the amount of £5,031 4s 10d due to them. This question remained unresolved, being raised again in March 1911, when the Bantry Extension Railway also became involved in the discussions. The secretary to the Cork County Council (as successors to the Grand Jury) informed the company that he could not recommend agreeing to wipe out the debts, suggesting instead the company making a cash offer. There the matter rested, the two companies retaining their independence until 1925.

As regards the IVR, the CB&SCR Act of 16th August 1909 made provision for the dissolution and transfer of the undertaking to the larger company with effect from 1st January 1909. This was to be subject to any dividend declared in the following month for the half year ended 31st December 1908 being available for distribution to the IVR shareholders. Section 9(1) of the Act laid down that £68,370 fully paid-up preference stock was to be created and separately distinguished as 'Ilen Valley Preference Stock'. Section 15 allowed for the baronial guarantee to remain in force until 21st July 1912.

Some station alterations

At Bandon, it was reported in February 1902 that the gas works adjoining the goods station, and which were the property of the Town Commissioners, had been seized for debt and gas production had ceased. The engineer saw little prospect of the gas works resuming production and suggested that enquiries be made as to exchanging the gas engine for an oil engine, or else obtaining a smaller gas power plant. This was approved by the board. At this time, the passenger station offices and platform were illuminated by oil lamps, while the goods yard and workshops remained unlighted.

The Bandon Town Commissioners forwarded a memorial in March 1903 requesting that engine drivers desist from the practice of blowing their whistles at Shannon Street. Kerr reported however on the dangers of people being in Chapel cutting, particularly in view of the private crossing there, and he could not agree to entirely discontinuing the practice. He did however concede that there were unlikely to be persons there at the time of arrival of the 03.30 mail and the 04.00 goods trains. Kerr's report was approved, it being agreed that drivers need not use their whistles until over Shannon Street bridge.

Several interviews were conducted in November and December 1913 with repre-

Railcars Nos 2627 and 2642 and an intermediate trailer are being spruced up at Albert Quay on 25th March 1961 prior to working the 12.15 service to Banting.
J N Faulkner

sentatives of the Cork brewing firm of Messrs Beamish & Crawford on the subject of constructing a siding into new premises acquired by them on the north side of the river at Bandon. Messrs Beamish & Crawford offered to supply all land required and way leave on their side of the river, and to give all their traffic to the railway for five years at existing rates. This was agreed to, the tender of Messrs R A Skelton & Co at £811 10s 0d, free ex steamer at Cork, for steelwork for the river bridge being accepted. The bridge and siding were both reported to have been completed by July 1914.

Improvements were carried out to Kinsale station in 1903/4. These included the construction of a new goods shed by Messrs Mann & Co of Cork at a cost of £345. In addition, a new engine shed was provided at the Cork end of the passenger platform, the turntable being moved to this location from the goods yard. At Drimoleague, some minor alterations were carried out to improve shunting movements. Mr John Atkins made application for a siding to enable him to remove timber from Ilen Wood about two miles from Drimoleague station. It was agreed to provide a temporary siding, subject to Atkins agreeing to a rate of 2s 10d per ton for carriage to either Bantry or Dunmanway. Atkins agreed to this and the siding was reported to be in place by July 1904.

A memorial was received in November 1903 from the inhabitants of Madore requesting the provision of a goods siding, previous applications having been made in 1889, 1890 and 1897. It was agreed in January 1904 to purchase a small piece of land and to construct a siding and a small goods store, at an estimated cost of £200. The works were commenced in October 1904 and were completed by the following February. The siding, facing to down trains, was on the up side, partly behind the passenger platform. It was worked by a one-lever ground frame, unlocked by a key on the section staff. At about the same time, a siding facing to up trains was installed at Aughaville, both being inspected by Colonel von Donop in April 1905.

The general manager informed the board in April 1904 of the requirement for making Ballinhassig a crossing station, a necessity, 'becoming more evident every day'. This arose from the increase in traffic following the opening of the Ballinphellic brickworks. Land was already available, having been pur-

chased under the powers of the 1900 Act. Work commenced in July 1906, Kerr reporting that when completed, it would considerably relieve traffic between Cork and Kinsale Junction, particularly on fair days. The new layout was described by Colonel von Donop in August 1907 as follows. The existing platform on the up side had been moved slightly back, and a new loop on the down side now served a new down platform, 350ft in length, and equipped with a shelter. The points and signals were worked from the existing signal cabin, which now had eleven working levers.

At the opposite end of the line, two matters require mention at Bantry. With the introduction of the steamer services on Bantry Bay and a consequent increase in tourist traffic, attention was turned to running passenger trains on to the pier. With a corresponding increase in goods traffic, it was decided in October 1903 to lower the level of the line on the pier and jetty, so as to bring wagon floors in line with the jetty dock so as to make it easier to transfer goods to and from the steamers. In August 1908, the general manager took advantage of Colonel von Donop's visit to the area to inspect a new siding (described below), to enquire as to the BoT's attitude to the running of passenger trains to and from the pier. The BoT were formally approached in December and agreed to the proposed working. Trains would arrive from Cork at the station passenger platform as normal, the engine would run round the train, haul it back to the entrance to the goods yard, and then propel it down to the jetty. Having exchanged passengers and parcels with the steamers, the train would be returned to the platform in the same manner.

In March 1907, a Mr W C Storer, who was manager of the Duneen Bay barytes mine, applied for the construction of a siding at Durrus Road for barytes traffic, also requesting a rate for carriage. The request was approved by the board, but 15 months later

we find a letter dated 1st June 1908, advising the BoT of new works near Bantry. What became known as Storer's Siding was in fact situated some 3½ miles nearer to Bantry, adjacent to mp56. A new connection facing to down trains, and worked by a key on the section staff, gave access to two sidings which served a mill on the up side of the line. In view of the falling gradient of 1 in 80 towards Bantry at this point, special instructions were issued for the working of the siding. All shunting had to be carried out on the sidings and under no circumstances were wagons to be left on the mainline below the siding points, with or without a brake van. The company originally involved in the operations here was the Bantry Bay Barytes Quarry Co Ltd, originally set up in 1872. It appears to have been reconstituted in 1875, after having gone into voluntary liquidation, trading under the name of the Liverpool Barytes Co.

In 1910, Storer requested the company to erect a wagon weighing machine at Bantry, it being agreed to remove one from Drimoleague, and to charge the Liverpool Barytes Co 1d per ton for all weighing done on their behalf. Later, in February 1911, the Barytes Co asked on what terms the company would provide loading facilities for lump barytes at Clonakilty station. They also sought a rate on lump barytes from Clonakilty to both Cork and Bantry Pier, the general manager being requested to discuss the matter with the company. The mine closed down in 1923 as a result of cheaper imports of barytes from the Continent, bringing about a loss of some 6,000 tons carryings annually.

The general manager submitted a memorial in October 1903 from the residents in the neighbourhood of the Chetwynd viaduct asking for a flag station to be erected at or near the viaduct. It was decided to contact the BoT to ascertain their requirements, an estimate of the likely cost to be prepared in the interim. On receipt of a reply from the BoT, it was decided to decline the request on the grounds of cost. In November however, the BoT appear to have had a change of heart, requesting a plan of the proposed station so that they might reconsider the matter. In the following February, approval was given, but, owing to the gradient, subject to no trains being allowed to stop there unless fitted with continuous brakes throughout. The board duly informed the memorialists that they could not see their way to constructing a flag station at this location.

Government control & world war

Within 24 hours of the outbreak of the European war on 4th August 1914, the railways in England, Wales and Scotland were placed under Government control. It was not until 22nd December 1916 however that an Order in Council placed railways in Ireland under the control of the Irish Railways Executive Committee. The IREC included members from the GS&WR, GNR(I), MGWR, D&SER and the NCC but not from the CB&SCR. It was agreed that in due course compensation would be payable by the Government so as to bring the net receipts during control up to the corresponding figure for the year 1913, subject to certain limitations on expenditure on maintenance and renewal of way, works and rolling stock. Allowances would be made for increases in wages and materials and a small proportion (6d per man per week) of bonuses granted to certain grades borne by the companies. Fare increases were not allowed during the war years, and it was not until 1st June 1918 that these were finally increased by 50%. Serious coal shortages also occurred in 1918 and these were to lead to cancellations of numerous trains, reductions in speed and the withdrawal of dining and through carriages. The latter did not of course affect the working of the Bandon system. Government control by the IREC ceased on 23rd September 1919, from which date control was passed to the provincial office of the Ministry of Transport in Dublin.

As early as September 1915 the general manager reported that a Munitions Committee had paid a visit to Cork to ascertain whether the company's workshops might be suitable for the manufacture of munitions. Nothing further transpired until the IREC directed an inquiry regarding the possible manufacture of wagons for the Government. The company replied that they had insufficient capacity at Cork to undertake this work and there the matter rested. Another minor disruption to the company was the departure in May 1917 of the assistant engineer, Mr Vereker, on his appointment to the 4th Irish Unit for Civilian Construction of Railways in France. He was to be paid one-fifth of his salary of £400 per annum plus expenses of 5s per day in France, but the company were expected to pay the balance. This would however form a charge against the War Office and they would refund it through the IREC. It might be mentioned that Vereker was a passenger on the SS *Leinster* when she was torpedoed en route to Holyhead in October 1918, he being one of the survivors.

Another connection at Ballyphehane

It will be recalled that a junction had been formed at Ballyphehane about a mile from Albert Quay at the time of the opening of the C&MDR, but due to differences between the two companies this connection had been removed in 1879 when the Macroom company opened their own Cork terminus at Capwell. A brief attempt was made in October 1898 to effect a connection at Ballyphehane, the matter being referred to the BoT for their views. It was pointed out that the CB&SCR only envisaged the transfer of goods and an occasional excursion train during the summer months. The IREC wrote to the CB&SCR in January 1918 submitting a communication from the Cork Chamber of Commerce suggesting the forming of a connection between the two companies' lines; a similar proposal was submitted by the Bandon Farmers' Association. The company replied to the effect that such a connection had been suggested to the C&MDR in January 1902 but that the latter company had declined to consent. Again in 1906, when the Act was being obtained for the CCR, a similar idea had been put forward with the CB&SCR offering to put in the connection at joint cost. They went on to say that they were fully aware of the advantages which would accrue to the mercantile and farming communities of such a connection.

In February 1918, instructions were received from the Admiralty requesting the company to make a working connection. The CB&SCR wrote to the BoT on 26th April informing them that, 'a Junction and Exchange Siding (for Government Goods traffic only)', had been put in between the two companies' lines. The C&MDR wrote a week later, referring to the connection enabling them to deal with naval and military traffic, 'for which object it has solely been constructed'.

Such was the opposition of the Macroom company to the installation of a junction that the actual connection in fact consisted of a siding placed between the two companies' running lines, with a facing connection from the Albert Quay direction. In October 1918 the IREC directed the Bandon company to urgently make the necessary arrangements with the C&MDR and the GS&WR to bring the new junction into use for, 'all public traffic except passengers', but only a month later they announced that they had decided not to proceed further with public traffic. With the wartime necessity for movement of troops and supplies gone and the junction no longer in use, the question of retaining the junction was under the consideration of the Ministry of Transport in London in 1920. It might be mentioned here that both Kerr and Johnstone served on the Cork Munitions Committee, Johnstone being on the Cork Board of Management for the manufacture of munitions. In a letter to the Surplus Government Property Disposal Board of the Ministry of Munitions, it was pointed out that the junction had been laid at the insistence of the Admiralty on land belonging to the railway companies. The total cost of the connection was £1,645, of which amount the CB&SCR had contributed £1,319. The Ministry of Transport envisaged that both companies would now take over the section of the junction laid down by them.

However it soon became clear that the Macroom company had no real interest in it, but offered a sum of £115 for their portion. The CB&SCR expressed an interest in the junction being retained for general public traffic, and in those circumstances would be prepared to pay their share of its cost. As the C&MDR were not interested in this scenario, the Bandon directors could not see their way to making any offer whatsoever. On the other hand, the Ministry of Transport found themselves unable, or unwilling, to issue an Order for the opening of the junction for general traffic. An interesting dilemma now came to light. If the land in connection with the junction came under the provisions of the Defence of the Realm (Acquisition of Land) Act of 1916, it was suggested that the removal or disposal of the works be postponed until later in the year, pending a possible change in the future organisation of the Irish railways. In the latter event, the junction might become of considerable value.

The Admiralty joined in the correspondence in April 1921, when they confirmed that the junction had been installed to enable the transfer of military stores from Haulbowline to Ballincollig barracks, so as to provide room for extensions to the Admiralty establishment at the former point. The Admiralty now contemplated reducing their establishment, and if the military should wish to return to Haulbowline, the junction would still be required. Another complication entered the equation, namely the transfer of power to the provisional government in September 1922. In May of that year, the CB&SCR made an offer of £200, on a scrap basis, for the junction and works, they being requested to increase this to £400, which they refused to consider. The C&MDR meanwhile reduced their offer to a mere £15, a figure which was accepted in September, at which time the CB&SCR handed over a cheque for £200. The junction was soon removed. However, one of the first decisions made by the new GSR board in January 1925 was for the reinstatement of the junction, details being given in Chapter Ten.

Munitions strike

On Tuesday 25th May 1920 a group of L&NWR workers at the North Wall, Dublin refused to handle munitions of war. In a short time almost every railway system in Ireland was affected and thousands of railway workers were suspended. Arising from these suspensions, services were severely curtailed or suspended. The general manager reported that on 28th June the 09.00 train had been held at Bantry station owing to the driver declining to work it when seven armed policemen endeavoured to join the train there. The driver and firemen and the guard of the train were duly suspended as were another Bantry driver and fireman who also refused to work the train. The board had little sympathy with the men concerned and ordered that they be dismissed. An appeal from the National Union of Railwaymen on the basis that the men were acting in strict accordance with BoT regulations, presumably as to the carriage of munitions on a passenger train, was declined.

A similar occurrence took place on 15th July when a party of more than 20 soldiers sought to travel on the 17.55 train to Kinsale, although on this occasion they were unarmed. The commanding officer reduced the number to 20 and the train then proceeded on its way after a delay of 22 minutes. Once again the NUR made an approach to the board, this time referring to the fact that the men had acted in accordance with the company's own rules (6 & 24) which stated that servants should not expose themselves to danger, the company responding by stating that in their opinion, 'the Rules in question were not involved'.

A meeting of delegates and general managers was held in Dublin at the end of August and it was agreed that in future men refusing to work trains with military personnel or munitions would only be suspended, trains so held up being withdrawn and no further attempt made to run them. At a further meeting in October, the Government made it very clear that the current situation could not be allowed to continue. They were in effect paying large sums towards wages of men who were refusing to work. They would now offer munitions and armed men, and the companies could dismiss men who refused to work such traffic. When the lines ceased to be economically workable, the Ministry would give an order for the closure of all or any sections which no longer paid their way. Alternatively the Government would introduce a Bill to terminate the agreement so far as the Irish railways were concerned.

Further suspensions occurred in November following refusals to work trains, various men being dismissed as a result. Such was the level of suspensions that all branch line services had been discontinued by mid-December 1920. Towards the end of December a countrywide conference of employees was held and a decision taken that work should be resumed without discrimination as to the class of traffic offering. Arrangements were now made to resume services, the general manager reporting that he had received instructions from the Ministry of Transport to re-open the line for traffic and to re-employ all men who had been dismissed as and when work offered for them. A full goods service was resumed two days later along with a two-train passenger service. Only the Clonakilty service did not resume, this service being reinstated on 3rd January 1921. It should also be mentioned that railways in Dublin, Belfast and Cork were affected by curfew regulations which prohibited people being out between 22.00 and 03.00. This resulted in shifts of men having to be re-organised in Cork yard.

End of Government control

Government control of the railways in Ireland came to an end at midnight on 18th August 1921. The Government announced in May 1921 that they would make a lump sum payment as compensation for claims arising from Government control. Under the terms of the Irish Railways (Settlement of Claims) Act of 1921, a figure of £3 million was approved for payment in full discharge of all claims against the Government. A tribunal, consisting of Sir David Harrel, John Mackie and Herbert Wilson, KC, was tasked with distributing this amount. The Irish companies agreed that a figure of £2,500,000 should be divided amongst the seven largest companies, the balance being divided up between the remaining 26 railways. The CB&SCR received a sum of £75,287, representing 3.012% of the £2.5 million. An amount of £91, based on the above percentage, was deducted as the Bandon company's proportion of the tribunal's expenses of £3,000.

In the run-up to the ending of Government control, the companies had to face up to what would happen in the future as they had for some years been operating in an artificial and unnatural environment. The eight-hour working day had been introduced, causing an increase in expenditure of some 255% whereas receipts had only risen by 96%. The country-wide wages bill in 1913 amounted to £1,554,690 whereas for the year 1920 it had risen to £5,848,470. In consequence of the removal of Government control the companies announced that higher paid employees were to receive 100% above pre-war rates, lower paid men receiving 150%. As an example, porters on

15s pre-war would now receive 37s.6d as against a current figure of 57s.6d.

Following a conference in London early in August, negotiations took place in Dublin but little progress was reported. Arising out of this a tribunal was set up under the chairmanship of William Carrigan, KC, to look into the matter of future wages. The tribunal issued an award in December 1921 which did not in fact provide for a uniform standard of wages. Railway companies were grouped according to their importance and financial position. The award was in the main against the principle of an eight-hour day and it confirmed a considerable cut in wages as made by the various companies. The award was to have come into effect as from 1st January 1922, this being postponed for two weeks to allow of further discussions. Negotiations between the companies and employees took place, it being made very clear that a railway strike at that time would be a matter of national disaster. The companies therefore agreed to a suspension for a further six months, but also agreed to increase wages by 4s per week until 5th May when a figure of 2s per week would be deducted. A further extension of six months to the end of 1922 was reluctantly agreed by the companies.

Further discussions took place in December 1922 attended only by the GNR(I), MGWR and D&SER. By this time the situation had worsened due to the effects of the civil war and the other companies, including the CB&SCR, stated that their financial position offered little prospect of agreement with the employees regarding the question of wages. The GS&WR went as far as to give notice that the system would close down with effect from 8th January 1923 due to its precarious position. The Minister for Industry & Commerce announced that the Government intended to maintain railway services when any company was unable financially to continue. They would however only pay the difference between receipts and expenditure, not wishing to be responsible for dividends to shareholders.

The War of Independence & the Civil War

The period from 1919 until mid-1923 was one of considerable civil strife, first with the War of Independence and then the civil war. Briefly, elections were held in December 1918, the Sinn Fein party securing a majority of the 105 Irish constituencies. They declined to take their seats in the Parliament at Westminster and an independent parliament or Dáil was set up in Dublin. Eamon De Valera, one of the leaders of the 1916 Rising who had evaded the death penalty, was appointed as Prime Minister, usually designated as President, of the Dáil in 1919,. Although so appointed, he spent some time fund-raising in the United States of America. Following his return to Ireland in 1921, a peace treaty was signed, whereby 26 of the 32 counties of Ireland were to have their own parliament, although remaining within the Commonwealth. The treaty was rejected by dissenting voices and it was not long before the country erupted in civil war. Prior to this however, we have to briefly refer to the War of Independence.

The first shots of the War of Independence were fired on 21st February 1919 by a group of Irish Republican Army volunteers from the 3rd Tipperary Brigade at Soloheadbeg in Co. Tipperary, two members of the Royal Irish Constabulary (RIC) being killed. Matters gradually escalated and the British responded by reinforcing the RIC at the beginning of 1920. In the early spring of that year, what became known as the Black and Tans began to arrive in Ireland. Contrary to popular belief, they were not, 'the sweepings of English jails, sadists and perverts let loose upon an innocent countryside'. Their enlistment to the police force was initially, at least, governed by the strict rules of the RIC. Later, in the summer of 1920, a second group, known as the Auxiliary Division, or 'the Auxies', were recruited to further augment the RIC. Between the two groups they instilled fear and hatred into the local populace, committing many atrocities.

De Valera stood for election as President of the Executive Council in January 1922, being narrowly defeated by 60 votes to 58. Arthur Griffith was duly elected President, De Valera and his associates withdrawing from the Dáil. This was probably the point in time when civil war became inevitable. With the Provisional Government in place to take over from Britain, the Black and Tans and the Auxiliaries were returned to Britain while British troops were also withdrawn. Whilst the Civil War had in reality begun earlier, the first major event was an attack on the Four Courts in Dublin on Wednesday 28th June 1922. The conflict was to last for almost a year, with considerable damage and destruction caused to the country's railway system. Liam Lynch, the Commander of the Irregulars in Munster, was killed in action in April 1923 and his successor, Frank Aitken, agreed with De Valera that it was time to call a halt to hostilities, a ceasefire following on 24th May 1923.

There were a number of incidents involving the CB&SCR during the War of Independence. The summer of 1920 saw several robberies involving mail trains, mainly around Kinsale Junction. By July of that year, the passenger service to Bantry had been suspended, while in December it became necessary to close all the branch lines. A restricted goods service operated between Cork, Skibbereen and Bantry. On the evening of 19th January 1921, shots were fired at the 17.55 down passenger train from Cork just after it had departed from Waterfall, luckily without any injuries.

The worst attack of this period however occurred just under a month later, on 15th February. A party of between 40 and 60 insurgents were lying in wait at Upton station, having received intelligence that a party of British soldiers would be travelling on the 09.15 train from Cork. On arrival of the train at Upton shortly after 10.00, the insurgents opened fire, killing six and wounding 17, one of whom died later from his injuries. It transpired that many of the British troops, who had come up by train from the military barracks at Kinsale, had continued their journey into the city rather than heading westwards. Those that had remained on the 09.15, numbering about 20, returned fire, killing two of the attackers. Among the other dead were signalman John Sisk and ticket checker Richard Arthur, as well as the Upton station porter. It was reported that the dead and injured were brought to Albert Quay on a special train. Subsequently the company granted a sum of £10 each for the funeral expenses of the deceased employees. Sisk's widow was in due course appointed a gatekeeper at 9s per week, plus war wages of £1 14s 6d, out of which she had to pay 2s per week rent. The company later received a sum of £100 for damage done to the carriages.

Two days after this shocking event, Scart bridge near Bantry was blown up, effectively stopping services west of Drimoleague. Clonakilty branch services were also cut about this time, following damage to the permanent way. Inchy bridge on the Ballinascarthy to Timoleague section of line was another target, rails being removed, leading to the derailment of *Argadeen* and her train. Once again, intelligence had reached the insurgents that a party of troops would be on the train, but they were disappointed as, for the first time in many weeks, no military personnel travelled on that morning – perhaps they had received counter-intelligence! Damage to *Argadeen* was slight and the line was back in operation in a few days. On 11th May 1921 the stationmaster at Bantry was held up by armed men, the goods store raided and four boxes of margarine and cigarettes were removed. The last recorded incident of this period was on 24th December 1921, when the 06.15 down goods was raided by armed men at Waterfall, nothing being taken on this occasion.

As related above, a bitter civil war broke out in June 1922 between Free State and Republican forces, its effects being felt most in the southern half of the country. As early as 2nd July, a number of IRA men demanded admittance to the company's locomotive works in Cork. They left after about two hours, taking with them a small piece of plate iron. They returned however on the following day and commandeered some plates and round iron. It was reported that they remained until 05.00 the following

morning, having in the interim kept eleven of the works staff employed cutting, drilling and turning. On the morning of 18th July, the 03.45 goods was raided at Drimoleague, a large consignment of groceries for Messrs Lowneys of Bere Island being carried off. On the following day, a consignment of 31 packages for the same customer were removed from the goods shed in Cork by seven armed men; an official receipt was given for the goods by the officer-in-charge.

Three separate raids occurred on 27th July. Twelve cans of petrol were taken at Clonakilty, a case of tobacco at Castle Bernard and five cases of soap at Durrus, while on the following day a further 50 cases of petrol were taken at Cork. There was an escalation three days later, when the pier at Baltimore was trenched and the rails removed. Glengarriff pier apparently also suffered damage about this time. Near Madore, rails were removed and an engine derailed, while on 8th August, Milleenaririg bridge was damaged by explosives, as the result of which, traffic could only be worked as far as Ballineen.

Chetwynd viaduct is blown up

Worse was to come as on the evening of 9th August the Chetwynd viaduct was damaged by explosives, one arch being severely damaged. All traffic was suspended and consideration was given to issuing provisional notice to all staff, a decision on the issue being postponed for a week. Within that week, four further bridges were damaged; Storer's near Bantry on the 12th, bridge No 8 near Waterfall two days later, and Ballymartle and Ballyhooleen (near Ballinhassig) on 15th August. Provisional notice was given to all staff on 16th August giving them ten days notice, the clerical staff being retained until 19th September. Messrs R A Skelton & Co. reported on 31st August, estimating the cost of repairs at £1,800, a figure which was accepted. The manager was requested to arrange with the military authorities for the protection of the work. Despite this, a workmen's train en route to the viaduct was fired on on 8th December, no damage or injuries being sustained. A week later, it was fired on again, work now being suspended.

In September 1922, the general manager reported that a proposal had been made by the military authorities to raise a battalion of railwaymen, to be armed and used for the repair, maintenance and protection of the railway system. The men so recruited would be paid by the companies, materials being provided in the normal way. The idea was that the Government would reimburse the companies under both headings at regular intervals. This suggestion was not well received by the men and appeared to be full of practical difficulties. Despite reservations on the part of both the companies and the men, the Railway Protection Repair & Maintenance Corps was set up in the autumn of 1922 under Major General Russell, who had previously been director-general of civil aviation. Amongst other means of transport used by the Corps were armoured trains and ordinary Lancia armoured cars modified with flanged wheels to run on rails.

General Russell approached the board in January 1923 advising that the Government were anxious to have repairs to the Chetwynd viaduct carried out as expeditiously as possible. He was informed that the men would be provided, immediately arrangements were put in place for their safe conveyance between Cork and the viaduct, which would require efficient patrolling of the line and the provision of an armoured locomotive and van. Furthermore, if the line was to be re-opened, it would require proper protection. Within two weeks it was reported that a number of men were employed plating an engine and van. In the interim however, further malicious damage had been caused to the company's system. Signal cabins and staff instruments had been destroyed by fire at Waterfall, Ballinhassig, Upton, Clonakilty Junction, Ballinascarthy, Clonakilty and Durrus, as had been the stations at Desert and Knockbue. On the night of 24th January 1923, the station house at Baltimore was completely destroyed, the carriage shed being demolished with the loss of four coaching vehicles.

Messrs Skelton & Co agreed in February to allow their men to return from London, repairs to the Chetwynd viaduct being sufficiently far advanced to allow passenger services to resume between Cork and Bandon on 20th February, passengers having to walk from one side of the valley to the other. Full services across the viaduct began four days later, services to Clonakilty and Ballineen commencing on 5th March. Services to Drimoleague and Kinsale began running on 12th March, with Bantry following a week later. The last section of line, that between Drimoleague and Skibbereen, was re-opened on 23rd May.

Towards amalgamation
At the end of April 1922 the Provisional Government appointed a commission to enquire into the position of railways in Ireland, the best method of their administration and the relations between the companies and their employees. Two reports were issued, the majority one stat-

ing that, in general terms, the Irish lines prior to the outbreak of war, had been considered as a sound investment, yielding a fair return on the capital invested. These returns had however been largely achieved through under-payment of railway employees. The report recommended State ownership under an independent railway board, a tribunal to be set up to ascertain the cash value of the undertakings taken over. The minority report agreed with most of the foregoing findings, but suggested the unification of railways in the State, these to be under Government control for three years. There was much criticism of the reports in the media, the *Freeman's Journal* saying that the State would have enough financial responsibility to concern itself for some time without involving itself in railways.

The Government appeared to be disinclined to introduce legislation and so a Bill was introduced by Thomas Johnson, TD, in November 1923 incorporating the principal recommendations of the majority report, including nationalisation. In the course of the debate, it was made clear the Government could not consider nationalisation, the Bill in due course being defeated. Long before this, in fact coinciding with the appointment of the Commission in April 1922, a meeting took place between representatives of the CB&SCR and the GS&WR to discuss the question of amalgamating the two companies. A fair measure of agreement was achieved, but when the matter was put to Government to see if they would sanction it and pass the necessary legislation, they stated they could not agree to a scheme involving only two companies pending the outcome of the Commission's deliberations. Further provisional agreements for amalgamation were concluded during 1923, involving the GS&WR, MGWR, C&MDR and the CB&PR. The D&SER did not wish to become involved with the GS&WR, preferring to go it alone or enter a grouping with the GNR(I).

The Government introduced a Bill in April 1924 for the re-organisation of the railways operating wholly within the State. The Railways Act of 1924 provided for the amalgamation of all the railways in the State, with a few minor exceptions. There were to be four amalgamating companies, the GS&WR, MGWR, D&SER and the CB&SCR, with 22 smaller companies to be absorbed. If the four larger companies failed to produce a scheme for amalgamation before 30th June 1924, a Railway Tribunal would be established with power to produce such a scheme.

The D&SER found themselves unable to agree a scheme with the other three companies. The L&NWR had in 1902 subscribed a sum of £100,000 by way of a loan towards the New Ross & Waterford Extension Railway, in addition to purchasing £87,000 of guaranteed stock of that undertaking. During the continuance of this loan, the L&NWR had the right to have a representative on the board of the DW&WR and its successor the D&SER. The London Midland & Scottish Railway, as successors to the L&NWR, under the terms of the Railways Act 1921, sought either a seat on the board of the new amalgamated company or repayment of the loan. The three other amalgamating companies refused to agree to either of these ideas. In addition, there was a separate agreement with the L&NWR in relation to receipts for cross-channel traffic, which in effect gave the D&SER an annual subsidy of £20,000. The LMSR refused to guarantee this sum unconditionally for the future.

In the short term, the three larger companies, the GS&WR, MGWR and CB&SCR, amalgamated as from 12th November 1924 under the title of the Great Southern Railway Company (singular). Early in December an agreement was confirmed between the LMSR and the GSR whereby the former received the right to nominate a director to the board of the Irish company. The Great Southern Railways Company (plural) came into being on 1st January 1925 with the amalgamation of the D&SER and the Great Southern Railway (singular), and the absorption of the minor companies. The Bandon company's remaining independent subsidiaries were finally absorbed into the GSR at the end of January 1925. So came to an end the independent existence of the CB&SCR. In the next chapter we will take a look at the major events which befell what became known as the Bandon section of the GSR and later Córas Iompair Éireann.

Ex GS&WR 0-6-0T No 201 working a cross-city goods train on the Cork City Railway on 18th March 1961, just two weeks prior to closure of the Bandon section.
R.M. Casserley.

Chapter Ten

THE POST-1924 ERA

At the January 1925 board meeting of the GSR, it was decided to reinstate the connection between the Bandon and Macroom lines at Ballyphehane. Work started in mid-January with a turnout from the Bandon line directly on to the Macroom line facing to down trains. A long trap siding was provided on the east side as a safety feature for up Bandon line trains. As first installed, the junction points were controlled by a ground frame at the junction. Macroom trains began using Albert Quay as from 2nd March, bringing about the closure of Capwell station for public use. Shortly afterwards, work began on the installation of a hand-generator in the signal cabin at Albert Quay so that the Macroom Junction points could be remotely operated. Whilst this work was completed in April, the new system was not fully operational until 9th August 1925. The line into Capwell remained unused for almost four years, the old station being utilised as a bus depot in 1929, for which purpose it is still used today. Thereafter, the line was occasionally used for the movement of oil tank wagons for re-fuelling the buses. Also resulting from the amalgamation, much of the repair and overhaul work on locomotives and rolling stock was transferred from Rocksavage to the ex-GS&WR works at Inchicore in Dublin, but following representations on behalf of the staff, some of the lighter repair work

work was retained at the former CB&SCR works.

In April 1925 the GSR board gave some consideration to the closure of the Courtmacsherry line due to the poor condition of the permanent way. In addition, the axle loading on the branch was only eight tons and this caused difficulties in finding additional motive power. It was decided to suspend services, this taking effect from 1st June. Local protests saw the intervention of the Department for Industry & Commerce who insisted on the necessary remedial works being carried out and the line was re-opened three months later. Later on, two diminutive ex-GS&WR 0-6-0 tank engines, Nos 90 and 100 were transferred there, and later still some of the ex-MGWR 'E' class 0-6-0 tanks also worked the line.

Approaches were made to the Cork Harbour Commissioners in 1927 by the GSR intimating their intention to apply for powers to enable the closure of the Cork City Railways. Although the line provided a vital connection between the otherwise isolated Bandon and Macroom sections and the remainder of the rail network, there is no denying that it had never operated at other than a loss. Originally it had been hoped that fish traffic from the west Cork ports would have provided a good income, but in fact by this time only about 2,500 tons was being carried annually, while livestock com-

prised no more than 1,200 wagons a year. Due in part to public outcry, the company decided not to proceed with their plans.

In the summer of 1929, the GSR introduced one of the four Clayton steam railcars it had purchased on the West Cork lines. An afternoon return trip was made from Albert Quay to Clonakilty, while in the winter timetable it ran in the early afternoon to Macroom and back before making a return trip to Bandon. This service also ran in 1930 but was withdrawn at the end of that year, despite an increase in patronage.

First closure

As part of a plan to reduce losses suffered, the GSR announced plans in 1931 to close a number of loss-making branches, including the line to Kinsale. In October 1927, Farrangalway had ceased to be a block post, the entire branch being operated as one block section and later on the 'one engine in steam' principle. A reduction in the service to one train each way daily in the summer of 1929 did little to stem the losses and in fact was probably counter-productive. Despite strong local opposition, the line was closed to all traffic as from 31st August 1931. Belatedly, at the beginning of 1934 attempts were made to have the branch re-opened, but by this time the GSR had already begun lifting the track. This latter was completed by the summer of 1934. Kinsale Junction was renamed Crossbarry as from October 1936, and around this time a number of stations countrywide were reduced to the status of halts, including several on the Bandon section.

However, despite the closures, losses continued to mount, leading to rumours of more closures. Part of the problem arose from increasing bus and car competition, which seriously eroded passenger receipts. In an attempt to counter this, legislation was passed in 1933 giving power to the GSR to take over not only the operations of the Irish

An unidentified ex WL&WR 4-4-2T shunting passenger stock over the Ilen River bridge at Skibbereen. Ian Allan Library

Omnibus Co but also those of Messrs John Wallis & Sons who operated road freight services. A second Act of 1933 reconstituted the GSR, reducing the company's capital from £26 million to £12.3 million. It also gave the Minister for Industry & Commerce powers to permit railway companies to end unremunerative services, provided adequate replacement road services were substituted.

Further closure threats came during 1934 involving the Baltimore and Clonakilty branches, these coming to nothing. Losses continued however to mount, the Bandon section alone recording a loss of nearly £20,000 for the year 1937. Arising out of these losses, the Minister appointed a tribunal in December 1938 chaired by Joseph Ingram to see how matters could be improved. In their submission to the tribunal, the GSR suggested the closure of 861 miles of unremunerative lines of railway, including the entire CB&SC section and the provision of alternative road services. The tribunal's report was published in July 1939, it being made clear that the tribunal were not entirely in favour of the withdrawal of rail services to the extent proposed. The fundamental importance of public transport from a national perspective and the role of the railways were pointed out. The report criticised the GSR under a number of headings, including its failure to rationalise its services under existing legislation. One member of the tribunal, Dr Henry Kennedy, in a minority report, suggested that state ownership of the company should be considered. In any event, the outbreak of the second world war in Europe in September 1939 put a halt to any of these closures being implemented. Following the amalgamation of the GSR and DUTC to form CIÉ, another review of transport was carried out in 1948 headed by Sir James Milne. Once again there were proposals to close a number of lines and, whilst the mainline from Cork to Bantry was to remain, the CB&SCR branches were to be closed.

The war years

As the war progressed, it had an increasingly adverse effect on the country's railways, particularly in the 26 counties where coal supplies quickly dwindled. The GSR had to rely on inferior fuels to the detriment of timekeeping. The timetable for the summer of 1939 had shown the usual three passenger trains each way daily, down from Albert Quay at 09.00, 13.05 and 17.30 with corresponding up workings. There were also three goods trains from Cork at 03.30, 07.15 and 19.05, the latter to Drimoleague only. Petrol quickly became scarce and travellers turned to the railway as bus services were curtailed. By July 1940 the 09.00 and 13.05 departures had been combined into an 11.25 to Skibbereen, providing connections to Clonakilty and Bantry; the evening depar-

Ex GS&WR 4-4-2T No 31 departing Albert Quay on the 17.30 to Baltimore on 11th April 1953. J N Faulkner

ture continued unaltered. Arising from problems with fuel, many trains were being severely delayed by poor steaming, extra time being allowed at various locations to enable crews to carry out fire cleaning operations. On the Bandon, a 22 stop was added at Ballineen for this purpose.

Further reductions in coal imports in the summer of 1941 led to additional cuts. One passenger train now left Cork at 17.00 for Skibbereen with connections for Clonakilty and Bantry. The corresponding up train left Skibbereen at 07.35 and arrived in Cork at 10.37. Some intermediate stops were cut out, such as at Aughaville and Durrus Road – Knockbue had already been closed since the mid-1930s although the platform and buildings remained. Goods services were reduced in November 1941 to operate on only three days a week, Tuesdays, Thursdays and Saturdays. By the summer of 1944 passenger trains only ran on Mondays and Thursdays, a daily service resuming in July 1945. It now looked as if services would return to normal but the winter of 1946/7 proved to be one of the worst in living memory with an extended period of heavy snow and severe frosts. There was severe disruption to transport in Britain and Ireland when coal supplies could not be moved from the collieries. Passenger services were again reduced to one train each way, with all cattle trains temporarily suspended. This latter move caused much disruption and anger amongst the farming community. Passenger trains again operated on three days a week as from 17th February, improving to four days a week on 24th May. Branch line services were suspended from 10th March. Full passenger services were reinstated on 16th June, the Clonakilty branch re-opening a week later.

Sugar beet traffic

An additional source of revenue presented itself during the 1930s. A sugar beet industry had first been founded at Mountmellick in County Laois as long ago as 1851, this early attempt failing after about ten years. In 1926 the Irish Sugar Manufacturing Co was established in Carlow. Within seven years this venture was also in difficulties and the government of the day, deciding that Ireland needed its own sugar beet industry, took the decision to establish Comhlucht Siuicre Eireann (Irish Sugar Co). Within 12 months the government had established three further factories, at Mallow, Thurles and Tuam, as well as taking over the Carlow facility. The Mallow factory opened for business on 15th November 1934, Thurles and Tuam following in December. The sugar beet industry proved to be one of the great success stories for the Irish State. By 1935 the four factories were producing 70,000 tons of sugar, thus substantially reducing imports, a figure which had risen to 89,000 tons by 1945. Fifty years later, with almost 90,000 acres of land under sugar beet, some 1.6 million tonnes of beet were processed into approximately 200,000 tonnes of sugar. Turnover for 1994/5 was £128 million with an operating profit of £24.7 million.

From the Bandon section's perspective, a good deal of sugar beet was grown in the Clonakilty/Courtmacsherry area, much of which was to be moved by rail. During 1938 an estimated 10,500 tons of beet were shipped out to Mallow from this region, requiring a daily output of ten wagons from Clonakilty itself, 13 from Timoleague and seven from Courtmacsherry. A circular for the 1941/2 season at Mallow Factory shows two wagons daily from Skibbereen, one each from Ballineen and Desert and two on Saturdays only from Dunmanway. These destinations were served by the ordinary goods trains. Special trains operated off the Bandon section to serve not only Clonakilty, Courtmacsherry and Timoleague, but also Ballinascarthy (four wagons), Ban-

Fianna Fail party, which had been in a minority since a general election in 1943, went to the country and was returned with a majority of 14. The bringing down of a government by opposition to a Transport Bill must be somewhat unique, although it had been precipitated by rumours of insider dealing involving GSR shares following the 1943 negotiations. In any event, the Bill was put before the Dail again in June 1944 and was passed with a comfortable majority.

Reynolds was appointed chairman of the new company with Edgar Bredin, the former general manager of the GSR, as the new general manager and Frank Lemass, the DUTC accountant and brother of the Minister for Industry & Commerce, as assistant general manager. The new company came into being on 1st January 1945. The inquiry set up in 1948 under the chairmanship of Sir James Milne was briefly mentioned before. This led in part to the passing of more legislation in 1950. Under the Transport Act, 1950, CIÉ was merged with the Grand Canal Co. and nationalised as from 1st June of that year. A Transport Tribunal was set up under the Act, which was to become involved in all decisions relating to the closure of branch lines, including those on which services had already been suspended. Additional borrowing powers were legislated for in the Act. Reynolds was replaced as chairman by Thaddeus C Courtney, who had commenced his railway career on the CB&SCR in 1916. One important section of the Act obliged the board of the new CIÉ to ensure that, 'taking one year with another, the revenue of the Board shall be not less than sufficient to meet the charges properly chargeable to revenue'.

The company failed to meet its obligations under the Act of 1950 in regard to breaking even. This failure led to another inquiry being appointed in July 1956, under the chairmanship of Dr J P Beddy, who had been a member of the 1938 tribunal. Beddy, who was thoroughly experienced in Irish public affairs, pulled no punches when the report was published in 1957. It was scathing of CIÉ's operation of the railway system. Beddy was of opinion that the services provided by the railway could be provided by other means of public transport, which would cost less to operate. Railways were an expensive form of transport more suited to high traffic densities. He recommended that the railways should be given a final opportunity, 'to show that their continuance can be justified in the national

don (five), Upton (three), and Ballinhassig (three) daily, as well as Upton, Crossbarry (three each), Clonakilty Junction (four) and Waterfall (two) on odd days during the week. A total of 41 wagons daily were scheduled to operate from the principal stations.

The beet campaign for the 1959/60 season commenced, as far as the Mallow factory was concerned, on Friday 2nd October 1959. The Bandon section had no less than 14 scheduled specials daily, with three each way daily to and from Courtmacsherry. These were arranged in such a way that no beet specials or ordinary goods trains would cross a passenger train at Ballinascarthy. As the campaign progressed, reduced loading of beet saw the cancellation of some of the paths laid down. Wagon numbers from Clonakilty and Timoleague during the 1959 campaign ran at 20 and 16 respectively. The closure of the Bandon section a little over a year later meant that all of this traffic had to be sent by road. Worse still, much of it went to private operators and was thus lost to CIÉ.

A new company is formed

Under the provisions of the Emergency Powers Order of February 1942, the Minister for Industry & Commerce appointed A P Reynolds as chairman of the GSR in succession to Sir Walter Nugent, Bart. Percy Reynolds, an accountant by profession, was already managing director of the Dublin United Transport Co. Negotiations took place during 1943 between the GSR and the Department for Industry & Commerce, leading in course of time to a Bill being brought before the Dail in May 1944, intended, 'to facilitate a long-term transport policy'. The Minister made it clear that there was nothing to be gained by, 'patching up', the GSR; what was needed was a new organisation, with a new legislative basis, a new financial structure, and a new relationship with Government. The plan was to merge the GSR with the DUTC and form a new company named Córas Iompair Éireann with a government-appointed chairman and six directors, who would be elected by the stockholders.

Following considerable debate in the Dail, the Bill was defeated. The governing

interest'. It did nevertheless recommend the closure of more than 100 stations and 1,000 miles of line, this latter including the entire Bandon system. The report further recommended the abolition of the Transport Tribunal set up under the 1950 Act, and the granting of powers directly to CIÉ to close lines. Other aspects of the report's findings do not directly concern us here.

Courtney, who was by now 63 years of age and in poor health, tendered his resignation as chairman of CIÉ to the Government in August 1958. He was replaced by 57 year old Dr C S (Todd) Andrews, formerly managing director of Bord na Móna (Irish Turf Board). Once again, the many changes wrought by Andrews do not concern our narrative. Suffice to say, however, that within six weeks of Andrews taking up his new appointment, the board of CIÉ discussed recommendations from the general manager relating to loss-making lines. Perhaps the most controversial closure of all was the suburban line from Harcourt Street in Dublin to Shanganagh Junction, near Bray. It was Dr Andrews who was responsible for the closure of the Bandon line less than three years later. Before dealing with the closure, however, we must take a look at some new traffic offering to the railway and the modernisation of the system as steam traction was withdrawn and replaced by diesel locomotives and railcars.

Dieselisation

Following on resolutions received from Bantry Town Council and Clonakilty Urban District Council towards the close of 1953, calling for the introduction of modern diesel trains for West Cork, CIÉ ran a trial trip with a four-car diesel railcar set from Cork to Bantry, Baltimore and Clonakilty on 24th February. This led to a timetable trial taking place on 4th March from Cork to Bantry and back. A diesel excursion was run from Bandon to Bantry on Palm Sunday, 11th April, in connection with a football match. In all, 705 people travelled on the eight-coach train. With the introduction of the summer timetable on 28th May 1954, a diesel train substituted for the daily steam service to and from Bantry, cutting 38 minutes off the steam timing. Numbers travelling quickly rose from an average of 20 daily to between 80 and 120. To improve the

image further, Albert Quay station was repainted and electric lighting was installed.

The summer timetable for 1955 introduced another innovation, the provision of a long-sought connection to and from Skibbereen out of the 12.15 down and 15.00 up ex Bantry. This gave Skibbereen a two-train service each way daily. The connections were however not maintained for the winter. By July 1957, all services on the Bandon were diesel operated except for the once-weekly goods to Courtmacsherry. A 'C' class diesel-electric locomotive had replaced the 4-6-0 tanks on the Cork to Bantry goods on 15th April, leading to a speeding-up of the service. This enabled a reduction in the number of locomotives employed on goods services from three to two. The Baltimore line was dieselised as from 21st May, the Clonakilty branch following on 3rd June. Finally, Courtmacsherry lost its steam engine on 26th May 1958 when C232 worked the first excursion of the year. An 'A'

class made the first trip over the Bandon in June 1958 with a trial train of two carriages and a heating van, travelling to Skibbereen and back; the 'A' class were not known to have operated any regular services on the C&B section.

The final closure

Preliminary notice of closure of the entire West Cork system was given in September 1960, a further notice being given on 12th January 1961, announcing the withdrawal as from 31st March of all services between Cork, Bantry, Baltimore, Clonakilty and Courtmacsherry. A report prepared for the board in February 1960 showed passenger receipts at £30,997, freight at £77,356 and sundries £676, giving total receipts for the year ended 31st March 1958 at £109,029. Against this, expenditure was shown as £177,336, giving an operating loss of £68,307. However after adding in fixed expenditure, the total loss on the Bandon section amounted to £91,029. Some sidings

Right upper: **Ballineen station looking towards Dunmanway with the small engine shed on the left; this was provided for the ballast engine. The ballast pit was located behind the trees on the left.**
W A Camwell, IRRS

Right: **4-4-2T No 480 (ex No 9) & train at Baltimore station.** Ian Allan Library

at Bantry were quickly removed in advance of the closure date.

Many protest meetings were held in an attempt to save the line, all to no avail. A Mr James O'Regan of Clonakilty took legal action against CIÉ in an effort to prevent the closure, which went ahead. When the case eventually came before the High Court in March of 1961, O'Regan announced that he was withdrawing his action. The threat of failure and the resulting legal costs which would inevitably be levied against him saw to this. The last 'public' train, which ran on Good Friday, 31st March, was the 18.00 from Cork to Bantry, reaching its destination 39 minutes late. The train was made up of railcar Nos 2641 and 2660 and intermediates Nos 841 and 1410 and carried 73 passengers, including a press party. A large force of Gardai travelled on the train, with a patrol car following. Additional Gardai were posted at stations, but none were actually required. The railcar returned to Cork with the press party aboard, arriving at Albert Quay at 23.30.

Lifting commenced at Baltimore on 12th March 1962, similar work beginning at Bantry a month later. By the summer of that year, strenuous efforts were being made by CIÉ to have parts of all the lines of the former CB&SC section lifted simultaneously. By October, the Baltimore to Drimoleague section had been lifted to the north end of Skibbereen station, the Bantry branch lifted westwards to Aughaville, the Courtmacsherry line almost entirely back to Ballinascarthy and the Clonakilty branch from there back to Shannonvale Siding. Lifting of the last section into Cork was finally completed by the summer of 1965. Albert Quay was retained as a goods depot, trains of goods wagons crossing the city to Glanmire Road. In mid-1967 some doubts were cast on the continued use of the cross-city link when the civic authorities expressed concern at the running of trains over streets and bridges, which operated on a one-way system for road vehicles. Despite these reservations, the line remained open and it was not until 10th April 1976 that the last movement took place. This involved the removal of a number of freight vehicles, including bogie fertiliser wagons, from Albert Quay.

Left: **4-6-0T No 471 (ex No 10) crossing the Ilen River bridge as it departs from Skibbereen for Baltimore. This was a substantial lattice-form iron bridge with a single span of 120ft.** H C Casserley

Below: **Skibbereen station in July 1956 with a Gaelic Athletic Association special which has just arrived from Clonakilty in charge of ex GS&WR 2-4-2T No 41. This had been one of the designs of H A Ivatt during his tenure aat inchicore in the 1880s.**
Photographer unknown, J W P Rowledge collection

Chapter Eleven

SERVICES

As described in Chapter One, the line between Bandon and Ballinhassig opened for traffic on 30th June 1849. We have no details of the service initially provided although we do know that a horse-drawn bus service ran twice daily between the latter point and Cork. With the opening of the line through to Cork in December 1851, a service of four trains was provided each way on weekdays; down from Cork at 06.15, 09.30, 14.00 and 17.15, with corresponding up workings at 08.00, 11.00, 15.30 and 18.30. There were two trains each way on Sundays, 09.30 and 17.15 down and 10.50 and 18.45 up.

A Cork businessman, Joseph Pike, approached the board in January 1858 to make arrangements for the carriage of his coal to Bandon. In this context, he offered to supply a number of wagons to carry on, 'an extensive coal trade with Bandon', and to connect his coal depot on Albert Quay with the company's terminus at his own expense. The local committee recommended the carrying out of this arrangement and to give Pike a preferential rate of 1s 3d per ton for at least 12 months. The normal rate for coal between Cork and Bandon at this time was 1s 9d. It was also stated that Pike envisaged bringing in a quantity of pitwood which would fill his wagons on the return journey to Cork. The board in London, however, suggested a rate of 2s per ton, but, following a meeting at the end of February, Pike agreed to pay 1s 6d per ton for coal to Bandon and the normal rate for pitwood. Should there be no pitwood for the return journey, the company were to have the free use of Pike's wagons. These latter were to be maintained in a state of repair by the company for 30s per annum. What seemed like a good deal for the company remained outstanding and by the following November, the committee considered, 'the treaty so far at an end', but they still agreed to allow Pike to make a connection from his store at his own expense.

An important instruction was issued to staff in August 1858 in relation to time-keeping. This circular, which most likely had its origins in an advice from the BoT, was prompted by an accident on an English railway attributable to, 'fast driving round a curve'. Whilst it was important that engine-

men and others should seek to have trains run to time so far as practicable, drivers were ordered not to make up lost time and to obey a number of newly imposed speed restrictions. Goods and cattle trains were to give strict precedence to passenger trains and, unless they were able to maintain a distance of eight miles or 20 minutes ahead of such a train, they were to be stopped at the nearest station to enable the passenger train to overtake them. The circular also referred to delays consequent on want of steam. Drivers and firemen were strictly warned, 'against a recurrence of such neglect and which cannot take place by proper attention to the Rules and Regulations laid down'.

In April 1859 a Mr Evans contracted for the construction of Upton Reformatory and Conran was instructed to put a siding in at Upton to more easily enable Evans to supply stone from Innishannon. It is not clear whether the siding was actually constructed at this time but its use would most likely have been shortlived. The want of lime for agricultural purposes in Bandon and the surrounding area was raised at about the same time. The nearest lime kilns were apparently at Muskerry, a distance of 14 miles, making the product expensive. It was suggested that the company might erect a lime kiln on their premises in Cork where it could be manufactured at a small cost and then sold in Bandon and at intermediate stations at a reasonable price. The construction of a lime kiln was still under active consideration in the following January, although there is no evidence that the work was ever carried out.

As early as February 1852 a special train was requested for a Southern Coursing Club meeting. It was agreed to run a train from Ballinhassig to Cork at 17.45 on 24th February. Then in May the board received a memorial forwarded by the Hon C B Bernard from some of the residents of Bandon protesting against Sunday excursion trains being run to their town. The secretary was instructed to reply but we are not privy to the board's decision in the matter, nor of course do we know what influence, if any, was brought to bear on the memorialists in the first instance. It is clear that excursions did continue to run on Sundays and that

these must have proved very popular with the people of Cork. A board minute of 3rd June 1858 directed the locomotive superintendent to bar the openings on the tops of wagons to make them safe for cheap excursion trips and, 'prevent parties from standing outside'. This situation seems to have lasted for the next six years as in June 1864 the board decided to increase Sunday fares due to, 'the want of carriages and the danger of carrying a great number of passengers without proper accommodation'.

The increase was also applied to Sunday traffic on the Kinsale line, which drew a response from the C&KJR secretary that they would act, 'very prejudicially on the traffic receipts of their line'. This comment drew little sympathy from the C&BR directors and in fact proved an opportunity to draw the attention of the Kinsale company's board to the unsatisfactory state of their permanent way. By now at least the shopkeepers of Bandon had come to realise the benefits to the town of Sunday excursions and an approach was made seeking to have the fares reduced again. It was agreed in June 1865 to reduce these to 2s 6d, 2s and 1s 6d, similar fares being charged to Kinsale.

By July 1861, the Post Office mail service had commenced to run, the timetable showing this train leaving Cork at 02.25 and arriving at Bandon at 03.30 with intermediate stops at Ballinhassig and Upton. From then on an early mail train was to run daily, with some minor alterations in departure times, right through to the 1914-18 War. In 1861, there was a down passenger at 09.20, a goods train ex Cork at 14.30 and the evening mail at 17.00, respectively arriving in Bandon at 10.20, 15.25 and 18.00. There were corresponding up workings at 07.40 (mail), 10.45, 15.45 (goods) and 20.35 (mail). There were also three trains each way on Sundays. The mail trains were first and second class only, all other trains, including the goods, carrying all three classes. Through fares from Cork to Bandon were 3s 8d, 2s 9d and 1s 8d, first, second and third class respectively, while returns were 5s 6d, 4s 6d and 3s. Sunday returns were considerably cheaper at 2s 6d, 1s.6d and 1s, obviously an early attempt at attracting excursion traffic.

Kinsale branch services

The propriety of reducing the number of trains on the Kinsale branch for the winter months was discussed in October 1863, it being agreed to have two trains each way daily, at 08.45 and 15.30 up and at 10.30 and 17.15 down. The entire question of the Kinsale traffic was reviewed in May 1865 when returns of passengers and goods were reported for a ten-week period ending on 6th May. These returns showed an average of 30.64 passengers daily from Cork to Kinsale and 40.77 in the opposite direction, corresponding daily receipts being £2 10s 1d and £3 3s 9d. From Bandon to Kinsale, average passenger numbers each way were 2.22 and 2.77 with receipts of 3s 4d and 3s 10d. Goods receipts between Cork and Kinsale averaged £4 16s 11d in both directions and between Bandon and Kinsale a mere 3s daily.

Notwithstanding the limited nature of the passenger traffic, the traffic manager considered the undue delay to passengers at the junction to be unreasonable and not calculated to encourage the pleasure traffic. It was suggested that all passenger trains from Kinsale should run through to Bandon and return to meet the down train from Cork at the junction. Having considered the report and its recommendations, the committee were of opinion that there was no traffic to be developed between Bandon and Kinsale and they could not therefore recommend the above suggestion. They also expressed the view that the development of pleasure traffic depended on low fares rather than on increased accommodation. The question of Kinsale services was raised on a number of occasions in future years. In March 1883 a service of only two trains each way was introduced, this decision being rescinded in the following month. Three trains operated daily in each direction for the summer of 1891 with an additional train on Thursday evenings from Kinsale to the junction to connect with the up mail.

Back to the mainline

By March 1867, basically the same service operated on the 'mainline' as six years earlier, including the mail at 02.25. By now however, the Kinsale branch was open and two trains were provided each way on weekdays, ex Cork at 10.30 and 16.20, the Bandon trains not providing connections. On Sundays, there were three trains to Bandon, two of which had connections to Kinsale. In addition, there was a 20.55 from Junction (Kinsale Junction), arriving Kinsale at 21.30. There were corresponding up trains on both lines.

Some nine months before the West Cork line opened, their Mr Parsons wrote informing the board that he intended running a train from Dunmanway in or about 17.30 and he considered there should be a connecting train from Bandon to Cork at about 18.30. This would obviate the necessity of WCR passengers being detained at Bandon for the normal departure at 20.35. There appeared however to be, 'many grave objections to such (an) alteration', and the local committee declined to recommend it to the board. By March 1867 the West Cork line had been opened for traffic with three trains each way between Bandon and Dunmanway. Whilst the three down trains are shown as connecting out of the 10.05, 15.45 and 18.15 arrivals from Cork at Bandon, the connections were not exactly an incentive to prospective passengers, respectively departing for the west 25, 45 and 250 minutes later. It was not quite so bad in the opposite direction, although there were frequent complaints from the WCR regarding the poor connections at Bandon. There was no Sunday service on the West Cork system.

A deputation attended the board on 30th November 1869 and handed in a resolution from a number of the inhabitants of Bandon requesting the attachment of a carriage to the down mid-day goods from Cork. Having been requested to report on the matter, the traffic manager said such a course would be most objectionable and would, 'embarrass the regular working of the traffic'. The request was therefore declined.

A similar service to that of 1867 was in operation in July 1873. By now the single fares from Cork to Bandon or Kinsale were 4s, 3s and 1s.10d, first, second and third classes, returns not being shown in the timetable. Three trains each way operated on weekdays on the West Cork line, the connections still being extremely poor. There were also two trains each way on Sundays. On this line, all three classes were carried by all trains, fares from Bandon to Dunmanway being 3s, 2s 6d and 1s 6d single. Connections were provided by coach out of the 08.45 and 15.00 down from Cork to Skibbereen, arriving at the latter three hours after departing Dunmanway. There was a further coach running on to Bantry in connection with the 15.00 down, total time from Cork being 5¾ hours for the 60-odd mile journey. The coach services only ran on weekdays.

Complaints having been made as to frequent irregularity in the working of the railway, the local committee investigated the matter in December 1877 and found a laxity in supervision. Whilst conceding that Richard Coghlan, the traffic and general manager, had been a zealous and trustworthy official of the company since its formation, his health had seriously declined and he was now quite unfit for outdoor duties. It will be recalled that on the occasion of the flooding at Bandon in 1873 he had walked through the floods and had contracted a disease of his lungs due to wet and exposure, a condition from which he had since suffered. It was therefore recommended that Coghlan be retired on a pension. The committee impressed on the board the importance of immediate attention to this matter as the want of supervision was, 'making itself painfully visible'. The board agreed to grant Coghlan his full salary for life. Alexander Gordon, the audit clerk, who had been assisting Coghlan, and since 1875 had in fact been undertaking a great part of his duties, was appointed his successor at a salary of £200 per annum.

Ex CB&SCR bogie composite carriage No 44B at Albert Quay on 10th July 1934. Built in 1906, this carriage had accommodation for 18 first and 34 third class passengers; it also included two lavatories. It was withdrawn in 1953.
H C Casserley

The amalgamated system

By July 1882, the lines to Skibbereen and Bantry (hilltop) station had been opened, the timetable showing the former as the mainline. The night mail now departed Cork at 03.00, arriving in Skibbereen at 06.10 with a Bantry connection arriving at 06.15, the two trains departing Drimoleague Junction within two minutes of each other. Other trains (on weekdays) left Cork at 09.20 and 18.00 for Skibbereen and Bantry, and 10.15 and 17.15 for Kinsale. There was also a 15.00 from Cork to Bandon only, this latter being balanced by an 7.30 up service. There were three trains each way on Sundays, including the night mail. The timetable also showed car connections by the 'Tourist Route' from Bantry via Glengariffe (sic) and Kenmare to and from Killarney. A request from the Earl of Bandon in February 1887 for the stopping of the 08.45 up train at Castle Bernard was agreed to, but only for persons, 'immediately connected with the Castle'.

By July 1888 an accelerated service was in operation, the 03.00 mail now arriving in Skibbereen at 05.40 and Bantry at 05.50. At this time, the Kinsale branch service was provided by a quick connection out of the mainline trains, although there was an additional 21.00 down from Junction to Kinsale. This timetable also shows an up train from Bandon on weekdays at 08.50 to Cork. The Clonakilty branch was now open and a service of two trains each way was provided on both weekdays and Sundays. There were two unusual workings on Saturdays only. These were the 19.00 from Clonakilty to Bandon and 19.15 from Castle Bernard to Desert, the latter apparently with a connection to Clonakilty. Notes in the tables show stops at various stations on market or fair days. For example the 09.20 from Cork stopping at Manch Platform on Dunmanway market days, at Knockbue on Skibbereen and Bantry market days and at Aughaville Platform on Saturdays only. Another note commented that return tickets were available for two days, those issued for journeys of 30 miles or more being available for three days after date of issue.

In connection with the opening of the Baltimore branch in May 1893, a service of three trains daily each way was decided on. Traffic however proved to be poor and it was agreed in October to discontinue the 15.00 down and 18.30 up on the branch for the winter months. One train was to operate each way on Sundays, but, if found to be unremunerative after a month, these trains were also to be withdrawn.

The 1901 and 1915 working timetables

The oldest extant working timetable which the author has discovered is that operative from 1st January 1901, printed by Messrs Guy & Co Ltd at 70 Patrick Street, Cork. This

'Bandon' 4-6-0T No 4 at Albert Quay on 19 April 1952. This was renumbered 463 by the GSR. J N Faulkner

gives us an opportunity to take a look at the passenger and goods services operating over the entire system. Baltimore is now shown as the outer extremity of the mainline. Down trains departed Cork at 03.30 (night mail), 07.10 (goods), 08.50 (passenger), all to Skibbereen; 11.20 (day mail) and 16.00 (passenger), both to Baltimore. There was also an 08.30 goods from Drimoleague to Skibbereen, returning from the latter at 09.40. In addition, there was a 10.15 passenger from Skibbereen to Baltimore, operating only on Skibbereen fair and market days. Sunday services consisted of the 03.30 night mail and a 10.30 passenger to Baltimore. In the up direction there was an 09.30 passenger from Baltimore to Skibbereen on fair and market days at the latter town, 07.30 (passenger) from Skibbereen to Cork (arriving 10.05), 11.50 (day mail) from Baltimore, 14.10 (goods) and 15.10 (mixed) from Skibbereen to Cork and the 17.35 (night mail & passenger) from Baltimore. Crossing points are shown in the timetable for all trains.

The Kinsale branch had two mixed trains each way on weekdays, at 08.50 and 17.12 from Cork, 08.40 and 15.20 from Kinsale. There were two passenger trains each way on Sundays, 10.30 from Cork and 21.00 from Kinsale Junction, 09.00 and 20.25 from Kinsale, both the latter running through to Cork. On the Clonakilty branch, the 08.50, 11.20 and 16.00 from Cork had connections from Clonakilty Junction, the first-named being mixed on the branch. In addition, there was an 11.50 goods train from the junction to Clonakilty and an 18.30 mixed from Cork. There were two trains on Sundays, a connection out of the 10.30 from Cork and a 20.35 from the junction. In addition to these, there was a mixed train at 17.45 from Cork which ran only on Sundays

preceding Clonakilty and Timoleague fair days. Finally, the Bantry branch, by then of course open to the town station, had connections from the day and night mails as well as from the 08.50 and 16.00 down passenger trains and the 17.50 goods, with corresponding up workings.

Special arrangements for various fairs were listed on the back page of the timetable. Ballineen fair had a special from Cork at 06.00, returning from Ballineen with cattle at 11.30. On Bandon cattle fair days a special passenger train departed Cork at 05.00 during the months of May to September and at 06.00 during the remaining months of the year. A second special, with empty wagons, left Cork at 06.30. Special trains of livestock departed Bandon as required until all brought to the station had been conveyed. A special also ran from Clonakilty to Bandon with passengers at 05.30 during the summer months and at 06.00 in winter, returning to Clonakilty soon after arrival in Bandon.

A special passenger train departed Cork at 17.45 for Clonakilty on the evening prior to fair day there. On the fair day itself, a special cattle train left for Cork at 11.30, extra specials running as required. On Kinsale fair day a special passenger train left Cork at 05.00 during the summer months and an hour later in winter; there was also a special cattle train at 12.00, extra trains running as needed. Finally, Timoleague fair produced a special ex Cork at 17.45 the previous evening. On the fair day itself a special cattle train left Ballinascarthy at 11.55, the regular Clonakilty goods being expedited on that day. Once again, extra specials ran as required.

The working timetable for June 1915 was printed by the Eagle Works of South Mall and Smith Street, Cork. The night mail now ran through to Baltimore, arriving there at 06.55, with a connection from Drimoleague to Bantry. There were two goods trains to Skibbereen, ex Cork at 04.55 and 10.45,

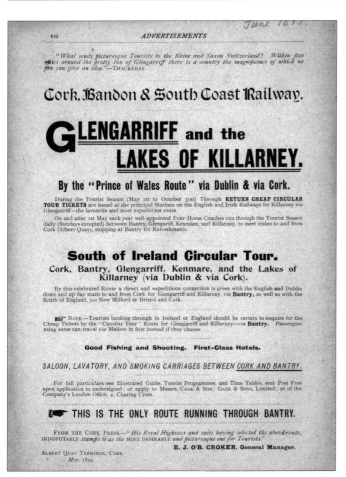

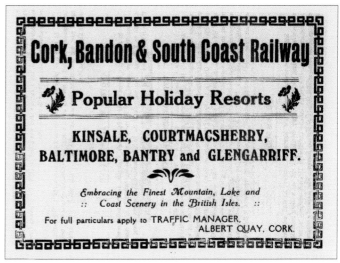

In the halcyon days of the late 19th and early 20th centuries, the railway companies serving the south and west of Ireland made considerable efforts to attract tourists to the undoubted scenic attractions of the areas they served. These are examples of some of the advertisements issued by the CB&SCR to attrat tourists onto their system. That on the left, from the *Railway Magazine* for June 1899, refers to the 'Prince of Wales Route', a phrase used by the company to attract custom. They were of course also in competition with the GS&WR for tourist traffic to Glengarriff and the lakes of Killarney. Author's collection

arriving at their destination respectively at 09.15 and 17.15. There was also a goods for Bandon at 06.00 from Cork, which occupied 82 minutes en route. The Baltimore passenger left at 09.00 and had connections to Kinsale, Clonakilty and Bantry, as did the 12.00 day mail. Finally, there was a passenger train for Baltimore at 16.15, arriving at 19.00. On Sundays, apart from the night mail, there was a 10.20 passenger to Baltimore and a 17.30 mixed to Skibbereen. There was a note in the down table stating that the ballast engine left Ballineen every Sunday at 17.30 to work the Clonakilty branch connection out of the 17.30 from Cork, returning to Ballineen from Clonakilty Junction at 20.32, except on the first Sunday in the month. Like the 1901 timetable, there were additional stops at stations on fair and market days.

Kinsale was served by one passenger and two mixed trains each way on weekdays, with three passenger trains on Sundays. Journey time from the junction was 33 minutes in the down direction, one minute less in the up direction. Trains stopped at Ballymartle in both directions by signal or on notice to the guard of the train. Tables 5 & 6 referred to the Clonakilty branch, there being two passenger trains, two goods and one mixed as well as a Timoleague line train from the junction at 17.20 on Mondays to Thursdays only. One mixed and two pas-

senger trains ran on Sundays. The light engine for Ballineen was scheduled to follow the western train to Bandon. Reference has already been made to connections out of passenger trains for Bantry. There was also a goods train from Drimoleague at 09.00 on weekdays, returning from Bantry at 15.30. Aughaville was not listed as a station, but a note stated that trains in both directions (both passenger and goods) would stop there if required. Likewise, the up and down day mail stopped at Durrus Road when required. The various special arrangements for fairs were similar to those in the 1901 timetable.

Services on the Courtmacsherry line are not shown in the timetables, but the *Blue Guide* for March 1916 shows trains from Ballinascarthy at 10.27, 13.25 and 17.36 with arrivals in Courtmacsherry respectively at 11.00, 13.56 and 18.08. The 13.25 down and the corresponding up train at 12.10 ran only on Fridays and Saturdays. There was no Sunday service at this time on the branch.

Due to rising costs, mainly the price of coal, the contract with the postal authorities for the conveyance of mails by special trains was discontinued in 1916. *Bradshaw* for March 1918 therefore shows the first train out of Cork as being the 09.30 to Baltimore, with a connection to Bantry. This was followed by a 12.40 to Bantry and a 17.15 to

Baltimore. There was also a Saturdays only train from Skibbereen to Baltimore at 16.10. The Kinsale and Clonakilty branches each had three trains in each direction on weekdays only. There was one train each way on the mainline to and from Skibbereen on Sundays. The tourist service to Killarney was shown operating, the connection out of the 09.30 down between Bantry and Glengarriff being by steamer on Thursdays and Saturdays, and on Tuesdays, Thursdays and Saturdays in the up direction into the 11.00 from Bantry. On the Courtmacsherry line, there were two down trains on weekdays at 11.00 and 18.45 from Ballinascarthy, with up trains at 08.05 and 16.15. There was also a 14.03 down on Saturdays only and a 15.05 on Fridays only, plus a 13.00 up on both days.

The question of only having two classes of travel on the company's trains was first considered in November 1905. The idea was approved of in principle and, with a view to carrying this out, it was decided in future only to refit first and third class carriages. A new first class fare structure was submitted in January 1907 based on singles at 1⅔d per mile and returns at 1⅔ of the single fare. These figures were in fact based approximately on existing second class fares and it was agreed to forthwith abolish second class and adopt the new first class fare structure as from May 1907.

Cutbacks

The First World War brought interruptions to services. The Chief Secretary wrote in November 1916 representing the advisability of stopping all excursion and special train traffic. Arising from wartime coal shortages, the IREC in March 1918 sought a revision in the company's timetable so as to effect a coal saving of 20%. Reluctantly, in April, the directors agreed to reduce the service to two trains daily on the mainline on weekdays with no Sunday trains on and after 15th April. In October 1919 an instruction from the IREC demanded a 50% reduction in coal consumption arising from a railway strike in Britain. Reference has already been made in Chapter Eight to the disruption to services resulting from the munitions strike in 1920.

The railway strike of 1919 was followed a year later by a miners' strike and this had the effect of passenger services on the mainline being again reduced to two trains each way daily, services being suspended entirely on the branches. More reductions followed in April 1921 in an attempt to further conserve coal stocks, with passenger trains now only running on Tuesdays, Thursdays and Saturdays. On the remaining three weekdays, only goods trains would operate. Later, the Civil War caused further problems, services being entirely suspended for a period following the blowing up of the Chetwynd viaduct.

Road services

Concurrent with the opening of the first section of line between Bandon and Ballinhassig, arrangements were made with Messrs Magan & O'Connor of Cork to provide a twice daily horse-drawn omnibus from Ballinhassig to the Imperial Hotel in Cork. Combined return fares between Bandon and Cork were 5s, 3s and 2s, first, second and third class respectively. Five vehicles were initially purchased by the company, each with seating for 28 passengers and hauled by four horses. This service left its legacy for many years after as the narrow road from the main road to Bandon up to Ballinhassig station was for many years known as the 'bus road'.

Following on the opening of the line throughout from Bandon to Cork, it was decided to dispose of the omnibuses. The Cork Steamship Co quoted £6 each for conveying them to London, consideration then being given to disposing of them locally. Road services were quickly provided to connect the railheads with outlying towns and in January 1855 we find a complaint being made against Sheehan, the driver of the car from Ballinhassig to Kinsale, for having only an open car, although the weather was 'intensely cold and the country being covered with snow'. We can only imagine what it must have been like to travel from say Ban-

don to Bantry in those early days. A week's notice was given to Sheehan of the company's intention to discontinue the service, but a month later it was agreed that he should run the car on his own account and receive two-thirds of the fares. Mention is made later in this chapter of road services operated in connection with the mail deliveries to western towns.

In May 1858, Charles Bianconi agreed to convey passengers on his car from Clonakilty to connect with the 07.40 train from Bandon to Cork for 1s each. It is apparent that not many passengers availed of this service as Bianconi was paid an amount of £10 14s 6d for the five months to the end of October. He complained to the company in October 1860 of the unfair manner in which he was being treated at Bandon station. As a result it was ordered that the drivers of all cars and their conveyances were to be excluded from the platform and yard at Bandon. This matter rumbled on for several months, a counter-complaint being made by David White, a coachman at Bandon. Resulting from an accident to Bianconi in 1867, he announced his intention to give up his business. Arising from this decision, the business was sold to Thomas Marmion, the road services from Bandon to Skibbereen and Clonakilty being taken over by him.

In June 1877 a letter was read from the secretary of the WCR seeking assistance towards the putting on of cars from Drimoleague to Bantry and Glengarriff. The directors agreed to give every facility in their power to the western traffic, but as regards cars from Drimoleague this matter rested with the WCR who had the haulage of the IVR line. With the opening of the line to the west, the road services changed from providing a basic connection with the trains for local people to that of a tourist nature, and we will consider further developments in that context.

Tourist traffic

Special trains were operated from time to time to cater for groups, as for example a train laid on in July 1854 for the Innoshannon Bazaar following a request from the Rev R Maunsell Eyre. Special fares were agreed for those attending the bazaar and in addition the company agreed to make a subscription towards the event. In the same month a party of 300 soldiers from the 59th Regiment travelled from Ballinhassig. Later, in August 1883, a request was made for special trains in connection with the visit of the Earl and Countess Spencer to Bandon. It was agreed to provide these at £6 per trip if paid for by the Earl of Bandon or £8 if paid for by the Lord Lieutenant. The County Inspector of Constabulary also requested a pilot engine to run before each train, this request being turned down, 'no engine being available for the purpose'.

Thackeray quoted the following: 'What sends picturesque Tourists to the Rhine and Saxon Switzerland? Within five miles around the pretty inn of Glengariff there is a country the magnificence of which no pen can give an idea'. With such beautiful scenery close by in counties Cork and Kerry, it is little wonder that the company became involved from an early date in tourism. The visit of the Prince of Wales to Killarney via the railway in 1858 drew the following comment: 'His Royal Highness and Suite having selected the above route, INDISPUTABLY stamps it as the MOST DESIRABLE and picturesque one for Tourists'. The company thereafter referred to the Killarney route as the 'Prince of Wales Route', although its significance as a tourist destination was appreciated prior to that.

As early as May 1852 the directors considered the question of the through booking of passengers to Killarney. Correspondence was entered into with the Chester & Holyhead and Great Western railways and the Bristol and Cork Steamship Company which resulted in an agreement with the Chester company whereby the C&BR received 2s 3d, irrespective of class, on each tourist going to Killarney over their railway. For the 1854 summer it was agreed to subscribe 3s 3d for first class passengers, second class remaining at 2s 3d. A Mr Fishbourne undertook to carry passengers between Bandon and Killarney.

These Killarney excursions really came into their own with the completion of the line to Bantry, a road connection initially being provided via Glengarriff and Kenmare. Consideration was even given to the erection of hotels at Castletown Berehaven and Collooney Lakes. In April 1895 it was announced that the GS&WR proposed stopping the up and down mails at Mallow with a connection being provided for Killarney and Glengarriff via Kenmare, which would facilitate tourists from England with a more expeditious route than that via Cork. To counteract this move, the company considered running an express train from Cork during the tourist season, contracting with a Mr Vickery to do the coaching onwards to Killarney.

Correspondence was received in September 1896 from Colonel Dickinson, chairman of the Development Syndicate (Ireland) seeking the company's moral support in their endeavour to acquire the coaches then worked by Mr Vickery as well as a number of hotels. This matter dragged on and in March 1897 we find Dickinson making enquiries as to a working agreement for a new coach service for the 'Prince of Wales Route'.

It was confirmed in July 1897 that George Vickery had in fact handed over possession of the 'Prince of Wales Route' to the Tourist Development Syndicate. In April of the following year, the general manager reported

(6)

Table No. 3. Kinsale Junc. to Kinsale.

Distance from Kinsale Jun.	STATIONS.		Week Days.			Sundays.			Wednesdays only.	
			26 Mixed.	Pass.	27 Mixed.	28 Pass.	Pass.	29 Pass.	Pass.	Pass.
MILES.			A.M.	P.M.	P.M.	A.M.	P.M.	P.M.	A.M.	P.M.
	CORK	dep.	8 50	..	5 12	10 30	..	..	..	..
	KINSALE Junc.	,,	9 40	..	5 51	11 5	..	9 0	..	..
4	BALLYMARTLE	arr.	9 50	..	6 1	11 15	..	9 10	..	..
	Do	dep.	9 51	..	6 2	11 16	..	9 11	..	..
8	FARRANGALWAY	arr.	10 1	..	6 12	11 26	..	9 21	..	..
	Do.	dep.	10 3	..	6 14	11 28	.,	9 23	..	..
10¾	KINSALE	arr.	10 13	..	6 24	11 38	..	9 33	..	..

Table No. 4. Kinsale to Kinsale Junc.

Distance from Kinsale.	STATIONS.		Week Days.			Sundays.			Wednesdays only.	
			30 Mixed.	Pass.	31 Mixed.	32 Pass.	33 Pass.	34 Pass.	Mixed.	Pass.
MILES.			A.M.	P.M.	P.M.	A.M.	P.M.		A.M.	P.M.
	KINSALE	dep.	8 40	..	3 20	9 0	8 25	..	..	..
2¾	FARRANGALWAY	arr.	8 50	..	3 30	9 10	8 35	..	..	..
	Do.	dep.	8 51	..	3 31	9 11	8 36	..	..	..
6¾	BALLYMARTLE	arr.	9 1	..	3 41	9 21	8 46	..	..	..
	Do.	dep.	9 2	..	3 42	9 22	8 47	..	..	..
10¾	KINSALE Junc.	arr.	9 12	..	3 52	9 32	8 57	..	..	..

Table No. 5. Clonakilty Junc. to Clonakilty.

Distance from Clonakilty Jun.	STATIONS.		Week Days.					Sunday.		
			35 Mixed.	36 Goods.	37 Dy Ml. Pass.	38 Pass.	39 Mixed	40 Pass.	41 Mix.	42 Pass.
MILES.			A.M.	A.M.	A.M.	P.M.	P.M.	A.M.	P.M.	P.M.
	CORK	dep.	8 50	..	11 20	4 0	6 30	10 30	5*45	..
	CLONAKILTY Jun.	dep.	10 2	11 50	1 28	5 11	7 53	11 37	6 56	8 35
5¼	BALLLINASCARTHY	arr.	10 16	12 8	1 42	5 25	8 7	11 51	7 10	8 49
	Do.	dep.	10 18	12 16	1 43	5 27	8 9	11 53	7 12	8 50
	CLONAKILTY	arr.	10 29	12 28	1 54	5 38	8 20	12 4	7 23	9 1

* Runs on Sundays preceding Clonakilty and Timoleague Fair days.

Left and on the page opposite: **Extracts from the CB&SCR Working Timetable for January 1901.** Author's collection

posed a charge of 1s per section or 2s 6d for the entire route, passengers to be given a receipt.

A complaint of another kind was raised in July 1901, namely the diversion of the American tourist traffic via the Macroom line. The general manager suggested that he should spend his holidays in America and arrange for the distribution of coupons there in order to secure the traffic as far as possible to the Bandon system. The board concurred with this idea, the Cunard Company offering a return ticket for £30. Croker was duly granted a month's leave of absence at the end of September 1901, a sum of £50 being given to him, to include his fare and expenses. The results of his trip are not recorded.

Back in circulation, Croker recommended in March of the following year the opening of a circular route from Bantry to Dunmanus Bay. Inclusive fares of 13s 6d, first, 12s second and 10s third class, would include luncheon at the Ahakista Hotel and tea at Bantry. The Development Syndicate agreed to do the coaching and provide the refreshments for 7s a head, this sum to be deducted from the above fares. In order to promote the new route, Crossley suggested that a number of influential gentlemen interested in the development of Cork tourism along with representatives from the press be invited to inspect it. The board agreed to provide a special train to Bantry and back and to contribute half the cost of the refreshments. At the same time, Croker reported that excursions to the Old Head of Kinsale operated by a coachman, Patrick Galvin, were very unsatisfactory, it being agreed that a new contract be awarded to Robert Acton of Kinsale.

The GS&WR wrote in June 1915 advising that owing to the poor condition of the road between Kenmare and Killarney, the motor service for that portion of the journey would be discontinued and replaced by a rail service. About this time, the TDC went into liquidation, Crossley advising that the motor service between Killarney and Bantry would in future be worked under the title of the Cork & Kerry Coaching Co. Shortly afterwards however, correspondence was received from Mr D Telford, liquidator for the Syndicate, informing the board that the Cork & Kerry Co ceased running the coaches as from 30th June, and that he had disposed of the fleet to the GS&WR. Crossley bought back the coaches from the GS&WR in July and announced his intention to form

that the Syndicate had opened a coach route from Macroom to Glengarriff and Killarney, a move which led to a protest from the CB&SCR. In response, the Syndicate enquired whether the company would arrange a circular tour from Cork to Glengarriff, outwards via the CB&SCR and returning via the C&MDR. This proposed arrangement was declined by the company. Complaints against the Syndicate surfaced in July 1899 when a Mr Graham, owner of the Glebe Hotel in Killarney, stated that the

Syndicate's coachmen were blackmailing his guests by demanding a charge of 2s 6d for box seats, a similar complaint being made by the manager of the Southern Hotel in Kenmare. In response to a letter from the general manager, Mr F W Crossley, on behalf of the TDC, commented that a regular charge was now being levied, not to generate additional revenue for the Syndicate, but to prevent the old established custom on the part of drivers of demanding money from passengers using these seats. He pro-a limited company and work the route himself. A board minute of 19th February 1920 confirms that Crossley was still operating the service at that time.

Post Office mail services

Hardly was the line open but Colonel Chatterton had an interview with Lord Hardwicke in April 1852 in relation to transferring the Post Office mails to the railway, a list of proposed charges being put forward. However the postal authorities considered the volume of letters between Cork and Bandon would not justify the expense involved. Lord Bernard wrote a year later enquiring whether any further approaches had been made to the Post Office, and it was agreed to send a deputation, to include His Lordship. Nothing appears to have arisen from this and, following suggestions in October 1854, an offer was made in December on the basis of £60 per annum for one day mail to be conveyed from Cork to Bandon by ordinary trains on weekdays only, £100 extra for one mail in each direction. In view of the low remuneration sought, the company were to be held free from any liability in respect of the mails. Regret was expressed by the directors that what was considered, 'the very liberal terms proposed', had been declined. A counter-offer of £40 for one day mail in the down direction was declined.

Finally, in February 1857, the secretary submitted a set of Post Office Regulations for the proposed conveyance of the mails. One of the proposals was for the running of a night mail between Cork and Bandon, but it was considered dangerous as the postal authorities required the journey (of twenty miles) to be completed in an hour. They also considered that the proposed starting time of the evening train from Cork should be deferred from 16.30 to 17.00. It appeared to them that the authorities should not have any objections as the mails conveyed by this train went no further than Bandon, 'and ample time is afforded after delivery in that town for parties to answer their letters, if necessary per the 8.40pm up train'. This comment gives an interesting insight into the public's writing habits in the mid-nineteenth century.

The locomotive superintendent raised another important matter, namely the necessity to have two drivers permanently engaged for the mail trains, leaving, 'only one man in the Shop for the repairs of all engines'; this indicated that drivers carried out repairs at this time. It was suggested that an engine fitter be engaged, who would be available in emergencies and in the event of staff leaving. Paterson also recommended the system of having an apprentice in the Works, which would be beneficial to the company's interests.

Although we have no details, an agree-

(7)

Table No. 6. Clonakilty to Clonakilty Junc.

Distance from Clonakilty.	STATIONS.	WEEK DAYS.					SUNDAY.		
		43	44	45	46 Day Mail. Pass.	47	48	49	50
		Mixed.	Goods.	Goods		Mixed.	Pass.	Pass.	Pass.
MILES.		A.M.	A.M.	A.M.	P.M.	P.M.	A.M.	P.M.	P.M.
	CLONAKILTY dep.	8 15	8 30	10 55	12 55	4 0	8 35	8 0	..
3¾	BALLINASCARTHY arr.	8 27	8 42	11 7	1 5	4 12	8 45	8 10	..
	Do. dep.	8 29	8 47	11 15	1 6	4 14	8 46	8 11	..
9	CLONAKILTY Junc. arr.	8 43	9 5	11 33	1 20	4 29	9 1	8 26	..

Table No. 7. Drimoleague to Bantry.

Distance from Drimoleague	STATIONS.	WEEK DAYS.					SUNDAY.	
		51 Nt. Mail Pass.	52 Pass.	53 Day Mail.	54 Pass.	55 Goods	56 Nt. Mail Pass.	57 Pass.
MILES.		A.M.	A.M	A.M.	P.M.	P.M.	A.M.	A.M.
	CORK dep.	3 30	8 50	11 20	4 0	5 50	3 30	10 30
	DRIMOLEAGUE dep.	5 26	10 53	1 17	6 3	9 16	5 26	12 30
6½	DURRUS ROAD arr.	..	11 10	a	6 18	..	..	12 46
	Do. dep.	5 41	11 11	1 32	6 19	9 30	5 41	12 47
12½	BANTRY arr.	6 2	11 31	1 52	6 39	10 0	6 2	1 7

Table No. 8. Bantry to Drimoleague.

Distance from Bantry.	STATIONS.	WEEK DAYS.					SUNDAYS.	
		58 Pass.	59 Goods.	60 Day Mail. Pass.	61 Mixed.	62 Night Mail. Pass.	63 Pass.	64 Night Mail. Pass.
MILES.		A.M.	A.M.	NOON.	P.M.	P.M.	A.M.	P.M.
	BANTRY dep.	7 12	10 0	12 0	2 55	7 10	7 35	7 0
5¾	DURRUS ROAD arr.	7 27	10 20	a	3 11	7 26	7 50	7 18
	Do.	7 29	10 23	12 19	3 12	7 27	7 51	7 19
12¼	DRIMOLEAGUE arr.	*7 45	10 45†	12 32	3 29	7 43	8 8	7 32

† The 10.0 a.m. Goods crosses 8.50 Down Train at Drimoleague.
a Stops only to pick up Passengers.

ment was reached with the Post Office as it was ordered in May 1857 that the common seal be placed on the contract for the conveyance of the mails by rail to Bandon, Bantry and Skibbereen. On the same day it was reported that Charles Bianconi had, 'placed all the horses for the mail and Day cars from Bandon to Skibbereen'. In advising this, Bianconi also sought to have the 10.40 up from Bandon altered to depart at 11.10, it being resolved to see how the traffic manager might carry this into effect. Two

years later, Bianconi was awarded the contract for the Cork to Bandon service, the Bantry and Skibbereen mails being given to Thomas Marmion of Skibbereen. Bianconi complained in March 1860 that he was not receiving sufficient remuneration for the Bandon mails, the company declining to make any alterations in the existing contract.

In December 1860 it was announced that the Dublin to Cork mails had been accelerated so as to arrive in Cork at 14.00 daily, the

Bandon being requested to alter the departure time of their train to 14.55 so as to allow of passengers from Dublin making the connection and also allowing time for the sorting in Cork of the western mails. The C&BR agreed to alter their train to leave at 14.30, this being reluctantly agreed to by the postal authorities, this change taking effect as from 1st February 1861.

A new agreement was concluded with the Post Office in January 1864 allowing for an annual payment to the company of £1,350, an increase of £350 over the existing contract. The agreement was for three years and was in respect of mails to and from Bantry and Skibbereen by rail and car. The company agreed to give the use of all trains, the postal authorities exercising no control over these trains except for the night mails. The company were obliged in return to give 15 days notice of any alteration in the hours of working of trains.

A complaint was made in July 1864 of the late arrival at Bantry of the mail car, it being stated that the driver had fallen asleep on

the car between Drimoleague and Bantry. On enquiry, it transpired that the driver had been plied with alcoholic liquor by passengers. The Inspector of Mails sought the removal of the driver in question, instructions being issued to Marmion that he was not to be again employed on mail cars. Marmion's contract came up for renewal in May 1865, at which time the WCR had hoped to be in a position to open their line as far as Dunmanway. It was however agreed to retain Marmion's services for another 12 months, this being later extended to 24th February 1867. A further extension was then agreed and in fact a three year contract was entered into with him in April 1867. Under this new agreement, he agreed to convey the mails from Bandon to Bantry via Dunmanway for £300 per annum, and from Bandon to Skibbereen via Clonakilty for £200 a year. Marmion sought an increase for the Skibbereen and Bantry mails in 1870, this being declined. As a result, he announced that he was making arrangements to offer his business for sale. He was subsequently offered an additional £25 per annum, and we find him still horsing the mails in 1873.

In February 1868 the Inspector of Mails enquired whether the company might carry the Kinsale mails, this being declined as it might, 'hereafter be used as a precedent to the injury of the C&BR mail service'. It was agreed that the Kinsale mails would as from 16th March be carried by the 16.20 ex Cork in charge of the train guard as far as the Junction, being taken over from there by road.

In August 1881 the company agreed to convey the night mails to Skibbereen and Bantry, with general use of all trains, for £1,500 per annum. In January 1885 a deputation waited on the board relative to the running of additional trains so that the midday mails might reach Skibbereen and western districts in sufficient time to enable letters to be replied to by the evening up mail. In response, the deputation were informed that the company had made a 'very liberal offer for the extra service required', but the Post Office had declined this. The question of additional services was raised in the mid-1890s, the Postmaster General declining to give any subsidy for these. The latter agreed in October 1895 to the payment of an additional £500 per annum for an additional mail service.

Various meetings between the directors and the postal authorities in 1900/1 led to a new five year agreement under which the company received an annual sum of £5,500 for the carriage of the mails, by ordinary as well as mail trains. This represented an increase of almost £2,000 per annum over the old contract. A further £50 a year was later included for the mail service between Skibbereen and Baltimore. Increases in the cost of coal and other materials during the war years led to six months notice being given in May 1916 to terminate the contract. This in effect brought to an end the running of the night mail train from Albert Quay, an institution which had been in operation for many years.

Baltimore station with C207 on a Drimoleague train on 15th September 1960. The single passenger platform was on the down side, opposite which was a one-time goods store and loading bank. The extreme right-hand line continued on to serve Baltimore Pier. Roger Joanes

Chapter Twelve

ACCIDENTS

Generally speaking, the Bandon suffered few serious accidents, more, as Colonel Rich was later to say, due to good fortune and the calibre of the permanent way staff and drivers. Only four months after the line opened between Bandon and Cork a Mr Tresilian claimed for alleged injury received while travelling on the line. With a view to finalising the matter, the company offered Tresilian an amount of 25 guineas without prejudice. In due course Tresilian accepted a sum of £100, having in the interim threatened to bring the matter to court.

An accident of a different nature occurred at Ballinhassig on Saturday 17th June 1854 when the 12.30 down train from Cork was wrongly diverted into a siding, coming into collision with three wagons. In this instance, Driver Anthony Guest, who we have already come across, by then the company's senior driver, stated that he had shut off steam at the top of the incline and was approaching the station at a slow pace perfectly prepared to stop if required. As he entered the station he found the signal all clear but noticed at the last moment that the points were set for the siding. Guest advised that there was nothing further he could do to stop in the short distance at his disposal, and that he and his fireman jumped off the engine just before the collision. None of the passengers were injured. It transpired that the pointsman, referred to as the policeman, had incorrectly set the points, giving as his excuse that he was engaged at the time in other duties about the station and he had had to run to the points on the train's approach. The committee found the driver blameless, the sole cause of the accident being the carelessness of the pointsman. This latter, who had given faithful service for five years, was ordered to be removed from Ballinhassig to, 'some other part of the line and a less responsible position'.

Ballinhassig was the scene of another accident on 10th March of the following year. The guard of the 16.10 down train reported that before leaving the station, he had satisfied himself that the doors of the carriages were all closed. On reaching Upton however, the porter there called his attention to the fact that one of the carriage doors was open. Some three hours later a message was received that the body of a Mr Allen was found on the track about a quarter of a mile from the station. It transpired that Allen was in possession of a Kinsale ticket. Most likely he realised that he should have detrained at Ballinhassig to take the coach and, realising his mistake, had endeavoured to leave the train whilst in motion. A claim was later lodged by his widow, but, as the Coroner's Jury had exonerated the company, liability was declined. Later, when the case seemed likely to go to trial, an offer of £90 was made and accepted.

Yet another accident occurred at Ballinhassig on 8th June 1872 when the 16.45 down to Kinsale ran into the rear of a preceding goods train. On investigation, it was found that it had been the custom for some time past to allow a goods train to leave Cork shortly before the departure of the 16.45. On arrival at Waterfall, both trains were normally held in the siding to allow the 16.20 up to go through. The stationmaster at Waterfall then despatched the goods, which stopped to discharge goods at Ballinhassig. On the evening in question, the passenger train left Waterfall only six or seven minutes behind the goods, neither the driver or the guard having been informed of the latter's proposed stop only three miles up the line. The normal course of action should have been to give precedence to the passenger train from Cork; apart from this, there was insufficient time allowance between the running of the two trains.

Problems at Cork

A report from the stationmaster in Cork in August 1871 highlighted a serious situation in regard to the use of the station by C&MDR trains. On the evening of Monday 14th August, a C&MDR special cattle train passed through the Cork distant signal at danger and collided with a shunting engine. It was also reported that a Macroom passenger train had gone through the same signal shortly before this accident, narrowly escaping a potentially more serious collision. On the matter being raised with the C&MDR, what was described as a most unsatisfactory reply was received from their manager. The board suggested that the two Macroom dri-

vers should be prosecuted for their violation of the signal rules, and that that company be charged with the cost of repairs to engine No 5. The account in the latter regard was duly returned along with a set of printed signalling instructions, the C&MDR placing the blame on the, 'unwarrantable conduct of the C&B Company's Engine Driver'. This latter was in fact Anthony Guest, the company's senior driver with 22 years service.

The C&MDR correspondence was forwarded to the board in Dublin, to prevent, if possible, 'the systematic persecution to which the Company's officials are so constantly subjected by a succession of frivolous and vexatious annoyances and unfounded complaints calculated to harass and annoy them in the discharge of their severe and onerous duties'. Following a meeting with two of the Macroom directors, some measure of agreement was achieved.

Adding insult to injury!

The traffic manager reported that on the night of Friday 15th August 1862, during shunting operations involving the 20.35 mail train, a young lad trespassing on the line about 100ft from the passenger platform at Cork was run over and seriously injured. He was immediately removed to the South Infirmary but he died some two hours later. A letter was received early in September from Mr McCarthy Downing applying on the part of the boy's father, Denis Sullivan of Skibbereen, for compensation. He was informed that the accident had occurred through no fault or want of care on the part of the company as the boy had been trespassing at the time. However the directors announced that they would themselves give a sum of £5 as charity towards any expense the father might have incurred. This drew the response that the offer was considered as adding insult to injury and they now increased their offer to £10. McCarthy Downing responded by stating that Sullivan was not prepared to accept this sum as a charity and sought a figure of £50. The directors stuck to their offer, which was finally accepted in July 1863.

An unusual accident occurred near Bandon on 11th November 1863. As the 02.25 down mail train was approaching, it collided with two wagons near Mr Shaw's flax mills about a quarter of a mile from the station, breaking the buffer beam of the engine. There were no passengers on the train at the time. The committee were of opinion that the accident was due to the wagons being blown off the siding on to the mainline owing to a violent storm. Conran was requested to take precautions to prevent a recurrence, by placing, 'choke blocks and lock', on the various sidings. There is no other record of a siding at this location so it would appear to have been shortlived.

A similar accident occurred some six years later adjacent to Chetwynd Viaduct when the 15.00 down train struck a wagon blown from a siding at Waterfall. On this occasion, the engine and a wagon were derailed, no injuries being initially reported to passengers. The driver was, yet again, Anthony Guest, who was awarded a gratuity of £10 and his fireman £3 10s 0d for their conduct in clearing the line promptly so as not to disrupt traffic unduly. Later, a Mr Patrick Gibson of Leeds complained of receiving severe concussion of the spine, the claim being referred to solicitors. A separate claim, for £90, was also lodged by a group of fish salesmen for loss of sale of fish attributed to the delay to the train, both claims being repudiated.

A potentially more serious accident occurred on 22nd June 1864 when the 09.00 train, consisting of an engine and tender, three carriages, a horsebox and two wagons, was completely derailed just beyond the mp8¼. The accident was caused by, 'one of the key joints being nearly out'. Luckily, none of the passengers or crew were injured. Seven rails were reported to be much bent and 24 chairs broken. The matter does not appear to have come to the attention of the BoT, the local committee investigating the accident. Conran was of opinion that Permanent Way Ganger Desmond was solely responsible for the accident, as he had failed to adequately examine the rail fastenings before each train passed. It was therefore decided to summarily dismiss Desmond.

A collision at Waterfall on 3rd November 1871 resulted in slight injuries to five or six passengers. The 17.45 down passenger train from Cork was delayed in departing, not getting away until 18.05, the delay being attributed to the late arrival of a train from Kinsale. The train in question consisted of an engine and tender, a composite, a third, a brake van, a carriage truck, seven laden wagons and a goods brake van. The train was assisted out of Cork by a banking engine at the rear. On approaching Waterfall station, the driver of the train engine shut off steam, but found that he required a little more steam to reach the station. It would appear that the driver of the assisting engine may not have shut off power, thereby causing some of the wagons, which were only

attached by means of a centre chain coupling, to become detached from the remainder of the train. The driver of the latter engine stated that after shutting off steam, his engine had fallen back and that at no time had he made further contact with the train. It was assumed that when the first portion of the train stopped at the platform, the errant wagons ran into it.

Colonel Rich was of opinion that the driver of the second engine kept steam on after the train engine had been shut off, thus slackening the couplings. Rich commented that the practice of sending a loose engine up behind a passenger train was objectionable and he felt that the goods wagons should have been separately worked to Waterfall. In the event, the board issued an instruction, forbidding the practice of sending an engine behind a passenger train. Rich also suggested that a distant signal and a second platform should be provided at Waterfall, and at all other stations where trains were scheduled to cross. Finally, he mentioned the desirability of fitting carriages and wagons with side chains in addition to centre couplings. This accident resulted in a number of claims being pursued against the company, a Daniel McSwiney alone claiming a sum of £2,000 for alleged spinal injuries; he subsequently accepted a figure of £300 plus costs.

Nervous passengers

The C&BR appears to have suffered a number of incidents involving passengers jumping or falling out of trains while on the move. One such incident occurred in December 1853 when a Mr Keen was reported to have fallen out of a carriage, no further details being given. Another passenger jumped out of the evening train on 10th March 1855, compensation being sought by his widow. This matter dragged on until August of the following year, when it was reported that an award of £90 had been made, despite the fact that the company were exonerated from blame. Whilst Counsel advised the company to appeal the case, the directors, probably wisely, decided to pay the amount in question.

On the evening of St Patrick's Day 1885, as the 20.30 up train from Bandon was midway between the latter point and Innoshannon, two men, John Finn and William Mahony, jumped from a third class carriage and were fatally injured. In this instance, it appeared that a row had broken out in the compartment, one of their companions having produced a knife. The BoT, probably jumping to the conclusion that the men were celebrating the national holiday, intimated that the company should not permit drunken men to travel on their line. The BoT were quickly informed that the men killed were not drunk, a fact confirmed by the Coroner.

It was decided in June 1887 to pursue a prosecution against two passengers, Messrs Deasy and Murray, who had jumped out of a train at Waterfall on the night of 29th May. They had approached the guard of the train while it was stopped at Ballinhassig, requesting that it be stopped for them at Waterfall, which he refused to do. When the train slowed there to exchange the staff, both men jumped off. The matter was discussed at the board meeting on 8th June, when it was reported that Deasy had disclaimed all knowledge of the case against him. This was despite the fact that his mother had already paid costs and had given a written undertaking that the offence would not be repeated.

A passenger returning from a football match in Clonakilty fell out of the 17.30 train near Manch Bridge on 3rd September 1904. The matter was reported as soon as the train reached its next stop at Dunmanway and a search was immediately made along the line. No body was found. Later however, it was discovered that the passenger in question had made his way home, where he was found singing in bed. It is reasonable to infer from this that alcohol may have played a part in this incident! The gentleman complained, hardly surprisingly, that his neck, shoulder and arms were very sore. He stated that he had been standing in the compartment with his back to the door. The Ballineen stationmaster confirmed that all door handles were turned when the train left his station, and it was probable therefore that the passenger had turned the handle himself.

The last of this type of accidents occurred on the evening of 5th October 1918 when the 17.15 down train stopped at Milleenarrig Bridge to drop off rations for the military guard on the bridge. A passenger, a Mr Cornelius Lynch, probably believing he had arrived at Dunmanway, opened the door of the compartment and fell into the Bandon River, which was in heavy flood at the time. Despite a thorough search of the river, no trace of him was found.

An accident of a slightly different nature occurred near Bandon on 7th October 1891. In this instance, a bull jumped out of a wagon, fell between it and a wall, derailing a total of eleven wagons. Sixteen head of cattle were killed and some of the drovers who were travelling on the train complained of being injured. The cost of repairs to the rolling stock, which included three T&CELR vehicles, amounted to about £300.

Axles rails and runaways

On the evening of 6th August 1870, the 17.50 down train for Bandon left Albert Quay about five minutes late. The train consisted of 2-2-2 tender engine No 3 of 1849, two composites and one third class carriage plus a brake van. As it approached Crossbarry level crossing, the rear axle of the tender broke on the inside of the journal, the tender tank came down on the broken axle, lifting the offside front wheel off the rails and causing the front axle to derail. This was the only vehicle to leave the rails and there were no injuries to passengers or crew. Colonel Rich in due course inspected the offending axle and expressed his surprise that such an amount of work could be obtained from so flawed a piece of metal. The axle in question had been running for 21 years, and, at the time of the accident, as little as one-eighth of an inch of metal remained sound. He went on to say that it afforded a strong example of the necessity for testing axles as, had this been done before being put into service, it must surely have given way. Aside from the damaged axle, Rich had some scathing remarks to make regarding the permanent way and the fencing.

Another accident occurred on the Kinsale branch on the afternoon of 19th March 1888, when a portion of the 15.05 up from Kinsale was derailed at a point known as Fooreen or Roberts' Bridge, about 2½ miles north of Ballymartle station and 1½ miles from Kinsale Junction. Injuries were sustained by four passengers, the engine crew and a permanent way inspector travelling on the engine at the time; none of these were serious.

The train, made up of a composite, a third, a brake van and a covered goods wagon, was hauled by 0-6-0T No 15, one of the two engines purchased second-hand from the Londonderry & Lough Swilly Railway just under three years previously. The train had departed Kinsale on time and had made scheduled stops at Farrangalway and Ballymartle. It was running at about 24mph on a falling gradient of 1 in 80 on a curve of about twelve chains radius when the engine left the rails without prior warning on the outside of the curve. It ran off to the right up the steep side of the cutting and fell back upside down across the rails, coming to rest about thirty-four yards from the point of derailment. The two carriages followed the engine, the composite (No 9) lying partly across the rails and partly on top of the engine, third No 4 falling across the line. The brake van and the leading wheels of the wagon were also derailed, although both remained upright.

Colonel Rich was sent over by the BoT to investigate the accident. Driver Abraham Harris, who suffered knee and shoulder contusions and bruising, reported that he heard a loud crack just as the engine derailed, this being confirmed by Fireman Jeremiah Carroll and Inspector James Long. Both Carroll and Long received minor head injuries and burning to their hands. Long, in evidence to Colonel Rich, stated that he had walked the part of the line in question within the previous ten or 12 days, finding nothing amiss. The rails here had been renewed about five years previous to the accident, while some new ballast had been added about nine months previously. Edward Murphy, the ganger for the length involved, stated that he had walked his length at six o'clock that morning and was within about six rail lengths of where the accident happened.

It was clear that a Vignoles pattern rail, 27 feet in length and weighing 68lbs per yard, had fractured as the engine passed over it. This rail had been supplied new in 1881 by the Rhymney Iron Co and was very little worn. It had broken in two pieces near the middle, the fracture being nearly vertical. A piece about 2½in long, 1½in wide and 1in deep had been chipped out of the rail top on the inside. The fracture indicated that the metal was hard and close grained. Colonel Rich's only recommendation was that the company keep more ballast on the outside of this type of rail, which would assist in strengthening the road.

As reported above, four passengers were injured, none seriously. The secretary was directed to write to Mrs Roberts thanking her for her kindness to the passengers and her attention to those injured. Arising from this accident, Mr Pike suggested that the company should place a certain sum every half year to the credit of an accident account to meet future liabilities. The company endeavoured unsuccessfully to claim compensation from the Rhymney Iron Co.

Another accident occurred on the Kinsale branch on 17th May 1892 when engine No 13 hit the buffer stops at Kinsale station. There is no reference to a train involved so it may well have been a light engine movement. In any event, it was reported that the engine was running in reverse and had no sandboxes on the rear wheels. It was ordered that the turntable at the Junction be put into repair and that sandboxes be fitted to the rear wheels of this engine.

Permanent Way Inspector James Long came to the attention of the board again early in 1895. The second ballast train was working at Kinsale Junction on 16th February when two wagons, left on the mainline for filling, were struck by the train during a shunting movement and ran away about half a mile into the section towards Upton. Kerr considered Long principally to blame as he was in charge of the train. His pay was reduced by 5s per week for a period of six months.

Flooding
Serious flooding of the line about a mile and a quarter to the east of Bandon led to the derailment of the 08.45 down passenger train on the morning of 16th January 1873. The train, consisting of a tender engine, brake van, a composite and a third, in that order, had departed Cork some fifteen minutes late due to the late arrival of an up train. In his evidence, the driver stated that he did not see the flooding until he was about thirty yards from it. As he could see that the line was dry a little further on, he decided to continue at slow speed, not realising that the ground beneath the track had been washed away. The line had earlier been walked in both directions by the milesman, who saw nothing untoward. The immediate cause of the derailment was the sudden bursting of its banks and the carrying away of an embankment by the Bandon River. The engine, tender, guard's van and composite carriage were all derailed. Two rails penetrated the carriage, causing serious injuries to some of the occupants.

Colonel Rich, who investigated the matter on behalf of the BoT, discovered that at the time of the accident, all the doors of the carriages were locked, and furthermore that the majority of the Bandon carriages were not fitted with steps. It was to be almost two and a half hours before the passengers were released and taken to Bandon. The guard was injured in the derailment and it took him about 15 minutes to get out of his van, whilst the fireman was busily engaged in drawing the fire. In the interim, the driver and the traffic manager, Richard Coghlan, who happened to be travelling on the train, made their way to Bandon station. However, finding the telegraph out of order, Coghlan decided to engage a car to take him back to Cork to summon assistance. This was in time to lead to Coghlan's premature retirement due to ill-health. Whilst no neglect was obviously intended, Rich criticised Coghlan's action, feeling that he should have remained to take charge and sent a messenger to Cork. He also commented on the inadequacy of the permanent way staff. Rich also recommended the improvement of the company's permanent way and that carriage doors should not in future be locked on both sides. Finally, he called for the fitting of steps to all carriages.

It must be unusual for a BoT inspector to find himself involved in an accident, but that is exactly what happened to Genneral Hutchinson on the afternoon of 29th June 1886. On that morning a special train had been laid on for a BoT inspection of the Clonakilty branch. In accordance with normal regulations, as the special proceeded through Ballinhassig tunnel, it was preceded by a watchman with a red lamp. It is not clear whether Thomas Sheehan fell or lost his footing, but he was struck by the engine and killed. The subsequent inquest found the company to be in no way liable, but the board decided, in view of Sheehan's long service, to grant his widow a gratuity of £20. Sheehan was in fact the second tunnel man to be fatally injured on the Bandon, as James Turner died in similar circumstances at Goggins Hill tunnel on 14th December 1867.

if necessary bringing someone from Dublin. In due course, Shea accepted a sum of £600 plus £100 expenses. This contrasted sharply with the allowances made to the two foot-plate men's families. Mary Kiely, widow of the driver was initially granted a weekly allowance of 7s.6d, and Twomey's father 5s, 'for the present'. In February 1888, the Rev L Cummins of Dunmanway wrote on behalf of Mrs. Kiely seeking a lump sum, 'to enable her to start in some business'. In the following June the weekly payments were stopped and she was offered a gratuity of £20, this being later increased to £50. Mrs Kiely declined to accept this figure, no further mention of her claim being made in the minutes.

An approach was made in June 1888 asking that Twomey be removed from Bantry to a hospital in Cork, Johnstone advising that a van would be required to be fitted up with a suspended bed. This was done in July. Johnstone also suggested that the allowance of 3s per week, previously paid to the nurses in Bantry, should be paid to Twomey's father in addition to the 5s already being granted. In due course, the total figure was increased to 15s per week, repeated requests for a further increase being declined. The company also paid a sum of £26 11s 4d to Bantry Union for the 54 weeks of Twomey's stay there. James Twomey died on 13th October 1900, following which his mother sought a grant. The family had been in receipt of a pension since the accident had occurred some thirteen years earlier. The board nevertheless agreed to grant a figure of £2 towards the funeral expenses.

Arising from the accident at Bantry, the manager suggested in June 1888 that in future all trains arriving at Bantry should stop before reaching the first facing points and not proceed to the platform until signalled. This suggestion was approved by the board, the engineer being requested to prepare the necessary plan and estimate for a trap siding.

Kinsale runaway
The most spectacular accident on the CB&SCR occurred on the cold but damp morning of 28th January 1915 when a special goods train from Cork came into collision with the 08.30 up mixed train standing at the platform at Kinsale station. This resulted in the deaths of two passengers on the latter train. The goods train had been running on a fairly regular basis for the previous three weeks, bringing materials in

On this occasion, Turner's widow was given a sum of £10. Following a request for a weekly allowance of 6s, in addition to the gratuity, the board agreed to give another £10 as a lump sum.

Runaway at Bantry
On the morning of Thursday 7th July 1887 the down night mail left Cork at 03.00. On board were Driver Patrick Kiely, aged 26, Fireman James Twomey and Guard James Galvin. Also travelling on the train that night was a Captain John Shea (in some references shown as O'Shea), late of the *Augusta*. The train consisted of ex-WCR 2-4-0ST No 11 hauling a composite saloon carriage, a composite van and eight loaded wagons. It would appear that the train approached Bantry (hilltop) station on time at about 05.50, but rather faster than was normal. The line fell on a gradient of 1 in 80 for almost four miles towards Bantry, only levelling out about half a mile short of the station. No 11, which was only a few months out of shops after a thorough overhaul, failed to stop at the normal point on the platform, ran across a turntable and struck the buffer stops. At this point, the line was on a six foot high embankment over which the locomotive fell, bringing with it the carriage, van and three of the wagons.

Kiely and Twomey were both thrown clear, although sustaining serious injuries. Kiely was badly burned and had suffered severe head and facial injuries to which he succumbed on the following day. The fireman suffered a fractured spine and ribs and also developed slight paralysis. Galvin was thrown against the brake wheel in the van, resulting in chest injuries. The *Cork Constitution* reported that Captain Shea complained of having received, 'a great shock

and some slight injury to his back', being removed to Vickery's Hotel in the town for treatment. The crew members were removed to Bantry Workhouse hospital, being too seriously injured to be transferred to Cork.

Details of the accident were immediately telegraphed to Cork, a special train being laid on to bring Gordon and Johnstone, along with two Cork doctors and some permanent way men and the necessary equipment to effect repairs. Johnstone reported that injuries to the engine consisted of damage to the water tank, cab, coal bunker, dome and chimney, due in the main to the carriage landing on top of it. Johnstone later informed the board that replacement parts for No 11 had cost a sum of £52. He also reported that the carriage was, 'very much shaken, the composite van not so badly'.

General Hutchinson investigated on behalf of the BoT and reported that the driver had reversed the engine when passing the Bantry distant signal, at the same time applying sand. Despite these measures, the train struck the buffer stop, situated some sixty yards beyond the normal stopping place, at a speed of about 10mph. The night watchman and the mail car driver, who were both standing on the platform awaiting the train's arrival, testified of hearing the engine's whistle being continuously sounded as it approached. All three of the crew were sober at the time of the accident, which was attributed to excessive speed on the approach.

Shea, who returned to Cork in August, later claimed an amount of £1,250 plus legal and medical expenses as compensation for his injuries. Reporting in March 1888, Mr Wright, QC, suggested that a specialist should be retained to examine Shea's eyes,

connection with the construction of huts at Fort Charles. On the morning in question, the train departed Cork at 06.40 with Driver Thomas Tyner, Fireman Bartholomew Gallagher and Guard Timothy Daly. The train of nineteen laden and two empty wagons was hauled by 0-6-0ST No 6 and weighed 206½ tons, just within the load allowed to this engine on a Kinsale line train.

The train appears to have run as normal, stopping only at Kinsale Junction and Farrangalway. In his evidence to the BoT inspector, Tyner stated that he approached the Kinsale distant signal at a speed of about 4mph, but despite applying his handbrake at this point, the locomotive began to skid and, despite reversing his engine, the train failed to slow appreciably and came into contact with the passenger train standing at the platform. This latter train was hauled by 4-4-0T No 7 and consisted of a composite van, a first, a third, and four covered vans. The rear vehicle was standing against the buffer stops and when the goods train collided with No 7, covered van No 67 reared up, telescoping the third and destroying two compartments. Realising that a collision was inevitable, Driver Patrick Walsh warned as many passengers as possible. Most had exited the train just prior to the collision. Unfortunately, Miss Ellen (also shown as Hannah) Lewis, aged 35 of Cappagh, Kinsale, and Mrs. Mary Hurley, 40 of Killener, Enniskeane, who were in the rear compartment of the third class carriage were killed. Six other passengers were injured, none seriously.

An inquest was held at Kinsale Courthouse on the following day, the Coroner, John J Horgan, presiding. The coroner stated that the CB&SCR was a well-managed concern under its general manager, John Kerr, and this was a deplorable accident. After hearing the evidence, the jury returned a verdict of accidental death due to the main platform line being open and the weight of the goods train excessive. They added a rider that it was desirable that a man should be in the signal cabin when trains were arriving.

Colonel P G von Donop was duly instructed to investigate on behalf of the BoT, his report being issued on 22nd February. There was no dispute that both the distant and home signals at Kinsale were at danger as the goods train approached, and that the points were set for the platform line rather than the goods yard. The driver admitted that he saw adverse signals, but he was simply unable to stop the train in time due to greasy rails. Colonel Von Donop could only conclude that this resulted from either want of care or want of skill on the part of the footplate crew. He did however suggest that a heavier brakevan be in future used on such trains. The van in use at the time of the accident was of only 7½ tons capacity. He criti-

cised the setting of the points, the front of the passenger train being situated only 160 yards from the down home signal. Furthermore, the goods train had been accepted at 'line clear' in contravention of normal block working arrangements. Even worse, the goods had been accepted from Kinsale Junction at 07.15, yet the stock for the passenger train was being marshalled only ten minutes before the arrival of the former. The operation of the signal cabin also came in for some criticism, the regular signalman not being on duty on the morning of the collision.

The BoT were duly informed in April that steps had been taken to enforce stricter observance of block working regulations and to replace all light brakevans with ten-ton vans. At the same time, it was decided to severely caution the parties involved in the accident, but not to take any further measures against them. In August 1915 an approach was made seeking compensation for Miss Lewis' sister, this being declined.

Staff fatalities

As recorded above, the Bandon were lucky as regards fatal accidents to passengers. They did however suffer the normal spate of accidents involving staff. One such occurred in February 1909. In the course of shunting operations in Cork yard on the night of 1st February, Driver J Robinson, in charge of a tank engine, entered the coal siding to remove four wagons. Having coupled up to these, he requested his fireman, 23 year old Michael McKeown, to release the handbrake. As he started, Robinson heard a shout from McKeown. On stopping the engine and looking out on the fireman's side of the engine, he found the fireman jammed between it and a wall. McKeown later died of his injuries in the South Infirmary. A verdict of misadventure was brought in, with no responsibility resting either with the company or the driver.

The crossing keeper at Ballyboy crossing, near Dunmanway, one D Crowley, was fatally injured after being struck by a special train on the night of Christmas Eve 1911. This was in fact the second such accident to occur at Ballyboy, Gatekeeper Mary Sheehan having been struck by a cattle special in April 1881. Both accidents occurred when the drivers ran through signals. In Mary Sheehan's case, the preceding train was not displaying a board at the rear to indicate a following special, whereas in Crowley's case, his widow admitted that they had not in fact checked to see whether or not the previous train carried a board. They had both wrongly assumed, possibly because it was Christmas Eve, that it was the last train to run, and they had closed the gates and removed the lamp from the signal post. Just as Crowley was retiring to rest, a whistle was heard and he ran to open the gates. He had

succeeded in getting one of these open, but, as he opened the second, he was struck by the train and killed.

In his evidence, the driver of the special stated that he had whistled for the crossing when he was some distance off and had shut off steam. His fireman said he could see a green light and informed his driver accordingly. The latter, without checking himself, opened the regulator and struck the gates shortly afterwards. The BoT officer, John Main, said he could not rely on the fireman's evidence; furthermore, if the driver was unsure of the position of the gates, he should have stopped short of them. That said, the accident was primarily caused by Crowley and his wife not checking the previous train. It was also clear that the gatekeeper was not in possession of a rule book, and it was urged that all gatekeepers should receive copies. Lastly, instructions should be issued that signal lamps should not be extinguished until broad daylight.

The last of our series of accidents to staff occurred at Clonakilty on the night of 16th January 1914, in the course of a shunting operation. The shunting was taking place under the direction of Porter F O'Regan. Having drawn two empty carriages, a brake van and a wagon out of the carriage siding on to the mainline, O'Regan uncoupled the engine and got into the brakevan to control the vehicles as they ran down a falling gradient to the passenger platform. Just prior to doing this, Porter Timothy Donovan had enquired where the wagon was going, to which O'Regan replied, 'it is all right'; despite this, Donovan appears to have uncoupled the wagon. As he was stepping back out of the way, he seems to have slipped, his right foot falling down between the running rail and the blade of the points.

Donovan was found lying about eight yards from his boot, and such were his injuries that death must have been instantaneous. The signalman, John Driscoll, confirmed he had heard the conversation between the two men and also saw the wagons running separately. Donovan had no right to become involved in the shunting movement, and his death was certainly caused by this neglect of duty. The BoT suggested that sufficient light be provided for after-dark shunting operations to clearly expose the fouling points.

Chapter Thirteen

LOCOMOTIVES

Locomotive acquisition on the Bandon can be divided roughly into three distinct phases. In the early years, new locomotives were purchased, most likely to manufacturers' designs with only outline specifications being laid down by the company's engineer and/or the board. During the second phase, corresponding largely to the chairmanship of Valentine O'Brien O'Connor, expenditure in all areas was held to a minimum. As related elsewhere, this was a period when the attention of the BoT had necessarily to be called to the affairs of the company. When, following often lengthy exhortations from the locomotive superintendent, it was reluctantly agreed to obtain additional motive power, the company purchased rundown engines secondhand from other companies. Most of these came from the GS&WR, of which O'Connor was also a director. Finally, following O'Connor's departure in 1873, the policy of buying new locomotives was reinstated. By the end of the company's independent existence, they were able to hand over to the GSR a fleet of 20 locomotives, only two of which were not considered worth overhauling, and scrapped in 1925 without receiving their new numbers. Two of the famous 'Bandon' 4-6-0 tanks in fact survived to be included amongst the final steam withdrawals by CIÉ in 1963, whilst another three had lasted until 1961. Before dealing with the locomotives themselves, we shall take a brief look at the various persons responsible for locomotive matters .

Locomotive superintendents

As was usual in the early days, matters relating to locomotives and rolling stock were dealt with by the company's engineer. We therefore find both Leahy and Nixon involved. John Barber was the company's first locomotive superintendent, remaining in that position until March 1855. He was replaced by John Paterson. In September 1856 Paterson informed the local committee that he had received an offer from a Russian railway company much more remunerative than his present post. He was prepared to remain provided his salary was increased. The board agreed to increase it from £2 12s 6d a week to £3, the salary previously paid to Barber. Paterson requested

leave of absence in December of that year, as he was reportedly recovering from a serious illness. In April 1857 however, he waited on the committee and informed them that he had received an appointment in Russia and would be leaving within three weeks. As his successor, he strongly recommended Thomas Conran, the senior fitter, as being fully competent to discharge the duties of locomotive superintendent. It was agreed to give Conran a month's trial at a salary of £2 3s 9d per week. In fact, Conran was ideally suited to the job and remained in charge for 30 years until his death in February 1887.

Conran was replaced by John J Johnstone, who had been the district superintendent at Bantry for some years. It seems likely, although there is no mention of the fact in the West Cork minute books, that J J Johnstone also looked after locomotive matters on the WCR. Johnstone's tenure was short as he died on Sunday 29th January 1888. His son, James W, who had served his apprenticeship as a fitter at the Inchicore works of the GS&WR and later at Messrs Dick Kerr & Co of Leeds, applied for the position but the board decided to advertise for a locomotive superintendent at a salary of £200 per annum, applications to be submitted by 15th February. Johnstone's application would also be considered along with any others received, but in the interim Maurice Reen, the Shop Foreman, was placed in charge. Reen later went on to become locomotive superintendent of the C&MDR.

After the various applications were considered at the meeting on 15th February, James W Johnstone was duly appointed at the salary named. He also served as engineer to the Schull & Skibbereen Tramway. So youthful looking was Johnstone junior that the board requested him to grow a beard so that he might command more respect amongst the locomotive department staff! He was to be the company's last locomotive superintendent, remaining in office until December 1924.

A cancelled order

The desirability of seeking contracts for locomotives and rolling stock was first considered by the directors at their meeting on 14th August 1845. The first order for locomotives was placed in October of that year

with Messrs Tayleur (later the Vulcan Foundry) of Newton-le-Willows. The design was believed to have been jointly prepared by Edmund Leahy and the contractors, four engines being ordered, three passenger and one goods. The passenger engines were apparently to have leading bogies and were probably to have been either of 4-2-0 or 4-4-0 wheel arrangement. The former was more likely as the Birmingham & Gloucester Railway, who appear to have influenced Leahy's thinking, used engines of this type. In any event, the 4-4-0 was not to be introduced into Britain for another 15 years and into Ireland for 32 years. All we know of the goods engine was that it was to be similar to the passenger engines, but without the leading bogie. On the other hand, Messrs Tayleur seem to have recommended to Leahy that the bogie arrangement should be abandoned and, as no alteration was proposed, perhaps they were originally to have been 4-4-0s. Leahy's patent drawing for the fireboxes appears to show a 2-2-4 type. We shall probably never know at this stage.

Leahy wrote to the board in February 1846 suggesting the addition of a partition in the firebox of each engine, thereby effecting a fuel economy and additional power. This was apparently but one of many ideas put forward by Leahy, who appears to have possessed an inventive frame of mind. The addition, which was estimated to cost an additional £90 for each engine, was accepted by the directors. Only a month later, Leahy wrote to Messrs Tayleur requesting them not to hasten with the construction of the engines as the line would not be ready for them. Also in February, following an inspection of the engines, Leahy waxed eloquent at the half-yearly meeting of shareholders when he reported that, 'they are executed in a most superior manner, so as to fully sustain the reputation of that establishment (Messrs Tayleur), not only in England, but in Europe. The workmanship and capabilities of these powerful engines surpass those of any locomotive yet constructed and induce the easy accomplishment of the highest speeds ever expected on the Cork & Bandon Railway or any other railway'. Praise indeed!

As reported elsewhere, Leahy was dismissed in July 1846 and was replaced by

Charles Nixon. With the line still not nearing completion, Nixon was instructed to write to the manufacturers in July asking them to suspend work. He in fact visited Newton-le-Willows in November and held discussions with a Mr Dobson. At this meeting, the question of dispensing with the bogie frames was raised, they being, 'both objectionable and expensive'. One bogie frame had already been completed and this was in due course shipped to Cork. It is not clear how far the construction work had gone, but the manufacturers agreed in December to accept the company's offer for cancelling the contract. It would seem that the materials already manufactured were used in the construction of some long-boilered 2-4-0 engines for the Eastern Counties Railway (Nos 172 to 181, maker's numbers 289-298). When Leahy sued the company in October 1847, J E McConnell of the L&NWR gave evidence to the effect that, having seen the drawings for the C&BR engines, they were an improvement on similar engines on the Birmingham & Gloucester Railway.

The Adams tanks

The board minutes would suggest that no further moves were made to obtain locomotives until January 1849. In that month, Nixon urged on the board small light-weight tank engines based on the patent combined locomotive and carriage designed by W Bridge Adams of the Fairfield Works at Bow in London. On 27th February 1849 Nixon made some journeys on Adams' first such engine, *Enfield*, on the Eastern Counties Railway (ECR). He reported that he had travelled a distance of 125 miles at speeds up to 50 miles per hour, 'with great steadiness', coke consumption being given as 10lbs per mile. The board agreed in March to the purchase of two of these locomotives and carriages, the latter with seating for 58 first and second class passengers.

Nos 1 and 2 differed from their ECR counterparts in that the engine and carriage portions were separate, and indeed a third carriage was soon ordered. The wheel arrangement was also altered from 2-2-0 to 0-2-2. These units were delivered from Bristol, having made the journey from London by rail, thus saving the C&BR £177 in freight charges. They were sandwich-framed engines with outside bearings to both axles. The firebox was semi-circular in plan and was surmounted by a plain cover on top of which was the safety valve. Water was carried in well tanks at either end of the frame. As was usual at this time, these engines had no cabs, the driver and fireman having to stand on a small space beside the rear water tank.

No 2 arrived in Cork on 16th July 1849, the first locomotive to be seen in the city, No 1 being delivered about a month later. No mention is made of how the engines were transported to Ballinhassig. They

appear to have given every satisfaction in service, the normal load consisting of two carriages, plus on occasions a horsebox and a carriage truck. By 1860 the two engines had become too small, by which time they also required boiler repairs. The locomotive superintendent therefore suggested their disposal and replacement by one passenger tank engine. They were still extant by August 1863 when it was decided to hold on to them, 'as they might answer for traffic on the Macroom Railway'. One was loaned to the WCR to enable their directors to go over and inspect their new line. One of them, probably No 1, was sold to the Cork Gas Company for £60 in December 1868. Both may in fact have gone to this source, where the driving wheels were reportedly used for a coke breaking mill.

For the next two engines, the company returned to Messrs Tayleur & Co. Type II, Nos 3 and 4 (maker's Nos 321/2) were delivered respectively in October 1849 and August 1851. They had outside sandwich frames and inside cylinders with outside valve chests and Stephenson gear. Both had water pumps worked from the inside eccentrics. The two engines were not identical. One of them had a luggage compartment on the tender, which was later removed. It is interesting to note that the diagram illustrating this compartment shows the gauge as 5ft, obviously an error on the part of the manufacturers. Referring to delays to trains in February 1852, the locomotive superintendent says these were due to the drivers not being acquainted with the gradients of the new line, rather than to the locomotives.

Following receipt of drawings from the MGWR, it was recommended that the fireboxes of engines be altered so as to use Scotch coal. No 3 having shown coal savings, it was ordered in August 1864 that all engines have their firebars altered accordingly. No 3 spent eight years in the shops, having repairs done only when the men were not otherwise engaged, the two engines being described as unfit for general use. She eventually returned to traffic in June 1882. The last report of her was in December 1890 when she broke a crank axle while shunting in Cork yard.

No 4 received a new copper firebox, brass tubes and new steel tyres in February 1874, at which time the two water pumps were replaced by injectors. She appears to have been loaned to the contractor for the IVR in May 1877, but had a defective axle three months later. She also was reported to be shunting Cork yard in June 1887, when it was recommended that she be stopped and replaced. She was sold to a Mr Younger in December 1888 for £125.

Sharps & a Fairbairn

Two engines were ordered from Messrs Sharp Bros, being delivered in September and October 1852 under Order No 254. They were shipped to Cork on the *Minerva*, one of the Cork Co's vessels. Nos 5 and 6 were 0-4-2 tender engines described as 'powerful goods engines'. No 5 was in trouble in February 1862 when she broke a crank pin on a passenger special in connection with Bandon Fair. This was believed to be due to defective manufacture, although it was admitted that it could not have been dis-

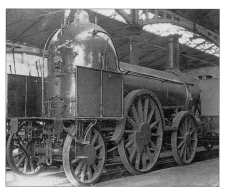

Right: **GS&WR 2-2-2 locomotive No 36 built by Messrs. Bury Curtis & Kennedy and similar in appearance to the C&BR engine purchased second-hand from the GS&WR in 1871.** Ian Allan Library

Below: **Ex GS&WR 0-4-2 locomotive No 101 originally from Messrs Bury Curtis & Kennedy and similar to C&BR No 8 purchased second-hand from the GS&WR in 1865.** Ian Allan Library

covered by inspection. She received a new firebox in July 1867 at a cost of £130, while in June 1871 it was reported that her cylinders were worn through. She was nevertheless still at work in a patched condition. A serious fault occurred in June 1887 when she failed on the 18.00 down at Waterfall due to the backplate of the firebox being forced off the stays, due it was believed to bad work done when the new firebox was fitted in 1867. By this time the boiler was twenty years old and it was not considered worth fitting a new firebox. She was in fact sold to Younger in December 1888 along with No 4.

No 6 received a new firebox in June 1866 at a cost of £132, new tubes being fitted four years later. It was initially decided in October 1876 to carry out extensive repairs to this engine, including new axleboxes and brasses as well as cylinders. There is no record of this work being done and it seems likely that it was decided not to proceed. No further mention is made of No 6, only BoT returns for 1879 indicating a drop of one in the stock.

The last new engine to be purchased for some years was Type IV, 0-4-0ST No 7, obtained from Messrs Fairbairn in March 1862 at a cost of £1,650. She appears to have been obtained specifically for the Kinsale branch, on which line she was working in March of the following year. It was reported

however that she had not done much work, and consideration was given to putting her on the mainline. Conran expressed the opinion that it would not be safe to do so and she remained on the branch subject to a speed limit of 15mph. Complaints came from the C&KJR board in July 1863 that she was defective, following which she was put on the mainline. By the end of July it was reported that she had only run 3,240 miles on the mainline and 939 on the branch since new. A complaint to Fairbairns elicited the reply that the engine was not designed for high speed and the fitting of a pair of hind wheels would probably solve the problems encountered.

The Vulcan Foundry, who had taken over drawings and patterns from Fairbairns, offered to supply a new axle, wheels and springs for a sum of £250 and she became an 0-4-2ST about this time, the exact date not being recorded. A new copper firebox was fitted in August 1873 along with a new steel crank axle. The purchase of 12 volute springs for No 7 in June 1874 proves that she was by now a six-wheeled engine. In addition, a reference to the breaking of a trailing axle in December 1875 and its replacement by a pair of wheels and an axle from an engine sold to Mr McSwiney (either Nos 1 or 8, probably the former) gives definite proof of the conversion. No 7 was put on shunting duties in March 1877 as she had

by now had several bad places on the boiler patched. She was however back on the Kinsale line in December 1881, the engineer considering her to be dangerous at this time due to lack of brake power and sanding.

It was decided to rebuild No 7 in 1889, new frameplates and wheels being ordered, the work being completed by May 1890. It is not clear whether she became an 0-4-4T or a 4-4-0T, Johnstone probably having a preference for the latter. If she did become a 4-4-0T, she probably also had the saddle tanks replaced by side tanks. The sale price of £70 would seem to indicate that little of the old No 7 was sold to Mr Jack in 1890.

Second-hand buys and a mystery engine

We now move into the second phase of locomotive development, namely the purchase of second-hand locomotives. As already alluded to O'Connor, the new chairman, was also a director of the GS&WR and he appears to have been of the opinion that money was saved by purchasing old locomotives from that company. The first of these engines was an 0-4-2 originally built by Bury Curtis & Kennedy in September 1846 and numbered 43 on the GS&WR. It was renumbered 102 in 1864 and was sold to the C&BR in December of the following year for £700, an enormous sum for such an old engine. This was particularly so as sister engine No 103 was purchased by the Athenry & Tuam Railway for £450, although admittedly five years later. It initially became C&BR No 8, being renumbered 1 in 1868 when the Adams engine of the same number was removed from stock.

No 1 was reported in May 1874 to be working but with the wheels very much in need of turning, a new set of tubes also being required. She was on the Kinsale branch in the following month with half of her tubes plugged, while in October she was described as being unfit for repair. No 1 was disposed of in November 1874.

The locomotive shown as Type VI, C&BR No 2 of 1867, is something of a mystery engine. Its existence cannot be absolutely proved, although the late Bob Clements was personally satisfied of its existance. What is more, if it did exist on the C&BR, we know absolutely nothing of its career on that line. What follows therefore is conjecture.

The Belfast & County Down Railway (B&CDR) purchased four 2-2-2 tender engines from Bury Curtis & Kennedy in 1848. One of these, No 4, was sold in March 1858 to Messrs Moore Bros in connection with their contract to construct the line from Comber to Downpatrick. It was last being recorded there in January 1860 when the B&CDR requested its removal. So far so good, but from here we enter the realms of speculation. It appears that this engine was most likely employed by Moore Bros on the Clonsilla to Navan contract early in 1861, on

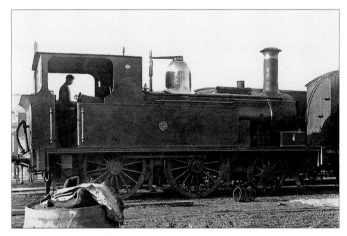

Left: **2-4-0T No 2 at Albert Quay, one of five engines from Messrs. Dübs & Co between 1874 and 1887. The boilers were similar to engines procured by the neighbouring C&MDR, differing only in having a dome with the Salter safety valves on the rear ring of the boiler. No 2 was rebuilt as a 4-4-0T in 1909 and was withdrawn in 1930 as GSR No 477 of class D18.**
Ian Allan Library

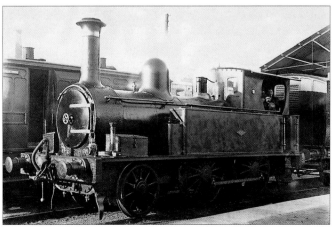

Left: **The first three Dübs 2-4-0Ts entered service in 1874, 1875 and 1877 respectively. No 8, seen here at Albert Quay, was supplied in 1877 and was withdrawn in 1920.**
Ian Allan Library

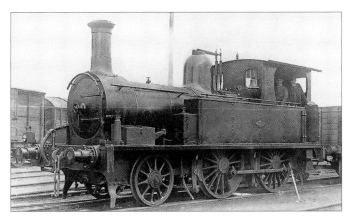

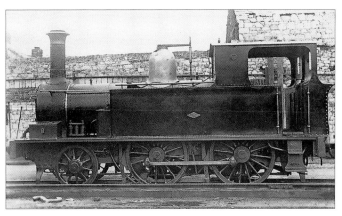

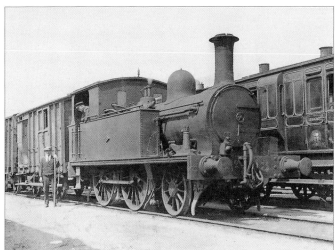

Above left: **Dübs 2-4-0T No 2 was built in 1875 and rebuilt in 1908 as a 4-4-0T. In this guise it became GSR No 477 in 1925 and lasted another five years being withdrawn in 1930.** Ian Allan Library

Above right: **The original Dübs 2-4-0T supplied in 1874 was not given its number, 1, until a year later. It became the company's third locomotive to bear this number. The first No 1, an Adams 0-2-2WT had lasted from 1849 to 1867. The second was an 0-4-2T purchased second hand from the G&SWR in 1865 which took the number of the Adams 0-2-2WT when it was withdrawn. In turn this number was passed on to the Dübs engine on the demise of the ex-G&SWR 0-4-2T in 1875.** Ian Allan Library

Right: **Delivery of the five Dubs 2-4-0Ts was spread over a 13 year period from 1874 to 1887. The penultimate locomotive No 13, which entered service in 1883 and is seen here shunting at Albert Quay, was withdrawn in 1919.** Ian Allan Library

Below: **2-4-0T No 1 on a goods train at Clonakilty Junction. Delivered in September 1874 from Messrs Dübs, she was finally withdrawn in 1930 as GSR No 482.** Ian Allan Library

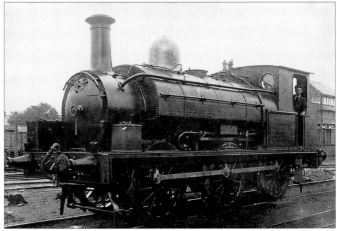

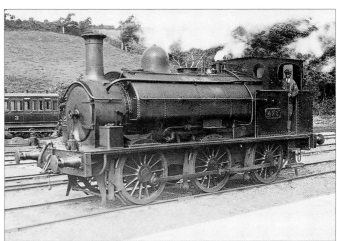

completion of which it may have been used on the construction of the Athboy branch. During this time, Messrs Moore Bros went bankrupt and the engine in use on the works was advertised for auction in April 1863, not apparently being sold at this time. Then, in January 1865, a locomotive corresponding in all known respects to No 4 was offered for sale by the Bankruptcy Court. At this time it was reported to be lying at the works of Messrs Courtney & Stephens at Blackhall Place in Dublin.

John Eaton, locomotive superintendent of the Ulster Railway, inspected this engine in February 1865 but reported that it was unsuitable for the Ulster's requirements. About this time, the C&BR offered £400

which was refused. Conran then inspected the engine in March, also advising on its unsuitability, having a preference for a coupled engine. Apart from any other consideration, its wheelbase was too long for the C&BR turntables of the time. This objection was hardly valid as the ex-GS&WR engine would have been as long as the B&CDR one. There are no further references in the board minutes until a cheque for £300 was signed in July 1867, this being referred to at the shareholders' half-yearly meeting the following February as being a payment out of revenue but charged to capital.

BoT returns for 1866 and 1867 indicate eight C&BR engines; C&BR Nos 1 to 7 and the ex GS&WR engine. The old Adams tanks

were removed from stock in 1868, leaving C&BR Nos 3 to 7 and the GS&WR engine, a total of six engines, yet the BoT returns for 1868 show seven. This appears to indicate the purchase of an additional engine. The £300 payment does not refer to GS&WR No 102, payment for which was made in two separate instalments. Furthermore, when another GS&WR engine was purchased second-hand in 1871 it was initially numbered 8, later becoming No 2, which would not make sense unless a No 2 already existed.

Type VII was another Bury Curtis & Kennedy engine, purchased second-hand from the GS&WR in July 1871, at which date it had accumulated a mileage of 293,094 miles since a rebuild about 1853. It had

Opposite page

Top left: **This is a view of one of the three locomotives acquired by the CB&SCR from the West Cork Railways. This was WCR No 3, renumbered 11 by the CB&SCR, a 2-4-0ST built by the Vulcan Foundry in 1877. This locomotive remained in service until 1904.**

Top right: **A later view of 0-6-0ST No 6, this time at Albert Quay, after receiving new boiler. Also note the enlarged bunker and new cab.** Ian Allan Library

Centre left: **No 6, an 0-6-0ST built by Beyer Peacock in 1881, is seen on 5th September 1901 at Ballinascarthy. In this year the locomotive was rebuilt with larger wheels. The original wheels were 4ft 2in in diameter, the new ones were 3in bigger.**

Centre right: **Seen here in its later guise as GSR No 473, this was a one off 0-6-0ST with 4ft 6in wheels built by Beyer Peacock for the CBSCR in 1894 and numbered 17. The locomotive was withdrawn by the GSR in 1935.** Ian Allan Library

Bottom left: **GSR 0-6-0ST No 473 at Cork on 15th September 1929. Numbered 17 on the CB&SCR, she was built in 1894 and lasted until 1935. This engine was one of two of the class fitted with 4ft 6in driving wheels. Clearly visible is the Beyer Peacock maker's plate on the centre splasher.** Late H.C. Casserley.

Bottom right: **0-6-0ST No 475 (ex CB&SCR No 5), one of a batch of five obtained from Messrs Beyer Peacock & Co Ltd of Manchester between 1881 and 1894. No two appear to have been identical. No 5 was introduced into service on 4th November 1887 and was one of two fitted with 4ft.3in driving wheels. These engines were based on a Beyer Peacock design for a Swedish railway compant in 1873, which was later adopted by W G Beattie in 1876 as a standard London & South Western Railway shunter. No 475 was withdrawn by the GSR in 1939.** Ian Allan Library

Right upper: **A view of the former CB&SCR No 6, seen as GSR No 472. The GSR applied the classification system used on the English Great Northern and latterly on the London & North Eastern Railway to its locomotives. Under this system No 472 and sister locomotive No 473 were members of the J24 class. No 472 was withdrawn in 1940.** Ian Allan Library

Right: **Another very clear photograph of No 475 on shunting duties at Victoria Quay in Cork. The sloping smokebox front as originally applied to these engines is plainly visible in this view.** Ian Allan Library

been purchased new in February 1848 as a 2-2-2 locomotive. As GS&WR No 38, it was rebuilt about 1852-3 as a 2-4-0. Within a week of purchase, Conran reported that it was working satisfactorily and required no outlay. She was initially numbered 8 on the C&BR, becoming No 2 in July 1872. By October of that year it was reported that No 2 was only fit for shunting as she had broken frames and hornplates. Little wonder that the GS&WR were disposing of her! Conran reported again in September 1876 that the 'old shunting engine' was, 'nearly past work and severe on the rails'. Some repairs appear to have been carried out by December but she was expected to barely last three months. If it was in fact No 2, Conran told the directors in May of the following year that he had taken her to pieces.

The last of the second-hand engines was yet another Bury Curtis & Kennedy engine, ex GS&WR No 24, purchased in November 1872. Conran reported having seen two engines for sale by the GS&WR, Nos 121/2.

The latter however was an 0-4-2 of 1854 and was not sold until 1882. It seems more likely then that Conran saw Nos 120/1, both of which were sold for scrap in January 1874. Two Bury singles were reported to be for sale in October 1872 and it was one of these which was purchased for £350.

Within a month of arriving on the Bandon, Conran reported that No 8 was unable to haul a train at ordinary speed owing to slippery rails and bad weather. Three days after this incident Conran stated that it was, 'entirely unfitted for our line; not able even for passenger traffic with more than five carriages for slipping'. It is hardly surprising to hear therefore that 12 months later she had only run 703 miles and she had been sold by February 1875. If ever proof was needed of the folly of buying other companies' cast-offs, surely this was as good an example as one could find!

Whether the debacle of No 8 was a contributory factor to the death of the CB&SCR chairman, O'Connor, in 1873, is unknown.

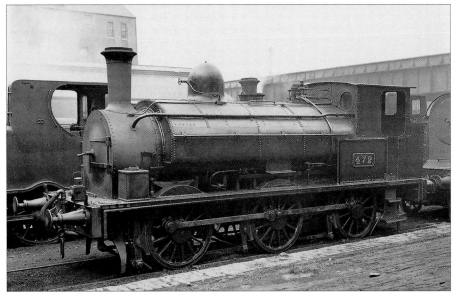

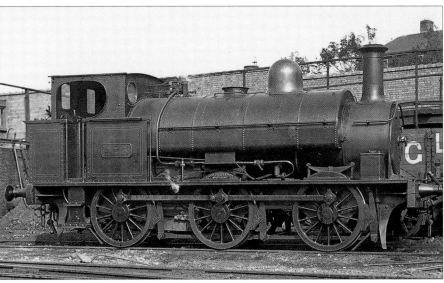

However, this was to be the end of purchasing second-hand equipment. Type IX represents five 2-4-0Ts acquired from Messrs Dübs & Co between 1874 and 1887. As built, all five were identical apart from slight variations in the shape of the cab sidesheets. The boilers were identical in known dimensions with those on the C&MDR engines, but differed in having a dome, with the Salter safety valves on top, on the rear ring of the boiler, whereas the Macroom engines had the domes over the firebox. At least three of the engines had Giffard injectors with clacks at the front of the front ring; all were replaced by faceplate injectors by about 1900. All had cabs narrower than the width of the tanks, with overhanging roof sand short sidesheets. The back weatherboard was flush with the back of the bunker, involving coaling via the cab. No 1 later acquired an enlarged bunker and new cab. A spare boiler was obtained in 1891, differing in having a small enclosed dome on the middle ring and Ramsbottom safety valves over the firebox. This boiler was only installed in Nos 8 and 13.

No 1 spent some three months in the shops during 1882 for a general repair. It was reported in September 1887 that she required a new firebox, this not being provided until February 1889. When she broke her crank axle in December 1902, No 1 had accumulated 582,429 miles. No 2 arrived in July 1875 and cost £2,100. She got a new firebox in December 1887. It had been intended to put in new brass tubes, but with increased metal prices, it was decided to install steel ones. A general repair in December 1895 saw new cylinders and tubeplates fitted. She was rebuilt in 1909 as a 4-4-0T.

No 4 cost £1,525 and was initially numbered 4A until the old No 4 was removed from stock in February 1888. She was fitted with the vacuum brake in April 1891, a spare boiler, not necessarily the original spare of 1891 but perhaps one from another of the class, being installed in 1896. There is little to report about No 8 which received the spare boiler in February 1891. She worked on the C&MDR for a couple of days in September 1878. It has in the past been stated that No 8 was converted to a 2-4-2T, but this is quite definitely not the case. Prior to the purchase of No 13 in 1881, tenders were received from three manufacturers for a new engine, the tender of Messrs Dübs being the lowest at £1,950. She was reported to have been involved in a buffer collision at Kinsale in May 1892. At the time she was running in reverse, with no sandboxes fitted to the rear wheels. Following this incident, it was ordered that they be so fitted.

West Cork acquisitions

Before proceeding with the principal company's future purchases, we must now take a look at the locomotives acquired from the WCR, three engines in all. The contractors, Messrs Kirk & Co offered, in view of the poor financial state of the company, to purchase engines from the manufacturers, Messrs J Cross & Co of St Helen's, Lancashire, and hire them at a percentage of the cost price. The WCR were to be responsible for the upkeep of the engines and were to have an option to purchase at cost price at the expiration of three years.

One engine was delivered to the West Cork sometime between August and December 1865. However in November of that year, John Eaton, locomotive superintendent of the Ulster Railway (UR) inspected what was presumably the second WCR engine at St Helen's, recommending to his board that they should make an offer for it, although this was later withdrawn. The contractors appear to have reneged on their deal as Messrs Cross advised in May 1866 that they were not prepared to let the two engines to the company on hire and unless some arrangements were promptly made as to their purchase, they would take away the engine already delivered. At this point the British & Foreign Plant Co became involved and set up a committee for the purpose of purchasing the engines and hiring them to the company. By the end of the year this deal was also in the balance and it would seem that there was some possibility of the neighbouring C&MDR purchasing the WCR locomotives and rolling stock.

Arising from a failure to keep up the monthly payments, the locomotives and rolling stock of the company was seized by the B&FP Co in June 1867 and as late as April 1868, John Wakefield, locomotive superintendent of the Dublin Wicklow & Wexford Railway, inspected the carriages with a view to purchase. Despite all these setbacks, Nos 1 and 2 were transferred to the C&BR in January 1880, becoming Nos 9 and 10 respectively. They were the only Cross locomotives delivered to Ireland.

Both engines were duly inspected and it was decided that with new plates round the bottom of the boiler they would be good for about five years. No 9 broke a valve spindle in October 1881 and was reported to be still working the Bantry branch after this happened. Such was the state of the company's locomotive stock that she had to be kept at work in this condition. No 10 suffered from the same problem in August 1886 while working Ballyboy Fair. Despite the notion that they would only be good for five years, both engines remained in service for considerably longer, No 9 lasting until March 1895 when she was sold for £65.

A West Cork minute of 28th October 1864 makes reference to the ordering of three locomotives from Messrs Cross & Co of St Helen's in Lancashire. However we know that this firm only delivered two 2-4-0 tank engines. It is possible that the third was to have been a goods engine. Two suggestions have been put forward by the late Bob Clements. It may have been an 0-6-0T which came into the possession of Isaac Boulton and later went to a colliery near Wigan, being named Hercules. This engine may have been similar to one supplied in 1865 to the South-Eastern division of the Portuguese Railways. The other suggestion is that it was also a 2-4-0T which a Mr Doherty had on the Maryport Docks contract between 1881 and 1884.

The third West Cork engine was a 2-4-0ST purchased from the Vulcan Foundry in 1877. As far as can be ascertained, it appears to have been identical to engines supplied to the Belfast, Holywood & Bangor Railway in 1876, these in turn being based on an 1863 design for the Belfast & County Down Railway. Two tenders had been obtained in March 1877, from Vulcans and from Burrowes & Son, both for £2,000. The latter was initially chosen but it is understood that it may have been an 0-6-0T and therefore felt to be unsuitable. This engine (WCR No 3 and later C&BR No 11) suffered a number of valve spindle failures, although this was virtually unknown with the B&CDR engines. As No 11 she was involved in the accident at Bantry old station in July 1887 when she ran through the buffer stop. This necessitated the purchase of a new cab and side panels. It was also involved in a derailment at the new Bantry station on the day following its opening to traffic. No 11 was sold for scrap in April 1905 for the sum of £75.

Beyer saddle tanks

The next type of locomotive to be acquired by the C&BR came from Messrs Beyer Peacock & Co Ltd, five engines being delivered over a 13 year period from 1881 to 1894; two during the tenure of Conran, one under J J Johnstone and two after the latter's son took over. The design for these engines apparently originated with Beyer engines supplied to a Swedish railway in 1873. This design was adopted by W G Beattie as a standard London & South Western Railway shunter in 1876.

The first engine for the Bandon, No 6, had 4ft 6in wheels but Conran appears to have decided that a slightly smaller wheel would be better and tried 4ft 5in in the next one, No 12. This however was not sufficient for J J Johnstone and the third, No 5, had 4ft 3in wheels. His son also used this size in No 16 but reverted to 4ft 6in for some reason with the last one, No 17. Apart from wheel diameters, there were other variations among the five engines. No 6 had Salter valves on the dome, while the remainder had Ramsbottom valves over the firebox and closed domes. No 6 also had a typical Beyer cab with short side sheets and the back cut away in an arc on each side. No 17 had continu-

Right: **Under the GSR and CIÉ quite a few 'foreign' locomotives found their way onto former CB&SCR metals. A number of ex-MGWR tank engines made the trip south far from their home territory. One of these, J26 class 0-6-0T No 557, the former MGWR No 112 built in 1891 by Kitson in Leeds, survived until 1959. The engine is seen here in 'The Quarry' with the Hibernian Road bridge behind it.**
J W P Rowledge

Below left and right: **Another long term resident on the former CB&SCR system was this 0-6-0ST No 299. Built by Hunslet in 1892 it was used in the construction of the Kenmare line and then by Fenit Harbour Commissioners. It passed to the G&SWR in 1901 and was finally withdrawn by CIÉ in 1957.** Left, photographer unknown
Right, J W P Rowledge

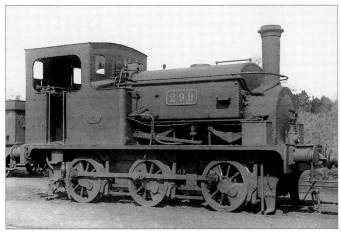

ous handrails round the sides and front of the smokebox, while the others had a rail at the front only. All were built with sloping smokebox fronts.

No 6 obtained a new boiler in 1922 with pop safety valves and a vertical front to the smokebox. The bunker was also increased in height and a new and better cab provided. No 12 appears to have had a vertical smokebox front by 1924 along with an enlarged bunker. No 5 had received an enlarged bunker by 1929 and received a GSR pattern chimney in 1933. Finally, No 17 never received the larger bunker and retained her CB&SCR livery to the end of her life in 1935.

Two Saints from the Lough Swilly

The Londonderry & Lough Swilly Railway was originally built to 5ft 3in gauge, but the decision was taken in 1885 to convert to narrow-gauge. As a result, all the original rolling stock and locomotives were auctioned off in May of that year. Conran was duly sent to the auction and returned with two locomotives and several carriages. Ex L&LSR 0-6-0 tanks Nos 4 and 5 were comparatively new engines, having been sup-

plied by Sharp Stewart in 1876 and 1879 respectively. They became C&BR Nos 14 and 15, losing their names, *St Patrick* and *St Columb* in the process. It was decided in July 1891 to put a bogie under the leading end of No 14 but it was to be February 1893 before she emerged as a 4-4-0T, No 15 following in March 1898. No 14 also received a new cab and bunker, No 15 receiving a new boiler, similar to the original but with Ramsbottom safety valves instead of the spring balance type.

No 14 was reported in July 1908 to be completely worn out and it was recommended that a new engine be ordered. She was possibly withdrawn in December 1908, although nominally in stock until the arrival of the new No 14 in April of the following year. No 15 was involved in a derailment on the Kinsale branch in March 1888 but apparently received little damage. She was fitted with a continuous brake in May 1893. Although a new No 15 was delivered in November 1910, the L&LSR engine was certainly still in use at least until 1914 when she was photographed during the reconstruction of the Shannonvale viaduct. She was loaned to Henry Ford & Son in Novem-

ber 1919, remaining there as a stationary boiler until January 1921. She appears to have been sold to Thomas Ward of Sheffield in July of that year, along with Nos 8 and 13.

Bogie tanks

Next to be considered are four 4-4-0Ts, two obtained from Messrs. Dübs and two from Messrs. Neilson. The story of these engines is complicated by differences between them and also doubtful figures as regards dimensions. First let us deal with the differences between those machines supplied by the two manufacturers. The Dübs engines, Nos 3 and 10, had laminated springs for the coupled wheels, whereas the Neilsons, Nos 9 and 18, had spiral springs. The former had standard CB&SCR sand boxes at the front of the tanks whereas the Neilsons had them under the top framing. The latter engines had footsteps at the rear bogie wheels, which the others did not, and they also had longer side sheets to the cabs. The Dübs engines had buffer beams rounded at the ends, the Neilsons did not. Finally, the whistles on the Dübs engines passed through the front plate of the cab, the other two through

Top left: **In 1891 the CB&SCR acquired its first 4-4-0 tank engines. The two locomotives, numbered 3 and 10 , were built by Dübs. No 3, seen here, was rebuilt as a 4-4-2T early in the early 1900s and was withdrawn as GSR No 479 in 1930.**

Top right: **Two further 4-4-0Ts, numbered 9 and 18, were supplied to the railway by Neilson in 1894. These were also rebuilt as 4-4-2Ts in 1898 and 1900 respectively. These were followed in 1901 by the only locomotive built by the company, 4-4-0T No 7, seen here on Victoria Quay and fitted with a bell to enable it to work on the CCR.**

Centre: **This fine portrait of No 7 was taken at Albert Quay. Renumbered 478 by the GSR, this locomotive was withdrawn in 1934 having worked on the Kinsale branch for many years up to the closure of the line.** Ian Allan Library

Bottom left and right: **As befits the only locomotive built at Rocksavage works, we have two further views of the engine. It is first seen in CB&SCR days at Albert Quay (left) and as GSR No 478 towards the end of its career.** Both, Ian Allan Library

the roof. To complicate matters further, the Dübs ones were later altered to conform.

Three rebuilds were carried out to these engines during their careers. Nos 9 and 18 were rebuilt as 4-4-2Ts with 3ft 6in radial wheels. This rebuild was carried out in an attempt to reduce axle loading. No 3 got completely new and longer cab side sheets when she was similarly rebuilt, probably in 1898. Both of the Dübs engines retained their Ramsbottom safety valves. No 18 had long pop valves by 1924, these being replaced by shorter GSR ones later. All had their copper-capped chimneys replaced by slightly shorter CB&SCR standard type, only No 18 (as No 481) getting a GSR one.

The second rebuild involved only No 10, which became a 4-6-0T in June 1906. The cab side sheets were not altered during the rebuild. The third rebuild involved Nos 3 and 9 which had their boiler centre line raised about 6ins. The fireboxes may also have been lengthened by a foot at the rear, which would have increased the grate area to about 17½ sq ft. When the first rebuilds were carried out, four sets of materials were apparently ordered. None of the rebuilds are referred to in the minutes.

All four engines had their boiler pressure at 135lbs per sq in by 1925. Originally the Neilsons had 140lbs and the Dübs 130lbs. In October 1922 the military authorities requisitioned No 3 and required it to be armoured. This work was duly carried out and she was handed over later that month. The armour plating was gone off her by May 1924. As regards No 9, she was not condemned until after the arrival of the new engine of this number. This may confirm

E L Ahrons' suggestion that the new No 9 was initially numbered 19.

Baldwins and& and a Cork built engine

As the turn of the century approached, the locomotive building industry in Britain was in the midst of a tremendous boom which coincided with a disastrous strike. Locomotive manufacturers were full up with orders and several railway companies turned to American manufacturers. The CB&SCR obtained tenders from a number of firms in October 1899 for new goods engines, varying from £3,000 to £3,600. Not only were these considered to be too high, but delivery times were also too long. Arising from this, Messrs Burnham Williams & Co (Baldwins) quoted £2,575 each for two inside cylindered engines, to be delivered in Cork within six to eight months. This tender was accepted in January 1900.

The first of two 0-6-2 saddle tank engines was reported to have run a few trial trips by 24th October, Johnstone commenting that the frame at the trailing end appeared weak and required strengthening. However, within a month the first signs emerged of the engines being overweight. The saddle tank was shifted slightly on one of the engines, but this does not appear to have improved matters substantially. The manufacturers suggested that the weighing machine in use was faulty, necessitating Johnstone arranging for a GS&WR engine to be weighed to check the machine. In due course Baldwins offered a figure of £100 in settlement, which was accepted.

Other alterations were made quite early on. Complaints had been made of the whistles disturbing people living near the line, leading to them being replaced by standard Bandon whistles. The engines arrived with steam brakes, initially with all blocks in front of the coupled wheels. Those of the trailing pair were soon altered to be behind. The sandboxes were moved from the top of the saddle tank, an additional one being attached to the front of the tanks, with the rear one inside the cab. Footsteps were originally of the American open type, these soon being replaced by standard ones.

By 1908, Johnstone advised that the American engines would require replacement within four years, and in fact No 20 was sold to Mr S Gould for scrap in August 1912 for £86. No 19 appears to have soldiered on until at least July 1914 when she was photographed on a special goods, the new 19 being on a passenger train on the same day. Whilst the purchase of these engines was regarded as a necessity at the time, they proved to be a poor bargain.

The only engine to be 'built' by the company was a 4-4-0 tank turned out from Rocksavage in 1901. Old No 7 was reported to be worn out by June 1897 and Johnstone suggested obtaining some parts at a cost of

£322 which would enable him to reconstruct her. It is difficult to know just where some of the materials used for this engine in fact came from. The boiler was most likely the spare Lough Swilly boiler bought in June 1895 at a cost of £495. It had been used in No 14 in 1896. The bogie probably came from old No 7, also the frames which were new in 1893. Johnstone's estimate for building the new No 7 could not have included new frames. The wheels were likely new, although the spare wheels for the Dübs 2-4-0T could possibly have been used. The crank axle was new, and it seems likely that the cab and bunker were also new.

The 'Bandon' tanks

Undoubtedly the best known of the CB&SCR locomotives were the batch of eight 4-6-0 tanks supplied by Messrs Beyer Peacock between 1906 and 1920, commonly referred to as the 'Bandon tanks'. Johnstone was instructed in May 1905 to prepare designs for a new engine. Two months later, Messrs Beyer Peacock tendered at £3,145 for a 4-6-0T, this being accepted. The new engine, No 11, arrived in Cork on 2nd June 1906 and was reported to be satisfactory. She had 1,000 gallon water tanks, but no difference was visible in the side tanks compared with the rest of the class, which had 1,100 gallon tanks. Tenders were obtained from various manufacturers in September 1908 for another new engine, similar to No 11, Beyer's tender at £2,575 being accepted. No 14 was followed by 15, 20 and 19 between 1910 and 1914. Beyer's tender for a further engine was accepted in April 1915, but a year later it was reported that the new engine had been held up by the Ministry of Munitions who declined to allow the manufacturers to complete her. Desperate for additional engine power, the chairman himself had an interview with the Ministry who refused to budge. They did however state that the company could have the boiler if they undertook to complete the work themselves.

The new boiler was duly delivered in August 1917. Beyer Peacock reported in February 1919 that work was progressing satisfactorily and that if a boiler was taken out of one of the company's engines and forwarded to them, they were hopeful of delivering the completed engine by April or May. It was in fact delivered in October 1919, an additional £2,104 being requested due to the necessity to repair the old boiler and provide a new copper firebox and stays. It appears that the Government may have contributed some of the additional cost as the cost of the engine as reported to the GS&WR in 1923 was nearly £1,000 less than it actually cost the company. Two more engines followed, Nos 4 and 13 in 1920.

The GSR fitted 'R' class superheated boilers with Belpaire fireboxes to five of the

class, one in 1935 and four between 1942 and 1947. No 468 reverted to an original boiler for two years before again being fitted with an 'R' boiler in 1950. Ross pop safety valves were fitted by the GSR to any members of the class not already so equipped by the CB&SCR. No 464 ran for a short time with a stovepipe chimney about 1940.

Four of the class spent time working suburban trains on the D&SE section. No 68 was the first to go there, being based at Dublin's Grand Canal Street shed for the summer of 1929. No 470 was the next to appear, arriving in Bray at the beginning of 1939, and, from that time until September 1956, there was generally one of the class allocated to that shed. No 466 joined No 470 for the summer service in 1939, but No 470 had left Bray by the end of that year. No 466 stayed in Bray until mid-1941, when in turn it was relieved by No 469 until the autumn of 1942. Thereafter, No 466 was the regular member of the class at Bray, and in December 1948 it was painted in the CIÉ green livery in line with a short-lived scheme adopted for locomotives working on Dublin suburban trains.

Might-have-beens

Between September 1890 and March 1915, corresponding with the order for the 4-6-0 tank locomotives, Messrs Beyer Peacock produced drawings of various locomotives for the CB&SCR. Some of these are worthy of brief mention as they would have been unusual on Irish railways. Two designs were put forward in December 1910. The first of these was for a large goods tank engine with a 4-8-0 wheel arrangement. A large boiler of 5ft 1¾in diameter, a grate area of 30.6 sq ft and heating surface of 1,786 sq ft would have provided ample power for any goods trains on the Bandon; there were to be four

safety valves on top of the firebox. The large boiler meant that the chimney and dome were squat to keep the maximum height from rail level at 12ft 10in. The cab profile however was similar to that on the 4-6-0T locomotives. Driving wheels were 4ft 5in diameter, with two inside cylinders of 20½in by 26in and a 180lbs boiler pressure, which would have produced a tractive effort of 27,830lbs at 75% pressure. With 1,800 gallons of water and three tons of coal, this engine would have weighed in at 77t 5c.

The second proposal of December 1910 was even more interesting. This was for an 0-6-6-0 Beyer Garratt. This design is of particular interest as the first Garratts actually delivered to any railway in the world were a pair of diminutive 0-4-4-0s in 1909 for the North East Dundas Tramway, a 2ft gauge line on the west coast of Tasmania. A E Durrant, in his work on Garratt locomotives, was of opinion that this initial design may have been offered to an obscure minor railway with little business potential, 'partly to placate Garratt and get him happily off the premises, and partly to ensure that they did not receive an order for two, odd non-standard locomotives which have been an embarrassment to design and build'. A further order in 1911 was for the 2ft gauge Darjeeling Himalaya Railway. The total weight of the Tasmanian 'K' class was only 34 tons and their haulage power was limited to 70 tons.

Bearing the above in mind, it is surprising that such an advanced design was proposed to the Bandon in December 1910. This was to have been a large engine with a 6ft diameter boiler and Belpaire firebox, giving a heating surface of 2,188 sq ft, grate area being no less than 34.8 sq ft. This latter was larger than that of the '800' class 4-6-0s introduced in 1939 by the GSR. There were

4-4-2T No 3, delivered from Messrs Dübs in September 1891 as a 4-4-0T. She was in fact the first of four very similar engines, two from Dübs and two from Neilsons. There were minor differences of detail in the two manufacturers' engines, although later rebuildings saw these disappear. A comparison with the photograph of No 9 on page 111 shows a standard CB&SCR sandbox in front of No 3's side tank, the front of the latter being rounded on the Dübs engines, and finally the whistle connection coming through the cab front sheet on No 3 whereas it came through the roof on the Neilsons. The Neilson water tanks were both longer and higher than those on the Dübs engines, the bunkers also being correspondingly higher.
Ian Allan Library

to have been four cylinders 16in by 20in with Walschaerts valve gear. The total length of the locomotive over buffers was 59ft 10in and weight in working order 87½ tons. Coal and water capacity were to be 3½ tons and 2,200 gallons respectively. Boiler pressure was 180lbs per sq.in and tractive effort a massive 30,100 lbs, again in line with the '800' class.

One can only but wonder at what might have been, had either the 4-8-0T or the 0-6-6-0 Garratt been built. Regarding the latter, it would appear that, despite Durrant's comments above, Messrs Beyer Peacock were somewhat awestruck with the Garratt concept and offered it to the Bandon without any really serious thoughts as to that company's requirements. The last design in this series came in March 1915, perhaps a little unusual because of the outbreak of war some six months earlier. This was for a more conventional 4-4-2T weighing in at 54 tons.

So we come to the end of the CB&SCR locomotive history. To complete the story however, we will take a brief look at the three engines which were purchased by the independent Timoleague company, and also a contractor's engine which may have been loaned to the Bandon for a short period in 1881.

Courtmacsherry tramway engines

The first engine bought by the T&CELR was an 0-4-2 tank supplied by Hunslet of Leeds in 1890 (their maker's No 520). Named *St Molaga*, her nameplates were

Below left: **Here we see Dübs and Neilson built 4-4-0Ts following their rebuilding as 4-4-2Ts. No 9 supplied by Neilson in 1894 only lasted for four years as a 4-4-0T. It became GSR No 480 and lasted until 1935.** Ian Allan Library

Below right: **The other Neilson built four coupled tank, No 18, is seen here on 6th September 1901, the year after it was rebuilt as a 4-4-2T.** Ken Nunn collection, LCGB

Bottom left: **The former No 18 became GSR No 481 and remained in service until withdrawn the mid 1930s.** Ian Allan Library

Bottom right: **Dübs built CB&SCR No 3 was fitted with armour in October 1922 at the request of the military authorities though this had been removed by 1924. As GSR No 479 she poses with her crew in Cork.** G Beesley collection

incorrectly cast as *St Maloga*, the locomotive being photographed with these by the manufacturers. *St Molaga* received a new boiler in 1922, generally similar to the original, but with two Ross pop safety valves replacing the Salter valves originally located inside the cab. The bell which this engine carried for use on the tramway section of line was presented by CIÉ to the Irish Railway Record Society, and has since been used as the chairman's gavel.

The second engine, *Slaney*, was purchased from the contractor, Robert Worthington, in December 1890. Originally built in 1885 by Hunslet (works No 382), she almost certainly worked on the Baltinglass to Tullow contract, and it was probably in connection with this contract that the name was applied. Later, she was used on the Palace East to New Ross works. The next move is not definitely known, but she most likely went to Trim. *Slaney* initially only had a slightly turned weatherboard, an open back cab being fitted about 1892, preceded by skirts which were removed within ten years – all three engines were so fitted for use on the tramway section. A broken cylinder and defective boiler plates led to her being condemned in August 1920.

The final engine to be looked at was another Hunslet, purchased by the T&CELR in September 1894, a 2-6-0T named *Argadeen*. This engine had cowcatchers fitted as new, these being removed between 1901 and 1920. The rear portions of the skirts were retained as footsteps. *Argadeen* was fitted with a new boiler in 1908,

although there is no record of this in the minutes. The late Bob Clements was of opinion that she might only have received a new firebox at this time. Then in August 1929, the boiler from the diminutive ex-D&SER tank locomotive *Imp* (Manning Wardle, 1906), with an additional ring added in front, was fitted at the Broadstone works in Dublin. Although *Argadeen* had gone into the shops in the previous October, the drawing for the replacement boiler was not prepared until March. This raises the possibility that the rebuild was only decided on after examination of the boiler in shops. The question raised is whether *Imp's* withdrawal in 1928 had already been decided on, or whether it was agreed to release a boiler for *Argadeen*.

Details of locomotives and their principal dimensions can be found in Appendices B and C.

Allman's Distillery engines

Two engines worked the distillery tramway at Bandon. The first of these was a diminutive 0-4-0ST built by Manning Wardle & Co in 1880 for Thomas Dowling of Cork for use on the construction of the Bantry extension railway. The engine was appropriately named *Bantry*. The C&BR approached Dowling in July 1881, seeking to borrow the engine while repairs were being carried out to company engines. There is no evidence that *Bantry* was in fact ever borrowed. She was valued by Johnstone at £400 in October 1881 and was to have been moved under her own steam from Drimoleague to Cork in

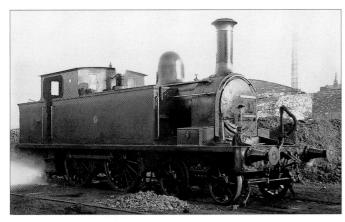

March 1883, but was found unfit. She was sold to William Martin Murphy and used by him on the Clara to Banagher contract. Murphy advertised *Bantry* for sale in May 1884 and she then returned to C&BR metals, having been purchased by J W Dorman for use on the Clonakilty extension works. Most likely after the completion of this contract, she was sold to Allman's Distillery, remaining there until she was withdrawn in 1920. She was affectionately known to C&BR men at Bandon as 'Allman's Coffee-pot'.

The second Allman engine was a much more modern locomotive, built new in 1920. It was a product of Messrs. Peckett of Bristol, being one of their standard 'Beaufort' type, an 0-4-0ST with outside cylinders. With the closure of the distillery, the engine was sold in 1930 to the GSR, classified M3 and numbered 495. It retained its original owner's name, still visible on the saddle tank for some years after passing into GSR ownership. She lasted into CIÉ days, not being withdrawn until 1949.

Bandon livery
We know little of the early livery applied to locomotives. By about 1880, they were painted an olive green colour. By 1914,

engines and carriages were painted in various shades of olive green with yellow lining. Engines had polished brass domes and some had copper-capped chimneys. Prior to the amalgamation with the C&BR, West Cork engines were also painted olive green, but with black and vermilion lining. Nothing is known regarding two of the Timoleague engines, but *Argadeen* was black with a rectangular nameplate, the name consisting of raised brass letters on a vermilion background. There was some dispute in relation to the livery on the two Baldwin engines as received from America. The company had specified sage green, panelled black and lined with yellow. Photographs show only a single yellow line, which presumably divided the sage green from a black border, though no difference is evident between the green and black in the photographs.

On the formation of the Great Southern Railway in November 1924, it was originally intended to re-number the Bandon engines in the series 510 to 529. However, by April 1925 the re-numbering scheme for the entire GSR had been settled on and they actually took up numbers in the series 463 to 482.

Below left: **0-6-2ST No 19, one of a pair purchased from the Baldwin Locomotive Works in 1900. They were the only American built steam locomotives purchased by an Irish railway. No 19 is shown in its original condition with two sandboxes on top of the boiler. She is also shown in what was apparently to be a short-lived lined livery.**

Below right: **One of the two Baldwin 0-6-2STs introduced in 1900 photographed at Ballinhassig, as witnessed by the aerial ropeway visible in the background.** Photographer unknown, Seán Kennedy collection

Bottom: **In this later photograph of one of the Balwdin tanks the sandboxes have been removed from the top of the boiler. In addition, standard CB&SCR steps providing access to the cab have replaced the open American type. Not noticeable is the provision of a standard whistle — this followed complaints from local residents.** Photographer unknown, Sean Kennedy collection

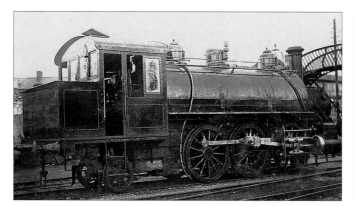

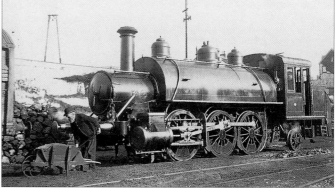

Above: **The most famous and long lived of CB&SCR engines were the eight 4-6-0 tanks built by Beyer Peacock for the company between 1906 and 1920. This is the Beyer Peacock works photograph of No 5. Delivered on 25th October 1910. She received a GSR 'R' Belpaire superheater boiler in 1944. This was replaced by her original boiler in June 1948, but two years later she again received an 'R' boiler which she carried until final withdrawal in March 1961 as CIÉ No 468. She was broken up at Dundalk Engineering Works in August 1961.**
Beyer Peacock Works photograph

Below left: **Very few 4-6-0 tank locomotives were built for service in Britian and Ireland during the age of steam but this unusual type certainly proved a success for the CB&SCR and its successors. An unidentified member of the class in seen in the yard at Cork before the GSR takeover.**

Below right: **All the 4-6-0Ts survived throughout the GSR era though two, Nos 465 and 469, were withdrawn in 1945. No 470, the former CB&SCR No 20 built in 1912, was not withdrawn until 1961. The locomotive is seen here on the turntable at Cork on 9th August 1935. R G Jarvis**

Bottom left: **No 463, the former CB&SCR No 4 built in1919, is seen at Rocksavage in CIÉ days. This locomotive lasted longer than the tracks it was built to run on surviving until the virtual end of steam traction in the Irish Republic in 1963 .**

Bottom right: **4-6-0T No 464 waiting to take over IRRS Special at Bandon on St.Patrick's Day 1961, just two weeks before the line's closure. This Bandon tank also lasted longer that the former CB&SCR system, it remained on CIÉ's books until 1963. C L Fry, Seán Kennedy collection**

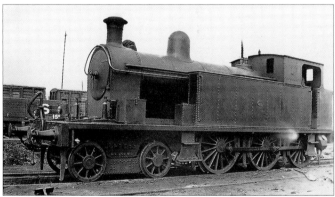

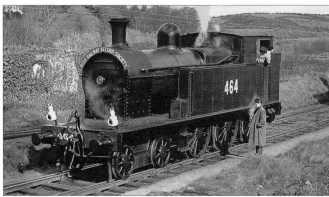

Chapter Fourteen

ROLLING STOCK

In August 1845 Leahy was instructed to prepare specifications for carriages, which he might consider best suited to the needs of the company. These were duly submitted to the board and approved in the following November, advertisements being placed seeking tenders. In December of the following year, a Mr Corlett wrote applying for payment for a, 'Model Carriage built for Mr Leahy'. The latter gentleman had by this time departed the scene and the board denied any liability for the payment. The first carriages of which we have any specific mention were three first and second class composites obtained in conjunction with the two Adams locomotives. Two carriages were initially ordered and it was intended that they be permanently coupled to the engines. However, as built they were separate and a third vehicle was ordered in March 1849. They were designed to carry 58 passengers and the first two lasted until scrapped in 1867 and the third one until 1872, although they had been converted into third class before their demise.

Captain Wynne's report of his inspection of the first section of line to be opened, that from Bandon to Ballinhassig, indicates that the company's rolling stock consisted only of the above carriages, adequate in Wynne's view for working nine miles of railway. As reported in the previous chapter, comparative trials were carried out in June 1850 between one of the Adams locomotives and the 2-2-2 tender engine No 3. It was reported that, 'every carriage and van in the possession of the company, all filled with human beings, and closed with two luggage vans heaped with 24 tons of ballast', were coupled to No 3. On one of the trial trips a total of 300 passengers travelled, indicating that at least five carriages must have been extant at this time and this must have included the two second class carriages, probably acquired earlier that year but for which the manufacturer is unknown. One of the second class carriages was altered to a first and second class composite in 1852, it being recorded in August that Robert Julian a Cork coachbuilder, had proposed to furnish three compartments of the second class carriages to make them fit for first class passengers for £63, this tender being accepted. He was also instructed to paint the royal arms

on, 'the present first class carriage'. Julian was paid a total of £74.11s.10d in the following September. The other second class carriage was turned into a first and second class composite in 1867, as a replacement for one of the aforementioned Adams vehicles.

On 27th February 1851, Mr Preston's tender was accepted at £142 for the construction of a portion of the new carrying stock. Tenders had already been obtained for ironwork and Preston most likely built only the carriage bodies, which were probably third class carriages if the two third class brakes which were recorded as being in existence at the end of 1862, were conversions from the Adams composites. Charles Nixon advised the local committee in April 1852 of the necessity of obtaining two additional thirds. These were approved and in the following month it was reported that Preston was manufacturing them at Bandon. It was stated that they were open saloons with cross-seats, 'and no divided compartments'. The C&BR rebuilt three of these thirds in 1871/3.

From the board minutes, we know that two additional composites were ordered from Brown Marshall & Co in April 1851 at a cost of £220 each. These were delivered in the following August, via Liverpool, by the Cork Steamship Co, and once again provided first and second class accommodation. As early as January 1853 the secretary suggested to the board the importance of establishing a means of communication between the passengers, the guard and the driver of trains on the company's line. He applied for, and received, permission to establish the system on one train of carriages. We do know that the traffic manager was requested in August 1857 to ascertain the probable cost of a third class carriage, but again the minutes are lacking in further detail. In May 1853 Nixon recommended procuring two additional composites and one third. It was agreed to have the engineer prepare specifications for the former, tenders to be sought locally in Bandon and Cork for the third. Tenders were received in July for the composites, these being referred to the secretary for further inquiry. There is, however, no further reference to the composites in the minutes and therefore it appears that they

were actually never ordered, but the third class vehicle was built by the company, the stock totals confirming these assertions.

Moving ahead to April 1860, the local committee considered the necessity of procuring additional rolling stock to meet the requirements of the traffic. It was thought that there would be an increase in traffic during the coming summer, particularly with the expected arrival of Brunel's steamship *Great Eastern* in Queenstown (now Cobh). Furthermore, the use of wagons for transporting passengers, as heretofore, was now considered objectionable. It was recommended by the committee that two thirds, each capable of carrying at least fifty passengers be procured as soon as possible, in addition to two more to be built by the company's workmen, the latter at an estimated cost of £135 each. Having been asked to consider his requirements for timber for the two carriages and six wagons, Conran submitted an estimate of £158 for 14 tons of oak, 10 tons of red pine and 12 tons of yellow pine. However, only one of the third class carriages was put in hand, and its completion in June was noted in the half-yearly report to shareholders of August 1860.

Meanwhile, the board had decided to obtain just one third class carriage from outside suppliers, the tender of the Dublin firm of Rogerson, Dawson & Russell at £245 delivered in Cork being accepted on 18th May subject to a 5% discount. The secretary was instructed to order cushions for this carriage, which was to have no letters painted on it, and it was delivered about July 1860. When the secretary drew attention to the continuing shortage of accommodation, the board decided that the other third class carriage should be constructed by the company's men and approval was given for the ordering of more timber, but it was decided to postpone the acquisition of upholstery until the following spring. Consideration was also given to the upholstering of the first class compartment of the four composite carriages as well as recovering the seats in the second class compartments, these carriages having been in use for eleven years.

Reporting to the board in January 1863, the locomotive superintendent indicated that there was a total of 15 passenger carrying vehicles, comprising four composites, one first, one second, seven thirds and two brake thirds. He stated that the four composite carriages were in very good working order; two of the first class compartments had been re-trimmed and the remaining two would be attended to during the year. He also reported that the first and the second were in good order, as were the seven thirds. The two brake thirds had been recently condemned and were soon to be replaced by two new vehicles in course of construction by the company's workmen, but this does not appear to have taken place until 1867 when they were replaced by two passenger brake vans. The carriage stock also included four carriage trucks and two horse boxes, one of the latter having just been constructed to replace, 'a bad one which will be converted into a goods wagon'.

In April 1863 the traffic manager recommended that an additional composite should be at once procured to meet the requirements of the Kinsale traffic, the board being requested to provide same, either by hiring or otherwise. In May Mr Dawson offered to supply the company with a second class carriage, 'as it stood at the Kingsbridge terminus…or it might be conveniently fitted up as a Composite at a short notice.' As it stood, it was painted green, with best springs, patent malleable wheels and Low Moor tyres. The secretary was instructed to ascertain the asking price as it stood or fitted up as a composite, the relevant figures being given as £262 10s 0d and £315 17s 6d. For the latter sum, Messrs Dawson would fit up the centre compartments as first class, with lining and cushions, and the end compartments with seat cushions only, of American leather cloth and best curled hair. In the event, an offer of £230 as a second was accepted, but the half-yearly returns show that it was in fact added to stock as a composite. This vehicle, originally No 2, survived into GSR days, having been converted into a first class carriage in May 1907 when second class was abolished. It became No 42 in 1908 and was not withdrawn until 1928.

The carriages are painted

George Miller, the locomotive superintendent of the GS&WR, examined and reported on the state of the locomotive and rolling stock towards the end of 1857, he being paid £5 5s 0d for his time and trouble. It was decided in March 1858, possibly following Miller's report, that the locomotives and rolling stock should be painted. Various tenders were received but were considered to be excessive. The locomotive superinten-

dent, Thomas Conran, stated that he had been in communication, 'with a party who is employed on an extensive Railway as Painter', who had agreed that the tenders were high.

In due course, a painter was procured to carry out the necessary work, but complaints were made in July that he was not working as speedily as he might. Two months later, further complaints were made as to, 'the great carelessness exhibited in the finish of his work', and it was decided to dispense with his services. The company's own painter was now instructed to proceed with the third class carriages and wagons. Later, a Mr Barry, who was already employed on the Cork Blackrock & Passage Railway, undertook to do the necessary work for 30s a week, this rate also being considered excessive. He was nevertheless taken on to paint one composite and one first, from week to week, 'for such time as he may give satisfaction'. The painting of rolling stock was to lead to some shareholders voicing objections at their half-yearly meeting in August 1859 to the unnecessary expenditure, the chairman in reply informing them that it was absolutely necessary for the preservation and cleanliness of the stock.

Rebuilding and replacement

The locomotive superintendent suggested in September 1863 that it would greatly improve the three old composite carriages if a third pair of wheels were put under them as this would make them last for several years longer. The suggestion was approved, but it was to be three years later before six more carriages were so treated. The traffic manager was still trying to persuade the board as to the want of additional accommodation in May 1864, leading to Conran being instructed to furnish an estimate for building one third class carriage, but noth-

ing seems to have come of this. In April 1865 the board decreed that WCR carriages were not to be used again, this indicating that the company had been loaned or hired stock from that company. Confirmation of the loan of WCR rolling stock to both the C&BR and the C&MDR appears in the WCR board minutes, an entry for 20th June 1867 stating that such loans be discontinued as some of the carriages, 'had been shamefully cut and injured'. It appeared in fact that the C&BR, having been loaned WCR carriages, had in turn loaned them to the C&MDR. One of the difficulties in using WCR stock was that the buffer heights of the two companies' vehicles were incompatible, ultimately requiring the raising of the company's stock to work with both the WCR and the C&MDR. This work, along with the addition of wheels to carriages, cost a sum of £426.

Like the locomotive stock, the history of the C&BR rolling stock is one of a constant shortage of accommodation and the acquisition of the minimum required to maintain a semblance of a service. This policy was to continue for a further period of time, and in fact, second hand vehicles were still being purchased in the 20th century. By 1867, most of the early stock was getting pretty worn. We have already noted that two third brakes were condemned in 1867 and in the same year rebuilding of the four original composites — the two Brown Marshall vehicles of 1851 and the 1852 conversions of the two seconds — commenced, the work being completed before the end of 1870. One of these composites was converted into third No 19 about 1882, another was withdrawn between 1886 and 1888 and a third one converted into a second and third class composite in 1889. Some of the underframe components of the fourth one may have been used in the construction of the saloon carriage described below, as the returns

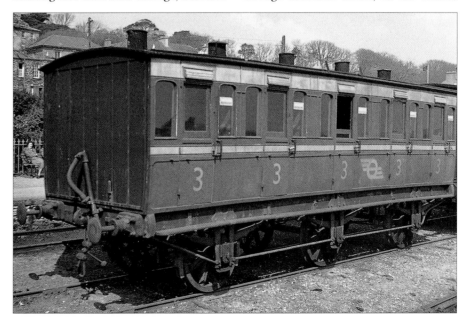

Six-wheeled third No 24B at Tramore on 21st April 1954. D G Coakham

Centre: **Six-wheeled Third No 15B at Cork.
This vehicle was supplied by the
Birmingham Carriage & Wagon Co in 1865
for the WCR. She was withdrawn in 1959.**
W A Camwell, IRRS

Below: **Six-wheeled Brake Van No 76B at
Albert Quay on 16th August 1952. This
vehicle dated from 1902 and was
withdrawn in 1957.**

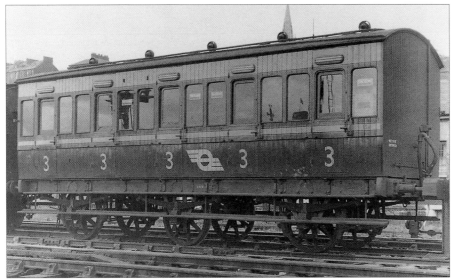

show the deletion of a composite in the
same half-year as the introduction of the
saloon.

Following the rebuilding of the composites the locomotive superintendent was urging the replacement of the old third class carriages, which he stated were past further repair. In July 1871, he said it was a good time to order three thirds, or to build them in Cork according to a pattern carriage he had just finished. Despite these urgings, it was February 1872 before a specification and tracing for the new vehicles were submitted to the board, the directors opting for two carriages at an estimated cost of £180, using old ironwork. One of these was completed in September 1872, the second at the end of January of the following year.

Conran informed the board in April 1873 that he had commenced altering the four-wheeled first class carriage No 5 into a first and second class composite by adding an extra compartment and turning it into a six-wheeled vehicle. This made it, 'uniform with the remainder of the carriages' and we can assume from this that all passenger-carrying vehicles were by then six-wheeled. No 5 was converted into a second and third class composite in 1878 and in 1889, following a further rebuilding, it became a third that lasted until 1901. The question of fitting steps on the company's carriages was raised in 1874, the engineer stating that he wished to know what was going to be done as the new line at Innoshannon station was now ready for use; for if steps were to be fitted, the new platform could be 15in higher. The provision of steps had previously been raised by Colonel Rich on behalf of the BoT and had now become urgent following the raising of springs on the rolling stock, which had made the carriages, 'decidedly too high for the platforms'.

In May 1875 the locomotive superintendent reported that he expected to commence a new second class carriage, and it appears that the underframe of one of the composites may have been used in its construction. However, as completed in 1876 this vehicle turned out to be first class saloon No 6. It was re-classified as third class saloon No 16 in 1896, and was destined to become the last surviving early Bandon carriage, not being withdrawn until 1913. Following completion of the saloon the locomotive superintendent sought instructions for the rebuilding of three old third class carriages which he considered were then nearly unfit for further service. The board approved of the suggestion and the replacement vehicles were completed in January, June and November 1877. All but one of the seven third class carriages rebuilt between 1871 and 1877 lasted until 1905/6, which is a testimony to the quality of work produced in the early days by the company's craftsmen.

The West Cork vehicles
The WCR, as we have already seen in Chapter Three, was an unfortunate company, beset with financial difficulties from the start. At a board meeting held on 29th April 1864, the directors of the WCR agreed with Mr Corry's suggestion of ordering rolling stock directly from the manufacturers. A committee comprising Messrs Corry and Kirk & Co were authorised to contract for the carriages and they recommended that the WCR accept the tender of Brown Marshall & Co, dated 30th June 1864, for passenger and goods rolling stock to the value of £12,407. The order, confirmed by the board on 31st August, included one first class carriage for £591 12s 0d, four first and second class composites at £525 12s 0d each, six thirds at £445.4s.0d each and two passenger brake vans at £340 16s 0d each. Three weeks later the WCR board agreed to Brown Marshall's request to allow the Birmingham Carriage & Wagon Co to carry out the contract made with them for rolling stock on precisely the same terms, Brown Marshall were to oversee the contract.

By March 1866, with the line still unopened, the rolling stock had been seized by the British & Foreign Railway Plant Co. and on 5th April Parsons, the traffic manager, attended the board to consider the question of hiring back from the B&FRP Co. the rolling stock required for the working of the traffic. Wood, the secretary, and Parsons attended a meeting of the B&FRP Co held the next day for the purpose of making the necessary arrangements, subsequently reporting that the B&FRP Co would agree to hire the rolling stock at a weekly rent to be mutually agreed on, and that a special committee of the Plant Co had been appointed to carry out such arrangements. The parties met again four days later, when the B&FRP Cos offered a ten-year lease-purchase arrangement for the rolling stock; the WCR to pay the sum of £30 weekly out of the traffic receipts for the use of the rolling stock. The rolling stock would become the property of the WCR at the expiration of the ten-year term, and the board agreed to this proposal on 12th April.

In August Messrs Brown Marshall were pressing for payment of a bill for £4,299

16s 2d falling due on 25th August, but the directors had to advise that they very much regretted that the WCR was not in a position to pay the amount, or any portion thereof. Brown Marshall agreed to a renewal of the bill for acceptance at three months, but when this fell due in November the company was in no better position to pay. Brown Marshall requested the board to consent to judgement being entered against the WCR for their claim amounting to £12,624 16s 5d, to which consent was given by the company. On 20th December 1866 Mr Sharkey, the company's solicitor, reported that proceedings against the company had been commenced by Brown Marshall.

As already recorded, the company was placed in receivership following a shareholders' investigation of its financial affairs. It was even found necessary to approach the B&FRP Co seeking a loan of £500 to complete unfinished works and allow of the opening of the line. At one point, in June 1867, the B&FRP Co stated that they were by then owed upwards of £1,300 for the hire of the rolling stock. The latter company considered that the traffic receipts of the WCR had increased sufficiently to allow an increase in the regular payments to £50 per week so as to reduce the amount due. The board agreed that, 'Those Gentlemen (the B&FRP Co) be informed that they have been misled as to the receipts, and the expenditure for working the line is quite equal to the receipts '.

A letter from the B&FRP Co, dated 26th September 1867, stated that the result of an interview with the WCR board had been reported to their directors. They were anxious to assist the WCR, but they stated that a condition prior to the entertaining of any proposition must be the payment of all arrears of the hiring account. On 31st October, Francis Mackreth, who, at the request of his colleagues on the board, had proceeded to Birmingham to confer with the B&FRP Co, reported the result of his interview. The board having considered the position, it was decided to write to the B&FRP Co. intimating that the removal of the rolling stock would place the company in difficulty, and might occasion the closing of the line and lead also to litigation. The board therefore requested the B&FRP Co to allow the rolling stock to remain for at least three months at a rent of £25 per week. The B&FRP Co replied stating that they had no intention of removing the rolling stock, but would require to be paid regularly for the hire of it. The board agreed to an immediate payment of £100, and to remit £50 every fortnight.

By September 1868 the situation was no better and at the end of that month the B&FRP Co sought to dispose of the rolling stock, the purchase of certain carriages being considered by both the C&BR and the DW&WR. The stock was, however, still avail-

able to the WCR the following April, but the company was desperately trying to find alternative sources and approached the Lancaster Wagon Company in regard to supply of rolling stock on deferred payment terms extending over 15 years. At the same time the B&FRP Co indicated that they would be willing to put an end to the existing agreement.

A tender from the Lancaster Wagon Co was considered on 19th May 1869 for the supply of two locomotives, three composite carriages, five third class carriages, two brake vans, twenty covered goods wagons, two carriage trucks, ten timber trucks and two horse boxes. The terms offered were a down payment of £3,675 and £750 per annum in quarterly payments to extend over ten years. The WCR was not prepared to entertain any proposition for the supply of rolling stock, except on terms of deferred payments. The board decided, however, that it would consider a tender on the terms proposed by the Lancaster Wagon Company's Agent; that was £750 per annum for 15 years, and requested them to tender on that or a similar basis. On 9th June it was reported that the Lancaster Wagon Co would not be willing to supply the rolling stock at £750 per annum for 15 years, but they suggested £1,000 per annum for 12 years.

Acting on a suggestion of the B&FRP Co, the Lancaster Wagon Co were approached in September to ascertain if they would purchase the rolling stock from the B&FRP Co and make arrangements for leasing a portion back to the WCR. On 17th February 1870 the secretary reported that the negotiations with the Lancaster Co had fallen through, and submitted a proposal from the B&FRP Co to lease the rolling stock at £20 per week or £1,040 per annum for twelve years. This offer having been considered it was resolved that the proposal for the lease and ultimate purchase of the existing stock be accepted in substitution for the terms on which the stock had theretofore been held, thus bringing to an end a period of almost 2½ years of uncertainty.

In December 1876 the WCR entered into correspondence with the Rolling Stock Company of Wolverhampton to enable them to purchase additional rolling stock, required in connection with the company's agreement to work the IVR extension to Skibbereen, for cash. The result was an offer to provide the funds, repayment to be over a period of seven years with interest charged at 7% per annum. The secretary was instructed to make an offer of 6% per annum interest for the advance, the consideration of tenders from the Bristol Wagon Co. and the Lancaster Wagon Co being postponed pending a reply. On 28th December it was reported that the Railway Rolling Stock Co could not advance the money to finance the rolling stock required by the WCR at a lower rate than 7% per annum interest.

Nothing more was heard about the matter until 13th February 1877 when a letter from the Railway Rolling Stock Co, repeating their offer to provide the money required to purchase the rolling stock at 7% per annum with repayments spread over seven years, was accepted. The draft agreement was submitted to the board on 6th June, but the WCR took exception to one of the clauses and requested an amendment. As the loan was secured on the existing rolling stock, it was deemed advisable to cancel the old agreement of April 1870, expiring 1st March 1882, and enter a new agreement for the remainder of the term, including repayment of the additional £2,000, spread over seven years. The additional rolling stock procured at this time included one additional third brake, for which dimensions and details of builder are unknown.

All but one of the passenger carriages obtained from BCW in 1865 were built to a length of 27ft 4in. The exception was the first class carriage, which was a four-compartment 24ft 9in vehicle. Originally No 7, it was rebuilt at Rocksavage in 1890 as a second and third class composite, eventually becoming third No 12 in 1901. It passed into GSR ownership in November 1924 and was not withdrawn until 1938. The first and second class composites and the third class carriages were all five-compartment vehicles. The four composites carried Nos 8 to 11 at first, No 11 being converted to third class No 18 about 1882 and possibly rebuilt at Rocksavage about 1912, as it lasted under GSR ownership until 1941 when it was converted into service vehicle No 211A. No 10 was similarly converted in 1892, becoming third No 24, and was probably rebuilt at Rocksavage in the early 1920s, as it was 1955 before it was withdrawn by CIÉ. The two other vehicles of this type were converted into second and third class composites in 1899, although they were still shown in the returns as first and second class composites until 1901. They subsequently became third class Nos 29 and 30 in 1902/3, No 30 being rebuilt at Rocksavage as a third brake in 1904, its body being used as a hut at Conyngham Road bus depot in Dublin, following its withdrawal in 1949. No 29 was one of the three carriages maliciously burnt at Baltimore on 24th January 1923.

Nos 8 to 16 in the third class list included the six third class carriages, the two BCW third brakes and the third brake obtained in 1877. Three of these vehicles, Nos 10, 11 and 13, were rebuilt at Rocksavage between 1913 and 1919 and survived in GSR ownership until withdrawn between 1939 and 1943. No 10 was converted into a service vehicle, No 210A in 1941 and No 11 was similarly treated in 1943 when it became Traffic

Department sleeping van No 221A. One of these vehicles, No 15, which was rebuilt at Rocksavage in 1920 was the last survivor of the former West Cork carriages, not being withdrawn until 1959.

Of the other third class carriages, No 14, was supposedly maliciously damaged in 1923 but, as it is shown as withdrawn by the GSR in 1928, it is more likely that it was one that was not rebuilt. Nos 8, 9, 12 and 16 were earlier withdrawals, No 8 being the first to go in 1895, it being recorded on 26th June 1895 that on taking it into the workshops, it was discovered that it was not worth repairing. The board having ordered it to be broken up, Johnstone reported on 11th September that the frame and wheels were converted into a truck for a travelling water tank. No 16, which might have been the third brake obtained in 1877, was replaced by saloon No 6 in 1896, No 12, which was possibly converted into a passenger brake van, was replaced by the former WCR first class carriage in 1901, and No 9 appears to have lasted until 1906.

Birmingham and Lough Swilly

We have seen that, with the exception of the two newest carriages supplied by Messrs. Dawson in 1860 and 1863, all other passenger carriages had been rebuilt at Bandon between 1868 and 1877. The next problem faced by the company was the question of obtaining additional carriages, and in August 1877 the locomotive superintendent reported on his examination of three carriages at the Swansea Wagon Works. He found that, although the carriages were of sound construction, they were not fit for second class but would be good enough for third class. This obviously did not suit the Bandon requirements as in September 1877 the manager, reporting on the need for extra carriage accommodation, recommended the purchase of three composites with one first class compartment in each, the remaining compartments to be second class. He further suggested that one third class, with a brake and a compartment for the brakeman, be obtained for attachment to all cattle trains so as to obviate the necessity of putting passengers into the guard's van, a procedure that he considered to be objectionable.

Thereafter matters moved quickly, for by 21st September the locomotive superintendent was reporting on his recommendation of the Birmingham Railway Carriage & Wagon Company's tracing and specification for the carriages. Birmingham's tender for supplying three composite carriages at £350 5s each and one third class carriage with brake van for £303 15s, delivered on Quay at Cork, was considered on 12th October and the board gave their approval, instructing that they be ordered. Delivery of the composites, originally Nos 12, 13 and 14,

commenced at the beginning of February 1878, and by 29th March the locomotive superintendent was able to report that all three had been running smoothly and cool for a week, also suggesting that it would not be well to varnish them for a few months. No 13 was subsequently renumbered, becoming No 1 sometime before 1902 and No 41 in the renumbering of 1908. All three of these 26ft 11in vehicles were reclassified as first class carriages in May 1907, Nos 12 and 14 being renumbered 49 and 51 in 1908, and all survived in GSR/CIÉ ownership until 1949.

The third brake, No 17, arrived in April, it being reported on 3rd May that it was working and fully up to specification. It was also a 26ft 11in vehicle, the body of which was completely renewed at Rocksavage in 1890. When No 17 was turned out at the end of April 1890 it was as a full third class carriage, Johnstone advising that it had cost £299 6s 0d to build the carriage, without the automatic brake. After about six years in service it was once again fitted up with a guard's compartment, Johnstone reporting this modification on 28th October 1896. No 17 lasted until 1947 when its body was scrapped following withdrawal by CIÉ; however, its underframe survived as a car carrier at Rosslare Harbour until 1963.

At the beginning of October 1884 Conran suggested that action should be taken in regard to the two composite carriages that would be required for the following season, and the board ordered that specifications and drawings be issued and tenders invited for the same. Tenders from Brown Marshall, the Birmingham Railway Carriage & Wagon Co, and the Metropolitan Carriage & Wagon Co were first considered on 21st January 1885, but the matter was postponed. It was not until 11th February that the tender of the Birmingham Carriage & Wagon Company at £490 for a first and second class composite and £540 for a first and second class saloon was accepted. Shortly afterwards the order must have been increased as a letter from the locomotive superintendent, dated 24th June, reported that he had inspected the four carriages being built at Birmingham and had to get some slight alterations made. He added that he did not expect they would be ready for delivery before the second week in July. Saloon No 16 was delivered on 20th July with the first and second class composite No 15 following a week later. Payment in the amount of £1,729 was authorised on 23rd September, £699 of which must have been for the two additional vehicles and the half-yearly returns indicate that two third brakes were added to stock at this time, which would have been Nos 22 and 23 in the third class list.

The first and second class composite No 15, which was a 29ft 4in. five-compartment vehicle, was altered to a second and third class composite about 1906 and was re-classified as a first and third composite in 1907, becoming third No 33 under the 1908 renumbering scheme. Unfortunately, it was completely burnt out in a malicious raid at Clonakilty on Sunday 14th January 1923. Saloon No 16 was shorter, being only 28ft 7in long, and less than two years after it was delivered it was recorded as being turned out of shops on 29th March 1887, having been cleaned up and varnished. The exact sequence of its renumbering is unclear for if it actually became No 56 in 1908, it would have had to be renumbered again following the introduction of new composite brake No 56 in 1910. However, it is known that it finally became No 60 in 1923. Following a rebuild in 1913, it was shown as having seating for 32 first class passengers, and it ran as a passenger carriage until 1949, when CIÉ converted it into breakdown van No 240A .

The pair of 25ft 10in long third brakes had interesting histories. Following the submission of a census of rolling stock in June 1889, from which it appeared that there were two carriages short, a partial renumbering of stock took place by which No 22 became No 19. Both vehicles had their brake compartments altered for luggage use only about 1913, and No 19 was one of the three carriages destroyed in the malicious burning at Baltimore station on 24th January 1923. The other third brake, No 23, survived for a short time in GSR days, being withdrawn in 1928.

Whilst the new carriages were under construction at Birmingham, a special board meeting was called on 4th May 1885 at which Conran reported on a visit to Derry and his inspection of the engines and rolling stock, which were to be disposed of by the Londonderry & Lough Swilly Railway. He stated that the two locomotives, one first class and two second class carriages were the only items of the stock on offer that were suitable for the Bandon. Having carefully considered the details and estimated prices, it was decided that Conran should attend the auction on Thursday 7th May, and he was empowered to bid for the two locomotives and carriages. On 13th May Conran

reported that as well as purchasing the two locomotives, he had secured one first class carriage for £180 and two second class carriages for £280. It seems likely that this stock was moved to Cork by rail, as Float Shears had to be hired at a cost of £35 from John Delaney in order to convey the two engines and three carriages from the north side to the south side of the River Lee, which would not have been the case if they had been shipped by sea. Delaney supplied the necessary men for wharfing the float, but was relieved of any liability for any damage, injury or risk to the stock whilst loading, unloading or during transit.

The Metropolitan Carriage & Wagon Co had built the three carriages for the L&LSR in 1878; the first class carriage was a 24ft 7in vehicle having been originally constructed as a first and second composite, a classification it reverted to as No 11 on the Bandon.

Following the abolition of second class in May 1907, No 11 was reclassified as a first class carriage again, and as such it became No 48 in 1908. Under GSR ownership it was reclassified as a third class carriage in 1938 and, following withdrawal by the GSR in 1943, its body was used as a hut at Cork. The two 25ft 11in carriages had a much more varied history and although they ran on the Bandon as second class at first, they were included in the third class list as Nos 20 and 21. They were reclassified as third brakes between 1889 and 1891, and were again reclassified in 1903 as passenger brake vans. They were, however, re-introduced to the third class list in 1911, each having just two compartments with seating for 20 passengers, and it is most likely that they were rebuilt at that time as they lasted under GSR/CIÉ ownership until 1955 (No 21) and 1959 (No 20).

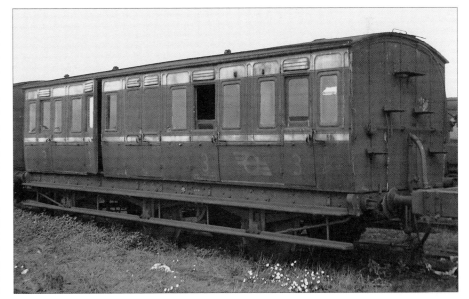

Right upper: **Six-wheeled luggage third No 59ʙ at Inchicore on 2nd October 1952. This was one of the ex DN&GR first/second composites purchased in 1909.**
D G Coakham

Right: **this bogie third, supplied by Lancaster in 1896. seating 60, this carriage remained in service until 1957.**
Photographer unknown, G Beesley collection

The short bogies

The year 1890 marked a watershed in the Bandon carriage history for it was in that year that the company introduced its first bogie carriage. Apart from rebuilds, and the vehicles purchased second-hand from the DN&GR — described below — all new passenger carrying vehicles from that date on were of bogie design. Until 1899 these were relatively short vehicles, all of which were permitted to work over the T&C section, but from 1901 onwards the length of successive designs was gradually increased.

Between 1890 and 1899 twelve short bogie vehicles were introduced; five third class carriages, five first and second class composite carriages, and two first and second class saloons. The first vehicle to be delivered was No 22, a 32ft 10in six-compartment third built by the Bristol Wagon Co in 1890. The origins of this particular order are interesting. On 12th June 1889 the manager submitted to the board the census of rolling stock, by which it appeared that there were two carriages short, and it was ordered that tenders be invited for two third class carriages. Tenders for two six-compartment bogie third class carriages were submitted on 3rd July from the Midland Railway Carriage Co, Birmingham Railway Carriage & Wagon Co, Ashbury and Brown Marshall, but a decision on the matter was postponed. A week later the lowest tender, that of Midland, at £495 each, was considered along with one from Edward Corry for the same type of vehicle at £420 each, and it was decided that Corry's tender should be accepted, provided that Mr Johnstone approved the tracing.

Johnstone recommended acceptance of Edward Corry's tender on 17th July, however, it was for only one bogie third class carriage at £485. The reason for the price increase and reduction in order quantity is not recorded, but whether it was the price or the builder, the Bristol Wagon Co, Johnstone may have wished to err on the side of caution with his first venture into bogie vehicles. This approach seems to have been justified when, on 14th August, Corry stated that the extra cost for the alterations required in the third class carriage ordered from him would be £26 15s 0d. The board decided to offer Corry £10 for the alterations and if this was not acceptable to him the order was be given to Midland at their tender price of £495. A week later Corry agreed to accept £495 for the third class carriage.

On 13th November Johnstone reported that the Bristol Wagon Co had offered to put the automatic vacuum brake on the new third class, which they were building at a cost of £38 10s 0d, and it was decided to have it put on. Progress thereafter appears to have been slow, as it was not until 21st May 1890 that Johnstone was able to report

on his inspection of the carriage at Bristol, noting that he found all the work very good and expected it to be delivered by the end of June. His estimate for delivery was, however, not to be fulfilled as it was 13th August before he could report that the new carriage had been received. No 22 was reclassified as a first and third class composite by the GSR and was not withdrawn until 1957. It was destined to be the only carriage supplied by the Bristol Wagon Co. to the Bandon; all subsequent orders being either awarded to the Lancaster Railway Carriage Co or constructed at Rocksavage.

Two weeks prior to his report on the inspection of the carriage at Bristol, Johnstone indicated that he proposed to lay down a bogie composite to replace No 5, lately converted to third class. The new No 5 (renumbered 43 in 1908) was completed by August 1891 when Johnstone reported that he had laid down the frame of another bogie composite. This latter vehicle, which was to be delivered as No 17 in 1892, became No 52 in the 1908 renumbering. Apart from the couple of body renewals completed in 1890, these two vehicles marked the beginning of the construction of complete carriages at the Rocksavage workshops. They were 33ft 11in long, five-compartment vehicles with seating for 16 first class and 30 second class passengers, the first of five vehicles to be built to this design. Rocksavage built composite No 7 (No 45 from 1908), which was ordered on 2nd August 1893 and completed in mid-1894, and two further vehicles of this design, ordered from the Lancaster Railway Carriage Co, were delivered in July and August 1899.

The two latter vehicles resulted from a report made by the general manager on 16th November 1898 recommending the purchase of five new carriages and the conversion of three old composites into third class carriages, which was postponed for further consideration. The matter was again considered on 11th January 1899, when it was agreed to order two new six-compartment first and second class composite carriages, but without lavatories, and to convert two of the West Cork first and second class composites to third class with a centre second class compartment, this being confirmed at the following week's meeting. In the intervening period, an offer from Robert Coey, locomotive engineer of the GS&WR, of 18 former Waterford Dungarvan & Lismore Railway carriages at a low figure was considered on 7th December 1898, as they might have proved useful for excursion traffic, but as they were four-wheeled vehicles it was decided not to recommend the purchase of any of them.

The tender specification for these two composites gives a good insight into the standard that the Bandon required at the time. The specification reads:

'To contain five compartments, two 1st and three 2nd class, mounted on two four-wheeled bogies. The body to be 34ft long and framed with the best selected Delaware or Quebec White Oak. The panels to be of well-seasoned mahogany, the inside sheeting and roof to be of pitch pine — in the 1st class compartments this sheeting to be covered with White Oak veneer and Walnut mouldings. The seats are to be fitted with sofa springs; cushions and backs of curled hair and covered with blue cloth to pattern. The 2nd class to have Wood's Patent Spring seats. Each end of the 1st class compartments to be fitted with one plate glass mirror and two sets of coloured photographs to be supplied by the Company. One 1st and one 2nd class compartments to be Smoking (to be marked on the glass) and situated together at one end. Each carriage to receive two coats of priming, five coats of filling, two of lead colour, two of lake metallic oxide, lined in yellow and lettered, transfers for letters and Coats of Arms to be supplied by the Company, and three coats of varnish. The underframe to be blacked and lined yellow and varnished on the outside, the bogies, wheels etc. to receive two coats of black.'

The tender closing date was Tuesday 7th March 1899, and on the following day Lancaster's tender at £775 each, delivered on the company's rails at Cork by 15th July, was accepted subject to a penalty of £20 per week to apply from 25th July. Johnstone, reporting in April, stated that he had inspected the timber for the new carriages and had found it very good. Letters received from the Lancaster Railway Carriage Co in July stated that they had not yet got the bogies for the carriages. It was pointed out that this was entirely due to the non-delivery by the Leeds Forge Co and was no fault of theirs, but despite the explanation the Bandon decided to hold Lancaster to their contract in regard to time of delivery. This must have expedited the work as the first carriage was delivered on 27th July, the second following on 11th August. They originally carried numbers 8 and 9, but became Nos 46 and 47 under the 1908 renumbering. As their delivery was outside the contract date, Johnstone enquired whether the makers were to be charged with penalties, but the board decided that these were not to be enforced. In May 1907 all five first and second class composites were re-classified as firsts, passing into GSR ownership in November 1924. Nos 46 and 47 were the first to be withdrawn in 1949, it was not until 1957 that CIÉ withdrew the other three vehicles of this type.

Having dealt with the composites, we must go back to 2nd August 1893 when the question of rolling stock suitable for running over the T&C was considered. It was decided that, as the existing stock was insufficient to accommodate the excursion traffic, the locomotive engineer be ordered to build a new composite bogie carriage to be ready for the next season and to get quotations for a third class bogie carriage. On 6th September 1893 Johnstone submitted tenders for the third class bogie carriage, that of the Lancaster Railway Carriage Co. at £490 being accepted. As early as November, Johnstone reported that he had inspected the new third class carriage at the Lancaster works and found everything very satisfactory, and No 25, another 32ft 10in six-compartment vehicle, was delivered on 22nd January 1894.

Three more vehicles to this same design, Nos 8, 26 and 27, were delivered in January 1896. It had been decided in the previous June to invite tenders for the three thirds and on 24th July Lancaster's tender at £499 each was accepted. In December the locomotive engineer reported that he had inspected the new carriages at the Lancaster works, and with the exception of the paint, which was rather light in colour, he had found everything very satisfactory. As the paint would darken with age, he had not objected to it. When the carriages arrived at Cork in January 1896 shipping damage was reported by Johnstone; one panel broken and paint damaged on the first one and three side lights broken on the second one, which he repaired at the builder's expense. No 8 was reclassified as a first and third composite by the GSR but reverted to all third class in 1941 before being withdrawn in 1957, the same year as No 25. Nos 26 and 27 had somewhat shorter lives having been withdrawn earlier in 1941 and 1948, respectively.

To conclude the story of the short bogies we must look at the two first class saloons built by the Bandon at Rocksavage. On 23rd May 1894 the locomotive engineer reported he had laid down the frame of a new lavatory saloon carriage, but it was 29th September in the following year before he was able to indicate that he had tried the new saloon. No 10, which was renumbered 55 in 1908, was built to the same 33ft 11in length as the composites, but the second of the saloons, No 18 (No 57 from 1908) completed in March 1896, is recorded as being a little shorter at 33ft 4in. There is no apparent reason for this change to what was a unique length for the Bandon, as the design of both of these saloons appears to have been identical in all other respects, consisting of two saloon style compartments and a lavatory,

seating being provided for 26 first class passengers. One interesting point about the second of these saloons is that the painting was carried out by piecework for £22. No 55 survived as a first saloon until its withdrawal by CIÉ in 1960, the last surviving CB&SCR passenger carriage, and No 57, following its reclassification as a third in 1938, lasted until 1948.

Longer bogies

At the end of November 1899, the locomotive engineer reported that he had laid down the frame for a second and third class composite carriage, and he asked the board's instructions as to whether it should be built with separate compartments or in saloons. Although it was noted that with saloons it would carry six passengers less, the general manager's report that second and third class saloon carriages were much wanted was taken into account and it was ordered that the new carriage should be built in saloons, with the seats in the third class saloon fitted with cushions. With this vehicle, completed in early 1901, the length was increased to 37ft 10in and it was provided with two open centre saloons for each class and two lavatories. Unfortunately, its original number cannot be stated with certainty but, following its reclassification as a first and third class composite in May 1907, it became No 54 in 1908. Its classification was never altered by the GSR and it lasted into CIÉ days, not being withdrawn until 1959.

Another two carriages were built at Rocksavage to the same length of 37ft 10in, first and second composite No 13 in 1902, and a second and third composite brake in 1903. The latter was reclassified as a first and third composite brake in May 1907 and became third brake No 31 in 1908. It is generally shown on carriage lists as built in 1905, but careful analysis has uncovered its true origin. No 31 was maliciously damaged by fire at Clonakilty on 14th January 1923 but fol-

lowing repair it lasted into GSR/CIÉ ownership and was not withdrawn until 1957. The first and second class composite, No 13, was reclassified as a first in May 1907 and became No 50 in the 1908 renumbering, but was unfortunately destroyed during the Civil War, although there is no reference to it in the minutes.

In early 1905 a new design of eight-compartment third class carriage was adopted wherein the length of the bogie vehicle was increased to 43ft 2in. It was decided to order four vehicles to this design, one to be built at Rocksavage and the other three under contract. On 1st February the locomotive engineer submitted tenders for three third class carriages and that of the Metropolitan Amalgamated Carriage & Wagon Co, Lancaster, at £720 for each carriage delivered, was accepted on the condition that delivery was completed by 15th May 1905, failing which payment would not be made until 1st May 1906. Within a couple of weeks Johnstone was reporting that he had inspected the timber and arranged details at Lancaster for the new carriages ordered, and had found everything in order.

In mid-April Johnstone again inspected the work done on the three carriages being built at Lancaster, and also the springs for them at Sheffield, and he reported that the work was not at all as far advanced as he had expected. Delivery was still promised by the middle of May, but despite this assurance the secretary was directed to write to Lancaster to express the board's disappointment at the poor progress made, and to impress on them the absolute necessity of delivery being made by 25th May, the date agreed upon. However, on the last day of May the locomotive engineer was reporting that he had an advice from the builders that the first of the three carriages had only been sent off on 29th May. Lancaster had written to the CB&SCR on 23rd May asking if they would accept delivery of the carriages and pay for them as delivered provided they

An eight compartment bogie third, four of which were introduced in 1905 and numbered 1 to 4. Numbers 1, 2 and 4 were supplied by Metropolitan, No 3 was built at the company's works at Rocksavage.
Photographer unknown, G Beesley collection

were forwarded within three weeks from date of their letter. The Bandon agreed to this provided the carriages were completed in accordance with specification. No 3, the vehicle built at Rocksavage to the same design, joined the three Lancaster carriages, Nos 1, 2 and 4, at the end of August. All four vehicles passed into GSR ownership and all were withdrawn by CIÉ in 1957.

The length was again increased for the three bogie carriages built at Rocksavage in 1906/07, two third brakes and a first and second composite. For this build a length of 46ft.6in. was adopted and this enabled the third brakes Nos 6 and 28 to be built with five compartments and a 19ft luggage and guard's compartment. Composite No 6 was a side-corridor carriage with three first class and four second class compartments with two lavatories located in the centre of the vehicle. It was initially reclassified as a first class carriage in May 1907, but in the following year it became first and third composite No 44. Third brake No 6 ran for a period up to 1928 as a composite brake and, having reverted to its original classification in 1928, lasted into CIÉ days until withdrawn in 1948. The composite lasted until 1953, and the other third brake, No 28, had the longest life of the three, surviving until 1953.

Finally, in 1908 the length for new Bandon bogie carriages was extended to 48ft 11in when the first of two first and third composite brakes, No 53, was turned out from Rocksavage, where an identical vehicle, No 56, was completed in 1910. These two carriages were constructed with two first class and three third class compartments separated by a luggage and guard's compartment in the centre of the vehicle. They both survived under GSR/CIÉ ownership without modification, No 53 until 1959 and No 56 until 1953. The last vehicle built to this length, and the last passenger car-

riage to be built new for the Bandon, was No 62, an open centre first class with 6 seating bays and two lavatories, completed in November 1914 at a cost of £955. It has sometimes been recorded that this carriage was to be used as a Tea Car on a possible through passenger service to Rosslare, but no contemporary evidence has been found to support this theory, and the absence of gangway connections also confirms that this was unlikely. The GSR proposed to fit gangways in 1934, but this carriage appears to have remained unaltered until withdrawn by CIÉ in 1954.

Second-hand from Greenore

To conclude this section on passenger carrying vehicles, we must now return to the start of the twentieth century when the Bandon twice availed of the opportunity to purchase second-hand vehicles from the Dundalk, Newry & Greenore Railway. On 1st May 1901 the locomotive engineer submitted a letter from Mr Burgess, advising that the L&NWR had some carriages for sale at Greenore. A week later Johnstone, having been to inspect them, reported that they were three five-compartment and two four-compartment cushioned thirds. He considered that they were in fair condition and, being fitted with automatic brake, would be worth £60 each for the five-compartment and £55 each for the four-compartment carriages, to which freight costs of £9 per carriage would have to be added. Having considered the matter, the board ordered Johnstone to make an offer of £275 for the five carriages.

When the L&NWR indicated that they wanted a separate offer for each carriage it was decided to leave the matter in the hands of the chairman, but on 22nd May the board discussed the matter again and decided to offer £55 each for the five-compartment carriages and £50 each for the four-compart-

ment carriages. In response to this offer the L&NWR intimated, through their local Agent on 12th June, that they wanted £90 and £80 respectively for the carriages, but it was decided not to increase the offer. This obviously put the L&NWR under some pressure, for by 31st July Burgess was indicating that he wished to see the general manager in Dublin. However, the CB&SCR board decided that this was unnecessary, as they were not prepared to increase the offer they had already made.

At a board meeting on 4th September, Johnstone reported by letter that the L&NWR had accepted the company's offer of £210 for two of the three five-compartment and the two four-compartment thirds, delivered at Dundalk, and by 16th October they had arrived in Cork. The L&NWR had built these carriages at their Wolverton Works in 1872 and 1876 for the DN&GR. On the CB&SCR, the two 27ft 6in five-compartment carriages replaced two old third class carriages Nos 5 and 9. The two 25ft 0in four-compartment carriages ran as second and third class composites at first; one being reclassified as third class Nos 7 about 1906, and the other becoming a first and third class composite when second class was abolished in May 1907 and then third No 32 in the following year. One of these vehicles was very badly damaged in the Kinsale accident of 28th January 1915, the two rear compartments being smashed and the body shifted on the frame. Although the CB&SCR initially considered that it was destroyed it must have been rebuilt as all four of these vehicles lasted well into GSR days, not being withdrawn from the coaching stock list until sometime between 1938 and 1941.

On 1st September 1909 the locomotive engineer reported that he had inspected four more carriages, which the L&NWR had for sale at Greenore, and he reported that they were six-wheeled four-compartment first and second composites with luggage compartments. He noted that they were in very good condition, being fitted with electric light and, as far as he could ascertain, the only portion that would have to be renewed was the draw gear. The board decided that the general manager should be authorised to purchase them at a total cost not to exceed £240, an offer of £200 to be made in the first instance. However, a week later the general manager submitted a letter, from Mr Burgess of the L&NWR, declining to accept less than £70 each for the four carriages. The general manager was authorised

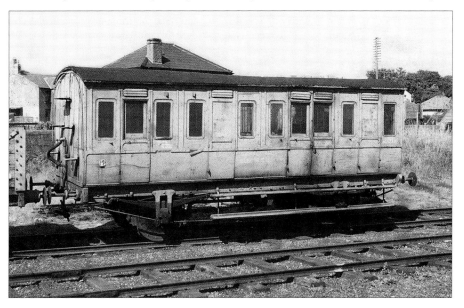

Ex CB&SCR four-wheeled third No 7 as Signal & Electrical Department Tool Van No 201A (she was so numbered in 1940). No 7 was purchased second-hand in 1901 from the DN&GR, where she was numbered either 5 or 15.
Photographer unknown, Author's collection

to purchase the four carriages in question, on the best terms he could, and on 13th October he was able to report that the L&NWR had accepted an offer of £55 per carriage.

The L&NWR had also built these DN&GR vehicles at Wolverton in 1872 and 1876. These 30ft 6in carriages were additions to the Bandon stock, becoming first and third composites Nos 58 to 61 inclusive. In 1923, No 60 was converted into third No 34, the vacant No 60 being taken up by saloon No 56 (formerly No 16). Unfortunately, one of these vehicles, No 58, was destroyed in the malicious burning of the station and carriages at Baltimore on 24th January 1923. The other three all survived into CIÉ days, it being between 1948 and 1954 before they were withdrawn.

Liveries and Numbering

Although it is known that the composite delivered by Dawson in 1863 was painted green, this may have simply been the standard colour applied by the manufacturer at that time to completed carriages. It is not known what colour was applied prior to September 1899 when the question of changing the colour of the company's carriages was considered. It was then decided that the next carriages to be painted should be coloured green. This would appear to have been the same shade of olive-green as used for the locomotives, and lining was yellow. Some time prior to 1914 a much lighter shade of green was applied to the upper panels, but olive green lined out in yellow was standard after World War I.

Following the abolition of second class in May 1907, the carriages containing second class seating were reclassified, first and second class composites becoming firsts and second and third class composites ordinary thirds, with the exception of the second and third class saloon which became a first and third class composite. In 1908 the passenger stock was renumbered; the thirds and third brakes retaining their original numbers, 1 to 30 with the former second and third class composites following as Nos 31 to 33. The first and second class composites took up a new number series, 41 to 52, the saloons following as Nos 54 to 57, with No 53 being retained for the new composite brake then under construction. Later additions took up following numbers in the appropriate sequence. After amalgamation into the GSR the Bandon stock was signified by the addition of the section suffix 'B' to the existing numbers, but early GSR withdrawals did not actually carry the new designation.

OTHER CARRIAGE STOCK

Luggage, parcel and brake vans
Four passenger vans appear to have been obtained in the early days and the company

constructed another one in 1857, which lasted until about 1882. In 1867 two old third class brakes and one of the early passenger vans were replaced by two new parcel and mail vans built by the C&BR, which appear to have lasted until about 1882-85. Another of the early passenger vans was replaced by a new mail van built by the company in 1870, which in turn was withdrawn about 1885. The last two of the early passenger vans disappeared sometime between 1879 and 1883. Two passenger brake vans, built in 1865 by BCW for the WCR at £340 16s each, were added to the C&BR stock in 1879, and lasted until 1898/99.

In April 1882 the locomotive superintendent reported that he was short of two passenger brake vans and six months later he had to raise the matter again stating that he was, 'very short of brake accommodation'. At the end of November the board accepted the tender of the Midland, Carriage & Wagon Co. for two passenger brake vans at £350 each delivered to Albert Quay. These two vans arrived at the beginning of August 1883, and lasted until about 1902. The next pair of vans was obtained as the result of a suggestion made by the chairman in June 1895; the tender of the Lancaster Railway Carriage Co, at £471 each, being accepted on 24th July. Delivery was made in the following February and these two vehicles eventually became Nos 71 and 72 in the renumbered passenger list of 1908. Both of these vans lasted into CIÉ days, one being withdrawn in 1948 and the other in 1960.

In February 1900 a tender from BCW to supply three 20ft 0in fish vans at £385 each was accepted. The specification called for the vehicles to be, 'fitted with one dog box at one end, with outside doors fitted with ventilators, and the other end a space covered with zinc so as to make a tray for carrying ice. Double doors to be oak-framed. Wrought iron wheels, 3ft 6in diameter on tread; each van to be fitted with one screw coupling and the vacuum brake. To receive two coats of primer, five of filler, two of lead colour, two coats of green lined yellow and lettered, and finally three coats of varnish.'

These fish vans were delivered in October 1900 and were assigned to the passenger van fleet. One of them, No 1, was destroyed in the malicious fire at Baltimore on 24th January 1923. The CB&SCR built three new 26ft 10in vans at Rocksavage between 1898 and 1902. Around 1902 former WCR third No 12 was converted into a passenger brake van. It was rebuilt at Rocksavage in 1922 and lasted in service until 1958 when it became service vehicle No 343A. There was a temporary addition to the van list between 1903 and 1911 during which period the two former L&LSR third brakes were classified as brake vans.

Horseboxes & Carriage Trucks
Two horseboxes were obtained in the early days, and Preston may have built these at the Bandon workshops in 1851. A new horsebox built by the C&BR in 1872 replaced one of them. Two horseboxes, built by BCW in 1865 for the WCR at £232 16s each, were added to the C&BR stock in 1879, and it appears that these might have been the two vehicles that survived into GSR days, the two earlier C&BR vehicles possibly being the ones withdrawn in 1907 and 1913.

There were four carriage trucks obtained early on and these were probably also amongst the trucks built by Preston in 1851. Two of these were withdrawn in 1870 and another between 1879 and 1883 and the last one in 1893. The WCR stock added in 1879 brought with it two carriage trucks that had been built by BCW in 1865 for £171 12s each. The two former WCR carriage trucks were withdrawn in 1879; the same year as the CB&SCR built two new carriage trucks — one completed in August and the other in November — which were the two vehicles that survived into GSR days.

GOODS STOCK

Early wagons
Our knowledge of the early wagons owned by the C&BR stems from a report to board made by the locomotive superintendent on 8th January 1863. At that time the company possessed 38 covered wagons and 17 open wagons and two timber trucks. The first goods vehicles appear to have been 12 covered wagons, probably built for the opening of the line in 1849, six of which were rebuilt by the C&BR in 1860 specifically for cattle traffic. About 28 open wagons had been built under contract in the Bandon workshops during 1851 by Mr Preston, and a further twelve covered wagons were also built under contract by Mr Walsh in 1855, all materials for their construction being supplied by the company. Although constructed by contract labour, these vehicles were always considered to have been built by the company. The board ordered the procurement of two timber trucks in February 1853, but it is not known where they were built.

The stock was increased by delivery of six covered wagons and six open wagons from Dawson in October 1857. In the period 1860-62 the C&BR rebuilt 16 of the early opens as covered wagons, and in 1861 they added three new covered wagons which they built at Bandon. The company's first goods brake van was built at Bandon in 1864 but it did not last too long as it was replaced by a new ten-ton van built by the company in 1871. In 1864 and 1867 the company built 12 new covered wagons (six in each year) to replace old ones which were

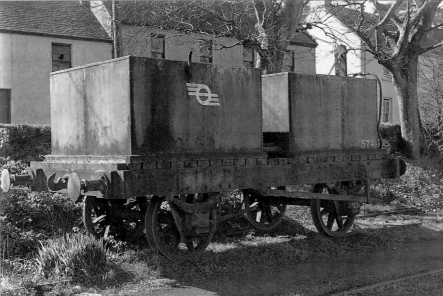

Top left: **Twelve-ton Open Goods Wagon No 603 at Cork.** Photographer unknown, J W P Rowledge collection

Centre: **Rectangular tank wagon No 574B, used for tar traffic at Courtmacsherry on 19th March 1961. From the appearance of the undergrowth and the lack of a coupling, at least at one end, it would seem that this vehicle had not been moved for some time.** D G Coakham

Below: **Six-ton open-ended wagon No 721B at Kingsbridge, Dublin on 20th April 1957.** D G Coakham

broken up, and in 1868 they rebuilt eight others.

In May 1869 an order was placed with the Lancaster Wagon Co, for the supply of six covered wagons at £90 each, the order being increased two months later by six additional vehicles of the same type. This was the first order to be placed by the Bandon with recognised wagon building companies, but was a short lived venture. In 1871 the company turned to the GS&WR for 20 second-hand covered wagons; although they only cost £7 each plus £1 per wagon for delivery, they came with a lot of problems and 18 of them were converted to open wagons in the following two years. By 1880 there were only eleven of them left running and the locomotive superintendent had them marked for light goods only. The company reverted to outside suppliers in 1873 when twenty covered wagons were ordered from the Bristol Wagon Co at £137 each, but the following order went to the home market when the South of Ireland Wagon Co of Cappoquin, secured a tender on 17th March 1876 for six covered wagons at £116 10s 0d each. This order was increased by a further six wagons in July, and on 31st August 1877 the South of Ireland Wagon Co's tender for 20 additional covered goods wagons at £97 10s 0d each was accepted.

The West Cork wagons

As recorded in the section on carriages, the WCR board agreed to the Birmingham Carriage & Wagon Co. carrying out the contract made with Brown Marshall for the supply of rolling stock to their company on precisely the same terms. The goods stock ordered in August 1864 comprised 20 covered wagons, ten open wagons, two timber trucks, and two goods brake vans. These vehicles were quite expensive; the covered wagons costing £168 each, the open wagons and the timber trucks £138 each, and the goods brake vans £217 4s 0d each. A further 20 covered wagons were ordered from the South of Ireland Wagon Co on 6th March 1877 at £97 10s 0d each, subject to the wagons being, 'the same as the last wagons supplied to the C&BR'. All of this WCR goods stock was taken into the C&BR list in 1879 and between December 1881 and July 1882 a total of 16 of the old WCR wagons were rebuilt as cattle wagons.

More new stock
Ten wagons were burnt at Bandon in August 1879. Seven were new and three old but all were in good condition — their timber work was completely destroyed. The South of Ireland Wagon Co completely rebuilt all ten of them, the seven newer wagons costing between £49 and £58 each and the three older ones £67 10s 0d, and for all intents and purposes they were considered to be new wagons. The company sought to procure four ten-ton hopper ballast wagons in 1879, but in the event four ordinary ballast wagons were obtained, but it is not certain whether these came from the Birmingham Carriage & Wagon Co or the South of Ireland Wagon Co The four ten-ton ballast hopper wagons were, however, eventually procured for £75 each from the Swansea Wagon Co in 1884. Dorman, the C&BR engineer, inspected the wagons at Swansea in May and reported that the gear for opening and shutting the bottom doors might prove ineffective, his fears being realised following delivery of the first two hoppers in July; the Swansea Wagon Co making the necessary alterations at their expense.

Meanwhile, 20 further covered wagons were obtained from the South of Ireland Wagon Co. in 1880 for £95 each and in March 1883 Brown Marshall secured an order for twenty covered wagons at £93 5s 0d each, which were all delivered by February 1884. Thus, by the end of 1884, we find the company in possession of a total of 170 covered wagons, 24 open wagons, 16 cattle wagons, four ballast trucks, four ballast hoppers, four timber trucks and three goods brake vans.

At the end of June 1887 a letter was received from the secretary of the Butter Market requesting that special wagons should be used for the conveyance of butter during hot weather and in November 1887 the locomotive superintendent was able to report that six wagons had been altered to suit butter traffic. Three of these wagons were subsequently cleaned, painted and equipped with continuous brakes in May 1896.

The expansion of the CB&SCR wagon fleet continued, the Birmingham Carriage & Wagon Co supplying 20 covered wagons in each of the years 1887 and 1890, the former at £83 each and the latter at £109 15s 0d each. The locomotive engineer laid down two ballast wagons in January 1888, which were turned out in August and December of the same year. December 1888 also saw the completion of a new goods brake van by the C&BSCR. In October 1890 it was Ashbury who won the tender for the supply of twenty covered wagons (£106 10s 0d each) and twelve ballast wagons (£86 each). The locomotive engineer enquired into the cost of fitting these wagons with through vacuum pipes and screw couplings, but when Ashbury quoted £7 15s 0d each for the work it was decided not to have them piped before delivery. It was to be March 1894 before this matter was raised again when it was decided to equip 20 wagons with the automatic vacuum brake for the purpose of running them in passenger trains for the conveyance of fish and perishables traffic. The construction of two more goods brake vans in the company's workshops was authorised at the end of April 1890, one being completed towards the end of the year and the other early in 1891.

In October 1891 the locomotive engineer recommended that some extra breakdown gear be got and it was decided to make enquiries as to the cost of a ten-ton locomotive crane. The following month it was agreed to accept the offer of Thomas Smith of Rodley at £450 for a travelling locomotive breakdown crane, provided the specification was altered to Johnstone's approval. The crane was ready for delivery by the end of May 1892 and was shipped in pieces and erected on site by the manufacturer.

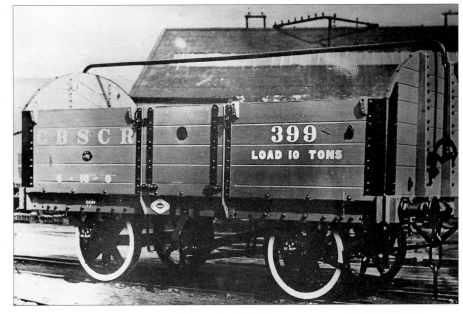

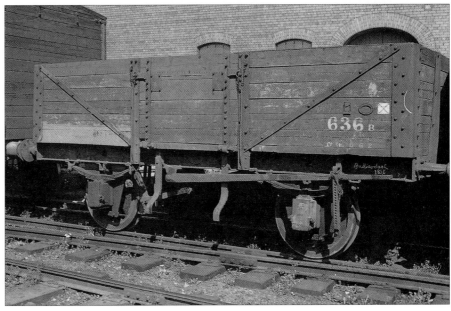

Right upper: **Pickering wagon No 399 at Cork. These wagons were purchased in 1904 for grain traffic, hence the tarpaulin rails and high ends.** Seán Kennedy collection

Right: **Twelve-ton open goods wagon No 636B at Albert Quay on 20th August 1954.** D G Coakham

Another goods brake van was completed in the company's workshop in June 1892 and in the following year three open wagons and three goods brake vans were turned out; the increase in the number of brake vans being occasioned by BoT requirements. In August 1894 the general manager reported to the board that owing to the insufficient supply of wagons it was, 'impossible to work the goods and cattle traffic with satisfaction to the public'. As a result of this report it was decided to obtain tenders for 50 new covered wagons and on 5th September it was agreed to accept the tender of the Bristol Wagon Co at £81 each and at the same time to call for tenders for 25 open wagons. The tenders for the latter wagons were submitted on 10th October and it was decided, once again, to accept that of the Bristol Wagon Co at £62 17s 6d. each for open wagons and £67 10s 0d each for timber trucks. A week later an offer was submitted for two goods brake vans at £137 each and it was decided to accept this in lieu of four of the 18 open wagons. By the end of 1894, 28 of the covered wagons and the two goods brake vans had been delivered; the delivery of the balance of 22 covered wagons, 14 open wagons and seven timber trucks being finally completed by 10th April 1895 following the replacement by the builders of two covered wagons that were lost in transit.

Two wagons were offered at £35 each by the CB&PR early in December 1900, this offer being accepted. Within a couple of days, however, this was withdrawn as it appeared that a higher offer had been received from the C&MDR. Despite a protest, these wagons were sold to the Macroom company.

The final phase

Following a lapse of over six years, new wagon construction commenced again in 1902 with the rebuilding of six open wagons as timber trucks and the delivery, in the following year, of six ten-ton open wagons from the Rocksavage workshops for £95 each. Complaints were made in July 1903 of a shortage of wagons for grain traffic. Johnstone was instructed to prepare plans for 20 ten-ton open wagons. The specification was to include framing of well-seasoned American white oak, sides, ends and floors to be of Baltic redwood, tongued and grooved. Length over headstocks was to be 17ft 8in with solid wrought-iron wheels of 3ft 4in diameter. The wagons were to be provided with Dean and Churchward either-side wagon brakes. They were to receive three coats of lead paint and to arrive lettered and numbered. Tenders for the supply of 20 additional wagons were received in the following October and that of Messrs R J Pickering of Wishaw at £98 10s 0d each was accepted; steel underframes were offered

Top: **Eight-ton cattle wagon No 158B, built in 1920, at Broadstone, Dublin on 23rd April 1954.** D G Coakham

Above: **Piped meat van No 167B, looking rather the worse for wear, at Kingsbridge, Dublin in April 1954.** D G Coakham

Top right: **Covered goods wagon No 41B at Athboy on 22nd April 1957. This wagon appears in a GSR Wagon List dated 1927 as a cattle wagon built in 1922!** D G Coakham

Centre: **Ten-ton covered goods wagon No 9B, built in 1912, at Glanmire Road, Cork on 20th August 1954.** D G Coakham

Below: **Ten-ton goods brake van No 761B at Glanmire Road, Cork on 20th August 1954.** D G Coakham

for an additional £10 per wagon. All of these open wagons were subsequently uprated to twelve-ton capacity. At least one of these Pickering wagons (No 399) was fitted with tarpaulin rails and higher, curved, ends. Apart from 20 wagons obtained from MCW via the GS&WR in 1921, described below, those from Pickering were to be the last wagons supplied directly to the CB&SCR by outside builders.

From 1904 the workshops at Rocksavage satisfied all the company's needs for goods wagons principally through renewals, many of which included conversions in type of vehicle. The last capital additions to the wagon stock were made between 1910 and 1912 when 20 open wagons, ten mineral wagons and 20 covered wagons were constructed as a result of the general manager reporting in April 1910 on the increase that had taken place in the quantity of goods carried during the previous ten years. The payment for these 50 wagons was met through the placement of £250 into a Reserve Fund each half year until the sum of £5,000 required had been set aside, the cost, however, being charged to the capital account.

Between 1905 and 1924 the covered wagon fleet was reduced by the renewal of 98 as cattle wagons, 44 as 12-ton open wagons and 15 as six-ton mineral wagons. At the same time at least 61 were renewed as covered wagons. The complete renewal of the cattle wagon fleet was accomplished through the replacement of the 16 original cattle wagons of 1881/2. In addition to the foregoing, 12 ballast wagons, three bolster wagons seven timber wagons and nine goods brake vans are known to have been renewed during this period, whilst two new goods brake vans were built, one in 1910 and the other in 1913. Four interesting six-wheeled goods vehicles were constructed at Rocksavage, two in 1913 and two in 1915. The first two were 24ft 6in 12-ton refrigerator vans which were built for perishable traffic running between Baltimore, Bantry and Rosslare, and the other two were 26ft 6in covered vans, all four being equipped with vacuum brakes. One goods brake van, No 753, and two timber trucks, Nos 712 and 713, were scrapped in 1921.

In March 1920 the locomotive engineer reported that he had received a quotation for the necessary ironwork for building 20 12-ton open wagons in the company's workshops, but the prices asked were so high, and the delivery so uncertain, that he obtained a quotation for complete wagons from the Metropolitan Carriage & Wagon Co at £396 each. At the same time he discovered that the GS&WR had 200 open wagons on order from the same firm at £391 each, so he wrote to Watson, the locomotive engineer of the GS&WR, asking if he could get twenty wagons for the CB&SCR on the same terms delivered in Dublin. Watson expressed his willingness to try and on 10th March he was able to advise that the GS&WR had agreed, subject to board approval, to

order 20 additional wagons on their own order with MCW for the CB&SCR. In the end the CB&SCR had to pay an additional £1,162 8s 2d as the original price of £391 per wagon had been subject to adjustment in accordance with variation in cost of materials and wages. They were initially numbered 10490 to 10509 in the GS&WR list, becoming Nos 631 to 650 on the CB&SCR.

In November 1924 a total of 431 revenue earning wagons — 100 open wagons (12-ton), 55 mineral wagons (six-ton), 144 covered wagons, four vans (six-wheel), 114 cattle wagons, and 14 timber trucks (including bolster wagons) — passed to the Great Southern Railway together with 13 goods brake vans and 22 ballast wagons, the latter including the four ballast hopper wagons

procured from the Swansea Wagon Co in 1884. As with the carriage stock, section suffix 'B' was allocated but, as a result of a major culling of CB&SCR wagon stock in the early years of GSR ownership, it is unlikely that any of the 106 vehicles withdrawn between 1926 and 1930 were in fact so renumbered. Following this substantial reduction in stock, there was a lull for a couple of years with only the odd vehicle being withdrawn until 1935 when 52 vehicles were taken out of revenue service. The period 1938-40 saw 47 more goods vehicles withdrawn, but World War II put a hold on the process and it was not until CIÉ came into being in 1945 that scrapping resumed again. Thereafter, withdrawals of former CB&SCR goods wagons continued at an average rate of about 12 vehicles per year and by the time of closure of the Bandon section in 1961 only 19 of the steel underframe wagons purchased in 1921 and one goods brake van (750B) remained in service.

Timoleague & Courtmacsherry stock

The Timoleague companies obtained two passenger carriages and 18 goods wagons from BCW in 1889 for the opening of the line. The two passenger carriages were 23ft 0in vehicles, No 1 being a third class and No 2 a composite first and third class. The goods stock comprised 16 covered vans (Nos 1 to 16) and two open wagons (Nos 17 & 18). In 1891 two more passenger carriages were procured, both 30ft 0in bogie vehicles. No 3 was a composite brake and No 4 a third class brake. A seven-ton brake van, for use on both passenger and goods trains, was purchased from BCW in 1918 and became No 5 in the passenger list. Five covered wagons and one of the open wagons had been withdrawn before 1925, but the remainder of the stock passed into GSR ownership, retaining their former numbers but with section suffix 'J' added.

Left upper: **Covered goods van No 4B, one of two such vans built in 1906, and fitted with a brake compartment. Photographed at Albert Quay on 16th April 1952.** D G Coakham

Left: **Ex T&CELR goods brake van No 5J at Cork in 1952. Built in 1918, 5J was rated at nine tons.** D G Coakham

Chapter Fifteen

A DESCRIPTION OF THE LINE

Much of the description which follows is based on a survey undertaken by Lt F V Yeats-Brown of the 3rd Battalion, King's Royal Rifles on behalf of the War Office in January 1904, updated as necessary to take account of previous and subsequent alterations. We are fortunate that this document has been preserved in the National Archives at Kew. This chapter gives a fairly comprehensive description of the line's principal features, and there will inevitably be some duplication with the historical chapters. It was however thought preferable to give as full a description as possible at this point.

The terminus at Cork, the largest station on the system, consisted of the main two-storey station building facing on to Albert Quay which accommodated the general manager and office staff, and also included the directors' board room. The original site was much smaller than in later years and could best be described as being 'Y-shaped' rather than rectangular. The entire area adjoining Rockboro Road was then in private use as a salt and lime depot. Additional lands were acquired in 1853 for the provision of a carriage shed but we do not know where this was situated.

Behind the main building were the passenger platforms. By 1869 three roads entered the passenger shed, the centre one used for the storage of carriages; this centre road was connected to both platform lines. At that stage the departure platform (down side) was longer than the arrival one as there was a connection on the arrivals side by means of a turntable to a carriage dock at an angle of about 45° and to a siding to the Hay Market, the latter at right angles to the running road. The two platforms had an overall roof for part of their length, this roof being extended at a later date, most likely at the same time as the arrivals platform was extended following the removal of the carriage dock. The original small signal hut stood on the down side just at the exit from the station, but by 1869 the cabin, still on the down side, was located opposite to where the Works were later situated.

Following the opening of the C&MDR in May 1866 a second engine shed was provided for the use of that company, while the goods shed, to the east of the departure platform, was extended by 40ft. A plan of the station in 1869 shows two engine sheds, one to the north of Gas Works Road, the other to the south opposite to the signal cabin referred to above; both had two roads, the second one having these lines continued for a short distance through the end of the shed. The goods shed had two roads running through it and these became one a little further north and ended in line with the main administration building. A trailing connection gave access to another long siding between the goods store and the passenger station.

The approach to the station was bisected by a level crossing at Gas Works Road and as early as 1869 complaints were being made that it was very dangerous. Even at that early period it must have been busy with movements in and out of both the passenger station and the goods yard. In 1877 a second goods shed was erected to the east of the existing one with a single road terminating in the shed itself, while a further long siding was provided beyond that again. A layout plan dated 1892 shows a few further alterations. There were still two engine sheds but by now they were both situated to the north of the level crossing. The one next to the end of the up platform had a single road while the shed adjoining the crossing had two roads, one of which continued through the crossing, and, by means of a small turntable, entered Rocksavage Works further to the south. The other major alteration was a long single-road carriage shed just to the south of the down platform.

Tenders were sought in June 1893 for the erection of a footbridge adjoining Gas Works Road level crossing, that of Messrs Arrol Bros being accepted in an amount of £428. The bridge consisted of three spans, 25ft 6in, 44ft 6in and 38ft, supported by steel columns on masonry piers, with a headroom of 14ft 6in. Various plans were put forward during the next ten years, including a new running shed and carriage shed. Following a trial in June 1899 it was decided to accept the tender of the Cork Free Wire Electric Lighting Co for the installation of ten arc lamps on 30ft high posts for the illumination of the goods yard; an additional five incandescent lamps were provided to light the footbridge and signal cabin

adjacent. By now the 43 lever timber built signal cabin was elevated over the down approach road to the station immediately north of the footbridge. Consequent on an increase in brick traffic from Ballinhassig, a brick siding was constructed into a field beside the cattle bank on the down side. Access was also provided on the up side and close to the level crossing, by means of a turntable, to the Cork Corporation stoneyard.

Major alterations became necessary following the passing of the Cork City Railways Act. A new bridge was designed to bring Hibernian Road across the approach to the station adjoining Rocksavage Works, this initially necessitating the demolition of the Bandon engine shed near the works and the cutting back of the carriage shop to make way for the new approach road on the west side. Later, in 1912, it also became necessary to remove the Macroom engine shed near Eglington Street to make room for the connecting line to the CCR. This ran alongside the western boundary of the station, leaving the premises by a gateway at the northwest corner. The opening of the Hibernian Road bridge in the summer of 1911 enabled the permanent closure of the level crossing in the middle of the yard. The adjoining footbridge was taken down, portion of it being later re-erected at Upton station.

Some alterations were also made to the main building about this time, the buffer stops being moved out thus enabling the provision of a new booking office and additional waiting rooms as well as a new refreshment room. A bookstall operated by Messrs. News Bros. was also included. One drawback to the CCR alterations at Albert Quay was that the station no longer possessed covered accommodation for locomotives stabled there. From that time onwards, important engines were stabled beneath Hibernian Road bridge, others having to remain in the open. The works at Rocksavage comprised a building 290ft in length where repairs were carried out to locomotives, in addition to which construction and repairs of carriages and wagons were performed. One locomotive was so heavily rebuilt as to be regarded as virtually a new build. In 1904, a total of 51 hands of all grades were employed in the works.

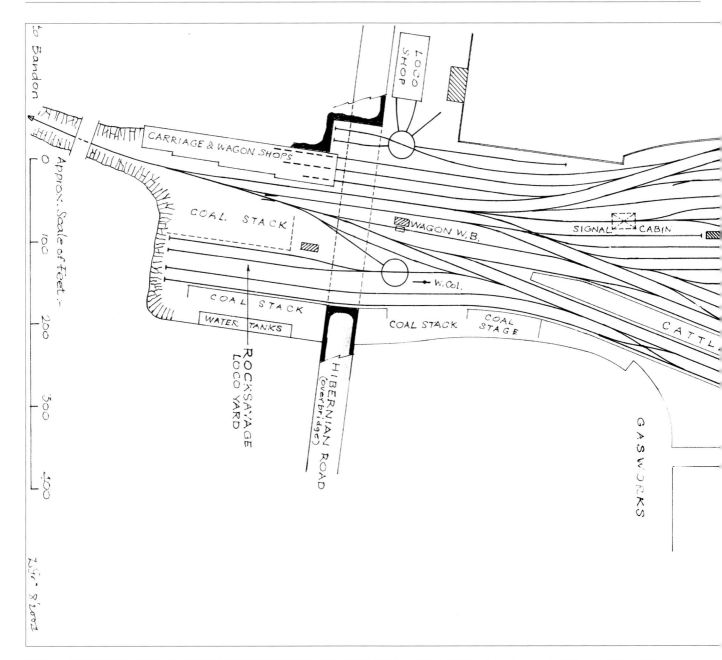

Left: **Former GS&WR 0-6-0T No 207, designed by Ivatt in 1887, brings a goods train over one of the lifting bridges over the River Lee, on the Cork City Railway which connected Albert Quay to the GSWR at Glanmire Road.** Ian Allan Library

Right: **This view taken close to the end of services on the railway shows a set of railcars, headed by No 2643, at the terminus and gives us a good view of Albert Quay's overall roof in the process.**

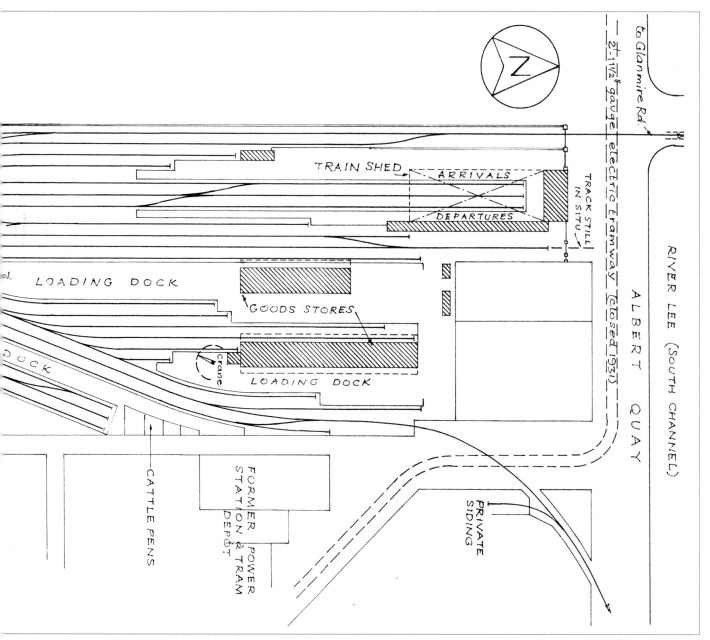

to Glanmire Rd.

2ft. 11½" gauge electric tramway (closed 1931)

RIVER LEE (SOUTH CHANNEL)

ALBERT QUAY

TRAIN SHED

ARRIVALS

DEPARTURES

TRACK STILL IN SITU

LOADING DOCK

GOODS STORES

Crane

LOADING DOCK

DOCK

CATTLE PENS

FORMER POWER STATION & TRAM DEPOT

PRIVATE SIDING

Leaving Cork the line ran through a short but deep cutting spanned by Douglas Road bridge, in effect a short tunnel. This point marked the limit of shunting. The line climbed for much of the next eight miles on a gradient of 1 in 100, necessitating the double heading of most trains out of Cork as far as the first station, at Waterfall. About a mile out on the up side at Ballyphehane was the site of the junction with the C&MDR. This junction was used between 1866 and 1879 when the latter company opened their own terminus at Capwell. During the First World War, the military authorities insisted on a connection between the two lines to assist movements to and from army barracks, so in 1918 a siding was constructed between the two companies' lines. As far as the CB&SCR were concerned the connection was by means of a facing connection at the Cork end, the C&MDR connection facing from the Macroom direction. This junction was removed in 1921 and a new junction was installed by the GSR in March 1925, which remained in use until 1950. This consisted of a straightforward facing connection off the Bandon line, while there was a siding on the down side trailing back towards Cork.

Approximately four miles from Albert Quay the line passed over the most impressive engineering structure on the line, the Chetwynd viaduct. Constructed of steel girders, the bridge consisted of four spans, each of 110ft, supported on masonry piers varying in height from 16 to 64ft to the springing of the arch. The base of the piers

measured 30ft x 20ft and the headroom over the main road below was 83ft.

Waterfall, the first station, approached over a level crossing, was a crossing place with two, staggered, platforms 276ft in length. The down platform, which had the station building and signal cabin on it, was on a loop, and behind it at the Ballinhassig end, was a goods siding. The up platform was lengthened in November 1870 to enable tickets to be collected here, and at the same time the goods siding was installed. The station building, 30ft in length, was originally of timber construction but was rebuilt with corrugated-iron in January 1896 at which time the original structure was reported to be falling to pieces. The stationmaster's house situated up the road from the station was of stone construction, while the signal cabin of eleven levers was built of brick. Waterfall became a halt under Albert Quay station as from September 1931.

Waterfall to Bandon

At milepost 8½ the line began a fall at 1 in 100, the down gradient going right past Kinsale Junction. Approaching Ballinhassig station the line passed through the first of two tunnels on the Bandon system. Ballinhassig tunnel was 880 yards in length and between 50 and 60ft below ground. It was partly brick lined where it passed through clay and had three ventilation shafts, each of approximately 3ft in diameter. Special instructions were included in the 1894 Appendix to the

Top left: **A train crossing Chetwynd viaduct in June 1951.**
T O'Brien, W McGrath collection

Top right: **A diesel railcar set at Waterfall station on 19th June 1959. The brick-built signal cabin contained eleven levers. Waterfall became a halt under Albert Quay in September 1931.** 'Stations UK'

Above left: **Upton station with an up train consisting of a three-piece AEC diesel railcar set. The Railway Signal Co signal cabin with nine levers is prominent in this view, with the station building just beyond it. The goods store is on the up side behind the wagon.**
Rev John Parker, Photos from the Fifties

Above right: **Bandon high-level station with a train bound for the west. The line on the right continues eastwards past the site of West Cork Junction to form a connection into Messrs Allman's Distillery. On the left is the subway providing access to the island platform, with the signal cabin provided by the Railway Signal Co beyond it.** David Lawrence, Photos from the Fifties

Working Timetable for trains working through the tunnel. Drivers of down trains were to be governed by the distant signal 200 yards from the tunnel mouth, carrying two arms, the upper of which was worked from the tunnel face but was slotted with the distant under the control of the station. In the up direction, the starting signal at Ballinhassig, situated at the end of the platform, was worked from the cabin and also by the watchman at the tunnel mouth. When special or other trains followed one another within a short period of time through the tunnel, the stationmaster was to see the following arrangement carried out. Any train following another within 15 minutes was not to be allowed to enter the tunnel from either end until the preceding train had been seen safely out of the tunnel. The tunnelman was required to stand in a position near the exit end and see the preceding train clear safely, when he was at once to return to the other end and signal the next train.

Ballinhassig station originally had a single platform on the up side with a 45ft corrugated-iron station building. The brick signal cabin of eleven levers was situated at the Bandon end on the up side of the line just beyond a level crossing. As related in Chapter Eight, in 1900 an aerial ropeway was erected from Ballinhassig station to the brickworks at Ballinphellic some 3¼ miles away. The end of the ropeway was situated on the down side and facilities included a trailing siding for the loading of bricks into railway wagons. There had apparently been a goods store located here in the early days, orders being given for its removal in January 1859.

Plans were drawn up and incorporated in an Act of 1888 for a diversion of the line for a little over a mile in length which would have seen the tunnel taken out of use and a new station constructed slightly to the west of the existing one. This work was never carried out, nevertheless the engineer reported in December 1889 that the new station at Ballinhassig had cost a total of £121 5s 7d. This doubtless refers to the replacement of the old timber structure by a new corrugated-iron building. Ballinhassig became a passing place in August 1907 following the addition of a new loop and 350ft long platform on the down side, the up platform having been moved slightly back to accommodate the new works. It became a halt under Albert Quay in November 1931. The War Office report of January 1904 states that the area to the north of the station was that chosen as, 'the ultimate line of defence against a force attacking Cork from the Bandon direction'.

About a mile west of Ballinhassig the line crossed the three-span brick Half Way viaduct, each span being 55ft wide. The falling gradient continued for a further mile at 1 in 100 before easing to 1 in 162 and then 1 in 111 to reach Kinsale Junction, known simply as Junction until 1888. The station was in a valley with rising ground to the north, while to the south the valley was flat and at the time of the survey was described as, for the most part, uncultivated.

Approaching Kinsale Junction, there was a level crossing at the Cork end with a turntable of 30ft diameter and also a water tank on the down side. There were up and down platforms, the latter, which included the corrugated-iron station building and a 26 lever signal cabin, having two faces, one of which served Kinsale branch trains.

The branch itself went off in the Bandon direction and soon turned southwards. A footbridge provided access from the 315ft long up platform which had a small shelter, while the stone stationmaster's house was located beside the station entrance on the up side. At the Cork end on the up side, Barrett's siding was an extension of the up loop. There was also a siding on the down side as well as a loop out beyond the level crossing, these being in effect an extension of the branch. The station became a crossing place in mid-1895. The turntable here was removed in 1935 and was never replaced; following the closure of the branch the name was changed in October 1936 to Crossbarry. It became a halt under Bandon as from 1st April 1938, but reverted to station status in July 1945 when it became responsible for the halts at Upton and Ballinhassig. It again reverted to a halt in September 1953, this time under the control of Albert Quay.

About a mile beyond Kinsale Junction the line began a short climb before beginning a further descent from milepost 15. Close to this latter point, immediately east of Crosses level crossing, was Brien's siding, access to which was by a facing connection; a loading bay was provided at this location. Upton station, variously known as Brinny (sometimes spelt Brinney) & Upton, Upton & Innoshannon Road and Upton & Brinny, was situated on a falling gradient of 1 in 170 and had a brick built station building on the single platform 288ft long on the up side. Towards the Bandon end was a nine-lever brick signal cabin, while on the down side was a goods loop serving a goods store and loading bank, the former measuring 60ft by 40ft. Upton became a halt in November 1931.

The nature of the country changed on leaving Upton, the line continuing to fall but on easier gradients, becoming hilly and well-wooded, while cuttings and Innoshannon or Kilpatrick tunnel were chiefly through rock. Beyond the tunnel the country opened out into the valley of the Bandon River. Innoshannon tunnel, the first railway tunnel to be brought into use in Ireland, was bored through rock and clay and was 170 yards long and about 60ft below ground level. Shortly after leaving Innoshannon tunnel the line crossed the Bandon River over Innoshannon viaduct. This bridge had two lattice girder spans each of 104ft on masonry abutments. As built it was of timber construction and was designed for double

track. This proved useful when the bridge was rebuilt in 1862 as very little disruption was caused to traffic.

Just to the west of the Bandon River bridge was Innoshannon station, also known as Innoshannon Road and Curranure & Innoshannon Road. As early as January 1846 an agreement was signed with Thomas Frewen to the effect that the company would erect and keep a station at the most convenient point to serve the village of Innoshannon. Despite a decision in August 1851 to discontinue the station here, there is some evidence that it was repositioned about 1856; it certainly appears in a timetable for July 1861 under the name of Innoshannon Road and simply as Innoshannon six years later. Receipts were furnished on a weekly basis during the latter half of 1871 leading to a decision to close the station as from 1st January 1872. Within a month, Mr Allman of Bandon was calling for it to be re-opened, while legal arguments were put forward that the company were obliged under the agreement of January 1846 to keep the station open. Resulting from this, instructions were given to re-open the station as from 1st July 1873.

Some delay occurred in completing arrangements, it being reported in January 1875 that the ticket office was ready but that nothing could be done until steps were provided on the carriages and the platform lengthened. By the following May it was reported that 50ft of the latter had been finished and gravelled. Correspondence took place early in 1891 with Moreton Frewen in connection with the 1846 agreement. Traffic was by now very small and Frewen conceded that he could not really enforce the agreement, particularly with new BoT signalling requirements. He did however seek compensation of £200 for the closure of the station and requested that a decent station should be put up at Upton, to be called either Upton for Innoshannon or Upton & Innoshannon Road. It was in fact closed in 1891, Frewen trying again in March 1898 to enforce the original agreement.

From Innoshannon the line descended towards the Bandon River and then climbed towards Bandon across open ground liable to occasional flooding. Bandon was sometimes known as Bandonbridge from the completion of the road bridge over the river at this point. In all the town had five stations at different periods, the original C&BR terminus later becoming the low level goods station. Approaching from the east, the 880 yard long siding to Messrs Allman's Distillery ran alongside the running line on the down side and crossed the main Bandon to Cork road to enter the distillery premises where there were two sidings and an engine shed for the company's own engine. On the up side a siding diverged to cross the Bandon River by a metal bridge to enter the premises of the Watergate Bottling Works, later Messrs Beamish & Crawford, this siding having been installed in 1914. Beyond this connection was West Cork Junction where the WCR line diverged to the west. A temporary wooden platform existed on the down side at the point of junction between 1876 and 1880. Entering the original Bandon station the Bandon Gas Works were on the up side between the railway and the river. Beyond this, a connection diverged across a turntable into the 50ft stone built engine shed with accommodation for one engine, and beyond this again were the goods store and cattle depot. Near the engine shed was a stone breaker capable of producing six wagon loads a day. There was also a forge and carpenter's shop employing from 12 to 15 men. The passenger station was to the south of the goods shed. Between 1880 and 1894, this station handled all goods and passenger traffic on both the C&BR and the WCR lines.

Further to the south of the old station and on a higher level was the new joint station opened in 1894. The accommodation here consisted of an office, booking office, general waiting room and ladies' waiting room, lamp room and engineer's office. The island platform was 100 yards in length, brick faced with ramped ends. Access was gained by means of a subway and ramp from the old C&B station, and from a road to the south of the line. The station itself was situated in the Bandon River valley and was built on an embankment 15ft high, with a falling gradient of 1 in 120 towards Cork. Adjacent to this station was the site of the original WCR passenger station, in use from 1866 to 1874. In the absence of an agreement over the payment of rent for the use of C&BR facilities at Bandon, the West Cork directors decided in 1874 to provide their own facilities.

The new station, situated about half a mile to the west adjoining their goods facilities, was generally known as Bandon West, although the platform name-boards simply referred to it as Bandon. This station was in use for passenger traffic from 1874 until 1880. It is most likely that it was also the site of the WCR goods station from the time of the line's opening in 1866 until 1880. The station was situated immediately to the west of St. Patrick's Roman Catholic Chapel, and adjoining a level crossing. This latter was later replaced by a bridge/tunnel for public traffic, although it remained in use to serve a convent. The station buildings were situated on the down side.

Bandon to Drimoleague
Castle Bernard, a private platform for the use of the Earl of Bandon, was situated on the up side immediately west of a level crossing of the same name. The platform, ramped at both ends, was stone faced and 150ft long with a brick built station house.

There was a siding on the down side with a trailing connection just beyond the western end of the platform. It was closed as a passenger station in 1891 although it remained in use for occasional goods traffic until the eventual closure of the line in March 1961.

The line, which had been climbing all the way from Bandon, reached a summit near milepost 23½ and then began a fall at 1 in 85 and then 1 in 300 to Clonakilty Junction. The subject of providing a station at this location was considered as early as July 1866, at which period it was referred to as Gaggin. Then in December 1881, the engineer submitted estimates of the likely cost of a passenger station at £50 and a goods station and siding at £115. After further consideration, the board came to the conclusion that, 'the making of the Clonakilty Railway is a very doubtful matter…also that it is not advisable to proceed with the Gaggin station at present'. There is, however, some evidence that a station may have been provided here prior to the opening of the branch.

There were two platforms at Clonakilty Junction, that on the down side being an island platform with a loop at the rear; the main corrugated-iron station building was situated on this platform as was the brick built signal cabin of 25 levers, two of which were spare. The up platform, reached by a footbridge at the Bantry end, had a small shelter. The footbridge also provided additional public access to the station from the road. Beyond the loop at the Cork end on the down side was a 30ft diameter turntable; the War Office drawing refers to a proposed engine shed at this point. Leaving Clonakilty Junction, the branch ran parallel for a short distance before deviating on the down side just as the mainline passed under the public road. A siding on the down side at the Bandon end ran for about 250 yards parallel to the mainline towards Cork from a point close to the turntable. Clonakilty Junction became a halt in 1931.

Leaving the junction the valley was undulating and began to open out, becoming flatter as it approached the next station at Desert. This was a small station with a single 95 yard long stone faced platform on the down side. On the platform was a corrugated-iron building 120ft long with a general waiting room and booking office. There was also a small lamproom on this platform. On the up side were two loops, the outer of which served a loading bank and goods store. The latter was, at the time of the War Office report, timber built with a corrugated-iron roof but was about to be replaced by an all corrugated structure. At the Cork end of the loop was a wagon turntable, which gave access to a siding running at right angles to the mainline; this 100 yard long siding served Farn cornmill beside the river.

A request was received in December 1885 asking that the name of the station be altered to either Farn or Farn Mills, this request being declined. A ballast pit was opened at this location in 1890. Desert became a halt in November 1930.

Beyond Desert, the country was undulating and after crossing the River Bandon the line ran on a low embankment, with boggy ground on either side until it reached Ballineen & Enniskeane station. Originally the river bridge was a timber structure, replaced in later years by a 13 span steel girder bridge on cast-iron cylinders. As related elsewhere in our narrative, there were at one time separate stations serving the villages of Ballineen and Enniskeane, but we have no details of the original station layouts. Ballineen and Enniskeane station was situated at the bottom of a short falling gradient of 1 in 116 and had both up and down platforms, each 110 yards in length and stone faced. The main station building, incorporating the stationmaster's house, was situated at the Cork end of the up platform with the brick signal cabin of 12 levers close by. At the Bantry end of this platform sidings gave access to a goods store, loading and cattle banks. The down platform was served by a loop and had a small shelter on it. Just beyond this platform, at the Bantry end, was a small engine shed and water tank, both provided for a ballast engine. There was also a 31ft diameter turntable.

Leaving Ballineen & Enniskeane a trailing connection gave access to a ballast pit complex between the station and the river. From here to Dunmanway, 7¾ miles away, the country was undulating, generally flat on the south side but rising to about 200ft on the north side. The railway ran parallel to the River Bandon. About a mile beyond Ballineen the country became thickly wooded on both sides, opening up again with large uncultivated fields or bad grass land. The line was now climbing for most of this section on gradients varying from 1 in 400 to 1 in 110.

Dunmanway, the Castle of the Yellow River, today has a population of a little over 2,700 and was a very flourishing town with a linen industry as well as two tanyards and two boulting mills, the latter capable of grinding annually 15,000 bags of flour. The station had two 120 yard long platforms with the stone and slated station buildings and signal cabin, the latter with 15 levers, on the up side. The down platform was served by a loop and had a small shelter. Behind this platform were the goods facilities consisting of cattle pens, loading bank and a goods store, the latter stone built and 98ft in length. These facilities were reached by means of another loop behind the platform. There was also a long siding off this loop running behind the goods store and towards the public road.

Leaving the station the line crossed the public road by a level crossing a short distance beyond which was a trailing siding on the up side serving Messrs Atkin's sawmill. The mill itself was operated by a Robey 140hp steam engine driving six saws, the largest of which could cut timber up to 2ft thick. The fields around Dunmanway were described in the War Office report as being small, the land on either side of the line often being boggy. About two miles beyond Dunmanway the gradient steepened to 1 in 80 and then ran through the narrow Gloundha defile, just wide enough for the railway and the public road and about 250 yards long, then opening up from some 60 yards wide to 300 yards. Beyond here, the line continued to climb on easier gradients before beginning a fall to the wayside station of Knockbue. It was approached over a level crossing and had a single platform on the down side only 40 yards in length with a small shed comprising a ticket office and waiting room with no lighting. Just before the platform was a small three-lever ground frame. There were no sidings here.

Drimoleague, also known as Dromdaleague, a town of approximately 4,900 people situated on the River Ilen, was described by Lewis in 1837 as having an excellent slate quarry but was in a very backward state agriculturally. It was nevertheless the most important station on the West Cork Railway system and was the junction for the Skibbereen and Bantry lines. As built it was a through station on the WCR's projected line to Skibbereen, only becoming a junction with the opening of the Bantry branch in 1881. The station prior to 1899 was situated about 60 yards to the west of the later station. The line approached from the east under a road bridge, passing a turntable and engine shed on the down side followed by the goods facilities and ran to an island platform, the down side of which accommodated Skibbereen line trains and the up side those to and from Bantry. There was a long trailing siding on the up side from the Bantry line almost back to the road bridge.

The post-1899 station consisted of a down through platform 390ft in length and an up, island, platform of 435ft between the Bantry and Skibbereen lines. The main station building, corrugated-iron built, was located on the island platform with the 31-lever brick signal cabin just off the western end. At the Cork end was a small stone engine shed and a turntable of 30ft diameter. There was a large water tank behind the turntable, the station having a water capacity of 15,756 gallons. The engine shed ceased to be used when diesel power was introduced in 1957 and was demolished in the autumn of 1958.

The down platform which was reached via a footbridge had a small shelter on it. Behind this platform, served by a loop which was connected at the western end to the Skibbereen line, were the goods facilities, consisting of a corrugated-iron goods store and loading bank. A cattle bank was located to the east of the overbridge on a siding extending towards Dunmanway for 190 yards. The junction between the two lines was situated immediately off the end of the island platform, the branch to Bantry swinging away to the right, both lines crossing the public road by level crossings.

Drimoleague to Skibbereen & Baltimore

As the line to Baltimore was for many years regarded as the mainline, we will continue the description of the line to that point. Leaving Drimoleague the line began a descent, which continued almost into the next station at Madore 3½ miles away. For more than a mile past Drimoleague this gradient varied from 1 in 88 to 1 in 77. Madore was another small wayside station with a wooden station building on the single 150ft long up side platform. There was also a stone built stationmaster's house behind the platform, while just beyond it was a six lever ground frame beside a level crossing. In later years a facing siding was installed at the Cork end on the up side to serve a small goods store and loading bank. Following a short climb at 1 in 567 followed by 1 in 102 of a descent the line more or less levelled out from here to Skibbereen.

Skibbereen (An Sciobairín or little boat harbour), described by Lewis as a market and post town with a population of 4,429, is situated on the south bank of the River Ilen.

Right upper: **Ex GS&WR 0-6-0T No 201 on a permanent way train at the up platform at Dunmanway. The main station building was of stone construction; the signal cabin contained fifteen levers.**
Photographer unknown, John Langford collection

Right: **Clonakilty Junction halt on 19th June 1959 with a down diesel railcar about to depart.** 'Stations UK'

Left: **Clonalkilty Junction with a Metro-Vick 'C' class Bo-Bo. On the right is railcar 2660, one of six built at Inchicore with a body designed by O V S Bulleid on an AEC underframe.** J L St Leger

Left lower: **Drimoleague station looking towards Skibbereen. At the far end of the station, the mainline to Skibbereen veers left, while the Bantry branch diverges to the right. Bottom right is the turntable with the single-road engine shed just out of view. The photograph was taken from the road overbridge at the Cork end.** J C F Pickenhahn & Sohn

At one time it was a centre for the manufacture of woollen goods, cloth, checks and handkerchiefs. The river was navigable for small coasting vessels and a considerable quantity of corn was at one time exported from here. Skibbereen was a terminal station prior to the opening of the extension to Baltimore and was also in later years the transfer point to the narrow-gauge Schull & Skibbereen Tramway.

As opened in 1877, the station had a single platform on the up side with a carriage shed situated behind it. As one approached the station there was a small signal cabin on the up side, immediately beyond which were the goods facilities. At the far end of the platform there was a small turntable giving trailing access to an engine shed. Beyond this again, a wagon turntable gave access to two sidings parallel to the river. Finally, there was a short loop to allow engines to run around their trains at the platform.

By the time the S&ST opened in 1886, the entire broad-gauge station had been re-located to the east of the platform. The S&ST station was situated behind the broad-gauge station, trans-shipment facilities for goods being provided. A shed for the tramway engine was situated between the passenger platform and the goods facilities. The main station building was of stone construction with a separate stationmaster's house. Signalling was controlled by a six-lever ground frame at the Cork end of the passenger platform. By the beginning of the twentieth century the engine shed and turntable had been removed to the Cork end of the station opposite the loading bank on the down side, the nearby turntable being of the usual 30ft diameter. One siding now ran parallel to the river on the down side of the line.

The opening of the Baltimore extension necessitated the construction of a bridge over the River Ilen. This was a 112ft span bridge of steel lattice on masonry abutments with a headroom of 20ft. The branch was of a switchback nature with gradients as steep as 1 in 60, passing through wild country, which the War Office report stated could be occupied against a hostile force approaching from the east. The only intermediate station was at Creagh with its single 249ft

platform on the down side of the line. The small station building also provided accommodation for the stationmaster. There were no goods facilities and the signals were controlled by a four-lever ground frame.

Approaching Baltimore, the country is quite hilly, the hills being bare or covered with furze and not much cultivated. Baltimore was supposed to have been a sanctuary of the Druids, the village with a population of about 460 in 1831 being situated on the east shore of a fine harbour. A substantial pier had been built here in 1833 at the joint expense of the Fisheries Board and Lord Carbery. The principal trade was the export of slate, copper ore, flour, wheat and potatoes, while imports consisted of timber, iron and coal. Approaching Baltimore the engine shed with the water tank of 8,500 gallons capacity overhead and a 30ft turntable were situated on the up side as the line emerged from a cutting. The single passenger platform, 252ft in length, was on the down side and on it stood the brick and slated station building which incorporated the stationmaster's house. The goods shed, 56ft long, a wooden building on a stone foundation, was on the up side as were cattle pens and a corrugated-iron carriage shed, the latter provided in 1899. The extension to the harbour commenced by a facing connection close to the turntable and ran round the back of the station on the up side to cross a small inlet prior to running on to the harbour itself. Here, the line separated into two parallel sidings, beside one of which was a fish loading bank. A cottage was built in 1896 to provide accommodation for engine crews on over-night turns.

Kinsale branch
Kinsale branch trains used the rear of the island platform at Kinsale Junction and deviated from the mainline on the down side. The line was steeply graded throughout with long sections at 1 in 76 and 1 in 80 in both directions. The first station on the branch was Ballymartle with a single platform just over 200ft in length on the down

side with stationmaster's house and offices. Also on the platform was a six-lever ground frame, there being no goods facilities. The summit was reached just beyond Ballymartle after a climb of more than 2½ miles at 1 in 80, the line falling away from the summit for more than a mile at 1 in 76. Farrangalway also had a single 175ft long platform but on the up side, on which were located the main station building and a seven-lever brick signal cabin. On the down side, served by a loop, was a 36ft goods store and a loading bank, beyond which was a house for the stationmaster. This latter was stone built but had a thatched roof. The signal cabin here was closed in October 1927.

Beyond the station was Farrangalway viaduct, a three span structure, each span being of 50ft with a 35ft headroom. Leaving Farrangalway, the line climbed at 1 in 100, then fell at 1 in 172, followed by rather more than a mile of a climb at 1 in 80 and then a fall on the same gradient right into Kinsale. This latter gradient was a contributory factor in the fatal accident at Kinsale station in January 1915, further details of which are to be found in Chapter Twelve.

Kinsale (Ceann Sáile or Tide Head) was formerly an important naval port and is today a noted tourist resort with considerable character and old-world charm. It was the scene in 1601 of an important battle involving British troops and a combined Irish and Spanish force. Its natural harbour was protected by forts on either side, these latter providing excellent views of the surrounding area.

Kinsale station had one single 345ft long platform on the down side which included a large station building incorporating accommodation for the stationmaster. Apart from a general waiting room, there were also separate first and second class waiting rooms. Sidings on the up side provided access to a carriage dock, goods store and loading bank, corrugated-iron carriage shed and cattle pens. The site of the carriage shed had previously been occupied by an engine shed. By 1904 a 50ft stone engine shed was located at the outer end of the platform with a 21ft 3in turntable just beyond it. Surprisingly for a terminal station, at the time of the War Office report, there was no signal cabin but a seven-lever ground frame on the up side at the outer limits of the station. There was one however by the time the BoT reported on the January 1915 collision. Interestingly, the staff instrument at Kinsale was located in the stationmaster's office rather than in the signal cabin.

Skibbereen station with C224 and train, Good Friday 1961. Behind the train the Ilen River bridge can be seen. The narrow-gauge S&ST was situated to the right behind the main station building.
J L St Leger

Clonakilty and Courtmacsherry

The Clonakilty branch diverged at Clonakilty Junction southwards on a short falling gradient of 1 in 80, almost immediately beginning a climb for somewhat more than a mile at 1 in 70 before easing to 1 in 300 to reach the line's summit two and a half miles from the junction. From this summit it fell on varying gradients to its lowest point at Ballinascarthy, the junction point for the Courtmacsherry line.

Ballinascarthy is located in a small valley with low hills on all sides except to the south. Its main claim to fame is that it was the birthplace of Henry Ford's father. To the west of the station is the Owenkeagh River over which the Clonakilty line crossed shortly after leaving the station. The station itself comprised an island platform 360ft long on the down side, with the station buildings constructed of timber. A separate stone built stationmaster's house was located just off the northern end of the platform. Branch trains used the rear face of the platform, the junction with the Courtmacsherry line being simply a set of facing points at the south end. There was a loop behind the platform on the down side, off which was a siding giving access to a timber built goods store. At the south end of the loop a short siding ran to a 17ft diameter turntable, beside which was a brick signal cabin with 15 levers. Finally, there was a water tank of 6,250 gallons capacity on the up side at the Clonakilty end of the platform.

The Clonakilty branch turned towards the southwest on leaving the station to cross over the river while the Courtmacsherry line departed roughly south-eastwards over a level crossing. From Ballinascarthy to Clonakilty the line see-sawed gradient wise with two mini summits. Nearly two miles south of Ballinascarthy on the up side a half mile long siding diverged. This siding was the property of the Shannonvale flour mill, owned and operated for many years by the Bennett family. The junction points were operated by a key on the section staff. The line was laid on a slight falling gradient all the way from the Clonakilty branch and ran

through a number of fields, then through a gate to a two-road terminus adjoining the mill building. The line was unusual in that it was from its inception operated in the up direction by horse power, gravity being used for empty wagons going down to the mill. The line lasted until the closure of the Bandon in March 1961 and was in its latter years operated by a grey named *Paddy*. His normal load was two wagons, which were normally brought up in the afternoon to connect with the 16.45 mixed from Clonakilty. Due to the gradients on the Clonakilty branch, wagons were only worked to and from the tramway by up trains.

Just beyond Shannonvale siding was the Argadeen viaduct over the river of the same name, a steel lattice bridge of 80ft span and with a clearance of 36ft above water level. Clonakilty (O'Keelty's Sept) is a tourist centre, the town having been founded by Sir Richard Boyle, later Earl of Cork. The station, lying as it did on the hillside overlooking the town, was approached on a falling gradient of 1 in 80. The station itself comprised a single 400ft long platform on the down side, which included the station office and accommodation for the stationmaster. Trackwork comprised two loops on the up side, the outer one of which served the usual goods store, loading bank and cattle pens. On the down side, at the Ballinascarthy end, were an engine shed large enough to hold one engine and a turntable of 30ft diameter. Nearly opposite the latter, on the up side, was a brick built signal cabin with eleven levers. It was proposed early in the twentieth century to erect a carriage shed between the turntable and the platform, but this seems never to have been built.

Although not strictly part of the CB&SCR, we will describe the line from Ballinascarthy to Timoleague and Courtmacsherry as, without the former, this section would never have been constructed. Timoleague (Tigh Molaga or the house of Molaga) owes its name to St Molaga who founded an Abbey there. Later, about 1240, the Friary was built on the site of St Molaga's ancient

cell. The Friary was sacked by the British in 1642. Courtmacsherry is a favourite seaside resort and provided many well-filled Sunday and holiday excursions from Cork and other venues down the years.

Leaving Ballinascarthy, the Courtmacsherry line veered away sharply south-eastwards to cross the main Cork to Clonakilty road by a level crossing. Ballinascarthy was in fact the highest point on the line which fell away on easy gradients, apart from three short inclines. From approximately mp4 the line turned southwards as far as Timoleague and then south-eastwards to the terminus. The first halt on the line was Skeaf (at 2m 42c but always incorrectly shown in working timetables as 3m) serving the village of Clogagh. Facilities at Skeaf were very basic, consisting only of a short earthen platform on the up side, a small shelter having been transferred here from Innoshannon when that station closed. Two miles further on the line met the River Argadeen which it crossed by the single span Inchy bridge. Near milepost 5 for a time a facing siding at Ummera served a ballast pit on the up side, while on the down side there was a small quay for sand traffic on the river.

Timoleague station boasted two level crossings, one at each end of its layout. There was a single platform on the up side, behind which, at the Ballinascarthy end, were a goods store and loading bank with two sidings. There was a loop on the down side, off which were two sidings serving a cattle bank. Close to the station were the remains of Timoleague Abbey and Friary. Between Timoleague and Courtmacsherry the line was in effect a roadside tramway, although at times on its own right of way, the maximum speed on this section being 12mph. Courtmacsherry station again had one platform on the up side of the line. On the down side on the approach was an engine shed, there having also been a 17ft diameter turntable here until 1950. On the down side opposite the platform was a loop, off which were three sidings, one of which extended to the small pier.

Drimoleague to Bantry

The last of the branches to be described was the 13 mile westernmost extension of the line from Drimoleague to Bantry. Gradient wise it was a difficult line with a short sharp climb of 1 in 80 shortly after leaving Drimoleague, followed by a drop at the same gradient for almost a mile and a half. Then began a continuous climb for almost five miles through Aughaville and Durrus Road, reaching a summit at mp53. This was followed by a fall at 1 in 80, steepening in places to 1 in 60 all the way to Bantry.

Aughaville was no more than a wayside halt for market day traffic, although a siding had been provided as early as August 1880 for the annual horse fair, at which time it was known as Ballyboy. There was a level crossing on the approach at the Drimoleague end. It would appear that a passenger platform was erected in February 1882. The sidings were removed in August 1888. It is not clear from the company's records, but it seems as if this siding was installed and removed each year. Durrus Road served the village of Durrus about six miles away to the southwest. It had a single platform 168ft in length on the down side, on which were situated a wooden station building and a seven-lever signal cabin. At the Bantry end was a level crossing, immediately beyond which, also on the down side, was a long siding accessed by a facing turnout and serving a goods store. Opposite to this latter was the stone built stationmaster's house.

Approaching Bantry, magnificent views were obtained of Bantry Bay and the mountains of the Beara Peninsula. Before this however, on the up side was a facing connection into Storer's sidings constructed in 1907 for the Liverpool Barytes Company. There were two sidings here serving the mill premises. Just beyond milepost 56 could be seen the turnout on the up side to the original Bantry hilltop station situated close to the Union Workhouse and about 94ft above sea level. The single platform was on the down side with a substantial building and

an overall roof over a portion of the platform. There was a goods store on the down side at the Drimoleague end, while on the up side there was an engine shed. A system of crossovers gave access to the latter and to a turntable right at the end of the line.

When the Bantry Bay extension was built, it passed on the town side of the Workhouse as it descended in a semicircle towards the town. The layout at the new station, which adjoined the harbour and the town square, consisted of a single platform 318ft long on the down side, on which were situated the station buildings, all timber built and comprising general and ladies' waiting rooms, booking office, parcels office, dining and refreshment rooms. Also on the platform was the stationmaster's house. There was originally no signal cabin, points and signals being controlled from an eight-lever ground frame at the Cork end of the station. A wooden goods store and loading bank were also located on the down side beyond the platform, while on the up side were an engine shed and 30ft turntable. There was a loop on the up side with various connections off it, one of which ran over a level crossing to the 100-yard long pier from which the steamers of the Bantry Bay Steamship Co operated.

Cork City Railway

Whilst this section of line was not part of the CB&SCR system, it did give that company access to the GS&WR and is therefore worthy of some brief mention. It also of course was responsible for major track alterations at Albert Quay, already described. The line ran along the western boundary of the station, leaving the Bandon premises by means of a gateway at the northwest corner adjoining Eglinton Street. Crossing over the main road, it crossed the southern channel of the River Lee by the Clontarf bridge onto the island between the two channels, with branches to Lapp's Quay and Anderson's Quay. It crossed the north channel on the Brian Boru bridge, making a trailing connection to Penrose Quay and running via Alfred Street and through the Clyde cutting before curving round to enter the GS&WR goods yard at Glanmire Road. A line also ran east after leaving Albert Quay station and proceeded to Victoria Quay. The two river crossings consisted of bridges on the Scherzer rolling lift bridge principle described elsewhere.

Chapter Sixteen

PERSONNEL

One of the first references to staff was an instruction to the secretary in December 1844 to employ a porter, presumably for the office, at 6s per week. As part of an economy drive in January 1852, it was decided to dispense with the services of the goods clerk in Cork, Frederick Lyster being requested to undertake his duties for an additional £10 per annum. Lyster later went as stationmaster to Bandon, his salary there being increased in May 1854 from £50 to £60 per annum. This latter compared with figures varying from £50 to £100 on the DW&WR and the W&LR, and from £36 to £60 on the MGWR. Despite the economies, the gatemen successfully applied for an increase in their remuneration in February 1854. It was announced in October 1856 that Lyster had been offered £100 per annum to move to Messrs Allman's Distillery at Bandon, but that he would prefer to remain in the company's service if he received an additional £20 to his salary, bringing it up to £80. The directors agreed to grant him another £10 and he remained on the staff. A board minute of September 1857 refers to a letter from Lyster in which he stated that his salary and his private income combined exceeded £100 a year, making him liable for income tax. He requested that the company look after the latter on his behalf, which they agreed to do. Lyster resigned his position in September 1865 when he was appointed manager to the neighbouring C&MDR.

In May 1857, Coghlan reported that he had received written resignations from seven of the gatemen, who refused to turn out for the 02.25 down train, despite the fact that they had been offered an additional 1s per week, and were not required to come on duty until 10.00 each day. It was ordered that two men be taken from the permanent way gang and five others employed as day watchmen at 6s per week. With wages at this level, it is hardly surprising that the company found it difficult to recruit staff! Two and a half years later, in October 1859, the permanent way labourers submitted a claim for increased wages, it being agreed to increase their pay from 7s to 9s per week. In the following month, it was directed that a boy be substituted for one man in each gang whenever an opportunity presented itself. Mr

Wall, the permanent way inspector, reacted by stating that he could not do with less than four men in each gang. The committee responded by suggesting that the number of gangs be reduced by one to seven, each one to take charge of three miles of line, instead of two and a half miles. In July 1861, the seven night gatemen were granted an increase of 2s to 9s per week, a claim for sentry boxes and fires being turned down.

In May 1857 two stokers (firemen) applied for an increase in their pay. They were offered 15s per week and informed that if they did not accept it, they would be dismissed. They had little option but to accept this figure and we find the same two firemen seeking a further increase three years later. At this time, the GS&WR and the CB&PR were paying their firemen a rate of 21s per week. The Bandon offered 17s 6d, which was accepted. In November 1872 the senior driver was receiving a sum of £2 10s 6d a week. Drivers on the MGWR received rates varying from 5s to 7s 6d per day, according to their grades. Minor allowances were made for nights spent away from their home depots, this not being a consideration on the Bandon system. All in all it can be seen that the company was not over-generous in its payment of staff. It is also worth recording that the Midland paid all of their staff a Christmas gratuity. That said, many members of staff lost all or part of these bonuses for misdemeanours committed during the year.

The question of payment for Sunday duty was raised by the permanent way gangers in April 1869, their claim being based on the fact that their colleagues on the C&MDR were paid 1s extra for Sunday work. It was agreed to grant this increase. In the following February, the signalmen at Cork sought and received payment for Sunday attendance.

A strike at Cork and staff reductions
Coghlan informed the board on 27th October 1871 that there was a likelihood of the company's men striking for higher wages, a claim having been lodged for an additional 4s per week and 4d per hour for all overtime worked after 18.00. Coghlan was instructed to enquire as to what other companies paid their employees. He duly reported on 3rd

November that the goods men at Cork had struck, despite having been offered 15s per week and 3d per hour overtime. This caused great inconvenience, necessitating the company refusing to accept goods traffic. Whilst efforts had been made to obtain men from Bandon and other locations, they had soon ceased work, having apparently suffered intimidation. All permanent way work was now stopped and the men transferred to Cork to replace those on strike. The secretary meanwhile reported that the GS&WR goods porters received 14s per week plus overtime, although the directors, now that the matter had been drawn to their attention, felt that the latter was not justified and intended to alter it. The engineer joined in the controversy later in November, when he advised that the permanent way men on the CB&PR had struck for 15s per week. He commented that the Bandon men, in receipt of only 10s per week, were unlikely to be satisfied with this figure. The directors decided to grant an increase of 2s to the men at the Cork end of the line.

January 1872 saw Conran complain of the long hours being worked by the goods train drivers, which he considered to be an unsafe practice. It was reluctantly agreed that a fireman be appointed to work all special and extra goods trains, this being cheaper than paying overtime. Conran also announced that he had given notice to the fitter and the viceman, thus saving a sum of £2 12s 0d per week. In June of the following year, the engineer reported that he had let four labourers and two carpenters go. In addition, another carpenter, who had been 25 years with the company, left following a refusal to grant him an increase. The board minute rather callously commented that, 'He was no loss as old age would soon have made him a burden on the Company'. About this time, the engineer also reported that a Mr Searles, engaged in painting signals at Bandon, 'was nearly beheaded…the Signalman having dropped the signal on the back of his neck'. The question of dismissing old hands in all departments was considered by the board in October 1887, 'simply because they were getting past their work'. It was decided that men who were past their work through old age or bad health should be dismissed. Men with 30 years service would get three months pay, men with between 15 and 30 years, one month's pay, while those with less than 15 years would receive nothing.

Some of the directors' decisions in relation to staff are difficult to comprehend. When a night watchman died in January 1864, it was decided to grant a sum of £10 for the benefit of his widow and three children. Likewise, when Thomas Healy, who had been a clerk for eight years, died, leaving his young son completely destitute, a sum of £10 was paid towards the funeral expenses. Yet in January 1874 they refused to grant a sum of £3 3s 0d for a coffin for the late hall porter in Cork, Cornelius Kelleher. Furthermore, the manager stated that he did not think it necessary to fill the vacancy, which would bring about a saving of 9s per week. Following further representations, it was agreed to pay Kelleher's funeral expenses; he had been in the service of the company for almost thirty years (he may well in fact be the porter referred to at the beginning of this chapter) and had died while on duty. A further request for a pension was answered with the comment that Kelleher had been retained, 'for several years as a pensioner more in consideration of his long service than usefulness'. Driver Anthony Guest died in November 1872 after 23 years service. His wife Priscilla applied for some assistance in December. In forwarding this request to the board in Dublin, the committee pointed out that Guest had been receiving his full wages of £2 10s 6d a week for nearly five months, he having been entirely incapacitated from performing his ordinary duties.

The year 1879 saw further economies becoming necessary to assist the company's finances. In July, Conran reported that he could save £2 10s 0d a week by postponing the rebuilding of six wagons, thus enabling him to reduce staff numbers. A month later he confirmed having given notice to two labourers, and having reduced the wages of other men in the works. These reductions were to lead to difficulties in recruiting additional staff, as the neighbouring CB&PR and C&MDR both paid higher wages. A minute of 24th October refers to the men in the locomotive department only being allowed to work five days. As regards the question of Saturday working, if necessary, it is interesting to relate the chairman's comments at the half-yearly meeting of shareholders in March 1879, when he shed an interesting light on industrial relations at that time, not only on the C&BR, but in industry generally. Having referred to the comparatively healthy state of the company's finances, McBirney went on to refer to expenses in the locomotive department. He stated that the hands were paid full wages for a half-day's work on Saturdays. This, he thought, was a pernicious system, as, if a man was paid a full day's wages, he should work a full

day, and in fact he had put up notices in his own factory to this effect. 'Labour now looked for the largest amount of remuneration for the least amount of work'. Seconding the resolution, J.H. Payne commented that the (half-day) system had proved a loss to the working classes who, during their half-holiday, spent their money and occupied their time, 'in a manner not at all satisfactory'.

The permanent way men sought a further increase in 1881, leading Dorman to recommend a reduction in the speed of all trains – 12mph down hill and 15mph up hill for all passenger trains, all goods trains to be restricted to 10mph, 'as slow speed disturbs the Permanent Way comparatively little'. The WCR men went on strike, although the disruption was short-lived. Arrangements were made to add 30 minutes to all train times on that section to take account of the speed restrictions. Those who remained at work were granted a bonus for the duration of the stoppage.

It was reported in February 1872 that the permanent way inspector had left to go to the neighbouring C&MDR at a salary of 30s per week. The directors appeared upset by this as they had recently increased his pay from 18s to 20s per week. Despite this, a ganger was promoted and given 18s per week. Likewise in April 1891, Maurice Reen, the locomotive foreman, also went to the Macroom company as their locomotive superintendent at a salary of £3 3s 0d per week. In an endeavour to hold on to Reen, the board offered him an increase of 4s per week to 56s. A replacement came from the Lancashire & Yorkshire Railway, he being paid £2 10s 0d per week.

The approaching opening of the Clonakilty branch led to some staff appointments being made in June 1886. Stationmasters were appointed to Clonakilty, Ballinascarthy and Gaggin (Clonakilty Junction), weekly salaries ranging from 14s to 21s, the latter at Clonakilty to include a house. The appointee at Clonakilty was William Coe, later to be appointed traffic inspector in January 1895 and superintendent of the line in January 1898. With John Kerr's appointment in October 1924 as a standing member of the Railway Tribunal, he had to resign his position as general manager of the CB&SCR. Coe was appointed acting general manager, a position which he held until the formation of the GSR a month later.

A list of stations drawn up in January 1898 indicates that they were divided into six categories for the purposes of stationmasters' pay. Class 1 (Cork and Bandon) men received £127 per annum by this time, while those at class 6 stations (Knockbue, Creagh and Ballymartle) each received 14s per week, not exactly over-generous figures. A list of these appears as Appendix G. By this time, DW&WR stationmasters' salaries

ranged from £52 to £169, depending on location. Passenger porters received 14s per week plus clothing, goods porters 15s, while signalmen were in receipt of between 13s and 18s, depending on location. The signalmen in Cork had had their salaries increased to 18s per week in January 1895, in addition to which they were to be supplied with a suit of clothes, 'suitable for Signalmen'. On occasions the company found it necessary to increase the men's wages simply because they experienced great difficulty in recruiting at the low rates of pay offered.

Towards the end of the nineteenth century, we see the beginnings of the trade union movement to look after the interests and welfare of railway workers. Railway managements refused to recognise these associations – we have already seen in Chapter Seven how the CB&SCR management refused to allow any intervention by the Amalgamated Society of Railway Servants in the dispute at Albert Quay involving Michael Buckley. As early as January 1890, the ASRS made unsuccessful attempts to negotiate rates of pay and hours of duty. In fact, following a meeting of the chairmen and managers of the principal Irish railways, held in Dublin in November 1897, it was agreed that no company would recognise the society, nor would they negotiate hours of labour, which it was contended was the sole preserve of the BoT.

War bonuses and the eight-hour day
Johnstone reported in December 1914 on revised hours of work on the GS&WR, he having been informed that these had been accepted by a majority of the men in the locomotive department at Glanmire Road. The CB&SCR directors decided to introduce these hours as an experiment for the winter months. Basically, the men were to work from 08.00 to 18.00 daily Mondays to Fridays, with 45 minutes for dinner between 13.00 and 13.45. Saturday hours were to be 08.00 to 12.45, making a working week of 54¾ hours, including the dinner period.

The question of a war bonus was first raised in February 1915. It was agreed to grant a bonus of 1s per week to apprentices and lads on wages not exceeding 12s per week. Stationmasters, clerks and servants on wages between 12s and 30s a week were to receive 1s 6d bonus, while those earning between 30s and 39s would be granted a war allowance of 1s per week. Wages were to be calculated on the basis of six days, that is excluding Sunday pay and overtime. The scheme was estimated to cost the company £1,700 per annum, was to come into effect as from 20th February and the bonuses were intended to remain in force for the duration of the conflict. Over the next few years, considerable additions were to be made to the bonuses, and by February 1918, the secretary reported that the figure for the year 1917 was £15,000.

Hardly was the war over when the general manager confirmed that he had attended a meeting in Dublin in January 1919, to consider the question of an eight-hour working day. It was strongly argued that this would necessitate the employment of a considerable number of additional men. Despite these arguments, Kerr reported at the end of January that the 48 hour week was expected to come into operation on Monday, 3rd February; he also reported that it involved an additional 15 men.

Clothing accommodation and discipline

It was decided in June 1851 to provide clothing for certain grades of employee, the tender of Mr E Cleburne being accepted at £82 13s 0d for clothing for one guard, 16 policemen and 20 porters and gatemen. Boots were obtained at 10s per pair in November 1859 from Mr Smith of Bandon. The tender of Messrs Ireland was accepted in September 1864 for the provision of clothing. However all was not well with the material supplied, as the locomotive superintendent complained two months later regarding the unsuitability of three coats supplied for the firemen, which were described as being too soft and open to keep out wet. In addition, the cord trousers were not nearly as good as those previously obtained. These were returned to Messrs Ireland for replacement. It should be said that this firm supplied many of the Irish railway companies with clothing, this being probably a one-off complaint.

Five years later they again successfully tendered for various items, including a suit for guards at £4, firemen £2, porters 27s 6d, a pilot coat for drivers at £2 5s 0d and lined oil coats at 17s 6d each. When tenders were sought in July 1878, that of the Upton Reformatory was chosen over that of Messrs Ireland.

Overnight accommodation for drivers and firemen sleeping away from Cork was provided at Bandon from an early date. Similar accommodation was provided at Skibbereen in 1880. Kerr was instructed in January 1896 to prepare plans and estimates for suitable houses for a similar purpose at Drimoleague and Baltimore. Two plans were drawn up, estimated to cost respectively £180 and £300. It was decided to invite tenders for the latter class of house at Baltimore only, the tender of J H Jones at £302 3s 7d being accepted in March.

Edward Scott, stationmaster at Innoshannon was transferred to Upton in August 1851, it being the intention to close the former station. Within a few months of his transfer, a Mr Sherlock was voicing complaints of incivility and uncourteous conduct on the part of Scott, the directors

vowing to take steps to prevent a recurrence. At about the same time, Sherlock sought permission to walk on the line between Upton station and his farm and one suspects that this may have led to altercations between the two parties. Twelve months later, in December 1852, it was reported that Scott was very slow in the performance of his duties and he was urged to use more expedition in starting trains from his station. Within a month of this, the Cork Committee expressed their great dissatisfaction with the arrangements at Upton, Scott being informed that he must immediately provide an apartment for himself, as otherwise it would be necessary to appoint another stationmaster as the directors could not, 'consent to the public being deprived of sufficient accommodation'. Despite Scott's apparent deficiencies, when the position of traffic manager was advertised in September 1856, he unsuccessfully applied for it.

Mr Blake, the stationmaster at Innoshannon in succession to Scott, came to the attention of the board in August 1854, having been found drinking in a public house in the village, presumably whilst on duty. This was said to be a repetition of similar incidents on previous occasions. It was decided to dismiss him, his replacement being William Loane, who was later transferred to Kinsale, where he died in service in April 1876. His replacement at Innoshannon appears to have been Robert Loane, probably a relative. Robert fell foul of the directors in May 1875 when it was reported that he had recently been before the Magistrates on a charge of being drunk and disorderly on the public road. He was fined £1 1s 0d and costs. The local board decided to dispense with his services.

Dismissal for a totally different reason befell Thomas Meredith, in charge of Ballinhassig. Meredith who had previously been a sergeant in the City of Cork Militia, had been summoned to attend militia drill on one day a week and at other periods when necessary. The board decided that it would not be advisable to retain any person who would be obliged to absent himself from the duties of his office, and he was accordingly given a month's notice.

When a stone was thrown at a passenger train near Ballinhassig in December 1856, breaking a carriage window, the permanent way gang were informed that any future such incident would result in their immediate dismissal for lack of proper vigilance. The co-operation of the local parish priest was also sought in preventing a recurrence, a reward of £10 being offered.

McCarthy, the Waterfall stationmaster, attended the board meeting on 20th August 1873 to explain why he had a horse grazing on the line. He was duly fined 5s and informed that any repetition would result in his immediate dismissal. The early months

of 1896 saw two further stationmasters up before the board to explain their actions. In January, George Evans at Ballymartle was reported to be, 'very unsatisfactory'. His accounts, though very small, were reported to be, 'invariably incorrect and his cash was £1 2s 6d short when last balanced by the Company's Auditor'. In addition, the Post Office had more than once remonstrated with him over his method of handling the ETS instruments, and he had repeatedly been checked for his indifference to the signals at his station. These various matters led to his dismissal.

In March 1896, Kerr reported that the points had recently been broken at Kinsale Junction, through carelessness on the part of the night signalman. This was apparently one of a number of such incidents at that station. Bad as this was however, it became clear that the stationmaster, the night signalman and the crew of the train involved had made no attempt to report the matter. Sullivan, the stationmaster, and the night signalman were both dismissed, while the driver and guard of the train were each fined one weeks wages for omitting to report the incident. Sullivan subsequently appeared before the board to give his version of events, despite which his dismissal was confirmed. The board did agree to appoint his son to the position on a month's trial.

One or two other individuals are worthy of brief mention. Mr Follis, in charge at Ballineen, was acquitted of manslaughter in December 1890 and was reported to have resumed his duties. In April 1888 a complaint was made by Mr Crane, DJ of Bantry, against Mr Rattray, stationmaster at Bandon on the night a Mr Gilhooley was being taken to Cork. On investigation, it transpired that Rattray was only endeavouring to persuade people to move back so that he could start the train. He had no intention of obstructing the police in the carrying out of their duties, an explanation which was accepted. In recognition of the very efficient and satisfactory way in which he had performed his duties, he was allowed, on his retirement, to occupy free of rent a new house being erected for the stationmaster at Bandon.

Various drivers came to the attentions of the board over the years. It was reported in July 1872 that Driver Peter Murphy had recently run through a set of points. Having considered Murphy's case, the local committee formed the view that Murphy was physically unfit to discharge his duties, due to what was believed to be rheumatism in his legs. However, on being referred to Dr Tanner, the company's doctor in Cork, it was discovered that Murphy was suffering from, 'paralysis of the lower extremities'. He had been in the service of the company for 23 years and it was therefore recommended that he be retired on pension. Instead, Murphy was put in charge of the stationary engine and boiler in Cork at 15s per week. The matter was visited again in August, when the committee considered that Murphy, after long service and unimpeachable conduct, had been, 'deprived of a lucrative berth by a dispensation of Providence, and reduced from £2 9s 0d to 15s per week'. It was therefore recommended that he receive an additional gratuity of £30 as had first been recommended by the board.

In March 1873, Conran reported that the 18.15 up goods from Bandon on St Patrick's Day had stalled approaching Ballinhassig station, necessitating the dividing of the train. The two sections were then taken forwards to Waterfall, where they awaited the passing of the up mail. However, when the latter arrived at Waterfall, it was discovered that Driver Donovan of the goods was incapable of taking further charge of his engine. It was therefore decided to send the fireman from the mail on as driver of the goods train. On being questioned, Donovan admitted having had a glass of whiskey at Bandon. He said this had gone straight to his head as he had fasted all day, being busily engaged in piloting and shunting from an early hour. Conran stated that this conduct was foreign to Donovan's character, he being described as diligent and sober in the discharge of his duties during his ten years service with the company. As this was his first offence, he was let off with a severe reprimand and a fine of £2. Two years later, Driver Patrick Donovan, perhaps the same man, was dismissed for being under the influence of drink. A petition on his behalf from his wife saw him re-employed as a shunting driver in Cork yard. Strict instructions were given that Donovan was not to drive any engine out of Cork, 'on any condition whatever'.

Dorman reported that the driver of the 08.45 up train from Bantry on the morning of 29th February 1884 had been suspended on his arrival in Cork, he, 'having the appearance of drink and being stupid looking'. On further investigation, it was discovered that the driver had been unwell for some days, but had decided to keep working. He had also worked longer hours than usual. He freely admitted having taken some brandy during the stop at Skibbereen as he felt particularly unwell at this point. He was confined to working in the shops at Cork for a week, being paid accordingly.

A driver was dismissed in February 1892 for having been found in a wagon at Kinsale, filling a bucket with porter from a cask. Finally, in May 1892, it was reported that Driver Murphy and his fireman had both left their engine unattended in Bandon yard on two separate occasions. When remonstrated with by the stationmaster, Murphy had been abusive. He ended up being reduced to the rank of fireman. A guard found asleep in his van in November 1884 was fined 10s in addition to receiving a severe caution.

During the long strike of 1898, referred to elsewhere, some of the more junior officials took on other duties to help keep the service running. One such was J W Dodds, the locomotive foreman in Cork. On 22nd July, whilst in charge of a special goods train from Clonakilty Junction, he ran through signals at Bandon and narrowly averted a collision with the down passenger train. Dodds was summoned before the board, but was simply cautioned; he resigned his position in February 1899. On the other hand, a regular driver who committed the same offence at Bandon in January 1900 was dismissed, despite the error being attributed to a slippery rail. 'It was no excuse for any locomotive man to say that because the rails were slippy the train passed from under his control'. Double standards!

Jeremiah Hallinan, gateman No 36, was suspended in December 1856 for being absent, 'and having his chains across the line…which were broken through by the 06.15 down train'. The board considered this a serious offence and directed that Hallinan be not only dismissed, but that he also be prosecuted. Having considered the matter further, the committee felt that Hallinan had been sufficiently punished by the loss of his situation, and suggested to the board that he should not be prosecuted. At the same time, they felt that all gatekeepers should be warned that in future any similar misdemeanour would be prosecuted to the utmost rigour of the law. Whilst some members of the board were of opinion that Hallinan should be prosecuted, the directors finally agreed to the committee's recommendation.

Eight months prior to this incident, another gateman, McCarthy, was dismissed for a similar incident. Several applications had been received, seeking this man's reinstatement, the committee refusing to countenance these. However, in consideration of McCarthy having received serious injuries during the construction of Goggin's Hill tunnel, rendering him unfit for active employment, it was ordered that he be paid the sum of £1. An unusual dismissal involved night watchman Dyer at Clonakilty Junction in August 1889, when the manager reported that trouble had been caused by the language of Dyer's wife, she having refused to keep away from the station.

In December 1873, one of the company's porters at Cork discovered a purse of gold, valued at £27 10s 0d. The full amount was subsequently handed over to its rightful owner, who was mean enough not to reward the finder. Believing that such acts of honesty should not go unappreciated and unrewarded, the board presented the porter in question with a gratuity of £1.

Health problems

A letter was read at the board meeting on 30th January 1895 from the Rev J J Sheehy, parish priest of Baltimore, asking that the wife of William H, a milesman, who had, 'suddenly become a lunatic', might be left in the house she held from the company. It was decided to leave her in possession and to give her half of her husband's pay for a few weeks to see how he progressed. The Rev Sheehy wrote again in July asking the company to re-employ H, but Kerr did not consider it safe to do so at that time. He was however given work in a temporary gang on a trial basis in November of the following year. It was reported, however, in December 1897 that H had once again been admitted to the lunatic asylum; on this occasion it was decided that he should not be employed again and that his wife should give up the cottage. It transpired that the family were still in possession of the cottage in March 1899, Kerr reporting that he had received an application from H seeking to be re-employed. It was still considered unsafe to do so, and he was allowed a month to remove his wife and family from the company's cottage. Another year went by and then H sought compensation for a plot of land, which had now been occupied by a new gateman at Creagh, this request being declined.

At least two other cases are recorded where employees suffered mental health problems (perhaps due to the stress of work!). In one case the decision was taken not to re-employ the man or to give him any financial assistance. In the second case, the man was the head porter in Cork with nearly 30 years service involved. He had been, 'deprived of his reason', but the governor of the asylum in due course stated that he was perfectly restored to health; a gratuity of £10 was awarded to the man's family in this case, but there is no mention of whether he was taken back into the company's service.

Another interesting case arose in October 1917 when it was reported that an up train from Skibbereen in charge of Driver John Ronayne had got stuck. It was stated that, 'the excitement appeared to have affected his head and he was slightly paralysed and remained so for two days'. It was decided to give him his full wages but to have him medically examined. In July 1919, Johnstone reported that Ronayne had been employed in the Shops in Cork, but had recently, 'developed the same complaint'. Johnstone was of opinion that he would not be fit for future employment. As Ronayne was only 59 years of age and had 43 years service, 34 of which were as a driver, it was decided to have him examined by the company's physician. Dr Kearney in due course confirmed that the man had paralysis of the left arm and leg and was unlikely to be able to work again. The company agreed to pay him a weekly allowance of 28s, during the pleasure of the board, being two-thirds of his previous wages as a driver.

Secretaries and traffic managers

In this context, details of the various locomotive superintendents can be found in the chapter dealing with the company's motive power. John M'Donnell was appointed the first secretary to the company, remaining in the post until April 1846, when he was replaced by Mr H Williams Wood. Wood duly announced his resignation in September 1856, he being appointed the company's agent in England. He agreed to come over to Ireland at any time the board required him to do so subject to being allowed £10 as travelling expenses. James Connell was appointed as from 1st October 1856. With effect from 1st January 1858, Connell's salary was increased from £150 to £200 per annum, he now holding the joint positions of secretary and accountant. Obviously with Connell's retirement in mind, George Townley was appointed as assistant secretary in November 1882, he succeeding to Connell's post when the latter retired in April of the following year. It was not long however before a special board was summoned to investigate bank lodgements and accounts, an investigation which resulted in Townley's suspension in November 1883. At this time, Gordon was requested to act additionally as secretary pro tem.

At a board meeting held on 23rd November 1883, attended by Townley, he admitted having applied company monies for his own purposes, and it was unanimously decided to dismiss him. Application was made to a Glasgow firm for the amount of certain cheques. Mr J J Mahony was appointed in January 1884 to replace Townley, but his sojourn was short as he tendered his resignation in April 1887. Gordon now applied for the vacant position but it was decided to retain him as traffic and general manager. Edward H Dorman, brother of the engineer, J W Dorman, was the successful candidate, being appointed in May, he to resign all other appointments and devote his entire time to the company's service. Dorman died at the end of January 1893 and applications were sought for a replacement in the following month, Robert H Leslie being duly appointed. Leslie remained with the company until its demise in November 1924.

It was resolved in August 1856 that a traffic manager should be appointed, the necessary advertisement being placed in the press. In due course, a number of applications were received, from as far away as the Lancashire & Yorkshire Railway. The list included three C&BR stationmasters; Frederick Lyster at Bandon, Edward Scott at Upton and Richard Coghlan at Cork. The successful candidate was Richard Coghlan. His salary was to remain unaltered for three months following his appointment. In May of the following year however, the matter was referred to the local committee with a suggestion that the terminus at Cork be fitted up for his residence, an expenditure of £30 being approved for the purpose. Coghlan remained on in this role until he resigned in December 1877 on health grounds. The board agreed to grant him his full salary for life after 32 years service.

Alexander Gordon, the audit clerk, was appointed in Coghlan's place, but in the dual role of traffic and general manager. He also held the position of secretary for a short while in 1883 with the unforeseen departure of George Townley. Gordon in turn died in December 1893, the board deciding to grant a sum of £200 towards a fund being raised in aid of his family. Edward J. O'Brien Croker was appointed general manager as from 1st January 1894 at a salary of £350 per annum. Croker only remained for another nine years, announcing his appointment as from 1st August 1903 as Irish traffic manager of the Great Western Railway at a much enhanced salary of £1,000 per annum. John Kerr, the company's engineer, was appointed to succeed Croker as general manager at a salary of £500 per annum, to include both posts. As already related, Kerr resigned in October 1924 on his appointment to the Railway Tribunal.

A notice soliciting subscriptions to a fund for the family of the late Alexander Gordon, former general manager, following his death in December 1893.
Author's collection

CORK, 7th December, 1893.

DEAR SIR,

The sad circumstances of the death of MR. ALEX. GORDON, for many years General Manager, Cork, Bandon, & South Coast Railway, have induced the Officers of the Cork Railways to hold a Meeting at which it was resolved to open a Subscription Fund for the benefit of his Family, and as a mark of esteem for his memory.

The case is peculiarly painful, as his death has left a Widow and Nine young Children unprovided for ; and in consequence of delicate health, and heavy demands on his resources, he was unable during his lifetime to make provision for his Family through assurance or otherwise.

The Fund to be raised will be invested in Trustees for the benefit of the Family.

The Committee, whose names appear below, earnestly hope that you will subscribe, and they will be glad if you will fill up and return the attached Form to the Honorary Secretary.

Subscriptions may be paid into the Bank of Ireland to the credit of the "ALEX. GORDON FUND," and will be acknowledged in the local papers.

Committee—
F. L. LYSTER, *Traffic Manager, Cork and Macroom Railway.*
J. J. O'SULLIVAN, *General Manager, Cork, Blackrock & Passage Railway.*
J. B. WILSON, *General Manager, Cork & Muskerry Railway.*
R. J. BULKELEY, *District Superintendent, Great Southern & Western Railway.*
DENHAM FRANKLIN, J. P., *Secretary, Clonakilty, Timoleague, and Courtmacsherry Railway.*

Honorary Secretary—R. H. LESLIE, *Secretary, Cork, Bandon. & South Coast Railway.*

Chapter Seventeen

REFRESHMENTS, HOTELS & STEAMERS

With a system of such a short mileage, it is hardly surprising that the CB&SCR had only two refreshment rooms during its independent existence, at Bandon and Bantry. As early as May 1852 a letter was received from the secretary of the C&BR recommending the establishment of a refreshment room at Bandon terminus, 'for the convenience of parties coming from the west'. Instructions were issued to enquire whether a Mr Loane would undertake this. There is no further mention of this matter in the board minutes and we must therefore assume that Loane expressed no interest.

Six years later a Mr Richard Dobbyn wrote to the board on the same subject. Whilst they considered that the accommodation of the public in such a venture was desirable, it would put the company to considerable expense and the local committee enquired on what terms Dobbyn might be offered the facilities. The board, after due consideration, expressed their opinion that he should give £100 per annum, the company in return undertaking the expense of building a refreshment room and any other attendant accommodation required at Bandon. By November 1858 it was resolved that no advantages were to be gained by the erection of a refreshment room and here the matter rested for a further nine years. Then in September 1867 the secretary was requested to ascertain what accommodation, if any, was available at Bandon for the provision of refreshment facilities. Conran in due course confirmed that there was a plot of ground suitable for such a purpose immediately adjoining the arrival platform. The cost of providing the facilities requested by a Mr Ward; that was first and third class rooms, two bedrooms and a kitchen, would be about £300. However the committee decided that a refreshment room at Bandon would not pay on such an outlay and once again the matter was shelved.

As already related, a new station was provided at Bandon in 1894 and in February of that year a letter was read from the manager asking what steps it was proposed to take in regard to refreshment facilities here. It was suggested that the company should supply luncheon baskets to passengers and the decision was taken to advertise for a refreshment contractor. It was announced in April

that a Mr Koenigs had declined to undertake the work at Bandon. It should be mentioned that Koenigs provided catering facilities to a number of railway companies about this time, including the GS&WR and the DW&WR. A Miss M Clarke of Skibbereen also declined to become involved. In May 1897 a Mr G W French made proposals but these were declined, presumably as being too underpriced. Work had apparently been carried out as instructions were given for the conversion of the room provided for refreshments into a waiting room.

Lady Bandon wrote in November 1898 on the subject of providing tea at Bandon station but it was decided that the stopover at the station was too short to allow of passengers availing of a refreshment room and it would therefore be useless to provide one. This seemed like the end of the matter but in March 1907 the general manager reported that constant complaints were being made of the want of refreshments on the line and he suggested that if the board would sanction an outlay of about £25, a small building could be erected on the platform at Bandon, and tea baskets supplied to the up and down afternoon trains. An arrangement might perhaps be made for the stationmaster's family to work it and a small rent be charged for the building and baskets, which would remain the company's property. The board agreed to this in principle and Kerr was instructed to submit a definite scheme for their consideration.

Kerr reported back to the effect that the stationmaster's family were quite prepared to undertake the working of a refreshment stall at Bandon, they to pay 5% interest on the cost of the building and 25% on the cost of the tea baskets and requisites, they also paying all expenses and the cost of refreshments. This was approved by the board and the 'tea house' was reported to have been opened for business in August 1907. Reporting to the board in January 1908, Kerr said the facility promised to be useful and he proposed to charge Rattray, the stationmaster, no rent for it up to 31st December 1907 and from that date a rent of four guineas per annum, payable half-yearly in June and December. In addition Rattray would be liable for making good any breakages or loss in tea baskets. The cost of providing the

facility was given as £30 for the building, £13 7s 7d for furniture and £12 3s 7d for baskets and fittings, making a total figure of £55 11s 2d.

The facility appears to have continued uninterrupted through the war years. Kerr made a report in February 1919 enclosing correspondence from the stationmaster at Bandon to the effect that tea baskets and ware had been purloined by American sailors, the loss to date amounting to 29s.6d. Rattray asked to be relieved of paying for the necessary replacements in the particular circumstances of the losses. The board decided to allow him half the cost of replacement.

Refreshments at Bantry
A lengthy report from the Development Syndicate (Ireland) Ltd was submitted to the board in March 1897 under the heading of tourism. The main thrust of the report was in relation to a proposed working agreement for a new coach service for the 'Prince of Wales' route and enquiring whether the company would give them land at Bantry for the erection, at the syndicate's expense, of dining and waiting rooms. About this time, a Mr George Vickery, who had been operating this coach service, had handed it over to the syndicate. The board approved of the idea and suggested that an agreement might be concluded if the syndicate agreed to extend the 'Prince of Wales' route to Castletown Berehaven at their own expense, erect a hotel there, and build refreshment and dining rooms at Bantry station, the latter to be subject to the approval of and under the supervision of the company's engineer. Kerr drew up plans, which were forwarded to the Development Syndicate in July.

The latter took some time to digest these plans and submitted amendments in the following February, these being approved of in due course. By May 1898 Kerr reported that as yet no steps had been taken towards the building of the refreshment and retiring rooms at Bantry as the Syndicate were bound to provide under a 20-year agreement signed on 14th May 1897. The secretary was instructed to write requesting that the buildings be available in time for the approaching summer season. A minute of 7th September of that year makes it clear that the work was still uncompleted. It was agreed at this time that the company would take over, at a valuation, the refreshment rooms at the close of the lease provided the Syndicate gave an undertaking to have them completed by 1st May 1899; this was to include the erection of a veranda not included in the original proposals. In October 1898 a letter was received from Colonel Dickinson, secretary to the Development Syndicate, undertaking to pay half the cost of bringing Bantry town water into the station, this being approved by the board.

Kerr reported to the board in June 1900 that the Lord Lieutenant had declined to grant a licence for the refreshment rooms for the summer season. In consequence, the Syndicate had opened them for light refreshments only. A more sinister matter was reported in January 1902, the board being shown a poster signed by a Captain Moonlight in which the West Cork Magistrates were warned to vote against the request for a licence. Reference was made to the Tourist Development Association and their agent, Vickery, 'the old Cromwellian cut throat and land grabber (who) has horses grazing on the boycotted farm at Newtown Bantry and is buying the hay and all the other produce off the boycotted farm from Edward Godfrey the grabber, perjurer, thief and fate falling son of the Reverend Godfrey Smith's old Kerry bastard and on whose head rests the blood of the late Mr Patrick O'Callaghan'. Any Magistrates voting for the licence would be, 'to Ireland and the United Irish League what Casey the informer was to the invincible (or any tourist travelling by what is known as 'The Prince of Wales Route' let them beware)'.

The Tourist Development Association wrote to the board in February 1913 enquiring if the company would be prepared to purchase their interest in the refreshment rooms, they being informed that the matter would be favourably considered. A figure of £200 was duly offered for the Association's interest in the premises and licence, including furniture. This was declined, a figure of not less than £300 being sought. Nothing further transpired until Crossley on behalf of the Association wrote in July 1915 asking what the company would offer, they deciding not to make any proposals at this time. Within a week however they received a letter from a Mr Telford, who had been appointed as receiver/manager to the Tourist Development Association, advising that he was preparing to put up for auction the interest in the 20-year lease.

The board stressed that they could not consent to the refreshment rooms being sold to a third party or to the transfer of the excise licence to anyone else. Arising from this the company offered £150, including all furniture and subject to clear title being obtained. Telford replied to the effect that he would recommend the Court to accept £150 for buildings and fixtures, the company taking over the furniture at cost. In due course this amount was reluctantly accepted and the board agreed to renew the licence for the current year at a cost of £8.3s.9d. Like that at Bandon, there is no reference to a refreshment room at Bantry in GSR days and we must assume that both were closed either prior to the formation of the company or very shortly afterwards.

On the independent T&CELR, a Mrs Lendrum wrote to the board of that company in June 1892 suggesting that such a facility be provided at least on excursion days. Whilst the idea appealed to the board, nothing further was done about it. A year later however it was agreed to let a room at Courtmacsherry to a Miss Coe to be used as a refreshment room, subject to her signing an agreement. One wonders if this was a daughter or other relative of the traffic inspector on the CB&SCR! Only nine months later, in March 1894, a Miss Peyton, sister of the Courtmacsherry stationmaster, was given the room for the season, 'on a small percentage (unspecified) of the receipts'. This was the last mention of the refreshment rooms at Courtmacsherry and they most likely had a short life.

Hotels

Reference has been made above to proposals for a hotel to be built by the Tourist Development Association at Castletown Berehaven. It will also be recalled that plans were drawn up for the construction of a hotel complex at Kinsale. Although the company never actually became involved in the running of hotels, they did on occasions make enquiries as to acquiring or building

them. For example, in December 1894 they enquired of a Mr French, probably the same gentleman referred to in connection with the refreshment room at Bandon, as to whether it might be possible to obtain the ground at Coloomey Lakes, and if so, upon what terms for building a hotel. It was expected that the company would have the exclusive rights of fishing and shooting attached to it.

In October 1895 it was reported that Lord Shannon's agent had been in Courtmacsherry and had informed the secretary that he thought it possible that the Demesne House there might be let for a hotel. If preferred, a site might be given for building one, but the matter was taken no further. In July 1896 a proposal for taking Lady Boyle's house and grounds at Courtmacsherry for use as a hotel was discussed, Mr Croker being authorised to offer £60 a year for the house and outoffices on a 35 year lease, and £20 per annum on a grazing lease for the adjoining land. If the venture proved successful after five years, it was suggested that the company would be prepared to pay a rent of £80 per annum for the house, they to expend £200 on improvements within two years from the date of the lease. These terms were in due course accepted, arrangements being made to set up a limited liability company with a capital of £5,000 in £5 shares to manage the hotel. This was however the end of the venture.

In January 1896 an application was submitted to the board seeking their moral support for the transfer of a licence for an old house in Baltimore to a new premises, which it was proposed to convert into a hotel and first class restaurant. In this context, either Coe, the traffic inspector, or the stationmaster at Bantry was requested to attend the Court in Bantry and make representations in favour of the application, 'in the interest of the tourist and excursion traffic'. A similar request was put to the board by the Tourist Development Association in regard to hotels at Glengarriff.

This rather inauspicious looking building at Glengarriff pier belonged to the Bantry Bay Steamship Company.

Steamer services

The first reference to steamers is in June 1854 when the traffic superintendent confirmed having made arrangements with the agent for the River Steamers to have an excursion on Whit Monday in connection with the railway. This appears to have been a one-off arrangement and it was to be nearly 30 years before the company's solicitors were requested to advise on the legality of the company chartering or subsidising a steamer between Bantry and Castletown Berehaven (variously called either Castletown or Berehaven; for the purposes of this account of steamer services we shall henceforth refer to it as Berehaven). This was in June 1881, the chairman advising six months later of two steamers for sale. Nothing further was done in this regard although the subject of obtaining a steamer for the fish traffic from Bantry was briefly discussed in January 1883. Enquiries were made of the Waterford Steamship Co to see if they would charter the SS *Erin* for three months, with an option to purchase. This project fell through however when it was discovered that repairs would cost about £300 against a value not exceeding £900.

In May 1883 a prospectus was issued for the Bantry Bay Steamship Co, which intended to operate a freight service between Bantry and Berehaven. In June, J W Payne stated that pending the final formation of a company, it had been decided to charter a steamer. The company agreed to bear half of any losses, Messrs Payne and Swanton bearing the balance. A thrice-weekly service commenced operation in the following year utilising the Belfast built SS *Countess of Bantry*, a small (92ft) iron hulled screw steamer.

The general manager reported in January 1888 on two matters involving the Clyde Shipping Co. This company had commenced operations in 1815 as a tug owner and entered the coastal trade in 1856. After this date, the passenger trade expanded and Clyde steamers were to be found plying in British and Irish waters, including those of west Cork and Kerry. A local steamer service operated between Cork and Dingle in County Kerry between the late 1850s and 1905. This service was taken over by the Clyde Shipping Co. in 1876, calls being made intermediately at Schull, Berehaven, Bantry, Kenmare, Sneem and Cahirciveen as and when required. One of the complaints was that the Kinsale Harbour Board had proposed making arrangements with them to ply between Kinsale and Cork. This service never materialised, but, if it had, it would undoubtedly have had serious repercussions for the railway company. The second was the loss of a large portion of the Bantry traffic, principally mill stuffs and pigs, a reduction in the railway rates being suggested to counter this. It was decided to

reduce the rates for mill stuffs to 4s 6d per ton and for pigs from both Bantry and Skibbereen from 2s to 1s 6d per animal.

It was reported in May 1900 that goods had been turned away due to insufficient lifting capacity at Berehaven, the company agreeing to contribute 50% towards the erection of a crane of seven tons capacity. The TDA approached the board in September 1899 advising that they were considering placing a small steamer at Bantry to operate to Glengarriff and to run excursions. Consideration was also given by the TDA to the establishment of a rest room and refreshment facilities at the (road) tunnel between Glengarriff and Kenmare. The company replied that they had in contemplation seeking powers in connection with steamer services and if these powers were granted they would consider the proposals put forward. Section 15 of the company's Act of 1900 gave authority for a subscription of not more than £10,000 to the Bantry Bay Steamship Co.

Following on the passing of the Act, Mr Somers Payne, managing director of the BBS Co represented the necessity of putting on a larger steamer as the *Countess of Bantry* was proving unable to cope with the increasing traffic offering. A suitable steamer would cost in the region of £6,000 and Payne requested that the company provide up to £2,000 as allowed for under the Act. This the company agreed to do, reserving the right to appoint an additional director to the steamship company. The SS *Princess Beara* was built at Greenock in 1901 and was steel-hulled and, at 115ft in length, was somewhat larger than the *Countess of Bantry*. The latter remained on the service however until 1935.

The SS *Valentia*, a steel-built triple expansion steamer built at Dundee in 1890, was offered for sale by the Clyde Shipping Co in November 1901. On hearing of this, the merchants of Bantry memorialised the CDB, who agreed to grant a subsidy of £500 per annum to the Clyde company in order to keep the vessel operating the west Cork services. The CB&SCR remonstrated strongly against this action, although in fairness the operation of the steamer provided the only economic means of transport to parts of the southwest at that time. Following further pressure from the railway company, the subsidy was withdrawn at the end of 1904 and the CDB undertook not to subsidise a similar service for five years. Apart from being, in the company's view, a violation of existing agreements, the action of the CDB would prolong the baronial guarantee tax on certain areas of west Cork. The withdrawal of the steamer service would make the Bantry extension railway self supporting. Within a few months the Clyde Shipping Co withdrew their steamer service between Cork and the south-western ports.

Meanwhile, discussions took place with the CDB in March 1904 in relation to a steamer service to Glengarriff and Adrigole, while Crossley met with the board on the same subject two months later. The Eccles Hotel offered a sum of £25 towards such a service for the 1904 summer season, the company agreeing to grant an additional £75, later increased to £100. It was reported that the new service commenced operating as from 1st July 1904. The question of running the service again during 1905 was considered in January. It was suggested that a definite proposal should be made to the TDA to run the SS *Lady Betty Balfour*, referred to in the company's records simply as the *Lady Betty*, in connection with the three day trains from the middle of May to the middle of September. The *Lady Betty Balfour* had been built for the Shannon Development Co by Bow McLachlan & Co of Paisley in 1897.

It was agreed to offer a subsidy of £80 towards this service, the Syndicate endeavouring unsuccessfully to have this increased to £100. Kerr now recommended that negotiations with the TDA be dropped and an attempt made to persuade the BBS Co to operate the service. Kerr reported in March that he was engaging the services of a marine engineer, a Mr Elwood, to inspect the *Countess of Bantry* and another steamer, the SS *Princess Louise*. Following the inspection, the latter was considered to be too old and too expensive at the asking price of £4,000. Another vessel, the Irish Lights steamer *Moya* was also briefly considered but was turned down due to her excessive draft of eleven feet, making her too large for Bantry Bay. In the event, the *Lady Betty Balfour* was chartered. At the end of the season, she was transferred to Warrenpoint in County Down, where she remained until World War I.

A third vessel was added to the BBS fleet in 1906, namely the SS *Lady Elsie*, built new at Greenock. With the arrival of this steamer, the CB&SCR agreed to guarantee traffic receipts of not less than £1,000 per annum for services, 'between Bantry and Adrigole, Glengarriff or any other localities in Bantry Bay eastward of the Roancarrig Light'. In addition they agreed to insure the new steamer for £2,500. This agreement was to remain in force for five years from 1st May 1906. Another clause in the agreement required the Steamship Co to make arrangements with the CDB for the construction of piers at Adrigole and Glengarriff, the latter being completed in 1907. Originally, passengers made their way on foot between the station and the pier but in 1908 the company extended passenger trains to make a direct connection on the pier, a small waiting shed having been erected there in 1906.

Correspondence was received from the CDB in May 1908 to the effect that a Mr

Michael Cottrell of Baltimore was seeking a subsidy of £120 per annum towards the running of a steamer between Baltimore, Hare Island, Sherkin Island and Cape Clear. The vessel proposed was considered to be too small and therefore quite useless for the proposed carriage of mails, goods and passengers, and as a consequence the company declined to offer a subsidy. The matter was raised again by the CDB in the following August, the company considering that such a service would not be of much use to them. On the other hand, the board felt that it might be well not to refuse entirely to subscribe, and they therefore offered a sum of £25 per annum for five years. The matter was resolved however when the CDB announced that they did not have the necessary funds available to subsidise it. It would appear from a board minute dated 26th January 1916 that a subscription of £6 had been given in 1915 towards a Baltimore to Cape Clear service, a similar amount being given for 1916. It was however made clear that this was not to be considered as an annual subsidy.

Passenger sailings on Bantry Bay ceased in 1936, the *Lady Elsie* being withdrawn and broken up. Goods services were operated by the *Princess Beara* which also provided a limited passenger service for the 1937 summer season only. There was an 08.30 sailing from Berehaven, returning from Bantry at 13.00, with connections provided into and out of the Cork trains. At the beginning of 1946, CIÉ began operating a road freight service between Bantry and Berehaven, a move which spelt the demise of the steamer. The latter had ceased operating by the summer of that year, the crew of seven being made redundant. So came to an end steamer services which had operated on Bantry Bay for more than 60 years. The *Princess Beara* was offered for sale for £6,000 and was broken up in 1948. CIÉ sought permission in 1949 to abandon the pier at Bantry, but, despite local objections, permission was granted. The timber portion of the pier was removed with the associated sidings being cut back.

Appendix A

LIST OF STATIONS, JUNCTIONS AND SIDINGS

Miles/chains	Station	Open	Closed	Remarks
Cork (Albert Quay) - Baltimore				
0.00	Albert Quay	1851	1961	
0.14	CCR Junction	1912	1976	
	Ballyphehane Jct.	See	text	a.k.a.Macroom Jct.
8.40	Waterfall	1852	1961	
9.26	Ballinhassig	1849	1961	
13.20	Kinsale Jct.	1863	1961	Renamed Crossbarry, 1936
15.24	Brien's Siding			
15.40	Upton	1849	1961	
	Innoshannon	1849	1891	
	Bandon WC Jct.	1876	1880	
19.64	Bandon [low-level]	1849	1961	Closed for passengers 1894.
20.00	Bandon [high-level]	1894	1961	
	Bandon WCR	1866	1874	
20.40	Bandon West	1874	1880	
21.60	Castle Bernard	1873	1961	Closed for passengers 1891.
24.03	Clonakilty Jct.	1886	1961	Initially known as Gaggin.
27.64	Desert	1867	1961	
29.40	Enniskeane	1866	1891	
30.00	Ballineen & Enniskeane	1891	1961	
30.40	Ballineen	1866	1891	
34.20	Manch Platform	c1869	1891	Used for race traffic after closure
	Dunmanway (1st)	1866	1877	Temporary station
37.56	Dunmanway (2nd)	1877	1961	
38.00	Atkins Mill Siding		1961	
42.00	Knockbue	1878	1961	
45.40	Drimoleague Jct. (2nd)	1899	1961	
45.60	Drimoleague Jct. (1st)	1877	1899	
48.78	Madore	by 1878	1961	
53.48	Skibbereen	1877	1961	
57.26	Creagh	1893	1961	
61.60	Baltimore	1893	1961	
62.00	Baltimore Pier	1917	1961	

Miles/chains	Station	Open	Closed	Remarks
Kinsale Jct - Kinsale				
13.04	Kinsale Jct.	1863	1961	Closed as Jct. 1931.
17.03	Ballymartle	1864	1931	
21.07	Farrangalway	1863	1931	
24.00	Kinsale	1863	1931	
Clonakilty Jct - Clonakilty				
24.03	Clonakilty Jct.	1886	1961	
29.20	Ballinascarthy Jct.	1886	1961	
31.00	Shannonvale Siding	1887	1961	
33.00	Clonakilty	1886	1961	
Drimoleague Jct - Bantry				
45.40	Drimoleague Jct.	1899	1961	
49.44	Aughaville	1886	1961	
51.78	Durrus Road	1881	1961	
	Storer's Siding	1907	c1920	
57.20	Bantry [Hill Top]	1881	1892	
57.60	Bantry [Town].	1892	1961	
58.60	Bantry Pier	1892	1949	
Ballinascarthy Jct-Courtmacsherry				
0.00	Ballinascarthy Jct.	1886	1961	
3.00	Skeaf	1890	1947	
5.00	Ummera Ballast Siding	1890		
5.78	Timoleague	1890	1961	
9.00	Courtmacsherry	1891	1961	
	Courtmacsherry Pier	1893	1961	
Cork City Railway				
0.15	Glanmire Road	1912	Open	GS&WR station.
0.00	CCR Jct.	1912	1976	
0.22	St. Patrick's Quay Sdg.	1912	1939	
0.30	Anderson's Quay Sdg.	1912	1963	
0.35	Lapp's Quay Sdg.	1912	1946	
0.57	Albert Quay	1912	1976	

Appendix B

LIST OF CB&SCR LOCOMOTIVES

No	Name	Type.	Maker.	Maker's No	Introd.	Rebuilt.	Wdn.	GSR No	Cost. £	Remarks.
1	*Rith Teineadh*	I	Adams	5?	6/1849		1868			
2	*Sighe Gaoithe*	I	Adams	6?	6/1849		1868			
3	*Fag an Beallach*	II	Tayleur		10/1849	c1870	12/1890		1,750	
4		II	Tayleur		1851		2/1888		1,850	
5		III	Sharp	698	9/1852		6/1887		1,920	
6		III	Sharp	699	10/1852		1879		1,920	
7		IV	Fairbairn		3/1862	1864/1890	6/1897		1,800	
8		V	Bury		12/1865		11/1874		700	EX GS&WR. Renumbered 1 in 1868.
2		VI	Bury		c1867	c1872			c300	
8		VII	Bury		1871		4/1877		300	Ex GS&WR. Renumbered 2 in 1872.
8		VIII	Bury		1871		11/1874		350	Ex GS&WR.
1		IX	Dübs	760	9/1874		1930	482	2,335	
2		IX	Dübs	861	7/1875	1909	1930	477	2,100	
4a		IX	Dübs	2323	11/1887		1924		1,525	
8		IX	Dübs	1072	9/1877		1920		1,840	
13		IX	Dübs	1877	7/1883		1919		1,950	
9	*Patience*	X	Cross	17	1/1880		1894			WCR1. Name removed by CB&SCR.
10	*Perseverance*	X	Cross	18	1/1880		1893			WCR2. Name removed by CB&SCR.
11		XI	Vulcan	806	1/1880		1905		1,925	WCR3
5		XII	BP	2902	11/1887		1939	475	1,500	
6		XII	BP	2046	2/1881	1922	1940	472	1,980	
12		XII	BP	2156	4/1882		1925	[474]	1,950	
16		XII	BP	3288	10/1890		1925	[476]	1,890	
17		XII	BP	3629	9/1894		1935	473	1,700	
	Bantry	XXI	MW	773	7/1881			Hire		To Allman's 1885/6.
14	*St Patrick* **	XIII	SS	2645	5/1885	1893/1896	1908		750	Bought secondhand from L&LSR
15	*St Columb* **	XIII	SS	2836	5/1885	1898	1910		600	Bought secondhand from L&LSR
3		XIV	Dübs	2777	6/1891	Vars.	1930	479	2,100	
9		XIV	Neilson	4741	11/1894	1898/1908	1936	480	1,825	
10		XIV	Dübs	3048	7/1893	1906	1933	471	1,945	
18		XIV	Neilson	4740	11/1894	1900	1935	481	1,825	
19		XV	Baldwin	18027	10/1900		c1914		2,575	
20		XV	Baldwin	18028	10/1900		1912		2,575	
7		XVI	Cork		1901		1934	478	325	
4		XVII	BP	5954	12/1919	1942/1950	1963	463	4,389	
8		XVII	BP	6034	11/1920	1946	1963	464	8,163	
11		XVII	BP	4752	5/1906		1945	465	3,145	
13		XVII	BP	6077	11/1920	1947	1961	466	9,163	
14		XVII	BP	5265	3/1909	1935	1959	467	2,770	
15		XVII	BP	5413	10/1910	1944/1950	1961	468	2,575	
19		XVII	BP	5822	6/1914		1945	469	2,975	
20		XVII	BP	5616	7/1912		1961	470	2,550	
	Slaney	XVIII	Hunslet	382	1885		1920			T&CELR engine
	St Molaga	XIX	Hunslet	520	1890		1949			T&CELR engine
	Argadeen	XX	Hunslet	611	1894	1929	1957			T&CELR engine
	'Coffee Pot' *	XXI	MW	773	1885/6		1920			Allman's Distillery
		XXII	Peckett	1556	1920		1949	495		Allman's Distillery engine to GSR 1930

* Unofficial name given by CB&SCR men at Bandon.

** These were the locomotive names on the Londonderry & Lough Swilly Railway which were removed following their purchase by the CB&SCR.

Manufacturers
BP   Beyer Peacock & Co. Ltd, Gorton Works, Manchester.
Cork CB&SCR Works, Rocksavage.
MW   Manning Wardle & Co, Leeds.
SS   Sharp Stewart & Co, Glasgow.

Appendix C

LOCOMOTIVE DIMENSIONS

Type	Wheels.	Cylinders	D.W.	B.P.	H.S.	G.A.	Weight*	Remarks.
I	0-2-2T	8" x 12"	5'0"				8 10	
II	2-2-2	14" x 20"	5'6"				20 00	
III	0-4-2	16" x 22"	5'0"		1036.8			
IV	0-4-0ST	14" x 22"	4'6"	100				
V	0-4-2	15" x 24"	5'0"	70			22 00	
VI	2-2-2?	15" x 20"	5'6"		1000			
VII	2-4-0	15" x 20"	5'8"	80				
VIII	2-2-2	15" x 20"	6'0"	80	1060	12.75	23 00	
IX	2-4-0T	15" x 22"	5'0"	120	830.5	11.20	32 00	
X	2-4-0T	15" x 22"	5'6"					
XI	2-4-0ST	15" x 20"	5'0"	c140	c766		29 15	
XII	0-6-0ST	17" x 24"	Vars	140	901	14.00	35 13	See text re Driving Wheel diameters.
XIII	0-6-0T	15" x 22"	4'6"		920	12.00	31 00	
XIV	4-4-0T	16" x 22"	5'6"	130/140**	838.5	14.50	41 02	** B.P. of Dübs engines 130lb, Neilson 140lb.
XV	0-6-2ST	18" x 24"	4'8"	160	1179.7	18.79	40 09	
XVI	4-4-0T	15" x 22"	5'0"	135	934	12.00	35 00	
XVII	4-6-0T	18" x 24"	5'2?"	160	1182.5	24.00	56 10	
XVIII	0-6-0ST	12" x 18"	3'1"		401		23 00	
XIX	0-4-2T	c10" x 16"	3'3"	140	360	6.20	21 17	
XX	2-6-0T	14" x 18"	3'6"	140	539	10.20	28 00	
XXI	0-4-0ST	9" x 14"	2'9"					Cyls. Also shown as 9¼" x 12" in some records.
XXII	0-4-0ST	10" x 15"	2'9"	160			18 00	

Abbreviations
D.W.   Driving Wheel diameters [ft.in]
B.P.   Boiler Pressure in lbs per sq in
H.S.   Heating Surface in sq ft
G.A.   Grate Area in sq ft
*Weight expressed in tons and hundredweights

A group of locomotives in 'The Quarry' at Rocksavage in July 1955, including Nos 90, 551, *Argadeen*, No 100 and an unidentified ex GS&WR tank engine. No 90 is the only one still in existance. G Toms

Appendix D

CARRIAGE STOCK

Saloons, Firsts & Composites	Seconds, Thirds & Third Brakes	Final CB&SCR No	Type	Builder	Year	Length ft in	Remarks	1923 Layout	1st Class	3rd Class	Withdrawn
1			Compo	C&BR	1868-70						c1882-86
2		42	Compo	Dawson	1863	24' 7"	To 1st in 1907	4-Compt. 6-wheel First	32		1928
3			Compo	C&BR	1868-70						c1882-86
	4		Compo	C&BR	1868-70						c1882-86
5			Compo	C&BR	1873		To 2nd/3rd Co 1878; 3rd in 1889				1901
6	16		Saloon	C&BR	1876		To Third Saloon No 16 in 1896				1913
	1		Third	C&BR	1871-77						1905
	2		Third	C&BR	1871-77						1905
	3		Third	C&BR	1871-77						1905
	4		Third	C&BR	1871-77						1905
	5		Third	C&BR	1871-77						1889
	6		Third	C&BR	1871-77						1906
	7		Third	C&BR	1871-77						c1906
7		12	First	BCW	1865	24' 9"	Ex WCR 1879; Rebuilt as 3rd No 12 in1890	4-Compt. 6-wheel Third		40	1938
8		30	Compo	BCW	1865	27' 4"	Ex WCR 1879; to 2nd/3rd Compo in1899, r/bt in 1904 and to 3rd No 30 c1906	5-Compt. 6-wheel Third		50	1949
9		29	Compo	BCW	1865	27' 4"	Ex WCR 1879; to 2nd/3rd Compo in 1899 and 3rd No 29 c1906	5-Compt. 6-wheel Third		50	1923
10		24	Compo	BCW	1865	27' 4"	Ex WCR,1879;to 3rd.No 24, 1892	5-Compt.6-wh.3rd.		50	1955
11		18	Compo	BCW	1865	27' 4"	Ex WCR 1879; to Third No 18 c1882	2-Compt. 6-wheel 3rd Brake		20	1941
	8		Third	BCW	1865	27' 4"	Ex WCR 1879				1896
	9		Third	BCW	1865	27' 4"	Ex WCR 1879				1901
	10	10	Third	BCW	1865	27' 4"	Ex WCR 1879	5-Compt. 6-wheel Third		50	1941
	11	11	Third	BCW	1865	27' 4"	Ex WCR 1879	5-Compt. 6-wheel Third		50	1943
	12		Third	BCW	1865	27' 4"	Ex WCR 1879; to Van in 1901				
	13	13	Third	BCW	1865	27' 4"	Ex WCR 1879	5-Compt. 6-wheel Third		50	1939
	14	14	Third	BCW	1865	27' 4"	Ex WCR 1879	5-Compt.6-wh.3rd.		50	1928
	15	15	Third	BCW	1865	27' 4"	Ex WCR 1879	5-Compt.6-wh.3rd.		50	1959
	16		Third	BCW	1865	27' 4"	Ex WCR 1879; 2nd/3rd Co in 1896 Rebuilt as Third 1890; Brake compartment added again 1896				c1901
	17	17	3rd Bke	Rocksavage	1878	26' 11"		4-Compt. 6-wheel 3rd Brake		40	1947
12		49	Compo	BCW	1878	26' 11"	To 1st in 1907	4-Compt. 6-wheel First	32		1949
13		41	Compo	BCW	1878	26' 11"	Compo No 1 c1896; to 1st in 1907	4-Compt. 6-wheel First	32		1949
14		51	Compo	BCW	1878	26' 11"	To 1st in 1907	4-Compt. 6-wheel First	32		1949
11		48	Compo	MCW	1878	24' 7"	Ex-L&LSR 1885; to 1st in 1907	4-Compt. 6-wheel First	32		1943
	20	20	Second	MCW	1878	25' 11"	Ex-L&LSR 1885; to Van 1903	2-Compt. 6-wheel 3rd Brake, rebuilt 1911		20	1959
	21	21	Second	MCW	1878	25' 11"	Ex-L&LSR 1885; to Van 1903	2-Compt. 6-wheel 3rd Brake, rebuilt 1911		20	1955
	22	19	3rd Bke	BCW	1885	25' 10"	Renumbered 1889 as No 19	4-Compt. 6-wheel 3rd Brake		40	1923
	23	23	3rd Bke	BCW	1885	25' 10"		4-Compt. 6-wh. 3rd.		40	1928
15		33	1st/2nd Compo	BCW	1885	29' 4"	To 2nd/3rd Compo c1906, To 1st/3rd Compo c1907	5-Compt. 6-wheel 5-Compt.6-wh. 3rd.		50	1923
16		60	1st/2nd Saloon	BCW	1885	28' 7"	To 1st in 1907	2-Compt.Saloon & Lge, 6-wh.1st.	32		1949
	22	22	Third	Bristol	1890	32' 10"		6-Compt. Bogie Third		60	1957
5		43	1st/2nd Compo	Rocksavage	1891	33' 11"	To 1st in 1907	5-Compt. Bogie First	40		1957
17		52	1st/2nd Compo	Rocksavage	1892	33' 11"	To 1st in 1907	5-Compt. Bogie First	40		1957
	25	25	Third	Lancaster	1894	32' 10"		6-Compt. Bogie Third		60	1957
7		45	1st/2nd Compo	Rocksavage	1894	33' 11"	To 1st in 1907	5-Compt. Bogie First	40		1957
10		55	1st/2nd Saloon	Rocksavage	1895	33' 11"	To 1st in 1907	2-Compt, Saloon & 1 Lav Bogie First	26		1960
	8	8	Third	Lancaster	1896	32' 10"		6-Compt. Bogie Third		60	1957
	26	26	Third	Lancaster	1896	32' 10"		6-Compt. Bogie Third		60	1941
	27	27	Third	Lancaster	1896	32' 10"		6-Compt. Bogie Third		60	1948
18		57	1st/2nd Saloon	Rocksavage	1896	33' 4"	To 1st in 1907	2-Compt, Saloon & 1 Lav, Bogie First	26		1948

Original No			Type	Builder	Year	Length ft in	Remarks	1923 Layout	Seats		Withdrawn
Saloons, Firsts & Composites	Seconds, Thirds & Third Brakes	Final CB&SCR No							1st Class	3rd Class	
8		46	1st/2nd Compo	Lancaster	1899	33' 10"	To 1st in 1907	5-Compt. Bogie First	40		1949
9		47	1st/2nd Compo	Lancaster	1899	33' 10"	To 1st in 1907	5-Compt. Bogie First	40		1949
19?		7	2nd/3rd Compo	L&NWR	1872	25' 0"	Ex-DN&GR 1901; 3rd No 7, 1906	4-Compt. 4-wh. 3rd.		40	1940
20?		32	2nd/3rd Compo	L&NWR	1872	25' 0"	Ex-DN&GR 1901; 3rd No 32, 1908	4-Compt.4-wh. 3rd.		40	1940
	5	5	Third	L&NWR	1872	27' 6"	Ex-DN&GR 1901	5-Compt.6-wh. 3rd.		50	1938
	9	9	Third	L&NWR	1872	27' 6"	Ex-DN&GR 1901	5-Compt.6-wh. 3rd.		50	1941
4	54		2nd/3rd Saloon	Rocksavage	1901	37' 10"	To 1st/3rd Compo 1907	4-Bay, 2 Lav, OC, Bogie Compo.	18	24	1959
13	50	50	1st/2nd Compo	Rocksavage	1902	37' 10"	To 1st in 1907	5-Compt.2Lav,SC,Bogie 1st.	32		1923
3		31	3rd Bke	Rocksavage	1905	37' 10"		4-Compt. Bogie 3rd Brake		40	1957
	1	1	Third	Lancaster	1905	43' 2"		8-Compt. Bogie Third		80	1957
	2	2	Third	Lancaster	1905	43' 2"		8-Compt. Bogie Third		80	1957
	3	3	Third	Rocksavage	1905	43' 2"		8-Compt. Bogie Third		80	1957
	4	4	Third	Lancaster	1905	43' 2"		8-Compt. Bogie Third		80	1957
	6	6	3rd Bke	Rocksavage	1906	46' 6"		5-Compt. Bogie 3rd Brake		50	1948
6		44	1st/2nd Compo	Rocksavage	1906	46' 6"	To 1st 1907;1st/3rd in 1908	7-Compt.2Lav,SC, Bogie Compo.	18	34	1953
	28	28	3rd Bke	Rocksavage	1907	46' 6"		5-Compt. Bogie 3rd Brake		50	1955
53		53	1st/3rd Co Brake	Rocksavage	1908	48' 11"		5-Compt. Bogie Compo Brake	16	30	1959
58		58	1st/3rd Compo	L&NWR	1876	30' 6"	Ex-DN&GR 1909	4-Compt. & Lge. 6-wh. Compo.	16	20	1923
59		59	1st/3rd Compo	L&NWR	1876	30' 6"	Ex-DN&GR 1909	4-Compt. & Lge. 6-wh. Compo.	16	20	1952
60		34	1st/3rd Compo	L&NWR	1876	30' 6"	Ex-DN&GR 1909; to 3rd No 34	4-Compt. & Lge. 6-wh. 3rd.		40	1948
61		61	1st/3rd Compo	L&NWR	1876	30' 6"	Ex-DN&GR 1909	4-Compt.& Lge.6-wh.Compo.	16	20	1954
56		56	1st/3rd Co Bke	Rocksavage	1910	48' 11"		5-Compt. Bogie Compo Brake	16	30	1955
62		62	First	Rocksavage	1914	48' 11"		6-Bay, 2Lav, OC, Bogie 1st.	38		1954

Non-passenger carrying Coaching Stock

No	Type	Builder	Year	Remarks	Withdrawn
71	Passenger Brake Van	Lancaster	1896		1948
72	Passenger Brake Van	Lancaster	1896		1960
73	Passenger Brake Van	Rocksavage	1898	R/n. 202A in 1940	
74	Passenger Brake Van		1899	R/n. 230A in 1946	
75	Passenger Brake Van	Rocksavage	1922	R/n. 343A in 1958	c1968
76	Passenger Brake Van	Rocksavage	1902		1957
77	Passenger Brake Van				c1911
78	Passenger Brake Van				c1911
1	Horsebox				c1913
2	Horsebox				1936
3	Horsebox			Ex WCR.	1941
4	Horsebox			Ex WCR.	c1907
1	Fish Van	BRCW	1899	Maliciously destroyed at Baltimore	1923
2	Fish Van	BRCW	1899		1949
3	Fish Van	BRCW	1899		1949
4	Carriage Truck		1871	R/b. 1952; To Wagon Stock 1961/2	
5	Carriage Truck		c1889		1941

T&CELR Carriages

		Type	Builder	Year		Remarks	1923 Layout
	1	Third	BRCW	1889	23'0"	From Contractor.	1 Large & 1 small compt. bogie
2		Composite	BRCW	1889	23'0"	From Contractor.	1 large 3rd & 1 small 1st Bogie
	3	Third	BRCW	1891	30'0"		3-Compt. Bogie.
4		Composite	BRCW	1891	30'0"		3 3rd & 1 1st compts. Bogie

Abbreviations

BCW	Birmingham Carriage & Wagon Co (later BRCW)	Lancaster	Lancaster Wagon Co	R/n	Renumbered
BRCW	Birmingham Railway Carriage & Wagon Co	MCW	Metropolitan Carriage & Wagon Co, Birmingham	R/b	Rebuilt
C&BR	company's works at Bandon (& possibly later at Cork)	Rocksavage	CB&SCR Works at Cork		

Appendix E

CB&SCR WAGON STOCK AS AT 1924

Year	Covered	Covered	Covered	Cattle	6-ton Mineral	12-ton Open	Ballast	Hopper	Bolster	Timber	Brake
No date		61 65 66 71 78 84 95 106 111 119 121 123 126 128 136 137 141 142 145 176 177 193 197 229 235 238 241 243 245 254 255 257 258 259 260 262 266 267 269 270 278 279 280 281 283 286 288 290 291 292 295 297 313 317 319 320 322 323 324 325 327 328 329 331 332 341 342 344 345 346 347 350 352 355 356 358 360	67 138 194 240 248 265 336	403 405 407 416 417 420 421 423 424 426 427	495 501 503 527 532 533 536		662 667 668 669 670 677	682 683 684 685	703	711 714 717 720	756 759
1903											
1904						557 558 559 560 561 562 563 564 565 566 567 568 569 570 571 572 573 574 575 576 577 578 579 580 581 582 583					
1905				401 402 404 406 408 409		551 552 553 554 555 556					
1906	1 2 3 4			410 411 412 413	504 505 506						
1907	5 6					584 585 586 587 588					
1908		68 150 188 271 294 296 326 349	104 138 233 237 284 289 293 318 337 340	117 425 (possibly 1905)	496 515 522 523	589 590 591 592 593 594	665 666 671 673 678		701	721	755 758
1909	89 115 209	38 58 108 130			517 520	595 596 597 598 599 600					
1910						601 602 603 604 605 606 607 608 609 610 611 612	674 675 676			723	761 762
1911				428 429 430 431 432 433	538 539 540 541 542 543 544 545 546 547	613 614 615 616 617 618 619 620				716 719	
1912	7 8 9 10 11 12 13 14 15 16	37 39 40		434 435 436 437						715 718	
1913	17 18 (6-wh Refrig)	92		34 42 48 50 70	510 526 550		672				763
1914		59		43 51 52 79 80 81 82 83 86 118	500 507 512 513 514 521 528 529 530 534 548 549						754
1915	19 20 (6-wh vans)	19 20 49 63		85 91 93 175 239 338	497 498 499 509 516 524 531		663				751 757 760

Year	Covered	Covered	Covered	Cattle	6-ton Mineral	12-ton Open	Ballast	Hopper	Bolster	Timber	Brake
1916				96 97 144 146 202 211 223	494 511 518 535	621 622 623 624 625 626 627 628 629 630					750
1917		76 109 110 111 112 113 127		36 53 54 64 69 77 87 90 99 100 103							752
1918				45 62 107 114 122							
1919		124 125 129		72 131 133 134							
1920		149		55 74 132 143 147 148 151 154 155 156 157 158							
1921				159 160 161 162 163 164 165 166 167	502 508	631 632 633 634 635 636 637 638 639 640 641 642 643 644 645 646 647 648 649 650	661		702	722	
1922				41 88 98 105 135 152	525				704		
1923				56 102 116							
1924				35 44 46 47			664				
Total	**23**	**110**	**17**	**114**	**55**	**100**	**18**	**4**	**4**	**11**	**13**

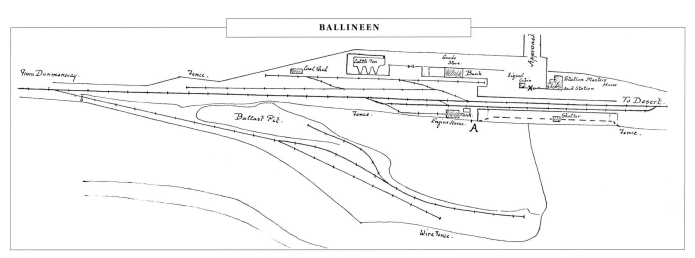

BALLINEEN

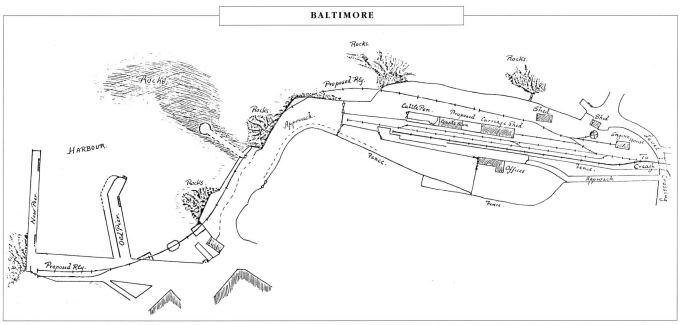

BALTIMORE

CHAIRMEN AND PRINCIPAL OFFICERS

CLASSIFICATION OF STATIONMASTERS, 1898

Chairmen

1844	Robert T Belcher
1845	Colonel North Ludlow Beamish
1852	General James C. Chatterton
1856	Valentine O'Brien O'Connor
1873	David McBirney
1882	William Shaw
1885	James Warren Payne-Sheares
1902	Joseph Pike
1920	Theodore F Carroll

Secretaries [1]

1844	Edward Billing (London)
1845	John M'Donnell
1846	Charles Nixon
1847	Humphrey Williams Wood
1856	James H Connell
1882	George Townley
1883	Alexander Gordon (Acting)
1884	J J Mahony
1887	Alexander Gordon (Acting)
1887	Edward H Dorman
1893	William J Scully (Acting)
1893	Robert H Leslie

Traffic Superintendents [2]

1856	Richard Coghlan
1877	Alexander Gordon

General Managers

1893	Edward J. O'Brien Croker
1903	John R Kerr
1924	William C R Coe (Acting)

Locomotive Superintendents

1844	Edmund Leahy
1846	Charles Nixon
	John Barber
1855	John Patterson
1857	Thomas Conran
1887	John J Johnstone [3]
1888	James W Johnstone

Engineers-in-Chief

1844	Edmund Leahy
1846	Charles Nixon
1856	William R LeFanu
1863	Cotton & Flemyng

Engineers

1872	James Dargan [4]
1873	John W Dorman [5]
1884	John R Kerr [6]
1910	F W Vereker (Assistant)

Notes

1. Title appears as Secretary & Accountant wef 1882.
2. Title appears as Traffic Manager wef 1872.
3. Johnstone was locomotive foreman as from date of WCR opening; also later traffic superintendent at Dunmanway.
4. Resident Engineer in 1872.
5. Dorman retained as Consulting Engineer until 1886.
6. Resident Engineer 1885/6.

Class	Station	Present Salary	Maximum at scale	Annual Increase. 1st year	2nd year	3rd year
1st	Cork Coaching	£127	£127			
1st	Cork Goods	£127	£127			
1st	Bandon	£108	£108			
2nd	Skibbereen	£84	£90	£6		
2nd	Dunmanway	£80	£84	£4		
2nd	Bantry	£70	£84	£5	£5	£4
2nd	Drimoleague	£80	£84	£5	£4	
3rd	Kinsale	£60	£70	£5	£5	
3rd	Clonakilty	£60	£70	£5	£5	
3rd	Baltimore	£65	£70	£5		
4th	Upton	£45½	£52	£5	£1½	
4th	Kinsale Junction	£39	£52	£5	£5	£3
4th	Clonakilty Junction	£52	£52			
4th	Desert	£45½	£52	£5	£1½	
4th	Ballineen	£46.16	£52	£5.4		
4th	Ballinascarthy	£46.16	£52	£5.4		
4th	Durrus Road	£46.16	£52	£5.4		
5th	Waterfall	17s.6d.	18s.	1s.6d.		
5th	Ballinhassig	17s.6d.	18s.	1s.6d.		
5th	Madore	17s.6d.	18s.	1s.6d.		
5th	Farrangalway	17s.6d.	18s.	1s.6d.		
6th	Knockbue	14s.	14s.			
6th	Creagh	14s.	14s.			
6th	Ballymartle	14s.	14s.			

Note: 5th and 6th classes are weekly figures, all others are annual.

PRINCIPAL ACCIDENTS

Date	Location	Killed	Injured	Remarks
17th Jun. 1854	Ballinhassig	0	0	Collision with wagons in siding.
10th Mar. 1855	Ballinhassig	1	0	Passenger fell out of train.
24th Nov. 1860	near Cork	0	1	Derailment due to fall in cutting.
15th Aug. 1862	Cork	1	0	Boy trespassing run over and killed.
26th Mar. 1863	Crossbarry	1	0	Workman killed.
14th Dec. 1867	Goggin's Hill tunnel	1	0	Tunnel watchman hit by train.
17th May 1870	near Waterfall	0	1	Wagon blown from siding.
3rd Nov. 1871	Waterfall	0	6	Two portions of train collided.
16th Jan. 1873	near Bandon	0	1	Train derailed due flooding of line.
Apr. 1881	Ballyboy crossing	0	1	Gate keeper hit by train.
12th Aug. 1882	Bandon	1	0	Pointsman killed by train.
17th Mar. 1885	near Bandon	2	0	Two passengers jumped out of train.
16th Jan. 1886	Bandon	0	4	Collision caused by fly shunting.
29th June 1886	Ballinhassig	1	0	Tunnelman killed by passing train.
9th June 1887	Waterfall	0	2	Backplate of firebox dislodged.
7th July 1887	Bantry hilltop station	1	4	Train overran station and hit buffers.
19th Mar 1888	Robert's Bridge	0	5	Broken rail caused derailment.
7th Oct. 1891	near Bandon	0	0	Animal jumped out of train and derailed part of it.
27th Sep. 1895	Clonakilty	0	6	Train collided with buffers.
3rd Sep. 1904	Manch Bridge	0	1	Man fell out of train.
6th July 1910	Bantry	0	1	Man jumped out of carriage.
28t Jan. 1915	Kinsale	2	6	Collision due to faulty block working.
5t Oct. 1918	Milleenarrig Bridge	1	0	Man stepped out and fell off bridge into river.

Appendix I

SIGNALLING

Electric Train Staff sections with staff colours, May 1894

From	To	Colour
Cork	Waterfall	Red
Waterfall	Ballinhassig	Green
Ballinhassig	Kinsale Jct.	Blue
Kinsale Jct.	Bandon	White
Bandon	Clonakilty Jct.	Red
Clonakilty Jct.	Desert	Blue
Desert	Ballineen	Red
Ballineen	Dunmanway	Blue
Dunmanway	Drimoleague	Red
Drimoleague	Skibbereen	White
Skibbereen	Baltimore	Red
Kinsale Jct.	Ballymartle	Red
Ballymartle	Kinsale	Blue
Drimoleague	Durrus Road	White
Durrus Road	Bantry	Red
Clonakilty Jct.	Ballinascarthy	White
Ballinascarthy	Clonakilty	Red

Signal Cabins, 1900

Location	Levers	Points	Signals	Cost
Cork	42	22	20	£6,149
Waterfall	12	5	7	£830
Ballinhassig	12	6	6	£468
Kinsale Jct.	30	13	17	£3,321
Upton	10	4	6	£905
Ballineen	12	6	6	£1,580
Dunmanway	18	8	10	£3,866
Ballymartle	6	-	6	£177
Farrangalway	10	4	6	£387
Kinsale	10	4	6	£720
Durrus Road	10	4	6	£521
Bandon	20	8	12	£5,493
Ballinascarthy	17	5	8	
Desert	2	4	1	£665
Clonakilty Jct.	27	12	13	£4,124
Drimoleague	31	16	15	£6,429
Skibbereen	17	5	9	£2,260
Knockbue	4	-	4	}£242
Madore	4	-	4	}

Top right: **Metropolitan-Vickers 'C' class Bo-Bo No C224 and an AEC railcar set at Drimoleague.** J L St Leger

Centre: **Bantry station looking west towards Bantry Pier with a Cork-bound AEC diesel railcar set at the single platform. Just to the right of the signal cabin can be seen a CIÉ 'P' class thirty-nine seater Leyland bus.**
David Lawrence, Photos from the Fifties

Bottom: **A goods train approaching Drimoleague. One of the two brake vans at rear is an ex-GNR(I) vehicle far from home.**
John Langford

Appendix J

LEVEL CROSSINGS AS IN APPENDIX TO GSR WTT 1935

GSR name of crossing	CB&SCR name of crossing	See Note	Station to which attached	Distance miles.yards	Signalled & Direction	Whether interlocked	Cottage attached	Notes
Cork to Baltimore								C. The gates at these places extend across the Railway Line when open for Public Road Traffic.
	Gas Works		Cork					
Castlewhite	Castlewhite		Waterfall	5.475	No		Yes	
Gortnaclough	Coakley's		Kinsale Jct.	12.410	Down		Yes	CN. The gates at these places are an exception to Rule 99 during the night only.
Killeen	Crossbarry		Kinsale Jct.	13.1165	No		Yes	
Lissnagroom	Sullivan's		Kinsale Jct.	13.1600	No		Yes	
Lisiniskey	Burke's		Kinsale Jct.	14.595	No		Yes	CX. The gates at these places are an exception to Rule 99.
Dunkereen	Deasy's		Upton	14.1610	No		Yes	
Crosses	Upton Station		Upton	15.555	Up		Yes	
Rockfort	Mahony's		Upton	15.1435	Up/Down		Yes	Rule 99 states: Unless special authority be given to the contrary, the gates at level crossings must be kept closed across the roadway, except when required to be opened to allow the line to be crossed.
Chapel	Regan's		Bandon	20.680	No			
Castlebernard	Castle Bernard		Bandon	21.640	No		Yes	
Enniskeane	Enniskean	CN	Ballineen	29.1265	Down	Yes	Yes	
Nedinagh	Inchafune		Dunmanway	34.1355	No			
Ballyboy	Ballyboy	CX	Dunmanway	36.505	Up/Down	Yes	Yes	CB&SCR names of crossings from 1905 Appendix to the Working Timetable.
Milleenananig	McCarty's		Dunmanway	36.1200	No		Yes	
Station Gates	Dunmanway Street	CX	Dunmanway	37.1600	Up/Down	Yes		Note 1: One of these was new in GSR days, the other was named Wholley's by the CB&SCR; it is not clear which is which.
Kilbarry	Kilbarry	CX	Dunmanway	38.925	Up/Down	Yes	Yes	
Cloonties No 1	Cronin's		Dunmanway	39.755	No			
Cloonties No 2	Clounties	CX	Dunmanway	40.15	Up/Down	Yes	Yes	
Garranes	Knockbue		Knockbue	41.1660	No			
Station Gates	Knockbue Station	CX	Knockbue	42.425	Up/Down	Yes	Yes	
Loughcrot	Loughrot	C	Drimoleague	42.1425	No		Yes	
Derrynagree	Hegarty's	CX	Drimoleague	44.170	Down	Yes	Yes	
Dromdaleague	Barry's	CN	Drimoleague	45.115	No			
Station Gates	Drimoleague Station	CX	Drimoleague	45.1365	Up/Down	Yes		
Garranes South	Clanchy's		Drimoleague	46.870	No			
Reenroe	Reenroe	CX	Madore	48.1000	Up/Down	Yes	Yes	
Station Gates	Madore Station	CX	Madore	49.523	Up/Down	Yes		
Cooragannive	Cooraganive		Skibbereen	49.1685	No		Yes	
Back of Town		CX	Skibbereen	53.1535	Up/Down	Yes		
Street Crossing	Skibbereen Street	CX	Skibbereen	53.1565	Up/Down	Yes		
Coronea No 1	Coronea No 1		Skibbereen	54.740	No		Yes	
Coronea No 2	Coronea No 2	CX	Skibbereen	54.1200	Up/Down	Yes	Yes	
Mallavonea	Note 1.		Skibbereen	55.550	No		Yes	
Bunlick	Note 1.	CX	Skibbereen	56.480	Up	Yes	Yes	
Creagh No 1	Crowley's	CX	Creagh	57.575	Up/Down	Yes	Yes	
Creagh No 2	Creagh Station		Creagh	57.1320	No		Yes	
Lackaghane	Daly's	CX	Baltimore	58.790	Up/Down	Yes	Yes	
Rath No 1	Seven Sisters	CX	Baltimore	59.820	Up/Down		Yes	
Rath No 2	Rath	CX	Baltimore	59.1135	Up/Down		Yes	
Church Strand	Santry's		Baltimore	60.880	No		Yes	
School Crossing	Connor's	C	Baltimore	61.270	Up/Down			
	Baltimore Station		Baltimore					
Clonakilty Jct. - Clonakilty								
Cashelmore	Stout's	CX	Clonakilty Jct.	26.230	Up/Down	Yes	Yes	
Ahalisky	Ahalisky		Ballinascarthy	28.1110	No			
County Home	Workhouse		Clonakilty	32.985	No			
Drimoleague Jct. - Bantry								
Station Gates	Hallahan's	CX	Drimoleague	45.1530	Up/Down	Yes	Yes	
Bog No 1	Bog Crossing No 1		Drimoleague	46.690	No			
Bog No 2	Bog Crossing No 2		Drimoleague	46.1650	No			
Inchingerig	Ilen Wood		Drimoleague	48.175	No			
Station Gates	Aughaville	CX	Aughaville	49.1455	Up/Down	Yes	Yes	
Station Gates	Durrus Station	C	Durrus Road	52.650	No		Yes	
Keilnascarta	Mines		Durrus Road	54.565	No		Yes	
Gurtnamuck	Neill's	CX	Bantry	57.1310	Down	Yes	Yes	
Old Barrack Road	Barrack Road	CX	Bantry	57.1650	Up/Down	Yes	Yes	
Station Gates	Bantry Station	CX	Bantry	58.15	Up/Down	Yes		
Station Gates		CX	Bantry Pier	58.790	Up/Down	Yes		
Ballinascarthy - Courtmacsherry								
Ballinascarthy		CX	Ballinascarthy	0.390	Up/Down		Yes	
Monteen		C	Ballinascarthy	1.1490	No		Yes	
Inchy Bridge		CX	Timoleague	4.500	Up	Yes	Yes	
Station Gates No 1		CX	Timoleague	5.1670	No			
Station Gates No 2		CX	Timoleague	6.145	No			
Kinsale Jct. - Kinsale (from CB&SCR Appendix to WTT, 1905)								
Ballintubber Wood			Farrangalway					
Finegan's			Farrangalway					

Appendix K

TICKETS

The CB&SCR issued the usual range of tickets on their services, all being of the Edmondson card type. First class singles were white, returns white with a skeleton R on the left half. Second class singles were blue, returns pink and blue, while thirds were buff for both single and return tickets, the latter with the skeletal R; in the case of third returns, the R was either red or black. As far as is known, child tickets were not issued by the company, with one known exception. This latter was a brown and white third class return issued in 1906 between Bandon and Cork, the word CHILD being printed on this ticket. It is assumed that adult tickets were normally used with the repeated station name removed by a special cutter from the bottom centre of the ticket.

A range of return tickets were available for special purposes. Tickets for military officers on leave were standard colours for first and third classes, but with the skeletal letters OL on the left half. Sailors and soldiers on furlough were catered for by the use of the letters SL. Third class weekend tickets sported the letters SM in red on the left hand (return) portion, while first class market tickets had a solid M overprinted in red. Some market tickets were known to have a brown right half with a central white circle, the left halves being white. Skeleton overprints were always on the left half of tickets and in most, but not all, cases the fare was pre-printed on the ticket. Privilege tickets were standard colours for both first and third class, with a skeleton P on the left half.

Bicycle tickets are known to have existed. These were horizontally striped in blue and white and were issued from a named station to any other station on the CB&SCR system not more than a certain number of miles distant. As an example, the author has seen such a ticket issued from Cork to any station not more than fifty miles distant, the fare being 6d. It is not clear whether similar tickets were issued for dogs and perambulators. Platform tickets were not issued by the CB&SCR, although in CIÉ days such tickets were available at Albert Quay.

In Chapter Eleven we have seen the importance of excursion traffic to the CB&SCR, particularly in relation to seaside excursions to Courtmacsherry. The company issued a range of somewhat colourful one-piece tickets for such trips. Known colours were green with a horizontal central stripe in pale red, and a red ticket with a central grey stripe. These tickets showed a return from an issuing station with no destination indicated. One exception to this was a ticket issued in this style in 1903 for an excursion from Cork to Courtmacsherry and back. No fare was shown on any of these one-piece tickets, nor was any space provided for it. Later excursion tickets were two-piece, coloured buff and green, with two central black wavy horizontal lines. The issuing and destination stations were both shown and fares were also indicated. A similar ticket in the same colours but without the wavy lines had a skeleton R on the left half. This was in respect of a special excursion from Kinsale Junction to Kinsale. In this latter case, space was provided to write in a fare.

The CB&SCR issued through tickets between their own line and that of the narrow-gauge Schull & Skibbereen Tramway. These were headed CB&SC & S&S RYS on the outward half and S&S & CB&SC RYS on the return half. Similar tickets were issued for the T&CELR, the initials of the latter company being shown as T&C. No such arrangements existed with the C&MDR, although of course no through passenger

traffic operated over Ballyphehane Junction after 1879. It might be mentioned that the Timoleague company issued their own tickets for internal traffic on their own line. Although the CB&SCR were members of the Irish Railway Clearing House, no through tickets to British railways have been seen.

Railway tickets issued in Ireland generally tended not to show a train number. An exception to this was the CB&SCR who used a special date stamp on certain special excursion trains; this applied in particular when a number of such specials operated from Cork to Courtmacsherry. It was the practice to have a date and train number vertically stamped on the left hand side of the ticket, a special ink date stamp being provided; the number appeared before the date.

The Bantry Bay Steamship Co, as we have seen in Chapter Seventeen, operated steamer services from Bantry Pier to Castletownberehaven and Glengarriff. Considerable tourist traffic operated over the latter route in particular, return tickets being issued bearing the heading CB&SC RY & BBSSCo on the right half with the titles reversed on the return half. The road part of the journey was operated by a GS&WR bus service with titled roll tickets. Road services also operated throughout from Bantry and these were catered for with two-piece third class tickets. The right half was for the road journey and was headed 'Car Portion', while the left half for the return rail journey between Bantry and Cork had the railway company's initials.

A diesel railcar set at Bandon on the last day of services. Standing in the open doorway is the noted Cork railway enthusiast and historian Walter McGrath.
J L St. Leger

Index

Also of interest...

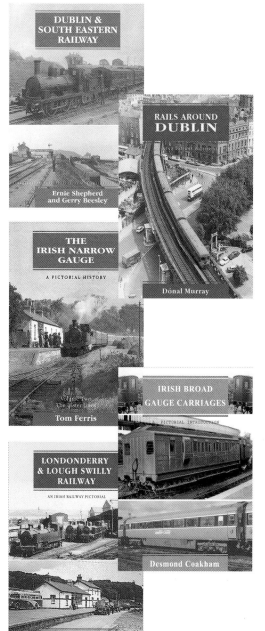

The County Donegal Railways Companion
R. Crombleholme, ISBN: 1 85780 205 5, 282mm x 213mm 112pp PB £14.99

The Dublin & Southern Eastern Railway
E. Shepherd and G. Beesley, ISBN: 1 857080 082 6, 282mm x 213mm 145 b/w photographs, maps, drawings 160pp HB £19.99

The Great Northern Railway: An Irish Railway Pictorial
T. Ferris, ISBN: 1 85780 169 5, 282mm x 213mm 112pp over 250 b/w photographs PB £14.99

Irish Broad Gauge Carriages – A Pictorial Introduction
D. Coakham, ISBN: 1 85780 175 X, 282mm x 213mm 96pp PB £14.99

Irish Narrow Gauge 1: From Cork to Cavan
T. Ferris, ISBN: 1 85750 010 9, 282mm x 213mm 112pp 250 b/w photos HB £15.99

Irish Narrow Gauge 2: The Ulster Lines
T. Ferris, ISBN: 1 85750 017 6, 282mm x 213mm 128pp over 280 b/w photographs HB £15.99

The LMS in Ireland
M. Kennedy, ISBN: 1 85780 097 4, 96pp 255 b/w photographs PB £12.99

Locomotives and Railcars of Bord Na Mona
S. Johnson, ISBN: 1 85780 045 1, 48pp b/w illustrations throughout PB £4.99

Londonderry & Lough Swilly Railway
S. Flanders, ISBN: 1 85780 074 5, 282mm x 213mm 64pp 170 b/w photographs PB £8.99

Modelling Irish Railways
S. Johnson and A. O'Rourke, ISBN: 1 85780 185 7, 282mm x 213mm 88pp colour & b/w photographs PB £14.99

Rails Around Belfast
A. Crockart and J. Patience, ISBN: 1 85780 167 9, 282mm x 213mm 80pp c200 b/w photographs PB £13.99

Rails Around Dublin
D. Murray, ISBN: 1 85780 144 X, 282mm x 213mm 80pp 200 b/w photographs PB £12.99

Sligo, Leitrim & Northern Counties Railway
N. Sprinks, ISBN: 1 85780 112 1, 80pp 178 b/w photographs PB £12.99

The West Clare Railway
J. Taylor, ISBN: 1 85780 122 9, 64pp b/w illustrations throughout PB £10.99

Midland Publishing titles are edited and designed by an experienced and enthusiastic team of specialists.

For a copy of our mail-order catalogue, or to order further copies of this book, and any of the titles mentioned elsewhere on this page, please either write, telephone, fax or e-mail to:

Midland Counties Publications, 4 Watling Drive, Hinckley, Leics LE10 3EY

Tel: (+44) 01455 254450 **Fax:** (+44) 01455 233737

E-mail: midlandbooks@compuserve.com **or visit:** www.midlandcountiessuperstore.com